Odessa, 1941-1944

A Case Study of Soviet Territory
under Foreign Rule

Odessa, 1941-1944

A Case Study of Soviet Territory under Foreign Rule

Alexander Dallin

With an Introduction by Larry L. Watts

The Center for Romanian Studies
Las Vegas ◇ Oxford ◇ Palm Beach

Published in the United States of America by
Histria Books, a division of Histria LLC
7181 N. Hualapai Way
Las Vegas, NV 89166 USA
HistriaBooks.com

The Center for Romanian Studies is an imprint of Histria Books. Titles published under the imprints of Histria Books are distributed worldwide.

All rights reserved. No part of this book may be reprinted or reproduced or utilized in any form or by any electronic, mechanical or other means, now known or hereafter invented, including photocopying and recording, or in any information storage or retrieval system, without permission in writing from the Publisher.

Second Printing, 2020

Library of Congress Control Number: 2020940664

ISBN 978-973-98391-1-2 (hardcover)
ISBN 978-1-59211-081-0 (paperback)

Copyright © 1998, 2020 by Histria Books

Table of Contents

Preface to the RAND Report 7
Preface to the 1998 Edition 9
Introduction "Alexander Dallin and Romanian Historiography"
    by Larry L. Watts 13
I. Odessa from Peace to Occupation 29
    Background 29
    Invasion 31
    Siege 38
    The End 48
II. Transnistria: Theory and Practice 55
    Romania and the War 55
    Transnistria: Vital Statistics 61
    The New Order 65
    Capture and Terror 72
    Transnistria: The Government 75
    Odessa: The Primăria 81
    Romanization 87
    Attitudes toward the Romanians 91
III. Social and Economic Trends: The Rural Areas 94
    The Setting 94
    Plus ça change 98
    The Peasantry 103
    The Harvest 108
    Social and Economic Trends: The Urban Areas 111
    Urban Society 111
    The "New NEP" 114

    The New Elite 121
    Industry, Management, and Labor 124
    Money, Prices, and Standards of Living 130
    The Criminal Fringe 137
    Social Change and Economic Initiative:
        Summing Up 139

IV. Education, Culture, Church, and Press 141

    Schools 142
    Higher Education 146
    Press and Propaganda 151
    The Arts 156
    The Church 161
    City Life 167

V. Politics: Attitudes, Ideas, and Action 172

    Major Trends of Attitude and Behavior 172
    The Communists 179
    Ersatz Politics 181
    Program for Tomorrow 182
    Emigre Politics 185
    The Nationality Question 193
    The Ethnic Elite 197
    The Ethnic Dumping-Ground 204
    Appendix: Forced Labor in Transnistria 213

VI. Moscow's Long Arm 217

    The Opportunities 217
    The Odessa Catacombs 221
    The Transnistrian Partisans 228
    The Partisans and the People 232

VII. The Last Phase 237

    Between Battlefield and Round-Table 237
    Military Government 243
    Again in Soviet Hands 248

VIII. Some Conclusions and Implications 255

Summary 265

Appendix 273

Bibliography 277

Index 293

Preface to the 1957 RAND Report

From mid-October 1941, to early April 1944, the city of Odessa and its hinterland were under foreign occupation. One of the largest Soviet cities to fall into enemy hands during the second World War, Odessa's experience was unique also for another reason: during almost the entire period it was under Romanian, rather than German, rule. As capital of the improvised, *ad hoc* province of "Transnistria," it became the object of Romanian policy disputes, experiments, efforts at self-enrichment, and exploitation. At the same time, it was the object of acute Soviet attention, including agents and partisans, while foreign observers — newspapermen and officials — and local residents intently watched the large and once flourishing city respond and adjust to a new and challenging situation.

In the study of the Second World War, the story of Transnistria has been well-nigh neglected. While scattered material is abundant, there exists no secondary study of any substantial value. Thus, the first aim of this paper is to provide an historical reconstruction of wartime Transnistria. The paper also seeks to analyze Transnistrian experience and see what lessons can be drawn from it. A comparison of Romanian rule with the German occupation in other parts of the U.S.S.R. during the same years reveals much of significance about the problems of occupation. Odessa under the Romanians also sheds a curious light on Soviet society: one can here study what happens — what aspirations and responses are disclosed — when Soviet controls are removed.

There are various limitations inherent in the subject-matter. Any *post facto* reconstruction, especially of attitudes and values, must be viewed with some skepticism. The sources contradict each other repeatedly. Contemporary observers were often in no position to have special insight into the subjects they dealt with; and memories inevitably tend to err when relied upon several traumatic years later, under drastically different material and political conditions. To mention but one major methodological hindrance, the refugee informants — who proved quite valuable — were exclusively urban intellectuals (in the broader Soviet sense of this term). This renders impossible a thorough study of workers' attitudes and behavior during the occupation. Because some work has already been done on peasant attitudes, however, the fact that informants were urban is less important. In some respects, it is fortunate to have so much of the material deal with the white-collar and intellectual strata under foreign rule; material on these groups in German-controlled areas is strikingly poor.

It should perhaps be added that the contrast between what happened in Odessa and in German-occupied areas proved somewhat less dramatic and less extreme than the stereotypes and myths among Soviet émigrés (typified by the polar images of "German rule — bad; Odessa — good") would have led one to believe. Nonetheless, in many crucial areas the differences were substantial — and where they were not, the reasons for this were significant — so that the author, at least, feels the investigation to have been justified, even though the evidence proved to be considerably poorer than had been hoped.

This study was produced for the Social Science Division of The RAND Corporation. The author owes particular thanks to Messrs. Melville J. Ruggles, Emmanuel G. Mesthene, Herbert S. Dinerstein, and Leon Gouré for their advice, assistance, and criticism. Appreciation must be expressed to the informants — Soviet refugees and Romanian ex-officers — who prefer to remain unnamed, and to individuals and libraries that helped survey the available materials or draw attention to obscure information: Professor John A. Armstrong, University of Wisconsin; Bibliothek des Instituts für Weltwirtschaft, Kiel; Signore Maurilio Coppini, Italian ambassador to Switzerland; Institute for the Study of the History and Culture of the U.S.S.R., Munich (which, thanks to the assistance of the American Committee for Liberation from Bolshevism, commissioned two manuscripts on wartime Odessa); Institut für Zeitgeschichte, Munich; Mr. Lev F. Magerovsky, Curator of the Archive of East European History and Culture, Columbia University; Mr. Ivan Maistrenko, Munich; Osteuropa-Institut, Munich; Dr. Joseph Schechtman, New York; Dr. Werner Stephany; Mr. Paul Sweet, German Documents Branch, Department of State; Professor Witold Sworakowski, Curator of the East European Collection, Hoover Library, Stanford University; and YIVO Library, New York.

Alexander Dallin

Preface to the New Edition

As the original preface to this manuscript indicates, it was written in 1956, on the basis of research and interviews conducted during the preceding several years. This explains some of its limitations. The author had access to some captured German army records and was able to interview some former residents of Odessa who after World War II found themselves in Western Europe, and a few officers who had served in the East during the war. Also available were some, though rather incomplete, sets of newspapers published during the war. But this was a time when American scholars had virtually no scholarly contact with, or access to, the Soviet Union or Romania.

What was manifestly lacking in this manuscript were, first of all, uncensored Soviet memoirs and archival sources, and second, virtually all accounts — official and unofficial — from the Romanian side.

Perhaps this publication will stimulate others to fill some of these gaps. Such additional sources — and others that have become available in the past forty years — would surely make it in many regards a far richer and far more precise account than the present manuscript. I would be delighted if this were to be one effect of its present publication. And yet, everything I have seen or heard since then suggests to me that the basic themes of what is described above and the general conclusions I reached at the time will apparently stand the test of time. Regrettably, not many survivors — either on the Romanian or on the Soviet side — remain alive to round out or correct this picture.

If the passage of time has reduced the seeming saliency of the experience, it has also crystallized some intriguing new questions. Those regarding Romanian policy and behavior I am hardly qualified to discuss.

Others, however, deal with the wartime experience of Odessa in the context of both Odessa's specific culture and tradition, and the broader Soviet experience, from the New Economic Policy of the 1920s to the post-Soviet transition of the 1990s.

How to explain the experience of Odessa under Romanian rule? One element was of course the greater permissiveness of the Romanian administration compared to the German regime to the north. It was, it appears, not a matter of Romanian compassion but rather a matter of laxness and inefficiency, perhaps a broader attitude toward authority and discipline, although there were many instances of terror, panic, and atrocities as well. There was also a slight element of political guile among probably a minority of the Romanians who hoped to annex "Transnistria" to a future Greater Romania and did not wish to antagonize potential subjects or "fellow-citizens."[1]

The behavior of the occupying administration is a significant variable, and the experience of the Odessa region prompts a comparison with the German regime in the Northern Caucasus, which was likewise comparatively lenient (for a combination of reasons: "Transnistria" and the Northern Caucasus, and to some extent Baltic areas, stand out by contrast with all the other of the former Soviet Union in the attitudes of the population toward the occupiers and toward forging a non-Soviet way of life). However, Romanian practice differed greatly from the German — including a popular sense that anything was possible, that anything could be bought or sold, and that there were exceptions to all rules. In any event, Romanian behavior was a necessary but not a sufficient condition for the emergence of the embryonic "civil society" (and to some extent, a "civil economy") that we observe in Odessa during the war.

What we find difficult to evaluate is the question to what extent Odessa — with its particular spirit, the values of its citizens, the tradition

---

[1] The Romanian wartime label of Transnistria or Transnistria, must be carefully distinguished from the post-Soviet usage of Transnistria. While the Romanian reference was to the area beyond the Dnestr River — i.e. in the Ukrainian USSR — the post-Soviet (Russian) usage refers to the area beyond the Dnestr within Moldova — i.e. the slice of territory centered on Tiraspol.

It is similarly important to bear in mind the charges in nomenclature and spelling for a number of locations introduced since 1991. Thus, the references in the text to Moldavia, of course, mean the current Moldova: the city of Nikolaev is now (in Ukrainian) Mykolaiv, and so forth.

of humor, spunk, and enterprise, defiance of convention, on the threshold of criminality — represented a unique phenomenon even after 25 years of Soviet rule. In many ways its tradition places it in a line closer to Marseilles and Naples than in a row with Leningrad and Sverdlovsk. But if this is so, it also implies that there lingered a flame more reminiscent of the years of the NEP (the New Economic Policy of the 1920s) than of the Stalin era — more Isaak Babel' and Il'f and Petrov than even Katayev and Fadeyev. Recent observers have confirmed the survival of this "something special" in Odessa.[2]

A different explanation (and these need not be mutually exclusive) would suggest that — from the perspective of the 1990s — Odessa was a remarkable forerunner of what we would now characterize as the values and attitudes of post-Soviet urban life, part of the transition to a non-communist society and economy. The flourishing of private enterprise, especially in the service sector, the remarkable growth of corruption and banditry; the ambivalence about politics; the search for creature comforts; the emergence of a (small) elite of *nouveaux riches;* and much else resonate with what emerged in the Soviet Union beginning with the years *of perestroika* and since. If Odessa was unique during the war, it was also because the development here was permitted, by default, to be more authentic than under the Germans in Kiev, Pskov, Smolensk, or Minsk.

In the end, both things may have been true. Odessa was and is unique, and that uniqueness showed during the war. But quite apart from its special flair, in a variety of ways that could not have been foreseen, the abortive experience under the Romanian occupation foreshadowed something of a pattern of post-communist development that has been observed, since 1989, in a variety of East European and post-Soviet settings.

The wartime experience must not be idealized by any means. Moreover, the popular mood began to change rather dramatically in 1943-44, as military fortunes reversed after Stalingrad, as economic conditions deteriorated and prices began to rise "astronomically," and as partisan activity reminded people of a potential Soviet presence. If, at the start, many residents of "Transnistria" seemed prepared to adapt to the new system, two years later, under conditions of war-weariness, Romanian rule was widely

---

[2] See, e.g., Maurice Friedberg, *How Things Were Done in Odessa* (Boulder, Colorado: Westview Press, 1991).

perceived as futile, unjust, or antiquated, while an upsurge of patriotism and wishful thinking led more people to think of the Red Army as the People-under-Arms, bearers of a new message.

The war years in Odessa remain a significant yet neglected experience which prompts provocative questions and deserves further study and reflection.

Alexander Dallin
Stanford California
August, 1997

Introduction: Alexander Dallin and Romanian Historiography

Larry L. Watts

As a long-time advocate for the republication of Alexander Dallin's manuscript, I am especially pleased at the reappearance of this remarkable work. It is remarkable for several reasons, not the least of which are the depth and breadth of his research and the fact that nearly half a century later western scholarship has produced no better, or even comparable, work on the topic.

As the author states, the principal goals of his study were to reconstruct and analyze the Transnistrian experience and its effect on the Soviet population, and to compare Romanian rule with the German occupation. On both points he succeeds admirably. Dallin was less concerned with the motivations and intent of central Romanian authorities and the variance in intended policies and actual implementation, issues of central concern to Romanian specialists. Paradoxically, even though he was explicitly focused on other aims and in spite of the almost total inaccessibility of Romanian documentation when it was undertaken, Dallin's work remains the most sophisticated regarding the Romanian occupation of Transnistria.

Faced with an uneven database, particularly minuscule in the case of Romanian, intent and policies were identified primarily through the prism of those who observed or experienced their effects.[1] At the start then, it is important to recognize the obstacles which confronted Dallin then and which still confront historians and analysts of Romania today. At the most general level, the availability of evidence and detail colors the subsequent nature of interpretation given the natural tendency to presume that state leaderships exercise relatively complete central control. More evidence and greater detail inform one of the conflicts, confusion, and failures that exist between intent and implementation and justify a less judgmental, more nuanced and "forgiving" interpretation of leadership intent. On the other hand, a paucity of evidence and detail promotes interpretations of more rigid central control and of a unity between intent and implementation, thereby justifying more simplistic and "harsher" interpretations of leadership intent. This continues to characterize scholarship on Romania during this period.

The presumption of more rigid central control is often confounded with unidirectional and policy-driven analysis in which a state and/or its leadership is evaluated on the basis of only its negative aspects while its positive aspects are neglected, ignored, or categorized as marginal and unintentional phenomena and thus not meriting serious attention. (Contrariwise, the same error is committed if one judges a state exclusively on the basis of its positive aspects, categorizing its failings as marginal or unintentional.) This approach is especially prevalent among belligerents and interested parties during wartime, tending to carry over into the subsequent historiography of the war as well.[2]

This is the case of the specialized literature on the region and on Romania in spades. There is a general and pronounced tendency to attribute the occurrence of all negative phenomena in wartime Romania and in Transnistria to purposeful Romanian intent, but to explain all positive phenomena as a result of Romanian incompetence in carrying out intent, usually because of a presumably greater distribution of venal characteristics among the Romanian people such as greed, corruption, and laziness.[3] It may be that specific events were primarily or partly the result of such characteristics. But this has to be empirically proven, not merely assumed on the basis of a cultural stereotype. While such analysis was not

---

[1] Perhaps the most pertinent materials now accessible are those in *Arhivele Statului Bucharest* (Bucharest State Archives) and *Arhivele Ministerului Apărării Naționale* (Archives of the Ministry for National Defense) in Bucharest and Pitești, and in the less easily accessible military cabinet records of Romanian wartime leader Ion Antonescu held in the *Osobii Arhiv* in what used to be the called the Central State Archives of the USSR in Moscow. There are also significant collections of pertinent American and British materials related to these problems that have been declassified since 1974 in the *United States National Archives* in Washington D.C. and the *British Public Records Office* at Kew, England.

[2] Compare, for example, the Second World War construct of the "Grand Alliance" and its effect on propaganda and subsequent historiography, with the differentiated treatment of the states and leaderships in the 1991 Yugoslav crisis. For an interesting discussion of the first case see Norman Davies, "The Misunderstood War," *The New York Times Review of Books*, June 9, 1994, pp. 20-22. For the second, sec Constantine P. Danopoulos and Kostas G. Messas, editors, *Crisis in the Balkans: Views from the Participants*, Boulder, Westview, 1997.

possible at the time of Dallin's work, it can and should be seriously undertaken today.

There is also a more specific effect of the uneven database deriving from the inter-relationships between Germany and Romania on the one hand and between the Soviet Union and Romania on the other. There is a general tendency in the literature, also evident here, to take German and Soviet pejorative statements and accusations directed against the Romanians at face value while questioning similar Romanian statements and accusations aimed at the Soviets and Germans as doubtful or unreliable. Obviously, the preponderance of German and Soviet sources necessarily reflects German and Soviet perspectives and biases to a far greater degree than it reflects the Romanian perspective and its biases.[4] Less obviously, as recent scholarship has discovered, the Germans exhibited a consistent tendency to present their wartime allies as morally inferior, especially in connection with atrocities and treatment of Jewish populations which the Germans themselves often staged or initiated but also with regard to "normal" abuses frequently committed by troops in combat and occupation forces.[5] This is not to assert that Romanian troops and local populations did not engage in atrocities. Indeed, there is ample evidence of this from a host of sources, many of them cited in this book. It is to assert that German reports pertaining to their allies' behavior cannot be assumed to be as complete and accurate as once thought and should be treated with the same degree of caution and skepticism as other sources, including Romanian ones.

Several factors make the relationship between the Soviet Union and Romania and thus the evaluation of Soviet sources dealing with Romania (and vice versa) more complex. First, for a variety of reasons, Moscow fostered

---

[3] This approach is so prevalent in the literature that the cultural stereotyping it represents, and the presumption of guilt and culpability implied within it, continue to go unremarked by serious scholars. Simply put, if Romanians did something bad they meant it. If they did something good, they did not. In fact, they preferred and attempted to do something worse but were prevented by their own incompetence and venality. Can this seriously be considered a valid framework for analysis? Dallin's findings can be read as a wakeup call for applying the same rules of empirical validation to Romania during this period as to any other object of historical inquiry.

[4] E.g., compare the evaluations of Romanian motivation and intent with those presented in Kurt Treptow, ed., *A History of Romania*, Iași, Center for Romanian Studies, 1997.

[5] Daniel Jonah Goldhagen describes how the German *Einsatzgruppe* often misattributed their carefully orchestrated atrocities to local populations and allies in his *Hitler's Willing Executioners: Ordinary Germans and the Holocaust*, New York, Alfred A. Knopf, 1996, pp. 518-520.

a denigratory attitude towards Romania ever since the founding of the Romanian principalities. This attitude survived into the Soviet regime in exacerbated form because of the union of then Tsarist-held Bessarabia with the Romanian Kingdom in 1918. Add to this the impact of Soviet wartime 'enemy image' projections and it becomes immediately understandable why pejorative attitudes towards Romania and Romanians dominated among Soviet citizens. Throughout the interwar period, and even during the Soviet-Romanian *rapprochement* of 1934-1939, the Soviet line on Romanian "imperialism" was maintained as a major aspect of Soviet public propaganda.

However, the greatest impetus to prejudicial Soviet appreciations came in two waves; the first after the Soviet occupation of Bessarabia and Northern Bucovina in June 1940, and the second after the opening of the Eastern Campaign one year later. The underlying cause was Moscow's need to brand the entire Romanian war effort criminal (the principal crime for which Romanian leaders were branded war criminals in the 1946 trials being "aggression against the Soviet Union"). This was necessary because international law still held Bessarabia and northern Bucovina to be Romanian territories under Soviet occupation at the start of the Romanian offensive, lending it the character of a just war (*jus ad helium*).[6] Not surprisingly, it became a matter of Soviet policy to play down Romania's defensive motivations for joining the campaign and to attribute and emphasize non-defensive motives to Romania, the baser the better. Predictably, Romanian intent and behavior in Transnistria was a central battlefield in this propaganda war.

These cautions aside, Dallin's findings and impressions regarding Romanian war aims, assimilationist policies, and the nature of Romanian control remain significant for our interpretation of Romanian occupation

---

[6] This was a unique situation. In Finland, for example, Helsinki was compelled to sign the Treaty of Moscow in March 1940, thus legally ceding Finnish territories lost in the Winter War to the Soviets and placing international law on the side of the USSR. Since Moscow evidently coveted more Romanian territory no such treaty was ever concluded over Bessarabia or Bucovina before the end of the war. Romania also had other defensive arguments for participating in the offensive. For instance, the Soviet seizure of several Romanian islands in October 1940, and the maneuvers and dispositions indicating Soviet plans for a preemptive attack. See, e.g., Brian I. Fugate and Lev Dvoretsky, *Thunder on the Dneper: Zhukov-Stalin and the Defeat of Hitler's Blitzkrieg*, Novato, CA, Presidio, 1997, and R.H.S. Stolti, *Hitler's Panzers East: World War II Reinterpreted*. Norman, University of Oklahoma Press, 1993. For the debate over the broader significance of Soviet offensive plans see John Erikson and David Dilks, editors, *Barbarossa: The Axis and the Allies*, Edinburgh, Edinburgh University Press, 1994, and Joseph L. Wieczynski, editor. *Operation Barbarossa: The German Attack on the Soviet Union June 22, 1941*, Salt Lake City, Charles, Schlacks, Jr., 1993.

policies and have been substantially borne out by subsequently accessible documentation. Unfortunately, they are also often neglected in mainstream literature dealing with wartime Romania and therefore deserve something more than passing comment.

Motivations for Entering the War

Dallin's finding that Romania did not annex Transnistria, and that only a small minority of Romanian officials entertained the idea, has been verified by Axis and Allied sources alike.[7] As he points out, Romania was well aware that Germany sought to persuade Romania to accept the territory as a trade-off for that part of Transylvania whose transfer to Hungary Germany had underwritten in 1940, something which the Romanians were loath to do. While this was an important motivation, it was not the primary one.

Another partial motivation was a carry-over of Romanian interwar efforts to implement a *rapprochement* with the Soviet Union which, given its military capabilities and outstanding claims on Romania like those of Imperial Russia before it, was perceived as a threat that could only be neutralized through the institution of a new less antagonistic relationship. In this sense Romanian reticence was much like that of Finland regarding participation in the siege of Leningrad. It was considered the straw that would break the camel's back in terms of earning the undying enmity of the Russians (or Soviets depending on the outcome of the war).

Additionally, and closer to the mark in identifying first priorities, Romanian self-interest in preserving the post-World War I *status quo* was closely linked to the recognition that Germany could never equal the resource and manpower base of the British and French Empires, the United States, and the Soviet Union. Once the Soviets joined the League of Nations in 1934, almost immediately after the Germans had left it and publicly condemned the Versailles peace arrangements, Romanians con-

---

[7] Perhaps the clearest statement of Romanian official policy can be found in *Foreign Relations of the United States 1941*, Volume I, Washington D.C., U.S. Government Printing Office 1958, pp. 326-327. Memorandum of conversation between U.S. Secretary of State, Cordell Hull, with Romanian Chargé d'Affaires, Brutus Coste, September 4, 1941. See also, *United States National Archives (USNA)*, State Department Records, Office of Strategic Services Research and Analysis Report #1518, "Rumania: The Present Situation," December 17, 1943, p. 14. The literary attempts of the pro-annexationists were meager in comparison with similar Finnish attempts regarding the annexation of Soviet Karelia. See, e.g., C. Leonard Lundin, *Finland in the Second World War*, Bloomington, Indiana University Press, 1957, pp. 125-142.

ceived of the looming conflict of great powers on the continent in terms of League defenders (supporters of the *status quo*) and League attackers (revisionists).

The continuity and prevalence of Romanian thinking in this regard is demonstrated by the fact that Romanian wartime leader Ion Antonescu had himself pioneered the military aspects of the *rapprochement* with the USSR such that, during 1934-1936, the bulk of Romanian forces were transferred from the Soviet front to the Western front with Hungary (which was already in a relationship of security cooperation with Germany).[8] By 1937, over 15 divisions — 70% of Romanian effectives — were on the Western Front, while only 5 divisions were on the border of the USSR.[9] Then Defense Minister, Antonescu was projecting a clash between the "German-Italian ideology" of revisionism and the *status quo* oriented "Franco-Soviet ideology," to which Romania adhered for obvious reasons.[10]

This appreciation of the military leaders and the military deployments that followed from it, approved and supported by the political leadership, were not seriously challenged until the German-Soviet co-invasion of Poland in mid-September 1939, despite the Molotov-Ribbentrop Pact. There was a broad consensus among Romanian military and political leaders that, along with the Allies, Romania would initially be fighting Germany and the Axis on a roughly equal footing and then quickly "gain an overwhelming superiority — militarily and materially — given the immense resources of America, of the Soviets, and of the vast colonial empires of the English and French."[11] This largely explains Antonescu's persistence in arguing with the U.S. representatives in early 1941 that only an American intervention and compromise peace could protect Europe from disaster as well as his readiness to admit in November 1941 that Germany had lost the war against the Soviet Union.[12]

---

[8] See, *e.g.*, *ASB,* fond Președinția Consiliului de Miniștri, dosar nr. 24/1934, f. 1-2, and *MAN,* fond 948/RSS3, dosar nr. 1 315, f. 116-120 and dosar nr. 1 414, f. 3; fond 948, dosar nr. 437, f. 547; and fond 332, dosar nr. 30, f. 4, 47 and 99-102.

[9] *MAN,* fond 948/RSS3 (General Staff-Operations), dosar nr. 380, f. 56, dosar nr. 456, f. 273, dosar nr. 1 362, f. 118; dosar 1 414, f. 184; dosar nr. 1 594, f. 6; fond 948, dosar nr. 416, f. 398-402, 407 and 490-495, dosar nr. 434, f. 65-70 and 152-155, and dosar 438, f. 627; fond 333, dosar nr. 601, f. 430-437; and fond Marele Stat Major, Secția 3 operații, vol. 1024, f. 120-121.

[10] *MAN,* fond 948, dosar nr. 438, f. 268-269.

[11] *MAN,* fond 948/RSS3 (General Staff-Operations), dosar nr. 1 706, f. 31-37, and fond 948, dosar nr. 493, f. 153.

Thus, Romania's primary motivation for resisting the annexation of Transnistria was its manifest self-interest in preserving the defensive nature of its war and its claim to the restoration of the *status quo ante*, which would presumably return it the territories of Bessarabia, Northern Bucovina, and northern Transylvania lost in 1940. This was reflected in Romania's repeated insistence from August 1941 until August 1944 on the application of the Atlantic Charter, co-signed by the U.S., Britain, and the Soviet Union, which explicitly refused to recognize any territorial modifications implemented during the war.[13]

This is an extremely important point for evaluating Romanian war aims and occupation policies and practices. If aggressive revisionism and imperial aggrandizement could be demonstrated to constitute Romania's primary motivation for joining the Eastern Campaign, then a number of presumptions can be made about Romanian intent and subsequent policies. For example, concern for international law was obviously not a priority. Therefore, subsequent atrocities and annexationist policies do not require detailed explanation for the understanding of Romanian wartime behavior. They logically follow from Romania's primary motivation. First cause, imperialism and revision, obviously took precedence over any concern for the restrictions of international law.

If, however, Romania was adamant on restoring the *status quo ante* and was attempting to adhere to the letter of international law in pressing its case, then the presumptions regarding Romanian intent and policies are quite different. Occupation policies must be evaluated in terms other than how they promoted policies of annexation and against the stipulations and restrictions of the laws of war, and atrocities require investigation as to their cause and the official reaction to them since they presumably deviated from intended Romanian behavior. First cause, defensive response

---

[12] See, e.g., *USNA*, State Department Records, 740.0011, February 25, 1941, Franklin Mott Gunther to the Secretary of State; *Ibid*, March 28, 1941, Gunther to the Secretary of State; and *Ibid*, 871.00/911, Telegram #960, November 15, 1941, Franklin Mott Gunther to the Secretary of State. Antonescu was equally insistent to the Germans that only a quick offensive against the USSR, launched and completed before the resources of the United States could be brought to bear, had a chance of success.

[13] See, e.g., *British Public Records Office (PRO)*, Foreign Office (FO) 371/43992, Document R1472, Telegram #5, January 21, 1944, Lieutenant Colonel Neame, Press Reading Bureau, Stockholm, to Political Intelligence Department, London, pp. 100-102. Antonescu was equally insistent with Hitler that his goal was to restore the status quo and reestablish Romanian territorial borders, not expand them. *USNA*, Modern Military Branch, OSS Record Group 226, Document #1196781, February 11, 1942, Ion Antonescu to Adolf Hitler, p. 2.

(the only validating reason for the use of force under international law), must be considered the primary motivation and apparent deviations from it investigated.

The degree to which our understanding of Romania's motivations for entering the war affects our interpretation of its subsequent behavior in very specific and important ways. To take one example germane to the study at hand, wartime administrations regardless of political coloration tend to institute draconian regulations, often stipulating the death penalty for a greater number of offenses that would not be deemed as such in peacetime. These measures to preserve order in periods of crisis are designed as disincentives rather than *post facto* reprisals, and are generally not carried out or are carried out in only symbolic fashion. If a presumption is made that the state authority values adherence to international law, then atrocities connected with such stipulations are the legitimate subject of detailed investigation to determine why and how the presumed deviation occurred and who is the responsible party or parties. It is not presumed that such draconian practices typify the policies and intent of the respective authority.

If, however, an *a priori* presumption of expedience rather than legality is made, then atrocities linked to such measures are considered a logical and inevitable consequence of them needing no further explanation. Moreover, even where there is no explicit evidence that such measures were implemented they are presumed to have accurately described normal regime behavior. For this reason alone, a serious reconsideration of Romanian occupation policies and Romania's role in the Second World War is very much in order.

Assimilationist Policies

Dallin was the first to establish that Romania did not adopt a program of assimilation or "Romanization" towards the resident Russian and Ukrainian populations, permitting the continued operation of their cultural establishments, schools, journals, and newspapers in a rather *lassez-faire* manner.[14] In part, as he notes, this was a reflection of Romanian political guile in that Bucharest was attempting to win hearts and minds in the region in preparation for the peace conference at the end of the war as well as to create as inhospitable a climate as possible for the reintroduction

---

[14] Subsequent work on Ukrainian history continues to omit this important detail, implying an effort to forcibly assimilate the Slavic population. See, e.g., Paul Robert Magosci, *A History of Ukraine*, Seattle, University of Washington Press, 1996, p. 625.

of Soviet-style communism. Also, in part, this difference with German occupation policies also reflected the fact that Romanians did not perceive the Slavs as *untermensch* as did the Germans, but rather recognized the necessity of long-term coexistence with what would inevitably be a large Slavic state to their cast no matter what the outcome of the war.

At the same time, however, there was an obvious "Romanization" effort in that the Romanian authorities did attempt to introduce or reintroduce Romanian history, tradition, and language to the "Moldavian" people — an ethnicity created by Stalin in 1924 in order to differentiate ethnic Romanians under Soviet rule from ethnic Romanians under Romanian rule and to foster the Soviet claim for Bessarabia and Romanian Moldavia.[15] To this end, the occupiers introduced Romanian literature, grammar, and text books, and established a Moldavian faculty at Odessa University. Whether this can legitimately be considered an assimilationist policy is an interesting question given the prior attitude and nationality policy of the Soviet authorities towards the Moldavians.

The transformation of the Moldavians to a privileged elite is in itself a partial explanatory variable for subsequent Soviet attitudes towards the Romanians and their administration. Moldavians under Stalin had not received anything approaching equal treatment and were consistently lower in the pecking order than either the Russians or Ukrainians. Thus, even had the Romanians implemented an impartial equality, it would have been natural for the resident Russians and Ukrainians to perceive the Moldavians as "getting uppity." Given that the average, presumably Slavic, citizen resented the study of Romanian as an imposition and sometimes insult, as Dallin points out, and further given that such things as bilingual signs were introduced and Romanian made the compulsory first foreign language, it is predictable that regardless of the "mildness" of occupation policies, and aside from the effects of Soviet interwar and wartime propaganda, a resentful attitude among the Slavic population would have developed because of this perceived assault on their relative social standing.

Central Control and Periodization

Dallin was the first to note that different periods of the Transnistrian occupation are distinguishable in terms of the policies followed by the Romanian authorities and their effect on the population. The first few

---

[15] Charles King, "The Moldovan ASSR on the Eve of the War: Cultural Policy in 1930s Transnistria," *Romanian Civilization*, IV:3 (Winter, 1995-1996), pp. 25-52.

months during the winter of 1941/1942 characterized by terror, chaos, and insecurity, followed, in the spring of 1942 and until the summer of 1943, by a relatively beneficent period for the local population, even in comparison with the pre-war Soviet regime. And finally, the period when the departure of the Romanians seemed imminent which was characterized more by the change of attitude by the occupied towards the occupiers rather than real changes in occupation policies and practices (at least until the Germans took over). A further aspect noted by Dallin that should inform later work concerns the German presence. Even though the bulk of German troops left Transnistria by the spring of 1942, the Germans did not disappear from the province, retaining a number of army echelons, a central coordinating staff, administrative headquarters for rail transport and operation of the port and coastal and antiaircraft installations, as well as offices for economic exploitation in Transnistria throughout the war.

Part of the cause for the seemingly radical change from the first few months of harshness and terror to the second period of mildness and even opportunity was thus evidently related to the fact that the front move through and out of the region, that German troops, including the dreaded *Einsatzgruppe*, and the bulk of Romanian troops moved out of the region with it, and that the military administration was replaced by a civilian one.[16] In this regard, it should be noted that due to the slow pace of authority transfer, the first official Romanian decree to the population of Transnistria was made public only on November 1, 1941, and the last regions (județe) were handed over by the Germans to Romanian control only in the spring of 1942.

Another part of the cause for these changes, again first identified by Dallin, was the existence of different and competing policy lines and interests within the Romanian leadership and between the Romanians and Germans. Unfortunately, this level of sophistication has not permeated mainstream specialized literature to any great extent.[17] While Dallin sketches the various approaches to the Transnistrian occupation, a number

---

[16] For example, the staff of the 4th Army based in Iași and in closest liaison with the Germans had proven an uncertain instrument even before the campaign. During the rebellion in January 1941, the 4th Army Commander publicly supported the Iron Guard against Antonescu. According to one authority, other senior Romanian officers, considered Antonescu only *primus inter pairs* and, as a consequence of "decades of close involvement in civilian government," insubordination and disobedience "continued to plague the officer corps." Mark Axworthy et al., *Third Axis, Fourth Ally: Romanian Armed Forces in the European War 1941-1945*, London, Arms and Armour, 1995, p. 60.

[17] See, e g., the treatment in Keith Hitchens, *Rumania 1866-1947*, Oxford, Clarendon Press, 1994, especially pp. 471-487.

of central power struggles also influenced the type and manner of policy adoption and implementation and their understanding requires a brief review of the conditions surrounding Antonescu's rise to power.

Antonescu was appointed the leader of the state by King Carol at the beginning of September 1940, after Carol had invited the Iron Guard into Government and while the Germans were insisting that the Guard remain in government.[18] From the start, the Guard, backed principally by Himmler's SD and the Nazi Party, fought with Antonescu over control of the state. Events came to a head in January 21-23, 1941, when the Guard mounted an unsuccessful coup against Antonescu. This did not end German support for a joint Antonescu-Guardist government, however, and together with the German Foreign Ministry, Hitler continued to insist that Antonescu rule with allegedly "healthy sections" of the Iron Guard. In order to placate the Germans that his refusal to do so did not mean greater unreliability of the Romanian leadership, Antonescu appointed a noted pro-German, General Iosif Iacobici, as Minister of Defense four days after the Iron Guard rebellion.[19]

Iacobici was an intimate of the German Minister in Bucharest, a frequent unofficial visitor to the German Embassy throughout 1941-1942, and was known to be "very close" to National Socialist circles as well.[20] On September 9, 1941, after the repeated failures and huge losses already incurred in the siege of Odessa, Iacobici was named Commander of the 4th Army responsible for the siege. As this was perceived a temporary posting given mistaken appreciations that Odessa would soon fall, Iacobici apparently retained the titular leadership of the Defense Ministry as well. On September 22, after the Romanian Chief of Staff was killed in a freak accident, Iacobici was named to that post, retaining his Command of the

---

[18] For a description of the dynamics between King Carol, the Iron Guard, and Antonescu see Larry Watts, *Romanian Cassandra: Ion Antonescu and the Struggle for Reform*, New York, Columbia University Press, 1993, especially chapters IV, V, and VI.

[19] General Colonel Dumitru Cioflina, coordinator, *Șefii Marelui Stat Major Român 1941-1945*, Bucharest, Editura Militara, 1995, pp. 17-19 and 75-76. Iacobici had actually fought against Romania as an officer with the Central Powers in World War I. On the other hand, the Germans did not yet consider Antonescu a "safe mail." See *Arhivele Institutului de studii istorice și social politice*, fond 10, dosar nr. 9G, f. 90; Hermann Neubacher, *Sonderauftrag Sudost 1940-1943: Bericht eines fleigenden Diplomaten*, Berlin, Musterschmidt Verlag, 1957, pp. 52-53; *Documents on German Foreign Policy 1918-1915*, Series D, Volume V, Document 169, pp. 235-236.

[20] Romanian and Allied sources are in agreement on this point. See, e.g., Ion Gheorghe, *Rumaniens Weg zum Satellitenstaat*, Heidelberg, Kurt Vownickel Verlag, 1952, pp. 223-224; *PRO*, FO 371/37374, Document R482, Telegram #31, January 22, 1943, D. Howard to Foreign Office, and FO 371/37376, Document R9441, pp. 19-20.

4th Army while relinquishing the Defense Ministry to Antonescu's *ad interim* leadership.

Thus, Iacobici, who still had his staff at the Defense Ministry, was simultaneously the Chief of the General Staff and the Commander of the 4th Army fighting to take Odessa, a completely *sui generis* concentration of responsibilities.[21] Following the explosion of Romanian Headquarters in Odessa on October 22, Iacobici requested Antonescu to approve the reprisals he ordered on the scene. The reprisals quickly became a massacre in which some 19,000 were killed. A massive cover up was mounted with the full complicity of the 4th Army Staff and the Headquarters General Staff; a feat which Iacobici was in a unique position to accomplish.[22]

At about the same time as these events, Iacobici was initiating a restructuring of the Romanian General Staff that would place it on an equal footing with the Ministry of Defense, making it and him independent of the Defense Minister's control and thus replicating Germany's independent *Oberkommand Wehrmacht*.[23] Antonescu had repeatedly refused Iacobici's earlier proposals in this regard even though the latter had German support. More to the point, the restructuring would create a position for Iacobici in which his authority would be second only to that of Antonescu and in which he would be empowered to take executive decisions in the latter's absence.

The discovery of this unauthorized initiative, previously rejected by Antonescu, led to an open and acrimonious conflict that was only partially resolved by Iacobici's dismissal on January 20, 1942. Iacobici then apparently sought out the support of Berlin and the Iron Guard. Finally, in a December 1942 *putsch* attempt mounted by the Germans and the Iron Guard, Iacobici launched an unsuccessful bid to replace Antonescu as chief

---

[21] Andreas Hillgruber, *Hitler, König Carol und Marschall Antonescu: Die Deutsch-Rumanischen Bezcihungen 1938-1944*, Weisbaden, Franz Steiner Verlag, 1954, p. 142 Antonescu was functioning at the time as Commander-in-Chief of the entire war effort as well as head of state.

[22] Axworthy (1995), pp. 143 and 217. See also the testimony at the war crimes trial reproduced in Marcel Dumitru Ciucă, *Procesul Mareşalului Antonescu: Documente*, Volume III, Bucharest, Europa Nova, 1995, p. 169. 19,000 is generally accepted the most probable figure but Soviet sources immediately claimed 60,000 deaths and a later Swedish pamphlet claimed 26,000. While in Soviet captivity Antonescu was compelled to sign two confessions, one claiming the massacre of 100,000 at Odessa and one 200,000.

[23] Cioflina (1995), pp. 20 and 95-98; *MAN*, fond 316, dosar nr. 25, f. 3-7.

[24] Order No. 19 of the Commander-in-Chief, Marshal Ion Antonescu to Army Corp General Iosif Iacobici, 20 January 1942 in *MAN*, fond Cabinetul Militar al Conducătorului Statului, dosar nr. 25, f. 3-7.

of state.²⁵ Along with the crisis in Romanian-German relations, Antonescu subsequently cashiered Iacobici from the army altogether.

Such dynamics as this, which obviously influenced both Romanian internal politics and external policies in sometimes radical fashion, were first hinted at by Dallin even though he was hampered by virtually no access to official and unofficial Romanian documents. Interesting questions remain as to whether and to what degree such power struggles affected the divergence in Romanian policies in Transnistria before and after the winter of 1941/1942.

Context

Perhaps the principal strength of Dallin's study is its comparative nature, making sense of the Romanian occupation through often direct references to German occupation policies. While Dallin was uniquely qualified to undertake this particular comparison given his earlier work on German occupation policies in the Soviet Union, there are a number of other comparisons that promise to further enlighten our understanding of the Romanian occupation and deserve consideration.²⁶

For example, there is no comparison of the Soviet occupation policies in Bessarabia and Bucovina that preceded the Romanian occupation of Transnistria. While the study of the Soviet occupation of these territories in 1940-1941 is still in its infancy, the potential for providing a valuable context for interpreting the subsequent Romanian occupation policies in the Soviet Union is selfevident.²⁷ Also useful in this regard would be comparisons with the Soviet postwar treatment of the respective populations in both Bessarabia and former Transnistria.

---

²⁵ *USNA,* Modern Military Branch, OSS Record Group 226, Box 993, Document #89221, Report #D-1692, August 2, 1944, and Ibid, Military Field Branch, Record Group 319, Box 968, File 092, August 18, 1943, Joint Intelligence Collection Agency, Middle East (JICAME), USAFIME, PIC Paper #14, "Political Alignments in Roumania, November 1942 to July 1943."

²⁶ See Alexander Dallin, *German Rule in Russia 1941-1945: A Study of Occupation Policies,* London, St. Martin's Press, 1957 (second edition, 1981).

²⁷ The significance of such a comparison is suggested in Dennis Deletant's contribution on Bessarabia in I.C.B. Dear and M.R.D. Foot, editors, *The Oxford Companion to World War II,* Oxford, Oxford University Press, 1995, p. 129. Initial attempts that merit attention include Valeriu Florin Dobrinescu and Ion Constantin, *Basarabia in anii celui de-al doilea Război Mondial,* Iași, Institutul European, 1995; Adrian Pop, editor, *Sub Povara Graniței Imperiale,* Bucharest, Editura Recif, 1993; and Ion Sișcanu, *Raptul Basarabiei 1940,* Chișinău, Republic of Moldova, Dacia, 1993.

Finally, in seeking to analyze Romanian policies in Transnistria it might be more useful, as originally suggested by Gerald Reitlinger, to treat the Jewish populations of Bessarabia and Northern Bucovina deported to Transnistria separately from the Jewish populations that remained under Romanian sovereignty throughout the war in the Old Kingdom and southern Transylvania.[28] At present, the Transnistrian deportations are generally interpreted as part of a Romanian Final Solution aimed at "dumping" unwanted ethnicities abroad (and murdering as many as possible along the way). Such an interpretation renders inexplicable the radical improvement of the treatment of deported Jews in the spring of 1942; Antonescu's guarantees, made in 1941 and 1942, of the physical safety of the rest of the Jewish population under Romanian control (some 320,000), and of his refusal to deport them to death camps in the autumn of 1942; aside from lending a schizophrenic quality to Romanian occupation policies generally. If approached in a differentiated manner, useful comparisons might then be drawn with other displacements of alleged "enemy aliens" during the war; for example, the evacuation of ethnic Japanese (also numbering about 120,000) from the Pacific West Coast in the United States during 1942 and the relocation of various minorities within the Soviet Union during the war (Volga Germans and, after their annexation, Poles, Lithuanians, Latvians, etc.).[29]

In conclusion, because of the stated intention of his work and the paucity of Romanian sources, Dallin could only present Romanian intention and policy from the perspective of those who experienced or observed their practical effects. At the same time, his insight has made this work the principal scholarly reference on Romanian occupation policies during the war to this day and a great boon to the historiography of Romania generally. I fully share Dr. Dallin's hope that the appearance of this work will spark further study of a long-neglected aspect of World War II history. I also share his belief that his basic themes and general conclusions will stand the test of time. Indeed, after almost half a century, one might argue that they already have.

---

[28] Gerald Reitlinger, *The Final Solution: The Attempt to Exterminate the Jews of Europe 1939-1945,* New York, Thomas Yoseloff, 1971, p. 426 and footnote 42. See also pp. 540-541.

[29] See, e.g., Page Smith, *Democracy on Trial: The Japanese American Evacuation and Relocation in World War II*, New York, Simon & Schuster, 1995, pp. 121-124; Roger Daniels, *Concentration Camps, North America: Japanese in the United States and Canada During World War II,* Melbourne, FL, 1981; and Norman Davies and Martin Macauley, "Deportations," in Dear and Foot, *The Oxford Companion to World War II, op. cit.,* pp. 295-296.

Odessa, 1941-1944

A Case Study of Soviet Territory under Foreign Rule

Chapter I

Odessa from Peace to Occupation

Background

At the end of the 18th century, after the conquest of the northwestern region of the Black Sea by Russia, the small Turkish settlement of Hadjibey was renamed Odessa. On a natural gulf, it soon became Russia's major maritime outlet on the Black Sea. By the early 20th century, it was a busy center of export and import, it had a fast-growing industry, and it attracted a motley of tradesmen and sailors, artists and immigrants. It was strikingly cosmopolitan and "Western" in character, partly because individual Western Europeans (like the Duke of Richelieu) had played a role in its initial development, but primarily because of its location and economic *raison d'être*. If St. Petersburg was Russia's northern window to Europe, its southern was Odessa.

To a basic Russian stock had been added a variety of other ethnic groups: Ukrainians, Moldavians, Bulgarians, Germans settled in or outside the city proper, and Jews, Armenians, and Greeks in considerable numbers Hocked to the port. There grew an urban middle class with material ambitions and cultural interests, leading to a further intensification of foreign influences and contacts. The first university in the new Russian areas in the south — *Novorussiia* — had been established in Odessa; foreign teachers, artists, and singers went there either as visiting performers or to settle. Odessa became known as "the Pearl of the Black Sea." The vigor of its cultural life, incidentally, continued pronounced — and a source of local pride

— in the Soviet era. By 1941, Odessa, with a population of some 650,000, had 18 academic and 29 technical institutes of higher learning, and 12 theaters.

Odessa had a special place in the history of the revolutionary movement. Here, in 1875, the first Russian labor organization, the "South Russian Union of Workers," was formed; here Leon Trotsky lived as a boy; here the mutiny aboard the legendary battleship "Potemkin" triggered the 1905 Revolution, which found widespread support among Odessa's urban proletariat and student body. During the Civil War, it repeatedly changed hands, being held at different times by Russian "Whites," Trench, Ukrainian nationalist, and communist forces. In 1920, it passed under Soviet control.

Under Soviet rule, Odessa changed. It did not benefit greatly from the industrial construction that expanded the productive potential of certain areas of the U.S.S.R. and transformed others. Its primary economic asset — the port — declined with the substantial drop in its foreign trade. Odessa attracted few outsiders and had little to offer that was new or unique. In the Soviet melting pot, Odessa, as a major city of the Ukrainian S.S.R., lost some of its specific color and became more like other Soviet cities. Yet, at the beginning of the Second World War, Odessa still had its specific reputation. Not unlike Marseilles, it was half-ironically, half-pejoratively held to be at once a source of shame and of pride. With its own jargon and humor, with a distinct laxity of morals and interminable jokes suggesting the existence of a semi-thievish fringe, it also stood for a spirit of inquiry and independent judgment, a quest for personal advantage and elbow-room not common under Soviet controls.

Periodically, Odessa had experienced typical Soviet crises — the end of the NEP, the break-neck industrialization-collectivization drive, and the Great Purges. Unlike other Soviet cities, it felt the Spanish Civil War: Soviet shipments to and from Spain went largely through Odessa. Odessa's hinterland, between the Bug and Dnestr Rivers, had undergone an evolution rather similar to the rest of the Soviet countryside. It was now dotted with collectives and state farms, interspersed with machine- tractor stations and electric power stations, the whole system thoroughly supervised from afar through an intricate system of controls.

Part of the hinterland included the Moldavian Autonomous S.S.R., which had been detached from the Ukrainian S.S.R., in line with early Soviet policy of fostering national groups within the U.S.S.R. The Moldavian Autonomous S.S.R. had also been created to keep alive claims to neighboring Bessarabia which united with Romania in the wake of the First World War. It was not until 1940, under the Hitler-Stalin Pact, that the Red Army marched into Bessarabia and Northern Bucovina to "reunite" these areas with the mother country. Moldavia was made the sixteenth full-fledged Union Republic.

Invasion

On June 22, 1941, the Germans struck. Like the rest of the Soviet Union, Odessa that day listened with consternation and disbelief to the radio address of Viacheslav Molotov. On the same day, the age classes from 1905 to 1918 were drafted.[1] Four days later, the Odessa garrison commander declared that the martial law *(voennoe polozhenie)* proclaimed on June 22 by the Presidium of the Supreme Soviet was in effect, and appealed to the population to uncover suspects and turn in violators of the detailed regulations, which ranged from the imposition of a curfew (2400 to 0430) to the prohibition of speculation.[2] The local papers, in the wake of Stalin's speech of July 3, demanded the "voluntary" formation of a "mighty people's *levée (opolchenie)*."[3] The registration of volunteers and conscription of the *opolchenie* were entrusted to the *oblast* and city committees of the Party.[4] Full-scale mobilization of other age groups did not begin until a month after the outbreak of war.[5]

By then, bombing raids on the city and the port, which had subsided after the initial attack on June 22, had multiplied and increased in effectiveness.[6] Perhaps more upsetting than the raids themselves were incidents such as the strafing by German planes of a column of students being evacuated by foot on the road to Nikolaev (presumably mistaken for soldiers, since they wore uniforms), and the bombing of port installations, where thousands were waiting to be evacuated by sea.[7]

---

[1] Odessa, Obl. komissia po istorii Otechestvennoi Voiny, *Odessa v velikoi otechestvennoi voine*, Odesskoe obl. izdat., Odessa, 1947-1953 (hereafter cited as OVOV), vol. 1, p. 14.

[2] *Ibid.*, pp. 28-29.

[3] *Ibid.*, p. 36.

[4] Anatolii Fadeev, *Gerroicheskaia oborona Odessy v 1941 g.*, Politizdat, Moscow, 1955, p. 15.

[5] Interview A (Compulsory military training was decreed throughout the U.S.S.R. on September 18, 1941).

The evacuation of men and materiel was a major preoccupation of the local authorities during the first two months of the war. The general "scorched-earth policy" made mandatory the removal or destruction of all tools, machines, stocks, and personnel. More specifically, a subsequent account relates, the State Defense Committee (established on June 30) "in the first days of July" ordered the evacuation of Odessa begun, with the removal of major enterprises, stocks of supply, and food stores as priority items.[8] That the German advance would continue was scarcely questioned, even if official Soviet communiqués avoided giving the impression of a serious, let alone catastrophic, rout.

Evacuation was rendered difficult by the disruption of communication and transportation lines, which had immediately followed the outbreak of war. Passenger trains did not operate until July 9, and then only sporadically; a few weeks later the rapid German advance to the north of Odessa cut the lines completely.[9] Numerous tourists, south for the summer, were another complication. Regular plane flights were canceled. Wires were accepted only on official business. Rather realistically, Valentin Kataev, the Odessa novelist, describes these initial weeks of war; his "hero" — a Moscow boy, trying to rejoin his mother in the capital — was finally put aboard a train; it got no farther than near-by Birzula (now Kotovsk), because a German plane had wrecked the railroad bridge ahead; after three days, the train returned to Odessa.[10] It was difficult to get away.

---

[6] Only a few bombs fell in the June 22 raid; the damage was chiefly in the outskirts. Though a crop of rumors grew out of the raid — Odessa seemed to generate them easily — an observer reports that the raids also gave rise to the feeling that perhaps air attacks were not so terrible as other forms of bombardment. When heavy air raids began in August, this attitude changed. Because they were more unpredictable in timing and impact, air attacks were generally feared more than artillery shelling. (Interview G. To preserve anonymity, informants are identified throughout this paper by alphabetical letter only.) Soviet postwar sources assert that attacks, sometimes as many as fourteen a day, aimed particularly at the port installations. During the period before Odessa's fall, the Germans reportedly made 360 air raids on the city. (Ia. M. Shternshtein, "Rabochic odesskogo porta v oborone goroda v 1941 g.," *Voprosy isotorii*, Moscow, 1956, no. 6, p. 100; Anatolii Fadeev, *Geroicheskaia oborona Odessy v 1941 g.*, Politizdat, Moscow, 1955, p. 31).

[7] Mikhail Manuilov, "Odessa during World War II" (MS in Russian), Research Program on the USSR, New York, 1952, hereafter cited as Manuilov), pp. 9-11; and Ia. Peterle, "Odessa — stolitsa Transnistrii," *Novoe russkoe slovo*, New York, June 1, 1952.

[8] Ia M. Shternshtein, "Rabochie odesskogo porta v oborone goroda v 1941 g.," *Voprosy istorii*, Moscow, 1956, no. 6, p. 99.

[9] Interview A. The last train to get through left Odessa on August 13 (*Voprosy istorii*, 1956, no. 6, p. 101).

Evacuation was directed by a special commission including Army, State, Party (and probably NKVD) elements.[11] As early as July 5, Communist Party members who were not locally indispensable were ordered to leave with their dependents. On July 8, the evacuation of industrial enterprises began. Other categories followed in the next weeks.[12] In early August, as rumors about the approach of the Germans multiplied, there were frantic efforts to get out "on one's own." The major avenue of escape was by sea, and thousands huddled for days in the port hoping to get abroad ships, knowing that they risked being bombed and strafed by German planes on their sea journey to Mariupol', Berdiansk, or the Crimea.[13] Others, younger and more enterprising, loaded their families on rented horse carts, or left by foot or bicycle. Sometimes, for no apparent reason, the militia would stop them on the road out of town and force them to return. More frequently, the authorities were happy to see anyone go who wanted to do so.[14]

As "Soviet patriots," or from fear, or a sense of duty, or from a combination of feelings, perhaps as much as 15 per cent of the population left voluntarily.[15] Others were urged, even compelled to leave. The prominent scientist and eye specialist, Academician V.P. Filatov, was flown out of Odessa at official behest, reportedly against his will. Among "intellectuals," only exceptional individuals seem to have been accorded such treatment. The university faculty, for instance, was given the opportunity to leave, but only about half took it.[16]

---

[10] Valentin Kataev, *Za vlast' sovetov,* Detizdat, Moscow, 1949, pp. 77-78.

[11] Manuilov, p. 9.

[12] Interview A; OVOV, Vol. 2, p. IV.

[13] Soviet vessels and sea transports made a total of 648 trips between Odessa and Sevastopol' alone during the six weeks' peak of evacuation. (*Krasnyi chernomorerts*, April 10, 1945, cited in Akademiia nauk, Institut istorii, *Ocherki istorii Velikoi Otechestveunoi vomy 1941-1945,* Moscow, 1955, p. 93). From the first weeks of the war on, later Soviet accounts claimed, the port of Odessa assumed the function of intermediary in the removal of plants from the Ukrainian and Moldavian hinterland to Novorossiisk, Mariupol', and Rostov. Not enough shipping was available to carry out this task. Passenger vessels (normally on the runs to the Crimea and Caucasus) were commandeered, but actually were used largely for evacuation of the wounded. (Shternshtein, *op. cit.,* p. 99).

[14] Peterle, *op. cit.*; interviews A and C.

[15] These estimates cover the entire period of evacuation, including those who left during the subsequent siege. In addition, of course, mobilization had removed a substantial number of adult males.

A far greater effort was made, from July on, to evacuate the equipment and key personnel of factories. By early September, German intelligence had ascertained the removal of the large Lenin plant, producing machine tools, with a peace-time contingent of some 6,000 workers, to Ufa; the "January Revolt" factory, which produced cranes and artillery equipment, with, normally, some 8,000 workers, was moved to Sverdlovsk; the administration of the Black Sea merchant marine, to Rostov; the giant October Revolution factory and some smaller war plants and chemical installations, to Rostov and Melitopol'. The André Marty plant and the turbines from the electric power stations were shipped off to the Urals, while the floating docks went to Mariupol'.[17] According to Soviet postwar sources, about 190,000 tons (the equivalent of some 10,000 freight cars) was disassembled and shipped out of Odessa, including equipment, machinery, and raw materials:[18]

	Incoming	Outgoing	
	Arrival at Odessa Harbor of Military Equipment, Arms, and Ammunition	Evacuation of Equipment, Raw Materials, etc.	Evacuation of Personnel
July 1941	5,300 tons	58,000 tons	46,000
August September October (1-15)	10,000 8,000	67,600 44,300 18,500	60,000? 67,000 civilians
Total	23,500 tons	188,400 tons	Probably about 200,000, but sources do not distinguish between civilians and wounded military personnel.

---

[16] Interview C. (The university was officially evacuated to Maikop, in the North Caucasus, and in 1942, when the Germans advanced into the Caucasus, removed to Central Asia).

[17] (OKW/Abwehr) Mares II, "Zusammenfassung aus Gefangenenvernelunungen und anderen Meldungen über Odessa und den Sektor vor Odessa," August 29, 1941, Captured Records Section, TAGO (hereafter cited as CRS), AOK 11, 35774/2; and (OKW/Abwehr) Mares II to AOK 11, Ic, October 9, 1941, CRS, AOK 11, 35774/2.

Evacuation, while substantial, went less smoothly than Soviet figures suggest. A number of ships carrying equipment and personnel were sunk on the way out; gossip-ridden Odessa spoke of "two out of three" ships sinking. In the chaos and confusion, a number of small plants and workshops were simply forgotten by the evacuation commission and received no instructions. Some of the cattle, fowl, and horses chased eastward on the roads from the farms of Odessa Oblast "safely" made it across the Bug (often, only to be overtaken by German columns there or farther east), but a considerable number of animals perished. There was considerable waste and disorganization in the removal of equipment.[19]

What contributed most to popular confusion about evacuation was the uncertainty about the ultimate fate of the city. The authorities at first aimed at total removal or destruction of factories, but, as will be seen below, reversed themselves when it became likely that Odessa would be cut off and would have to marshal all that it could of its own resources to withstand a prolonged siege. In mid-August, after most machines were gone — the precise date cannot be established — an order suddenly went out to convert plants into repair shops for armored vehicles and artillery pieces, and to improvise "Molotov cocktails" and other rudimentary weapons.[20]

All this could not but have a most unsettling effect on the local population. There was apparently a goodly measure of pessimism, intensified by the depressing impression created by the passage of retreating troops through the city in early August, and by the appearance of deserters from the frontlines, who sought to hide in the city; and there was some feeling

---

[18] Odessa, Obl. Komissiia po istorii Otechestvennoi Voiny, *Odessa v velikoi otechestvennoi voine* (hereafter cited as OVOV) Odesskoe obl. izdat., Odessa, 1947-1953, vol. 2, p. IV; Shternshtein, *op. cit.,* pp. 101, 103, 106-107. The Lenin plant reopened and resumed partial war production after three months, in Sterlitamak; in 1943, it received a special government award. The Kirov plant went to Sol'-Iletsk (Chkalov Oblast). The Khvorostin (jute) plant, evacuated from Odessa in July 1941, went through Novorossiisk to the Kuibyshev area. The Vorovsky sewing (tailoring) shop wound up in Irkutsk Oblast. The Lysenko Agricultural Institute was in Uzbekistan; the Filatov Institute worked on wounded with eye injuries, first in Piatigorsk, later in Tashkent. Some of the evacuees from stage and opera were evacuated to Kirghizia, then toured the Briansk Front and performed in Kuibyshev (OVOV, vol. 2, pp. IX-X, 91-129; *Izvestiia,* April 12, 1944). On the evacuation of the university, see below, Ch. IV.

[19] Manuilov, pp. 9-12; interview C.

[20] Some pertinent details on this reversal and the difficulties connected with the operation of the improvised war plants are described in one of the few Soviet memoirs dealing with the siege of Odessa, G.I. Penezhko, *Zapiski sovetskovo ofitsern, Sovetskii Pisatel,* Leningrad, 1949.

of weary indifference as supplies dwindled, enemy air attacks increased, and hope for the city vanished. In the first days of the war, hoarding of available supplies and foodstuffs had begun on a considerable scale. "Panic" in the sense of frantic and often aimless activity manifested itself primarily among those who sought to leave the city but could not. There was an atmosphere of nervousness and rumors; and individual instances of people being shot for violation of military orders reverberated widely. A Soviet account admits that a destruction battalion formed in the port, among other things, was compelled to "fight with panic-makers."

But there is no indication of overt discontent, not the slightest suggestion of any effort to help speed the Germans' or Romanians' arrival, or of actual sabotage. There are hints of dissatisfaction, even in workers' circles, about the way the Party brass "take care only of themselves" — similar resentment was reported in Moscow during the crisis in October, 1941.[21] By and large, this resentment remained confined within an axiomatic acceptance of the Soviet side as "one's own." The best indication, perhaps, of the failure of the population to break its ties with the Soviet regime is the "spy mania" which developed in Odessa (as in many other localities) during the first weeks of war. Had there been widespread willingness to break with the Soviets, anxious and zealous "spy hunting" would not have been so widespread. Not only Komsomol activities but ordinary citizens would apprehend "enemy agents." Such activity tended to be nonsensical. Two beggars were arrested on suspicion of espionage, and two university instructors were "caught" by a crowd because one was smoking a cigar and the other wore a Tyrolian hat.[22]

By mid-August, however, a more stable, more austere mood came to prevail. The crucial factor in bringing this about was the military situation, which left the city no choice but to settle down to a long siege. By the end of July, the German Eleventh Army and the Romanian Fourth Army had reached the Dnestr. With quite heavy casualties, the Germans crossed the river and broke through the Soviet defense lines. Once across, the mobile German columns sallied forth rapidly, taking Kotovsk and Voznesensk on August 7 (thus cutting Odessa's two rail links) and racing on across the Bug. The Romanian army — smaller, less skillful, and not so well

---

[21] Shternshtein, *op. cit.* p. 100. See also Leon Gouré and Herbert S. Dinerstein, *Moscow in Crisis*, Free Press, Glencoe, IL, 1955.

[22] All the foregoing, interview A; Manuilov, pp. 11-14; Mares II, "Zusammenfassung," *op. cit.* See also Fred Virski, *My Life in the Red Army*, Macmillan, New York, 1949, p. 132.

equipped — lagged behind, but took advantage of the initial crossing to widen the bridgehead and advance southeastward from the Dubosary — Grigoriopol' area toward the Black Sea port.[23]

Odessa faced the prospect of being cut off. The Germans, to the north, had already by-passed it. The so-called Maritime Group of the Red Army had retreated from its positions near the Romanian border but, by August 7, found itself cut off from the rest of Soviet forces. It was now reorganized into the Maritime Army for the defense of Odessa.[24] Rather, its commander, Lt. Gen. G.P. Safronov, initially prepared to abandon the city and ordered the further evacuation of troops and equipment from the port. Yet in fact there was an ambiguity about Soviet plans for the city's future. On August 8, the commander of the Odessa garrison proclaimed a state of siege. Curfew was extended to cover the hours from 2000 to 0600. Entry into the city without special permits was barred. "For all diversionary acts (shooting from attics, giving light signals, operation of radio transmitters) house owners, managers, and superintendents will be held responsible."[25] On August 10, when Odessa was practically cut off, the construction of defense fortifications — three concentric semi-circles around the city, with the open side toward the sea, the widest as far as 25 kilometers from the city, the nearest within 6 to 10 kilometers — was hastily begun. Work on anti-tank obstacles, artillery installations, and barricades within the city limits was also started.[26]

Evacuation or defense? With Odessa virtually cut off, the decision had to be made. On August 16, Rear Admiral G. Zhukov, commander of the Odessa Naval Base — apparently on his own initiative — countermanded an order of Lieutenant General Safronov, commanding general of the Maritime Army, concerning the departure of four vessels (Dnepr, Azov, Pestel', and Rostov) with troops and military equipment. Insisting that they were needed to hold Odessa, Zhukov wired a detailed plan for the defense of the city to Admiral F.S. Oktiabr'ski, commanding admiral of the Black Sea Fleet. On October 18, Oktiabr'ski and another member of

---

[23] For the most detailed accounts of military operations before Odessa see, on the Soviet side, A.D. Borisov, *Odessa-gurod-geroi*, Voenizdat, Moscow, 1954 (hereafter cited as Borisov), and, on the German side, *Deutsche Heeresmissiou in Rümanien*, "Beobachtungen aus dem Felszug gegen Odessa," MS, 1941-1942, CRS, DUM R 17058.

[24] M.A. Stepanov (ed.), *Deistviia voenno-morskofo flota*, Voenizdar, Moscow, 1956, p. 97; Fadeev, *op. cit.*, p. 19.

[25] OVOV, Vol. 1, p. 67.

[26] Borisov, pp. 13-15.

the Black Sea Fleet's military council, N.M. Kulakov, reported Admiral Zhukov's plan with a favorable recommendation to the Supreme Stavka. The following day this body approved the decision to hold Odessa and decreed the formation of the "Odessa Defensive Rayon" (discussed below) under Zhukov's command. Characteristically, Safronov was dropped and replaced by Major General I.E. Petrov as commander of the Maritime Army. On August 20, the Germans intercepted a message signed by Marshal Budennyi, commander of the South Front, to the military council of the Odessa Defensive Rayon: "I order that Odessa must not surrender under any circumstances."[27] The siege had begun.

Siege

Odessa was under siege for two months before it fell to German and Romanian forces (see map 1). By agreement between the German and Romanian commands, the Romanian Fourth Army was to affect the capture of the city, helped only by small — almost nominal — German detachments, particularly artillery and other specialized services. Initial plans called for its being captured by early September.[28] However, as early as August 20 the Romanian command began to realize that the rapid push for Odessa had failed. In spite of their considerable numerical superiority — about 6:1 in manpower and 5:1 in artillery — the Romanians were compelled to dig in and begin systematic attacks and infiltrations.[29] Axis artillery began shelling the port.

By mid-September, their supplies low, their casualties high, and morale rapidly dropping, the Romanian troops had failed to seize any of the pivotal points in the defense line. Seeing the difficulties in which their "allies" found themselves, the Germans on September 9 established a new command of "German Troops before Odessa" *(Befehlshaber der Deutschen Truppen vor Odessa)* under General L'Homme de Courbière, and provided for a German liaison and advisory officer for each Romanian unit. Hitler had promised the Romanians the loan of the entire LIV Corps but failed to transfer any troops except for one division briefly assigned to rear-area

---

[27] Shternshrein, op. cit., p. 102; Budionnyi order, intercept, August 20, 1941, CRS, DHMR 27638/3. (Soviet histories tend to date the beginning of the siege as of August 10).

[28] CRS, DHMR 27638/3; and Deutsches Verbindungskoniniando 2 bei 4. rum. Armee, "Richtlinien fur Einsatz deutscher Truppen," n.d., CRS, 132 ID 13907/10.

[29] The Romanian forces amounted to about eighteen divisions, the Soviet forces to about three divisions.

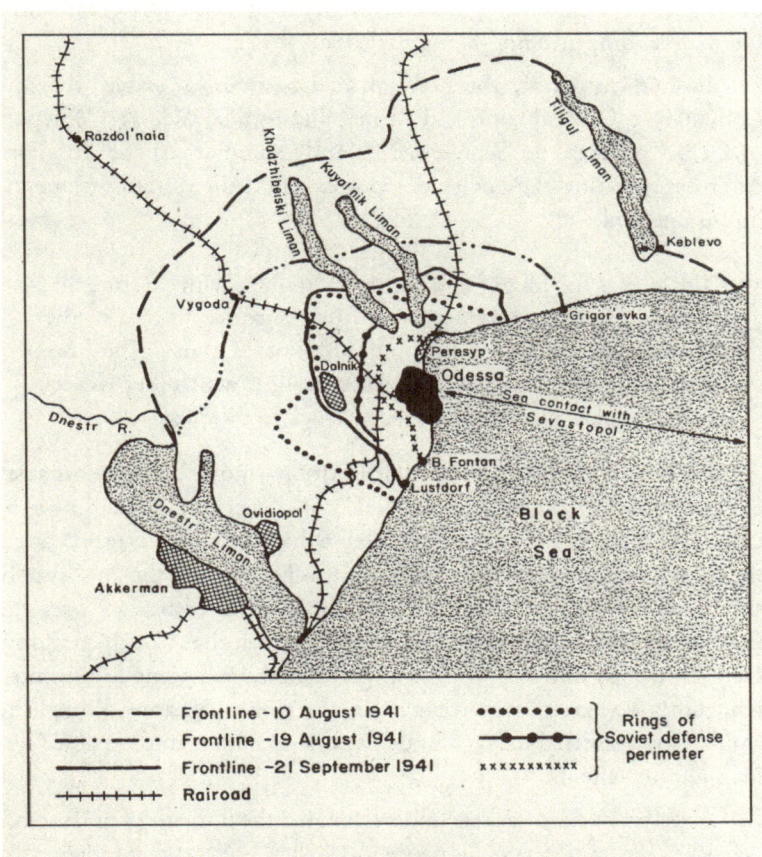

Map 1 — The Siege of Odessa

security near Ochakov. The Red Army, meanwhile, had reversed its earlier evacuation policy and was now pouring in troops, ammunition, and equipment from Sevastopol by sea, and the Red Navy maintained vessels (including the cruiser "Komintern") off-shore to reinforce the city's defenses with long-range guns and to guard against any Romanian or German landing attempts along the coast.

By mid-September the situation had become so "stable" that the Romanian command confessed its inability to take Odessa.[30] A report of Gen. Courbière on September 19 aptly summarized the situation. After enumerating the Soviet manpower and artillery reinforcements, he commented:

> The enemy has fought and continues to light with extreme bitterness. He has a very active air force, superior to that of the Romanians. He is being supported by naval guns... The Russians have the advantage of the interior line, which they cleverly use by rapidly moving troops by truck to the decisive sectors.

He maintained that the Romanian troops, moreover, were exhausted. The appointment of Defense Minister Jacobici as commanding general of the Fourth Army on September 9 had brought no real change; the Romanians were, on the whole, badly officered, and the poor supply situation was further complicated by the absence of bridges over the Dnestr. The Romanian command had demanded that Courbière throw German troops into action to help get the advance going again; most reluctantly lie agreed to participate in the next operations, though he would have preferred to stay out or else first to obtain considerable German reinforcements.[31]

Apparently, the attackers underestimated the difficulties of the city's defenders. From the bases along the Adzhalyk, northeast of Odessa, the Axis artillery could shell the port and vessels leaving and entering it. Yet the defense was predicated on the continued operation of the port. "At that moment," a Soviet account frankly acknowledges (referring apparently to September 15), "the Supreme High Command appealed to the defenders of Odessa to hold out a few more days, during which they

---

[30] Ibid.; G. Barbul, *Mémorial Autonescu — le 3' homme de l'Axe*, Ed. de la Couronne, Paris, 1950, vol. 1, p. 136; Borisov, pp. 16-36; Antonescu to Hitler, August 17, 1941, CRS, DHMR 76152.

[31] Bfh. deutscher Truppen vor Odessa, Ia, to HGr. Süd and AOK 11, September 19, 1941, CRS, Russland 13103/2.

would receive help in troops and arms." The Stavka ordered a small landing at Grigor'evka (Dofinovka), which was successfully carried out on September 22, knocking out the menacing artillery installations with the aid of two rifle divisions specially brought in from Novorossiisk, and causing a few days' confusion in German and Romanian quarters at the front.[32] Odessa gained a breathing spell. On September 24, the Romanian dictator, General (and now, since the Russian campaign, self-appointed Marshal) Ion Antonescu, informed the head of the German Military Mission in Bucharest that he must abandon the siege: casualties were stupendous, and he had no replacements or supplies. After some recrimination, by October 1 he had agreed to continue the siege, but only on Berlin's promise of reinforcements in men and heavy weapons. On October 5, Hitler informed Antonescu that, because of the capture of Kiev, he could spare some German divisions to help before Odessa. Troop movements did begin, and by October 17-20 the first additional German contingents were expected at the Black Sea.[33]

Achieved at a high price — but, in the process, inflicting severe casualties on the enemy — the successful defense of Odessa was, tragically or paradoxically, just then ordered terminated. By the beginning of October, the order was given to prepare to abandon the city.

During the siege, the population of Odessa was only vaguely aware of these high-level decisions, which were reflected indirectly and slowly in events within the universe of its own experience. Chiefly, it felt the pul-

---

[32] Stepanov, *op. cit.*, pp. 103-107; Shternshtein, *op. cit.*, p. 107; Fadeev, *op. cit.*, p. 50; Korück 553, "Betrifft Landung russischer Kräfte bei Grigorjewka an der Nordküste des Schwarzen Meeres ca. 25 km östlich Odessa," September 24, 1941, CRS, Korück 20383/8; Borisov, pp. 36-40.

[33] Deutsche Heeresmission in Rumänien, "Gliederung und Zustand des rumänischen Heeres," CRS, DHMR 18026; Ion Gheorghe, *Rumäniens Weg zum Satellitenstaat,* Welsermühl, Wels, 1952, pp. 188-190.

Earlier, Antonescu had opposed having Germans participate in the capture of Odessa, because they would reduce the glory the Romanians would gain by seizing it alone. The following excerpt from the diary of Halder, the Chief of the German General Staff, is indicative of this problem:

18 August 1941: "Colonel Metz (liaison officer AOK 11): Attack on Odessa will run into trouble if there is no German HQ on the scene... Outrages by Romanian soldiers."

21 August 1941: "The Romanians think they cannot take Odessa before the beginning of September. That is too late. No Odessa — no Crimea... Sodenstern (on phone): Field Marshal son Rundstedt emphasizes necessity for speeding the capture of Odessa. Antonescu obstinately refuses any help from us. The Führer must step in."

Franz Halder, *Diary,* English mimeographed ed., vol. 7, pp. 50, 54, and 58).

sation, with almost frightening regularity, of Romanian attacks in daytime, and of nightly counterthrusts by Soviet troops — army regulars, recent recruits and "green" city-dwellers, NKVD units, and especially marine infantry, which (often after considerable quantities of vodka) fought savagely.[34] To the roar of artillery in the distance, to the flashes of shells and to the accompaniment of increasingly frequent air attacks by German planes, life within the defensive perimeter continued.

In addition to the usual Soviet state and Party organs, there was (as indicated above) the Odessa Defensive Rayon (*Odesskii Oboronitel'nyi Rayon*, or OOR), created on August 19 by order of the Supreme Command. Its commander was the commander of the Odessa Naval Base (which was now also given full control over a part of the Black Sea Fleet); its deputy commander, the commanding general of the Maritime Army which did much of the land fighting in the Odessa area. This merging of land and sea forces was apparently intended to facilitate defense and supply operations and, so far as can be judged, was a successful administrative device.[35] The Odessa Defensive Rayon promptly issued new orders providing for greater restrictions, wider draft, the recruitment of forced labor, and severe punishments for evasions and violations.

While the OOR was concerned largely with military matters, civilian affairs seem to have been concentrated in the hands of a small group of handpicked officials, trusted and in effect selected by the Communist Party. On August 22, the formation of three-man teams — *troikas* — was approved for the city as a whole and for its rayons. These amounted in effect to a minimum government, to consist of the first secretary of the (city or rayon) Party organization, the chairman of the (city or rayon) soviet, and the chief of the local NKVD (or militia).[36] The precise relationship between these organs and the military command remains

---

[34] Interview C; Borisov, p. 19; *Bol'shain Sovetskaia Entsikloediin*, 2nd ed., Moscow, vol. 30, p. 525.

[35] Borisov, p. 28; Stepanov, *op. cit.*, p. 101.

This device perhaps merits special attention as it is unlike both other forms of total local wartime control adopted in the Soviet Union: Moscow and Leningrad defense operations and decisions were directly in the hands of the State Defense Committee (GKO), while from mid-October, 1941, the defense of other cities (for instance, Sevastopol, Tula, Rostov, Stalingrad) was entrusted to special City Committees representing "total" State, Party, and other public authority responsible to the GKO. (A.M. Sinitsyn, "Chrezvychainye organy soverskogo gosudarsrva v gody velikoi otechestvenntoi voiny," *Voprosy istotii*, 1955, no. 2, p. 35).

[36] OVOV, vol. 1, p. 74.

unknown. It appears to have been one of distinct division of functions. Evacuation of civilians was in the hands of the Party, while the evacuation of troops and supplies was the responsibility of the military council of the OOR. In fact, however, the Party (though perhaps later exaggerating its part)[37] maintained some preponderance in such fields as the draft of civilians and the registration of volunteers for the army. It also assigned new political commissars to such military installations as the naval base at Odessa, and it barred the military from sharing in the maintenance of law and order, including watch duty, civilian defense, and fire-fighting, in Odessa.[38]

The primary task of government was to do "all to help the front." This involved obviously getting manpower for the army. A resolution of the *obkom* on August 22 shows the basic approach: all capable of bearing arms must serve in the army.[39] An order issued the next day provided for the mobilization of all males from 16 to 50 (other reports give an age range of 18 to 56 and 17 to 65). Exemptions were hardly ever granted. However, evasions continued — to the point where it was announced they would be punished by shooting. Instances of malingering and self-amputation continued to be reported, as were desertions from the units at the nearby front — perhaps not so much for want of patriotism as for lack of arms, training, and food. Without uniforms, barely instructed in the art of throwing a "Molotov cocktail," the new recruits were rushed to the frontlines, and inevitably sustained heavy casualties.[40]

Another major task was getting manpower for the construction of fortifications around and within the city. On August 13, it was decreed that each city rayon must supply at least 3,000 men and women for this task.[41] Five weeks later the local soviets, civilian defense posts (MPVO), and other public organizations were empowered to draft any resident for urgent defense construction and for repairing bomb damage. In theory

---

[37] Soviet postwar sources tend to overstress the role of the Communist Party in all these endeavors, and in assessing these claims this tendency should be borne in mind. In fact, however, the Party appears to have played far more important a role than the somewhat denatured organs of the state.

[38] Fadeev, *op. cit.,* pp. 16, 32; Shternshtein, *op. cit.,* pp. 101, 103; Stepanov, *op. cit.,* p. 110.

[39] *Ibid.*

[40] Manuilov; pp. 15, 23, 25; interview C; Peterle, *op. cit.,* (OKW/Abwehr) Mares II, "Zusammenfassung," September 3, 1941, CRS, AOK 11, 35774/2; Borisov, p. 17.

[41] OVOV, vol. 1, pp. 71-72.

every able-bodied citizen was to give thirty days' labor (presumably, per year) to public duties. For the moment, everyone was to spend five days at such tasks. In many instances, workers were marched in groups, directly from work, to dig trenches or erect barricades. Sometimes such construction brigades would be supplemented by accidental groups; for instance, all passengers would be taken off a streetcar and put to work — to get excused one needed a written exemption. Such work might involve a few hours of lugging sacks of sand or rocks or taking up the macadam.[42] Within the city a giant network of defensive installations arose: 243 huge barricades of rocks, pieces of pavement, iron and steel girders, or sandbags, often many feet high, across the main thoroughfares.[43]

Odessa — like the rest of the Soviet Union — established destruction battalions *(istrehitel'nye bataliony)* in line with NKVD orders issued before the end of June from Moscow.[44] The city was divided into nine militia districts, and each was to establish its own unit. These battalions were to mine and destroy important facilities that could not be evacuated — key plants, buildings, and bridges; presumably they were thereafter to operate as stay-behinds.[45] Each unit, it may be noted, had its NKVD representative and was staffed largely by Party and Komsomol members.[46]

War production, improvised as it was, inevitably occupied a good deal of attention and was the major task of those unable to fight — women and old men. There were almost no tanks on the Soviet side

---

[42] *Ibid.,* pp. 71, 183-184; Borisov, p. 17; Peterle. *op. cit.*; Mares II, "Zusammenfassung," *op. cit.*

[43] Fadeev, *op. cit.,* p. 24; Paul Werner, *Ein sclnveizer Journalist sieht Russland,* Walter, Olte, 1942, pp. 176-177. For photographs of the Odessa barricades, see also OVOV, vol. 1, pp. 215, 245; *Bol'shaia sovetskaia entsiklopediia,* 2nd ed., vol. 30, foll. 532; and (AOK 11, Ic), *Bessarabien-Ukraine-Krim,* Eric Zander, Berlin, 1943.

The construction of Odessa fortifications was under the direction of Arkadii Khrenov, who was credited with a crucial part in the Soviet breakthrough in Finland in early 1940. (*Soviet War News,* no. 51, September 8, 1941, p. 3.) Soviet accounts have stressed, apparently with sonic factual basis, the inventiveness and ingenuity of port and city technicians and engineers in improvising loading, production, and assembling without the requisite parts and facilities. More dubious are Soviet postwar claims about the systematic overfulfillment of work norms in besieged Odessa.

[44] For background and details, see War Documentation Project, "Organization and Control of the Partisan Movement in World War II," by John A. Armstrong and Kurt DeWitt, HRRI, Maxwell AFB, 1954.

[45] The establishment of destruction battalions was begun in Odessa as early as July 2 (Sec Appendix).

[46] (OKW/Abwehr) Mares II to AOK 11, *Ie, op. cit.;* Fadeev, *op. cit.,* p. 16.

before Odessa; any improvised armored vehicle or train, any repaired machine guns or mortars were of help to the troops. One is led to suspect, however, that — given the evacuation of most equipment and some of the personnel, and the lack of raw materials and supplies — local production made a rather minor contribution to the defense of the city.[47]

The distribution of food and other goods was a further area of official preoccupation. Because of the initial hoarding and the failure to obtain further supplies, food stores had closed by mid-August. On August 25 a ration-card system was introduced, providing, among other items, for the daily issuance of 400 grams of bread per capita; the adjacent farms and mills were enjoined to speed the harvesting and milling of corn and grain for the city. Meat, fats, and sugar were likewise rationed. While there were shortages, there was no wholesale famine.[48]

Other problems were more acute. The water supply had been a sore for many a year. Odessa drew its water from a reservoir some 15 miles from the city, and often, particularly during the summer, some dry sections or the higher floors of buildings would run out of water. The Romanians seized the reservoir in late August and cut off the supply. As a result of a systematic drive to dig artesian wells, 58 wells were functioning before the siege was over. Strict regulations forbade the waste of water (for instance, the use of fresh water to flush toilets). In late August the daily quota was 1/4 pail per person; in mid-September the city soviet instituted a card system for water, allowing one pail a day per person. There were, however, variations from city section to section, and shortages continued to the end.[49]

One official decision did not involve restrictions and shortages. In the words of a refugee, "given the lack of water and of suitable shelters, the big source of relief was that they put supplies of export goods and foodstuffs from the port storehouses on public sale. For the first time in a long time, people had plenty to eat and wear."[50] Evidently realizing that it would be impossible to evacuate some of the stocks, the authorities

---

[47] Among Soviet accounts, see, above all, Penezhko, *op cit.*

A Soviet account claimed that the Odessa workers "built and handed over to the Red Army command two armored trains." *(Soviet War News,* no. 44, London, August 30, 1941). Others speak of mortars and hand grenades produced in Odessa.

[48] Mares II; "Zusammenfassung," *op. cit.;* Borisov, p. 24; Fadeev, *op. cit.*, p. 33.

[49] Mares II, "Zusammenfassung," *op cit.;* OVOV, vol. 1, pp. 73, 135; A. Chekaniuk, *Narodne opolchennia v hervichnyi oboroni Kyeva I Odesy,* Ukrvydav., Moscow, 1943, p. 33.

[50] Peterle, *op. cit.*

decided to raise morale by throwing open for distribution (at the end, apparently, without cost) huge quantities of goods. According to a German source, 15 million rubles' worth of textiles were involved; a refugee speaks of the distribution of prodigious quantities of tea, destined for sale all over the Soviet Union but stuck in Odessa when the war broke out.[51]

Officials in the field of propaganda were kept constantly busy. To counter Axis propaganda, it was forbidden to pick up German and Romanian leaflets, though actually their content soon became known. According to Soviet sources, there were about "a thousand" agitators working on the defense plants, barricades, antiaircraft points and other installations in Odessa.[52] Soviet sources state that radio, and also movies, continued to operate under the siege. Individual radio receiver sets had been ordered turned in, under threat of severe penalty, early in the war, and all that was left was the system of centrally-controlled piped *radio-tochki*. Refugees from Odessa, incidentally, unanimously stress the role of rumor during the siege, and agree on the surprising reliability of the rumors and the speed of the "grapevine" system of transmission.[53]

When the siege began, the Party *obkom* (*oblast* committee) and *gorkom* (city party committee) sounded the alarms: the enemy is at the gates; every house must become a fortress; every means must be used against the enemy — not merely conventional weapons, but even "boiling water poured on the heads of the cannibals." A new publication, *In the Fight for Native Odessa (V boiakh za rodnuiu Odessu)*, published articles, reports of accomplishments by military and civilian personnel, and verses composed to fit the occasion. Its slogan, repeated time and again, was: "Odessa was and will remain Soviet." Soviet propaganda stressed examples of individual heroism and reiterated exhortations to steadfastness, bravery, and self-sacrifice. On September 16 a decree of the Supreme Soviet awarded decorations to about forty officers and men fighting before Odessa; this was widely publicized in the beleaguered city.[54] There was little attempt to conceal the seriousness of the situation; yet, to the end — even after the decision to leave had been taken — there was no official hint of abandonment:

---

[51] Mares II to AOK 11, Ic, *op. cit.;* "Zusammenfassung," *op. cit.*; interview A.

[52] Chekaniuk, *op. cit.,* p. 31.

[53] *Ibid.,* p. 34; Interviews B and C; Mares, "Zusammenfassung," *op. cit.*

[54] OVOV, vol. I, pp. 67-68, 100-101, 138-141, 151-153.

The sacred task of every citizen (read a leaflet-poster widely distributed about the end of September) is to give all his strength, and if need be his life, for his fatherland and our native city. Odessa was, is, and will be the impregnable fortress of Bolshevism on the Black Sea.[55]

Subsequent Soviet accounts stressed the "agitation" work conducted in the port area. All the devices of indoctrination were used: arousing hatred for the enemy, fostering pride in accomplishment, and eulogizing individual heroes. The media ranged widely from "thematic discussions, newspaper reading, political news reports, and brief addresses to intimate talks." Admittedly there was a "differentiated approach:" the major effort of Party and political personnel was concentrated on key elements in production and security such as crane operators and foremen.[56]

The effect of all this on the population cannot be gauged reliably. According to one informant (who has proved to be generally astute but whose contacts were limited to intellectual circles), people were "influenced, but confused by the conflict between accounts of heroism and of the apparently smooth course of events given in Soviet propaganda, on the one hand, and, on the other, the rumors of Soviet retreats and failures, the stories of mass surrenders, and visible evidence of military difficulties." As the siege progressed, lower-level Party officials frankly doubted the optimistic official line but could not perceive the actual trend of events. Few people believed that the city could hold out indefinitely, but vague rumors and fantastic stories circulated about impending Soviet help or even of a British landing in the Balkans that would push up the coast of the Black sea to join the defenders of Odessa.

Some residents moved from the port or the center of town to the less exposed western and eastern coastal peripheries (such as Bol'shoi Fontan). In the center of the city banditry developed. Groups of teenagers and others — including apparently some deserters but chiefly "professional" criminals and near-criminals from Odessa — attacked stores, buildings, and individual passers-by, particularly at night under the protection of total darkness.[57] Post-Stalinist Soviet accounts have admitted that agitators in Odessa had the job of "stop(ping) treasonable chatter and exposing provocateurs' rumors." The last night before the city was yielded, it is asserted,

---

[55] OVOV, vol. I, p. 133.

[56] Shternshtein, *op. cit.*, p. 104.

[57] Mauilov, pp. 16-17; interviews A and C; Peterle, *op. cit.*

"diversionists" started fires in the workshops in the harbor, presumably to alert enemy aircraft. Such instances appear to have been exceptional.[58]

Everything seemed to contribute to insecurity — lack of news, nights made sleepless by air attacks, a changed pace and a changed set of values. Many of the most stalwart civilians, on whom the Soviet authorities could have relied, had left with the Red Army or had been evacuated before the siege began. Paradoxically, the regime sought to hold a city whose population included more than the usual proportion of inhabitants who were indifferent or hostile to the system. There was certainly no evidence of the determined fanaticism needed for a long siege. Yet most residents continued day after day to trudge to their assigned places of work and fulfill their duties, both hoping for and fearing the inevitable change ahead.

The End

In September, the command of the Odessa area had ordered preparations made for winter warfare.[59] The situation was becoming increasingly difficult, but there was no likelihood that fighting would soon be over, if replacements and supplies continued to arrive from the Crimea. It was therefore a considerable shock when the OOR received orders from the Stavka to prepare to abandon Odessa.

The evidence on the Soviet decision to yield the city is contradictory. A contemporary article by Major General I. Petrov[60] states that the evacuation was ordered on October 6, to be completed on the 15th. For eight days, he asserts, rear area troops, artillery, trucks, tanks, staffs, and miscellaneous equipment were being removed right under the Romanians' noses. The dates and perhaps other details conflict with subsequent Soviet accounts. According to Borisov's semi-official booklet on the defense of Odessa (written, it is true, in 1954, and inclined to endow the decision retroactively with greater wisdom than may have inspired it at the time) the factors influencing the Soviet High Command were the Germans' seizure of Perekop, which threatened to doom the Crimea, and the renewal of the German offensive to the north. The Axis advance into the Crimea and along the Black Sea shore was especially a threat:

---

[58] Shternshtein, *op. cit.,* p. 109; Fadeev, *op. cit.,* p. 17.

[59] Borisov; p. 41; Fadeev, *op. cit.,* pp. 60-61.

[60] Major General I. Petrov, "Pravda o bor'be za Odessu," *Kramaia zvezda,* October 22, 1941.

The Supreme Command (writes Borisov)... concluded that the time had come when the further defense of Odessa had lost its usefulness. With the retreat of our troops who had operated in the Crimea, the situation in which the Odessa Defense Rayon found itself worsened considerably. In ease of enemy penetration to Mariupol* and Rostov, Odessa would find itself far in the enemy's rear. Besides, for reasons of terrain, it could not be utilized by the Soviet command as a bridgehead for a powerful counter-attack against the foe.[61]

Other sources assert that the Stavka's decision to yield Odessa was taken on September 30 and that the withdrawal was to be completed by October 15.[62] The decision called for the transfer of all troops and equipment to the Crimea, to strengthen the lines there. Despite this, on October 2 the Soviet troops started a counter-attack of their own in the Dal'nik sector, which failed; in turn, on October 9, the Romanians staged an all-out offensive, which yielded but little. To explain the mounting of a Soviet attack after the decision to leave had been taken — and, at that, one costly in men and materiel — postwar Soviet historiography has been compelled to assert that the attack was a maneuver calculated to confuse Axis forces.[63] This purpose at least was achieved. To the end, the Germans and Romanians had no idea of the Soviet evacuation; not until the 15th, the night before it ended, did German aerial reconnaissance seem to have spotted the embarkations, which, of course, became more obvious toward the end. The withdrawal was difficult to plan and even more difficult to execute. A detailed evacuation schedule was drawn up including timetables and sequences according to which equipment, troops, and civilians were to be loaded. Artillery and troops capable of going into action immediately in the Crimea (they were intended for the vulnerable Ishun position) rated priority in removal. Then came valuable factory equipment and army rear units. In actual fact, however, the plan was disrupted: "The worsening situation in the Crimea," a Soviet account admits, "made it necessary to shorten the original time span for the evacuation of Odessa."[64] Yet the abbreviated schedule was not met. The special commission in the port supervising the evacuation — and consisting of representatives

---

[61] Borisov, p. 41.

[62] Fadeev, *op. cit.*, p. 62; Shterushtein, *op cit.*, p. 107.

[63] *Borisov,* pp. 42-42. See also F.D. *Vorob'ev* and *V.M.* Kravtsov, *Pobeda sovetikikh vooruzhennykh sil,* Moscow, 1953, pp. 101-103.

[64] Stepanov, *op. cit.*, p. 109

of the army, navy, local civilian (presumably State and Party), and port authorities — took even a day longer than the original plan had called for.

Kataev correctly states:

> Almost all citizens of Odessa guessed that the city had been ordered abandoned. Rumors about this had been circulating for a long time. They were confirmed by the fact that nightly transports left the harbor with troops, goods, and artillery.[65]

The chaos and destruction were apparent to all, particularly in the last 24 hours. What could not be taken along was wrecked. Horses were shot in the port and their corpses piled up near the piers. The town was littered with abandoned equipment and parts of uniforms — some from soldiers who had hidden and changed into civilian clothes. For several days, the city was full of the ashes of burned papers. The dams from some of the neighboring *limans* (river mouths and inlets), particularly to the northeast of the city; already had been blown up earlier during the siege to obstruct the Romanians' advance — the old workers' section of Peresyp', on the outskirts of the city, was flooded, and the streets, even the lower stories of buildings had been under water for months — and this added to the picture of destruction. The harbor was full of wreckage — materiel dumped to prevent its being captured by the enemy, or ships sunk by enemy action; port facilities were either evacuated or blown up. In the city the barricades loomed monstrous and utterly useless, since Odessa was being abandoned without any fight within its limits.[66] The night of October 15, the local daily, *Chernomorskaia Kommuna*, appeared for the last time with the banner headline, "Odessa was, is, and will be Soviet." Then the artillery duel suddenly stopped as the last Soviet forces embarked and left at dawn. A mysterious sense of suspense pervaded the city as news spread that "they" — the militia chief, the admiral, the local Party officials, the troops holding the nearest sector — had left.[67]

---

[65] Kataev, *op. cit.,* p. 106; Shrernshtein, *op. cit.,* p. 108.

[66] An additional irony was that the obstacles, erected well in advance of Soviet departure, permitted not only pedestrians but cars to pass through. (Karl Sedlatzek, "Siegreicher Einzug in Odessa,"*Hamburger Fremdenblatt,* October 18, 1941).

[67] Manuilov, pp. 9-10; 30-31; Borisov, pp. 18, 43-44; Mares, "Zusammenfassung," *op. cit.* Peterle, *op. cit.*; Werner, *op. cit.;* G. Costa, in *Corriere della Sera,* October 18, 1941, reprinted in *Rumänisches Blut für das neue Europa,* Bucharest, 1943, pp. 82-83; Fritz Zierke, "Jenseits des Dnjestr," *Völkischer Beobachter,* Berlin, July 19-20, 1943; LIV AK, Ic, "Gefangenenvernehmung," October 29, 1941, CRS, AOK 11, 22409/121.

Only the Romanians didn't know it. Startled by the sudden silence and the ease with which their detachments suddenly managed to advance, they entered Odessa on October 16. But their attack was into a void. What they gained in captives and booty was trivial. They pushed down to the port, and found nothing remaining but wreckage. They had literally missed the boats.

Reports of Soviet atrocities in connection with the evacuation deserve at least passing mention. They come, of course, entirely from hostile sources, and while perhaps partially based on fact, remain unproven. One informant, a lawyer in Odessa until 1944, asserts that it was common knowledge that the Soviet authorities shot the political prisoners in the local jail (or in the custody of the NKVD) before leaving.[68] Another account, reported in September, but apparently not fully accepted by the Germans in Kirovograd, had it that in late July, while the railroads were still operating, 800 political prisoners had been sent out from Odessa in sealed cars. One version had them maliciously starved or suffocated en route — only corpses arrived at Kirovograd; another version accepted the "facts," but did not elaborate on Soviet intention. There was a kind of corroboration in the two versions about a "shipment" having taken place.[69] It was also claimed that the NKVD shot some *Volksdeutsche* — ethnic Germans — before Odessa was abandoned.[70]

Perhaps the most widespread, most tenacious, yet most fantastic tale tells of the discovery, during the Romanian incumbency, of corpses in Odessa harbor. None of the refugee informants presented the story as fact and there is at least the suspicion that it was a Romanian propaganda plant.[71] As apparently reported in Odessa newspaper under the Romanians, corpses of wounded Red Army men were discovered in the course of repair work in the harbor. It has been suggested that the Soviets were attempting to evacuate them, but were frustrated by a German air attack that sank the boat. The wartime version, however, insisted that the wounded were tied down and must have been deliberately drowned. The most detailed postwar reconstruction of these allegations appears in a Ukrainian book recently published in Canada.[72] It includes testimony from two independent sources that a closed ambulance bearing Soviet

---

[68] Interview B.

[69] Deutsches Verbindungskommando, *op. cit.*

[70] Manuilov, p. 27.

[71] Interviews A, B, & C; Manuilov, p. 32.

wounded soldiers was found in Odessa harbor. As to whether this was an accident in the rush of evacuation or, as some allege, a fanatical attempt to keep the wounded from falling into enemy hands, one can but speculate.[73] Some doubt remains, moreover, whether the entire incident ever really did take place, since Tarapanov, the scavenger who reported the "discovery at the bottom of Odessa harbor, had himself been a victim of Soviet terror and was violently anti-Soviet by conviction.[74]

Originally, as has been shown, there were few if any overt manifestations of popular dissatisfaction with the Soviet regime. What strictures were made — and they were voiced more freely and frequently with the passage of time — were looted in a deeper loyalty to the homeland — and, inevitably and implicitly, to its government.

A certain breakdown of loyalty did develop, but it was more of a gradual corrosion than anything expressed in hostile acts.[75] Soviet failures in the war produced a breakdown of public respect for Soviet authority The moment when the Red Army (along with the "leading Party and State

---

[72] Fedor Pihido, *Veykn vitchyzniana vima*, Novy Shliakh, Winnipeg, 1954, pp. 112-114 (Pihido asserts that some nonpolitical criminals in Odessa prisons were released a few days before the city was abandoned, while others were shot by the NKVD (pp. 114-115). See also Petr Ershov, "Strannyi konets," MS, p. 61.

[73] Another atrocity tale concerns a mass grave at Tatarka, near Odessa. In early May of 1943, various foreign officials, including the Italian consul (whose report on the visit is available), were shown the corpses at Tatarka, in different states of disintegration but entirely unidentifiable. Witnesses produced by the Romanians claimed that the victims, buried with their personal effects, had been killed by the Soviet authorities in 1939. (Italy, Ministero degli Affari Esteri, file "Fossa di Tatarca," Maurilio Coppini, despatch, May 8, 1943, Italian War Records, National Archives, Washington, D.C., Box 1267, frame 1014833). There are reasons to doubt the Romanian version: I) the Tatarka story was never publicized; the Axis propaganda machine would not have failed to use it if the evidence were solid; 2) the above visit come on the heels of the Katyn and Vinnitsa atrocity publicity, and the Romanians may well have been led to the Tatarka story in search of further propaganda of a similar nature; 3) Tatarka is known to have been the locale of some anti-Jewish atrocities perpetrated by the Romanians themselves in the fall of 1941; 4) both the date, 1939, and the fact that the victims were buried with personal effects, permit some doubts even if the above factors were not involved.

[74] Interview G.

[75] The only ones who were obviously disloyal to the Soviet regime were the deserters from the Red Army, many of whom hid in the city. By and large, they seem to have been helped by the local residents. There were instances of soldiers hiding in private apartments in daytime and risking to leave only at night, or not at all. On the other hand, some denunciations of such hiding deserters are also known. Both protection and informing appear to have been motivated more often by human emotions than by any pervasive political sense of duty or lack thereof.

cadres")[76] left coincided rather closely with general popular disillusionment in the system; this disillusionment did not, however, produce any hopefulness about impending Romanian rule.

Even without a willingness to turn one's back on the Soviet order — though obviously already some were willing to — there were harbingers of it in unorthodox and spontaneous behavior. Even Kataev implies, in his mass scene at the pier, that Soviet controls no longer sufficed to keep order among the thousands milling and pressing to get aboard boats.[77] Families were separated and their belongings lost.[78]

One refugee suggests the general atmosphere in the last weeks: "Somehow a weakening of Soviet power was felt; people dared more." Just what they dared remains a bit vague. In the last day or two, looting assumed major proportions; the Soviet militia no longer sufficed or wished or dared to maintain order; looting, however, did not reach its peak until after the Red Army had gone. The expectation of defeat was voiced far more publicly and loudly than would normally have been safe.[79] The only known "political" action resulting from the breakdown of Soviet authority was an incident which occurred a full month before surrender, immediately after German planes had dropped virulently anti-Semitic leaflets. A group of "young hooligans" — about 16 or 17 years old, appearing to be students or apprentices — ran through the streets of a poorer section of Odessa, shouting the old pogromist slogan, *Bei zhidov, spasai Rossiiu* ('Beat the kikes and save Russia'). The Odessa militia failed to intervene, either because it was afraid to court trouble or because it felt too weak.[80]

From a military point of view, the siege had lasted so long largely because *both* sides were weak. The Red Army had over a period of two months tied down a considerable number of enemy divisions, diverted some forces from other sectors of the front, and inflicted heavy casualties. However, almost all the victims were Romanians, not Germans; the equipment tied down included scarcely any heavy weapons and a minimum of planes and armor; and the siege did less to upset the German military timetable than did other engagements elsewhere.

---

[76] The problem of stay-behinds is discussed in Chapter VI.

[77] Petia was carried away by the crowd and pressed against the very gangplank."

[78] Kataev, *op. cit.*, p. 78.

[79] Interview C.

[80] Interview C. See also Manuilov, pp. 23, 28; and interview A.

Paradoxically, the decision to yield was made just as German troops were about to be diverted to Odessa. If German-Romanian intelligence was so poor as to permit the escape from the beleaguered city of the entire garrison and most of its supplies, Soviet intelligence was equally poor in prompting the command to yield precisely when holding out for an extra few weeks would have tied down an entire German corps.

The siege of Odessa permitted the Soviet propaganda mill to build a new myth. Odessa, along with Sevastopol, Leningrad, and other Russian towns, was elevated in December 1942, to the status of a "hero-city," and there was a wholesale award of decoration to its defenders.

During and even at the end of the siege the prevalent state of mind of the population was exhaustion and confusion. Evacuation was no index to loyalty: many stayed who were normally in no sense anti-Soviet, and some who left were disposed to turn against the regime. Nor was "loyalty" itself a constant: conditions and circumstances were apt to make yesterday's Communist tomorrow's ardent advocate of a new order. Yet it can be stated that, politically, the siege and evacuation left considerably fewer friends of the Soviet order in Odessa than had been there before the war. At the same time, the Romanian troops who entered the city had undergone an extensive, unaccustomed experience of strain, shock, and deprivation scarcely more pleasant than that experienced by the city's own inhabitants. This, one may suggest, tended to make them apt to react as weak and beaten troops, disposed to seek comfort and help, and unlikely to impress their new "subjects" as superiors. By a peculiar concatenation of circumstances, the siege had contributed to the creation of a situation in which the psychological gap between victor and vanquished was small. Both yearned for a spell of normal life, a respite, a breath of clean air.

Chapter II

Transnistria: Theory and Practice

Romania and the War

Romania, which had undergone a series of domestic upheavals during the previous year, found the German invasion of the Soviet Union a unique opportunity. Under its self-styled dictator, Ion Antonescu, it espoused a pro-German orientation and abandoned its traditional pro-Western sympathies. Romania stood to gain by joining with its new "ally," who had in effect occupied it. Bucharest thirsted to regain Bessarabia and Northern Bucovina, lost to the Soviet Union the year before, and to give vent to its long-standing hostility against the Eastern Slavs. Humiliated and angered by the German-Italian arbitration of its conflict with Hungary, Romania sought in every way possible to press its claim to Transylvania, a large part of which had been ceded to the Magyars. Unstable politically, economically, and militarily, Romania was a dictatorship; the monarch (young King Mihai) and his regent-mother (Elena) were revered but hardly assertive figureheads; it had its apparatus of terror but used it relatively casually, tending to let some political foes survive. Berlin took Romania into its confidence when the war against Russia was being planned, months before the attack. It took little persuading to get Antonescu to pledge military aid to the Germans. Indeed, of all the "allies" and satraps of the Reich, he was the only one "in" on the preparations for invasion. Romania thus entered the Eastern war in search of glory and "justice" (the recapture of its lost provinces); it also entered in a spirit of acquisitiveness and revenge.[1]

It seems impossible to trace just where the idea of a Romanian "Transnistria" arose. In the 1930s there had existed in Romania a small *Asociația românilor refugiați transnistreni* — i.e., a society of refugees "from beyond the Dnestr," refugees from the U.S.S.R. Romanian eastward expansion was alluded to in conversations between Hitler and Antonescu in January and again in June, 1941, though still in vague and problematic terms.[2] Hitler, it would appear, personally pressed Romania to take over Soviet soil — in part, to reward Romania for participating in the struggle and assure its continued alliance and assistance; in part, as a crude maneuver to "compensate" in Romania for its loss of Transylvania to Hungary and to make it shift the direction of its territorial covetousness from west to east.

Given these ends, the logical area to assign to Antonescu was that east of Bessarabia. Bessarabia lay between the Prut and Dnestr; one could carve an analogous province between the Dnestr and Bug Rivers — a large, fertile, and reasonably well populated area, with Odessa as its capital. A convenient rationale to conquest was provided by Moldavian (or Romanian, as they were now called) settlers in this area; a large part of the Dnestr-Bug area had actually been set up as the Moldavian Republic under Soviet rule. This then was the land beyond the Dnestr — Transnistria (Trans-Dnestria) as politically-minded Romanian scholars were prompt to call it.[3]

---

[1] For accounts of Romania in 1941, see Henry L. Roberts, *Romania,* Yale University Press, New Haven, 1951; Henri Prost, *Destin de la Roumanie,* Berger-Levrault. Paris, 1954, and the concise statement in Arnold and Veronica Toynbee (eds.). *Hitler's Europe 1939-1946,* Royal Institute of International Affairs, London, 1954. On Romanian-German relations, by far the best study is Andreas Hillgruber, *Hitler, König Carol und Marschall Antonescu,* Steiner, Wiesbaden, 1954.

[2] The following discussion is based on a variety of sources, which are in general agreement on this subject: Evgenii Tverskoi, "Rumynskaia okuparsiia oblasti mezhdu Bugom i Dnestrom v 1941-44 gg.," MS, Russian Research Center, Harvard University, 1951 (hereafter cited as Tverskoi); *Hitler's Europe,* p. 606; *Trial of the Major War Criminals,* International Military Tribunal, Nuremberg, 1947, vol. 7, p. 163; Otto Bräutigam, "Überblick über die besetzten Ostgebiete während des 2. Weltkrieges," MS, Institut für Besatzungsfragen, Tübingen, 1954, p. 19; "Transnistrien und die Rumänen," *Ostland,* vol. 20, no. 24, December 15, 1941, pp. 428-432; interview F; Ion Gheorghe, *Rumäniens Weg zum Satellitenstaat,* Welsermühl, Wels, 1952, pp. 192-193.

By the start of the invasion on June 22, 1941, German policy-makers were aware of the "compensations" to be made to Romania. Even the relatively ill-informed economic planning staffs knew that special arrangements had to be made because "Odessa will be transferred to Romanian possession."[4] There were those in official Berlin who strenuously objected; they were largely in the group that sought a pro-German Ukrainian puppet state. The Ukraine, already due to lose Galicia and at least temporarily divided into areas of military and civil government, was now due to forfeit an "inalienable" part of its territory. This seemed unsound in principle, as well as stupid tactics, to the Ukrainian-oriented wing of the newly-formed Rosenberg Ministry for the Occupied East. Rosenberg's deputy for political affairs, Dr. Georg Leibbrandt, himself a *Volksdeutscher* born near Odessa, submitted in mid-July a formal memorandum to prove that the future Ukraine needed Odessa as a harbor (it was impolitic to mention the more blatantly political arguments),[5] but to no avail. Hitler's staff, with the consent of the military, went ahead on formalizing the arrangements with Romania.

There were also dissenting voices in the Romanian camp. There is evidence that Antonescu himself, although certainly not averse to receiving this territory, was not eager to annex it. It appealed to him above all as a pawn to trade in postwar negotiations. Transnistria would increase his bargaining power for Transylvania. Some considered this game chimeric. Iuliu Maniu, the veteran leader of the Peasant Party — in semi-retirement and in effect under house arrest — commented in disgust that Romania would do well to beware of its "trances" — Transylvania and Transnistria. In 1943, the German press admitted that "there had been... fears in Bucharest about whether Romania had done well in assuming so difficult a task." However, in the summer of 1941, Bucharest seemed "entranced."

Bessarabia and Bucovina were promptly reoccupied and on July 25, 1941, officially reintegrated into Romania. The "liberation" of Transnistria was next on the agenda, with German armies leading the way over much

---

[3] The notion of giving Odessa to the Romanians was not new. In 1885, it was part of a fantastic masterplan to dismember Russia, which was attributed to Britain. (See S. Korlf, *Russia's Foreign Policy*, Macmillan, New York, 1922, p. 34). Similar rumors were current during World War I.

[4] OKW/Wi Rü Amr (von Gusovius), memo to Stab I/0, July 4, 1941, CRS, Wi/ID, 2.1174.

[5] Leibbrandt, "Odessa als ukrainischer Hafen," Document 1044-PS, (July, 1941). (Document series cited refers to evidence introduced at the Nuremberg trials).

of its territory.⁶ On August 4, as if in anticipation of conquering it, a government-financed Romanian weekly entitled *Transnistria* appeared, which sought to show that historically and geopolitically that province was a logical and necessary complement to Romanian Moldavia.⁷

With operations proceeding at a more rapid pace on the southern front, Hitler, on August 14, 1941, wrote Antonescu concerning plans to turn over vast stretches of Soviet territory to Romania. The Führer even spoke of the Romanians occupying the area "between Dnestr and Dnepr" — a territory far in excess of Transnistria. Three days later, on the 17th, Antonescu replied, assenting to Hitler's plan with the following stipulations: the Dnestr-Dnepr region was to be divided at the Bug river into two spheres, one lying between the Dnestr and the Bug, i.e., Transnistria; the other, to the east between the Bug and the Dnepr. In Transnistria, Romania would immediately take responsibility for law and order, administration, and economic exploitation. In the eastern sphere, Romania offered security forces only once the fighting there was terminated. Romania, said Antonescu, lacked "means and specialists" to provide this sphere with civil government. Thus, Antonescu turned down a chance (which Germany might not actually have given him) to expand further to the east. Obviously aware of his inferior status *vis-à-vis* the Führer, Antonescu proceeded in his letter to ask Hitler to specify the rights and duties of the Romanian administration in Transnistria.⁸

On the basis of this exchange of views a working agreement — at times erroneously called a treaty — was signed on August 19 in Tiraspol between the Romanian and German commands.⁹ Antonescu, who had just promoted himself to marshal, thereupon proceeded to decree the establishment of Romanian occupation government in the Dnestr-Bug area. The German military command, in control there — or,rather, in control of as much as had been occupied by the 11th Army— continued to

---

⁶ See also Tverskoi; R.MfdbO., IIIa, "Vermerk über die im OKH starrgefundene Besprechung wegen Übernahme eines Teils der Ukraine in Zivilverwalnmg," August 27, 1941, Document 194-PS; *Hitler's Europe*, pp. 624-628; and Fritz Zierke,"Jenseits des Dnjestr" *Völkischer Beobachter,* July 19, 1943.

⁷ Often quoted in other publications. No files of the original have been located. For some excerpts, see *Ostland,* vol. 20, no. 24.

⁸ Antonescu to Hitler, August 17, 1941, Document USSR-242 (full text), in National Archives, Washington, D.C.; for excerpts in English, see *Trial of the Major War Criminals*, vol. 7, pp. 317*ff.*

⁹ See *Ostland,* vol. 22, no. 3, February 5, 1943, pp. 54-55.

insist, with ill-concealed hostility for the Romanians, that the terms were overly vague and that there was much still to be ironed out.[10] A three-day conference took place from August 28 to 30, 1941, at Tighina, on the Bessarabian side of the Dnestr, across the river from the provisional "capital" of Transnistria, Tiraspol.

The result of the conference was a compact signed by the chief of the German military mission to Romania, Major General Hauffe, and a representative of the Romanian General Staff, Brigadier General Tătăranu. The "Convention of Tighina" confirmed the arrangement outlined in correspondence between the heads of state but left open the northern border of Transnistria. It spelled out in some detail the rights and duties of the two occupying powers as to sea and rail transportation, economic exploitation, and security troops. The plan to have Romania assume responsibility for the security of the Bug-Dnepr area (roughly, south of the Uman'-Cherkassy line) remained alive, but in the following weeks was tacitly abandoned. Thus, Bucharest found its rights to Transnistria confirmed and, as it were, recognized by international (though military, rather than diplomatic) agreement. It should be noted that no mention was made of annexing or incorporating the province into Romania.[11]

Anticipating developments, it may be well to add that this agreement was never formally abrogated, though disputes — for instance, over the northern border of the province — continued to flare up time and again. Hitler would occasionally urge Antonescu to annex Transnistria, but Antonescu would delay, fearing that the Germans were trying to lure him eastward.[12] Individual Romanian staff officers would tell the Germans that they knew Transnistria would not be annexed before the end of the war, and that even then there would first have to be a plebiscite.[13] When pressed by Hitler to enrich himself at the expense of the Ukraine, Antonescu is reported to have suggested a trade: let Romania regain Transylvania,

---

[10] AOK 11, O.Qu./Qu.2, to OKH/Gen.Qu., August 26, 1941, CRS, Korück 20383/7.

[11] "Vereinbarung über die Sicherung, Verwaltung und Wirtschaftsauswerrung der Gebiete zwischen Dnestr und Bug (Transnistrien) und Bug und Dnjepr (Bug-Dnjepr Gebiet)," Tighina, August 30, 1941, CRS, DW Num. 4; full text also in CRS, DHMR 76152; Document 3319-PS, pp. 33-38. The agreement was followed by a German order of September 4 establishing a border along the demarcation line separating Transnistria from the German Army Group South Rear Area, and stipulating what persons and goods were to be permitted across in either direction.

[12] Gheorghe, *op. cit.*, pp. 192-193.

[13] SD Report 100.

cede Transnistria back to the Ukraine or its German successor regime, and compensate Hungary for its loss by giving it the Galician districts of Stanislav and Kolomea — an ingenious albeit impossibly intricate and unrealistic scheme.[14] Berlin did not bite, and Budapest certainly would not have either. Romanian-Hungarian tension and recrimination were on the increase, and did not abate until the end of the war.

Before the end of 1941, it was clear that Transnistria would never take the place of Transylvania in Romanian hearts. The German Military Mission in Bucharest warned that Bucharest had even found it opportune, after the capture of Odessa and the successful penetration of the Crimea, to weigh withdrawing from the war: it was felt Romania had done its duty, kept its promises, gained what it wanted, and lost more than it had been prepared to invest. The Romanian court, including young King Mihai, apparently opposed the venture across the Dnestr. When the king visited the Romanian troops fighting farther east in the summer of 1942, he ostentatiously avoided stopping and inspecting Odessa.[15] It became clear after the recapture of Bessarabia (wrote the Germans) that the majority of the Romanian people considered the war against Russia an unnecessary adventure, and that "the entire enthusiasm for Transnistria was... an artificially kindled brush fire."[16] Transnistria was looked upon as an object of plunder, but of no value as a permanent possession. "The effort to deflect the Marshal (Antonescu) from Transylvania by territorial acquisitions in the east must already be considered to have failed."[17]

Berlin was dissatisfied with Romanian performance in military matters, as well as economically and politically; yet Marshal Goering was aware

---

[14] Bräutigam, *op. cit.,* p. 19.

[15] Air Vice-Marshal Arthur Gould Lee, *Crown Against Sickle,* Hutchinson, London, (1950), pp. 33-34, 41-42.

[16] Such an attitude was, moreover, bolstered by the stand of the Western powers. The United States, for instance, informed Romania in September, 1941, that (while tacitly sanctioning the recapture of Bessarabia) it considered Romanian expansion beyond the Dnestr as an inimical act. (See, for instance, Andreas Hillgruber, *Hitler, König Carol und Marschall Antonescu,* Striner, Wiesbaden, 1954, p. 143). The well-informed *Neue Zürcher Zeitung* (July 1, 1942) seems to have overstressed matters a bit by reporting that "There is unity in Romania on the question of rejecting the political annexation of Transnistria. One seems to count on a future population exchange between the Romanians of Transnistria and the Bessarabian minorities." Other organs, particularly of the Romanian extreme right, such as *Porunca Vremii,* were at the same time arguing for annexation.

[17] Deutsche Heeresmission in Rumänien, memorandum, n.d., CRS, DHMR 76152. See also Erich von Manstein, *Verlorene Siege,* Athenäum-Verlag, Bonn, 1955, pp. 210-212.

(as he told General Thomas, head of the Economic and Armament Branch of the High Command) that "one must be very cautions with Antonescu;" he is "quite a stubborn mule but the only one in Romania who sticks to the pro-German line."[18] Especially during the following year — 1942 — there were frequent disputes between Germany and Romania (with the Italians occasionally involved) over deliveries of oil and grain to the Reich. At first Romania reluctantly yielded to German insistence that all "excess" grain from Transnistria (presumably after feeding the Romanians) be transferred to the Germans, but Bucharest soon balked and backed out of this informal commitment. The Germans had hoped for as much as one million tons of grain; bitter recriminations to Bucharest were to no avail. Finally, in November 1942 — when Germany and Romania were exchanging mutual accusations over the situation at Stalingrad — Mihai Antonescu, the foreign minister, told Berlin that the Reich could count on no grain from Transnistria.[19] As the war proceeded, the German-Romanian alliance was subjected to increasingly severe strains; the Transnistrian situation contributed much to the deterioration of the alliance.

Transnistria: Vital Statistics

On August 19, the very day the Tiraspol agreement was signed, Antonescu appointed a governor of Transnistria, with Tiraspol as his temporary capital; actual rule was to start the next day.[20] Henceforth Transnistria's status was ambiguous; Romania had proclaimed its sovereignty over it, but firmly desisted from annexing it. Its position has been compared to that of Poland under the Germans: in substance, a dependency completely at the mercy of the occupying power, yet with some of the attributes of separateness, perhaps because there was no sound ethnic or political basis

---

[18] OKW/Chef Wi Rü Amt (Gen. Thomas), "Aktennotiz über Vortrag bei Reichsmarschall Goring im Sonderzug am 7. Marz 1942, CRS," Wi/ID 329.

[19] Mackensen, dispatch to AA. October 9, 1942; Killinger. dispatch to AA, November 25. 1942; Weizsacker to legation Bucharest, December 5, 1942; Killinger to AA, December 9, 1942; Clodius to AA, December 26, 1942; all AA, reel 244, frames 160544-49, 160/75-76, 160838-39, 160841-42, 160931-38.

A side issue contributing to the deterioration of relations between Berlin and Bucharest was the discovery by the Romanians that some German agencies (apparently of the SS) "illegally" exported grain by having ethnic Germans buy up grain in Transnistria with funds brought into the province surreptitiously by German officials.

[20] Antonescu, decree, August 19, 1941 (German trans.), forwarded by Romanian General Stall, August 20, 1941, CRS, Korück 20383/7.

for annexation. Some Romanian wartime maps of *Romania Mare* — "Greater Romania" — showed Transnistria as part of the state; others did not. Romanian law did not automatically apply in Transnistria; nor could Romanians or Transnistrians cross from one area to the other freely. In practice, Transnistria's government was entirely separate from that of its occupying power; it had a Romanian civil governor and an administration that was a composite of Romanian and indigenous elements.

Transnistria, in which were included part of the Moldavian and of the Ukrainian SSRS, had an area of 39,733 square kilometers (about 10,000 square miles). Its total prewar population of 3.4 million had, according to Romanian sources, meanwhile dropped to about 2,250,000.[21] Nearly one out of five lived in or around Odessa. Odessa had grown comparatively little in the Soviet period — from about 500,000 to some 620,000; what with evacuation, mobilization, and migration, it had declined to an estimated 300,000 at the time the Romanians took over. In the following months some residents returned from rural areas and captivity; almost the entire Jewish population was forced to leave. Thus, Odessa's population fluctuated, ranging between 300,000 and 400,000 in 1942-1943, and dropping, in April 1944, on the eve of the Germans' and Romanians' departure, to 230,000.[22]

There was a considerable disproportion among demographic groups. As a result of Soviet mobilization and evacuation, the adult males were direly under-represented. In rural areas, the Germans complained, they could find no males between 25 and 50 years of age.[23] One source suggests that only 45,000 persons in the city were males above 21 years of age; there was perhaps another 15,000 in the age group between 18 and 21. Of the 230,000 surviving in April, 1944, fewer than 100,000 were employed; of these, fewer than 40,000 were males capable of military service (presumably a rather broad category that included persons earlier

---

[21] One suspects that these figures may be inexact. A census was held in early 1942, but results were never published. Romanian data speak of a density of 58.5 per square kilometer.

[22] *Bukarester Tageblatt,* August 20, 1943; *Der Deutsche in Transnistrien,* Odessa, vol. 2, no, 19, May 16, 1943; Karl f. Müller, "Das Land zwischen Dnjestr und Bug," *Deutsche Ukraine-Zeitung,* Rovno, July 26, 1942; "Transnistrien," *Mitteilungen der Gengraphischen Gesellsehnft Wien,* vol. 86, no. 4-6, pp. 198-200; Hans-Joachim Kausch, "Rumäniens Anteil: Der Aufbau in Transnistrien," *Deutsche Zeitung im Ostland,* Riga, August 17, 1943; *Der nahe Osten,* Istanbul, vol. 13, no. 1, January 1, 1943, p. 9, and no. 16, August 15, 1943, p, 373; *Novae slovo,* Berlin, February 7, 1943.

[23] LIV, A.K., Ic, to AOK 11, Ic/AO, August 4, 1941, CRS, LIV A K. 15420/9.

listed as underage).[24] Among adults, it seems reasonable to assume a ratio of 2:1 between women and men.

Transnistria was unusual in its ethnic composition. Exact figures are lacking, but the bulk of the rural population was Ukrainian and Moldavian, along with a strong admixture of Russian, *Volksdeutsche,* and other nationality groups. The urban population was overwhelmingly Russian, with a high proportion of Jews and, in Odessa particularly, of Greeks and Armenians. It should be noted here that this area, especially its southern part, was closer to a "melting pot" of nationalities than most parts of the U.S.S.R.; settled entirely from the outside, it had no "indigenous stock." As a result, the nationality question played a rather subordinate role in this area.

Odessa was the only large city. Tiraspol, the temporary capital, had had only some 30,000 inhabitants.[25] A few other towns — Rybnitsa, Dubosary, Mogilev-Podol'ski, Balta, and Zhmerinka — were about the same size.[26] Many of the first reports speak of the reduction of population at the time of occupation. Only 5,000 of the 10,750 residents of Berezovka were there when the Germans arrived in August 1941; in the inner boroughs of Anan'ev, there were only 1,500 left out of an estimated 5,000 to 7,000.[27] Soon, however, some men and women came out of hiding; others returned from near-by farms or from the road, to which they had taken in futile flight; prisoners came home; and deserters from the Red Army registered as legal residents. There was also a small immigration into Transnistria from areas of German rule, despite German and Romanian barriers of all sorts; by hook or crook some succeeded in moving into the wealthier and reputedly more comfortable Transnistria.

The port and industry of the Odessa region were both now wrecked, but its agriculture had also played an important part in the Soviet economy. Its soil was rich; its wheat, and also fruit-growing, vineyard culture,

---

[24] *Bukarester Tageblatt,* June 21, 1943; AOK 6, AWiFü, "Lagebericht," April 23, 1944, CRS, Wi/Id 2.361.

[25] Exact statistics on urban population were not published by the Soviet authorities after 1926, except for data on individual large cities, released in 1940. The Romanian and German authorities do not seem to have found authentic material on the subject either. A rough German estimate spoke of 60.000 prewar residents in Tiraspol — a rather unlikely figure.

[26] See, e g., *Der Deutsche in Transnistrien,* vol. 2, no. 19.

[27] Ortskommandantur Ananjew, "Lage in Ananjew," August 19, 1941; O.K.II/939, "Einsatz in Beresowka," August 15, 1941; and O.K. II/662, "Einsatz in Tiraspol," August 19, 1941; all CRS, Korück 20383/10.

and cattle-breeding, made it a productive agricultural region. Only 5 per cent of the land was forest; over 70 per cent had been under cultivation.[28] For Romania, as well as for wartime Germany, its agriculture was bound to be important.

The lateral borders of the province were well-defined by the Dnestr and Bug Rivers, and the southern by the Black Sea, but the northern boundary of Transnistria remained to be defined (see map 2, p. 139). Field Marshal Keitel, in a memorandum on August 24, 1941, spoke of it as following roughly the northern border of the Moldavian SSR (approximately the Kamenka-Savran'-Pervomaisk line). The "Convention of Tighina" six days later did not fully satisfy Romanian aspirations: though generally reluctant to take any Soviet territory under its wing, the Romanians also illogically sought to increase the area to be administered by them, particularly that adjacent to Bessarabia and Bucovina. On September 3, Romania requested — and received — from the Germans a northward expansion which included the areas of Mogilev-Podol'ski, Zhmerinka, and Tulchin.[29] Negotiations about other borders continued for months, but without results.[30] Rosenberg, who distrusted the Romanians, meanwhile sought and claimed to have obtained Hitler's consent to moving the border a trifle westward at Nikolaev, located right across the Bug River from Transnistria. He justified this with the statement that "as things stood now, the Romanians can look into all (German-run) wharf installations" at Nikolaev.[31] Not even this change was made, however. The following summer (1942) the border question flared up with new complexity. The German foreign office did not deem the Tighina accord binding, because it had been concluded between the two armies, not the two states. The foreign office wished to leave the question open; the German army had lost interest, because the territory had been turned over to civil government; the Rosenberg Ministry and the Naval High Command sought to recover some of the territory, including Ochakov, but without prospect of success.

---

[28] In addition to standard sources on economic geography, sec I.G. Farben, "Transnistrien," Microfilm PB 73518, Library of Congress, Washington, D.C.

[29] „Vereinbarung...," *op. cit.;* OKW/WFSt/IV/Verw. (Keitel), "Sicherung und Verwaltung des Gebietes zwischen Dnjestr-Dnjepr," August 24, 1941, CRS, DHMR 76152; OKW/WFSr/IV/Verw. (Warlimont), circular, September 4, 1941, CRS, EAP 99/99.

[30] Auswärtiges Amt (Mackeben) to Stutterheim, November 11, 1941, CRS, EAP 99/87.

[31] Rosenberg, "Vermerk über Unterredung beim Führer am 14.12.1941." Document 1517-PS, *Trial of the Major War Criminals*, vol. 27, p. 272.

What ensued were weary and futile negotiations that contributed further to German-Romanian tension.[32]

The New Order

The German forces entering the area first established the customary network of komendaturas — local military government offices. The operation of military government, even on a local basis, was difficult; there was confusion, some of it from lack of directives, some from lack of interest in it, and some from lack of equipment and personnel to administer it. There were also clashes between German and Romanian officers and staffs, each accusing the other of abuses or looting. The pattern of military occupation can be seen in Tiraspol, where the German army established a komendatura (as did the Romanians), appointed a fifty-year-old Moldavian bookkeeper, Mikhail Ivanovich Zelinski, as mayor, and ordered the screening of personnel for an auxiliary police, the restoration of water and electric power, the repair of roads used by the army, and the conscription of Jews to clear rubble. Elsewhere, e.g., Berezovka, the man picked for major had also been major under the Soviets; of his four deputies, one was a Russian, one a Ukrainian, one a Moldavian, and one a *Volksdeutscher* — this probably showed more equity and circumspection than was customary. Soon after occupation the population would be ordered to turn in all arms and ammunition — and machine guns, pistols, rifles, grenades, and rounds of ammunition (often abandoned by the Red Army) poured into receiving points — though probably only because of the dire punishment threatened in case of disobedience.[33]

Here and there a crisis would occur. In the town of Kodyma a local woman claimed to have overheard a conversation or rumors of impending Communist sabotage (the burning of the harvest), and reported this to the Germans. The latter promptly shot a number of residents as hostages, committed cruel atrocities in the Jewish section of Kodyma, and threatened similar retribution if sabotage occurred. For a few days a mood of real panic prevailed.[34] There were no major excesses, except for those committed

---

[32] RMfdbO and Auswärtiges Amt), "Aufzeichnung über die Frage 'Grenzziehung Transnistrien' an Hand der in der H.Abr. I vorhandenen Vorgänge," October 5, 1942, CRS, EAP 99/1143.

[33] See sources in note 27 above.

[34] AOK 11, file on Kodyma, August 1, 1941, CRS, AOK 11, 35774/6.

by the SD's (Security Service of the SS) special action teams (the so-called *Einsatzgruppen*). The command of the 11th Army was primarily interested in securing the rear, establishing a *modus vivendi,* and pushing on to the east. "On the whole," the Germans reported on September 2, "the population is entirely willing to work and glad to... have been liberated. Only rarely does one encounter sabotage groups..."[35]

By late August, Romanian officers began to claim that they had been appointed "prefects" and were to replace the German komendaturas; two weeks later, by mid-September, all the military government units of the German army (technically, Army Rear Area 553) had moved eastward, out of Transnistria. The only officers left were in Tiraspol and in Berezovka, to help transient German military personnel.[36] There were two exceptions to the general evanescence of German influence and control. In the ethnic German *(Volksdeutsche)* settlements of Transnistria, the Reich reserved special rights and inhabitants received privileged treatment.[37] For instance, in the Kuchurgan area — which included the settlements of Selz and Mannheim, southeast of Tiraspol — the Germans replaced the initial Romanian administrators, established a German-style village government consisting of a village *Schulze* (mayor), a scribe, and a village council.

> Village-wide assemblies were convened (reported the regiment in charge); those to be appointed were determined by acclamation, and then they were installed by the responsible sergeant by a handshake...

Confirmed later by the German district administration, these local appointees, gathered in one of the larger *Volksdeutsche* villages to elect an area *Schulze*. In the villages, three-men courts were also picked, as were special appointees for school and church affairs and animal husbandry.[38] The Germans maintained certain agencies in Romanian Transnistria. Keitel, in his memorandum of August 24, 1941, had specified that a central German coordinating staff would continue on the spot — preferably in Odessa. The German army's transport administration was to assume responsibility for the repair and operation of the trunk rail lines. The German

---

[35] Beauftragre der Chefs der SiPo u. SD beim Bfh. rückw. H. Geb, Süd, "Tärigkeit," September 2, 1941, CRS, AOK 11, 35774/6.

[36] Korück 553, "Übergriffe deutscher Polizei-Organe im rumänischen Verwaltungsgebiet," October 5 and 6, 1941, CRS, Korück 20383/8.

[37] See Chapter V, for a discussion of the *Volksdeutsche*.

[38] "Schutzmassnahmen auf Aufbauarbeit der 6 /I.chr-Rgt 'Brandenburg' z.b.V. 800 in den deutschen Siedlungen... (13.8. bis 25.9.41)," CRS, AOK 11, 35774/3.

army was to provide coastal and antiaircraft installations along the Black Sea.[39] Virtually all of these provisos stemmed from German self-interest or from distrust of their militarily inferior Romanian "ally." The German-Romanian Convention of Tighina (August 30)[40] fully spelled out the Reich's prerogatives in each of these fields, and also in communications and economic liaison. Pursuant to it, a German commandant had charge of the port of Odessa and regulated its security, reconstruction, and use.[41] An over-all liaison staff (*Verbindungsstab*) replaced General Courbière's operational headquarters; at first under Panzer General Lutz, and from December, 1941, under Lieutenant General von Rothkirch, it had command authority over virtually all the diverse German army echelons remaining in Transnistria.[42]

In addition to the military (and some counterintelligence personnel), the German maintained diplomatic representatives in Transnistria. One of the subordinate German ministers in Bucharest, Pflaumer, was made Antonescu's titular adviser on Transnistrian affairs — but without voice or authority.[43] Since Transnistria was, as it were, foreign territory, Germany in the late spring of 1942 opened a Consulate General in Odessa. Its head, Dr. Werner Stephany, technically reported to ambassador Killinger, the Nazi fanatic who represented the Reich in Bucharest. There were also occasional visits of German officials and dignitaries to the area — SS General Lorenz came in July, 1942 (in connection with the *Volksdeutsche* question), and Reich Minister of Transportation Dorpmüller in October 1943 (in connection with problems of shipment and evacuation).[44]

Romanian rule began with a peculiar situation. For nearly two months, while Odessa itself was being fought for, the Romanians had had only the rural hinterland to occupy. They seemed reluctant to establish a full-fledged administration with part of the area still in enemy hands. The greatest hindrance to the establishment of civil rule was the Romanian

---

[39] Sicherung und Verwaltung...," *op. cit.*

[40] Vereinbarung...," *op. cit.*

[41] Verbindungsstab der deutschen Wehrmacht in Transnistrien, "Merkblatt," February, 1942. CRS, DHMR 29221/1.

[42] OKH/HPA to VSt DW Transnistrien, wire, December 9, 1941, CRS, DHMR 76152.

[43] Deutsche Heeresmission in Rumänien, *op. cit.*

[44] *Der Deutsche in Transnistrien,* vol. 1, no. 3, August 2, 1942; *Bukarester Tageblatt,* October 3, 1943.

troops themselves, chief disrupters of the very law and order they were supposed to maintain. It was not without reason that the Soviets, after the war, charged that the Romanians in Transnistria had as their slogan, "Plunder and Romanize."[45]

The reasons for widespread pillage are not hard to determine. The Romanian army had never had the discipline needed to make it immune to opportunities for personal advantage. It was, moreover, expressly invited to live off the land. Revenge had inspired the entire campaign — and seemed to sanction abuses and retribution. The Romanian soldier received but 2 lei a day, a trilling sum, and often not even this was paid. As the Romanian army had never properly organized its supplies and reinforcements, the troops were more or less compelled to take what they could.[46]

But this does not wholly account for the wanton destructiveness, the physical mistreatment, rape, and manslaughter frequently reported by the more highly disciplined German army. (Acts of *individual* terrorism and abuse were punished by the Germans; but collective acts on a much vaster scale were both ordered and carried out by them). A fat dossier could be made of German reports to higher echelons about Romanian pillage, requisitioning without pay, and destruction of buildings, equipment, or food-sniffs; also of their senseless looting of useless items, discrimination in the distribution of food and supplies and the assignment of jobs, and a variety of other offenses. The reports are too numerous and come from too widely-scattered sources to have been concocted by anti-Romanian officers.[47]

Things reached the point where General Schobert, CG of Eleventh Army (killed soon after), wrote Marshal Antonescu a frank letter of complaint. Coming from the pen of a German professional military man who

---

[45] U.S.S.R., Extraordinary Commission, "Soobshchenie Chrezvychainoi Komissii po ustanovleniu i rassledovnniiu zlodeianii. O zlodeianiiakh. sovershennykh nemersko-rumynskimi zakhvatchikami v gorode Odesse i raionakh Odesskoi oblasti," June 13, 1944 (International Military Tribunal Document USSR-47, hereafter cited as Document USSR-47).

[46] Vierjahresplan, Geschäfrsgmppe Ernährung, Georg Reichart, "Bericht," November 15, 1941, CRS, Wi/ID 58.

[47] O.K. Katarshino, report to Korück 553, August 20, 1941, CRS, Korück, 20383/10; "Schutzmassnahmen...," *op. cit.*; Beauftragte des Chefs der SiPo u. SD beim Bhf. H.Geb. Stid. "Bericht über das Verhalten der rumänischen Besatzungstruppen," September 2, 1941, CRS, AOK 11, 35774/6; 2./123, "Meldung," August 8, 1941, CRS, LIV AK 15420/9; UV AK., Ic, "Übergriffe rumänischer Soldaten," August 17, 1941, CRS, LIV A.K. 15420/9; Leonid Sobolev, *Dorognmi pobed v Buhhnreste*, Voenizdar, Moscow, 1944; AOK 11, IV Wi, "Tätigkeitsbericht," August 25, 1941, CRS, Wi/ID 2.515.

was not disposed to sentimentality or compassion for the native population, it makes striking reading. It was, after all, addressed to the head of an allied state. Living off the land, he wrote Antonescu, does not mean wanton rape or senseless destruction. "The plunder by Romanian in the occupied areas has assumed such proportions that one must anticipate a political aversion (against the Germans) on the part of the Ukrainian population." Schobert requested, in the interest of victory and pacification, that the sternest measures be taken against violators of discipline.[48]

In the following months, there was some improvement, especially as combat troops moved on, as transportation and supply facilities operated more smoothly and as the civilian gendarmerie replaced the military police. But the German army still had reason to complain about Romanian behavior[49] — and if *they* did, one may safely assume that local residents had even more reason to complain. Until the end of 1941, the use of force remained widespread and the most usual "vehicle of change."[50]

In Odessa proper, the "new order" was quickly established.[51] One can scarcely speak of an "interregnum" between Soviet and Romanian rule. The Romanian troops entered suddenly, obviously unprepared for the seizure. Groups of 20 to 30 men would be assigned to a street or section, would find billets, and post the first orders. Romanian behavior was, as one refugee put it, "without special dignity or airs;" the few Germans who arrived, on the other hand, inspired both awe and fear. The new authorities almost at once proclaimed a list of "don'ts" under pain of death. All orders were to be obeyed; arms were to be turned in; 9:00 p.m. was set as the curfew hour; all public gatherings were forbidden; all Red Army men were to report and register.

---

[48] General von Schoberr to Marshal Antonescu, August 15, 1941, CRS, Korück 20383/ 7.

[49] In turn, the Romanians lodged complaints about the Germans whenever they could be shown to have committed abuses, forcibly removed machines, or the like.

[50] Dr. Ihnen, OKVR, "Tätigkeitsbericht für die Zeit vom 15 XI.-15.XII.," December 15, 1941, CRS, DHMR 76152; AOK 11, IV Wi, "Tätigkeitsbericht," August 6, 1941, CRS, Wi/ID 2.580; AOK 11, IV Wi, April 15, 1942, CRS, Wi/ID 2.580 (summary report, no title).

[51] The following section is based on interviews A, C; Peterle, *cit.*; Tverskoi; Manuilov, pp. 34-37; *Rumänisches Blut für das neue Europa*; *Bukarester Tageblatt*; Werner, *op. cit.*, pp. 176-180; Petr Ershov, "Strannyi koners"; Rafael Lemkin, *Axis Rule in Occupied Europe*, Carnegie Endowment, Washington, D.C., 1944, pp. 565 ff.

Other orders dealt with the repair of public utilities.[52] "Water, light, and bread" were the three main objectives which the city administration gave as its first task. Difficult enough in normal times, it was made more difficult by the destruction already by the Soviets and by the further destruction done by such agents as continued to operate in the area.

The task of the new authorities was also complicated by the lawlessness of both sides, the population and the army. Looting in Odessa, it will be recalled, started on the eve of the Red Army's departure. Now it became more widespread. Who started it, who engaged in it? No one seems able to tell. "As usual, when authorities change," one refugee explains, "there appeared 'dark elements'" who looted stores and apartments abandoned by the evacuees. According to another informant, there was a sequence to the looting: food stores first, then furniture and household equipment, then useless things, in an increasing pitch of "acquisitiveness" as long-frustrated desires to use hands and elbows were released. A good many of the looters were teenagers. Here is how a novelist describes it; in an unpublished manuscript he writes:

> On the way home, Lilia noticed in the buildings of the sanitarium (on the outskirts of Odessa) groups of village boys, racing each other home from the sanitarium... They were stealing the belongings of the resort pharmacy. They carried containers of all shapes and sizes, jars and glasses, rubber syringes... boxes with pills and medicine; someone had carried off the pharmacy scales.
>
> "In town they're taking darned near everything from the stores and warehouses, it's awfully crowded, and nobody's stopping you," an eight-year-old boy proclaimed with the excitement of sensational news...[53]

The sanitariums were, indeed, among the first buildings pillaged, and soon cases of poisoning from stolen medication were reported. The *neft'baza* (gas station) was likewise early wrecked. The sugar supply at the *PO* (the consumers' cooperative) was looted. A few people tried to stop the looters, but in vain. It seemed to be a kind of release after long tension. At the root of the pillaging were need and deprivation, but once begun, "everything went." Curiously, the drive was not merely acquisitive; it was also destructive — some statues (for instance, of Stalin) and some buildings (apartments of hated officials) were completely wrecked. Looters

---

[52] Text of order of October 16, 1941 in OVOV, vol. 2, p. 6.
[53] Ershov, *op. cit.*, p. 3.

fought each other, or ganged up to deprive others of some particularly cherished spoil. Not only state property but the goods of neighbors who had left were shamelessly appropriated.

Many, of course, did not join in the looting — from fear, principle, or lack of "know-how." And after a few days, the pillage subsided. "On the streets there are few people; the shops have been looted; there is no light; no streetcars are running... It is scary in town."[54]

The people as a whole were neither overjoyed nor irrevocably hostile to the new order; they were insecure and wondered about the future. The Romanians themselves acknowledged that many feared them more than they had feared Soviet terror.

The same novelist describes October 17 in a suburb of Odessa: All day long fishermen and their wives would drop in to talk it over with N: "What does it all mean? And won't it even be worse than before?"[55]

The Romanians were not necessarily evil, but they were foreigners, hungry and lousy strangers, who could not even make themselves understood. Who knew what they were up to? An Italian newspaperman gives a scene form the second day of the occupation: an elegant old piano is standing on the sidewalk, abandoned by some evacuee or a looter who had changed his mind... a girl goes by, stops to play some chords, and a few people gather... furtively she sits down to play, but "without joy..." just then a Romanian officer appears down the block... the music stops... he only smiles and walks on... and the playing resumes...[56] Except for some shooting at night, some arrests by day, except for the wiry young looters, for the hungry and frustrated who joined them, except for the few busy-bodies who already began to "adjust" to the new regime and were writing memoranda and manifestoes to the Romanian authorities, Odessa was quit and tired.

The ordinary householder experienced the Romanians in a special way. Hungry Romanian patrols would go from house to house, from apartment to apartment, ostensibly seeking *puşcă* (weapons), which were to have been surrendered. It did not take housewives long to discover that their guests' interest could be easily deflected from official duties to food, above all to sugar. Indeed, Odessa residents soon spoke of "sugar patrols,"

---

[54] *Ibid.*, p. 30.

[55] *Ibid.*, p. 22; Hans Schumacher, "Im Government Transnistrien," *Deutsche Allgemeine Zeitung,* October 14, 1943.

[56] *Corriere della Sera,* October, 21, 1941.

because visits usually ended with sugar or the entire sugar container (especially if it was silver) in the pockets of the soldiers. A cup of tea with sugar came to symbolize a willingness to cooperate with inspecting patrols. However, there was a limit to the sugar residents had, and when the patrols started multiplying, coming back under spurious pretexts to the same apartments within hours of each other, residents began to insist that patrols indicate the completion of their inspection. The verdict, "VERIFICAT" (verified), written in chalk, adorned the doors of Odessa houses. But not even this deterred some Romanian patrols; the same door might have five, six, or more "VERIFICAT"s — witness of a once abundant sugar supply.[57]

All this did little to inspire awe of or respect for the Romanian troops. Two specific acts committed by the Romanians soon furthered the alienation: their acquisition of "prisoners of war," and the mass retaliation for an act of Communist sabotage.

Capture and Terror

The Romanians ordered all males to report, with their Soviet passports, to certain schools or other official buildings to be registered and to have a Romanian visa entered into the passport. Jews were to report to separate registration boards. Used to Soviet insistence on "documentation," the population accepted this without undue surprise or concern, and by and large heeded the order. It was amazing, refugees state, how many males had apparently managed to stay in Odessa. On the day of registration non-Jews soon realized that the armed guards at registration points would not let them out; soon there were huge crowds inside, milling around aimlessly, waiting to be processed. At 6:00 p.m., all (except a few who, by pull or bribes, had managed to get out) were marched off to a local barracks. From there, thousands — these civilians picked at random — were sent to Romania as "prisoners of war." The rationalization was that any adult male must have been a Red Army soldier, an official, or a Communist. Few *bona fide* captives had been taken in Odessa; the Romanians, therefore, devised this way of acquiring at least 7,000 prisoners. Many of those taken had no connection whatever with the Red Army or the military. According to German intelligence there were soldiers in Odessa:

---

[57] Peterle, *op. cit.;* interview C; Manuilov, pp. 37-40.

...several times this number remain in the city in civilian clothes. All these elements have served their military service in the Red Army and have either remained behind on their own or else were purposely left behind.

But these were often in hiding. It was simpler to send off the "registrees" — white-collar workers and janitors, intellectuals, and laborers.

In Romania the prisoners were for the most part assigned to farm labor. After some months, they began to be "released" from prisoner-of-war status. Some died in captivity; those who came back generally told tales of abominable conditions, but not of systematic cruelty or shooting.[58]

The feeling of having been trapped, cheated, and mistreated persisted, despite the reversal of policy toward the prisoners — which coincided with a general trend on the part of the Romanian occupying authorities toward a more liberal course. By the spring and summer of 1942, some prisoners from Transnistria were being returned; even Soviet accounts were constrained to admit this. Their return had practical results especially in the rural areas, relieving the shortage of manpower on the farms.[59]

The Romanians did seek and succeed in getting the Germans to release Transnistrian prisoners, arguing (as did the "Bessarabian wing" in Transnistrian politics) that Transnistrians had a status comparable to that of Romanian citizens. The status was certainly not identical, however; the Romanian army — *for pragmatic reasons* — did not demand and did not even permit military service of Transnistrians.[60]

There continued to be prisoner-of-war camps in Transnistria, even in Odessa itself. Though poorly kept, housed mostly in buildings wrecked by aerial attack, the prisoners were still better off than their countrymen in Germany. In the last year of the occupation the Germans even permitted local residents to help care for them. Russian girls brought food, and the women's auxiliary of one of the few Russian organization permitted — veterans of the First World War — gave prisoners prepared parcels, food, and tobacco. Lectures and religious services were

---

[58] Manuilov, pp. 37-40; Peterle, *op. cit.*; interview E; Abwehrstelle Rumänien, "Bericht über Wahrnehmungen in Odessa," November 4, 1941, CRS, DHMR 29222.

[59] Valantin Kataev, *Za vlast' sovetov*, 1949 ed., p. 359; interview A; German Consulate, Odessa, dispatch, February 26, 1943, AA, reel 1273, frames 342512-15.

[60] Tverskoi.

eventually allowed in the largest camp in Odessa. These efforts in their behalf, it is reported, were genuinely appreciated by the captives but failed to dispel their profound skepticism of anything that came to them by or through the Germans.[61]

The awareness that there were prisoners of war, both wrongly so-called and genuine, helped perpetuate the feeling of distance between the population and the Romanians. Instinctively and unthinkingly, the people felt closer to and commiserated with the captives; their hostility to the Romanians seems not to have diminished when the Romanians relaxed their policy and permitted prisoners to be aided.

Acts of terror and atrocities committed by the occupying forces naturally also aroused violent feelings of hostility among the native population. The Romanian authorities started taking hostages within a few days of the occupation. Moreover, "suspects were seized and hanged on poles or from balconies" for the most insignificant violations of orders, though more serious violators sometimes would be treated dilatorily and laxly. On October 17, it was reported, the Romanians shot Soviet citizens who had membership cards in MOPR or the Osoaviakhim. On October 19, the Romanians began taking action against the local Jewish population, detailed elsewhere in this paper. But terror reached its peak after October 22, when the former NKVD headquarters on Marazli (later Engels) Street, occupied by the Romanian staff, was blown up by a Soviet agent. Retaliation was prompt, cruel, and indiscriminate. Public posters threatened the execution of hostages at varying ratios, up to 100 for every Romanian soldier, and 200 for every Romanian officer or German killed. And, in the words of a factual *Abwehr* report:

> ...on the morning of the 23rd (the day after the explosion), about 19,000 Jews were shot on a square in the port, surrounded by a wooden fence. Their corpses were sprinkled with gasoline and burned.

Thousands more were allegedly taken to Dal'nik and there massacred in anti-tank trenches. But not only Jewish residents were apprehended; and, in the initial frenzy of retaliation and terror, any suspicion sufficed for hanging. This reign of terror — of perhaps no more than ten days — cast a cloud of gloom over Odessa. Refugees report that women and children would become almost hysterical at the sight of long rows of gallows, for instance, along the trolley line leading out of the city. Others tell of groups

---

[61] Manuilov, pp. 121-124.

of arrested citizens being chased over Soviet-laid mine fields to make the mines explode — with many casualties.[62]

When the notorious German *Einsatzgruppe* "D" moved out of Transnistria, to Nikolaev and the Crimea, it left memories of terror and mass annihilation. As time went by semblance of order descended. True, for a while, it was almost routine to hang anyone caught with a Party membership card or an army paybook. Then this ceased. Terror from then on was more localized, more pinpointed against individual groups — such as Jews or partisans — and more "legalized."[63] Yet the early days of horror left what seems to have been an indelible mark on the people and prevented them from identifying themselves with the Romanians. Soviet life had, of course, accustomed the population to violence and terror. It was the unabashed publicity; the almost proud display of cruelty; and the means of execution which shocked the people. A secret murder in an NKVD jail was accepted far more readily than a public hanging or the burning of hostages. Deep down, one suspects, there was a feeling that there had been some tortuous rationale for Soviet terror; that of the new lords seemed utterly unjust.[64]

Transnistria: The Government

A decree-law promulgated by Antonescu on August 19, 1941, but not publicized until later, established the government of Transnistria. It outlined the structure of government and gave as the first tasks of the administration: to supervise the resumption of normal economic life,

---

[62] Peterle, *op. cit.;* Ershov, *op. cit.,* p. 27; Document USSR-47; Mathias Carp, *Cartea neagră,* SOCEC, Bucharest, 1947, vol. 3, p. 199; OVOV, vol. 2, p. 20.

[63] As late as November 3, 1941, it is true, the Romanian command provided the death sentence for any injury to the occupying personnel, sabotage of their equipment, or concealment of food supplies from them. *(Odesskaia gazeta,* no. 4, November 5, 1941). On November 20, after two Communists had killed two Romanian soldiers, the number of retaliatory hostages for every terror act was raised to 500. (OVOV, vol. 2, p. 7). There is no evidence that the decree was actually enforced.

The relative decline of terror after the first months is documented by Soviet postwar figures. In Golovanevsk rayon, a total of about 1,000 persons were liquidated under the occupation. Of these, 908 perished before the end of 1941. (Ia. Iarovyi, "Ne zabudim, ne prostim!" *Bol' shevtstskoe znamia,* May 6, 1944; OVOV, vol. 2, p. 26).

[64] See also SD Report 100; interview C; Korück 553, *op. cit.;* O.K. Ananjew, *op. cit.;* E.I. Mamukov, "Rumynskaia okkuparsiia Odessy i Transnistrii v 1941-1944 gg," MS (hereafter cited as Mamukov), Institute for the Study of the U.S.S.R., Munich, 1955, pp. 19-20.

particularly agriculture; to repair roads, railroads, and bridges; to establish an indigenous police subject to the supervision of the Romanian gendarmerie; and to open schools and churches. This order included both a slight demagogic appeal to the new subjects and an interesting definition of their prerogatives: "All citizens of the province will enjoy civic rights, except for the right to engage in any political activities whatsoever."[65] The Transnistrian government was publicly proclaimed on October 17, the day after Odessa fell.[66] Up to December 1942, the governor's headquarters was Tiraspol; it then was moved to Odessa,[67] and the restored Vorontsov Palace was used both as the governor's residence and as his official headquarters.

The civil governor was Professor Gheorghe Alexianu.[68] The holder of a chair in administrative law at Cernăuți University, a close friend of the "Number Two Man" of Romania, Mihai Antonescu, (Alexianu and Mihai Antonescu had co-authored the volume on Romanian law in a comparative-law series published in Paris before the war),[69] Alexianu had the reputation of being both "the only liberal" in the Romanian government and the sponsor of the anti-Semitic measures under the Goga regime a few years earlier. Alexianu was apparently a Western-type intellectual with megalomaniac tendencies, some administrative ability, and a good deal of vitality.[70] His secretary-general was Emil Cercavski (or, in Russian spelling, Cherkavski).[71]

---

[65] Antonescu, decree, August 19, 1941, *op. cit.*

[66] Joseph B. Schechtman, "The Transnistria Reservation," *YIVO Annual of Jewish Social Science*, New York, 1953, vol. 8, p. 178; Prost, *op. cit.*, p 163.

[67] Many refugee informants dared the establishment of the Governorship as of early 1943, clearly not aware that it had been functioning elsewhere for over a year.

[68] The substitution of civil for military government did not involve, of course, the complete removal of Romanian troops. Until 1943, one Romanian "fortification division" was stationed in and around Odessa, and three other divisions, formed almost entirely of reservists undergoing training, were stationed in Transnistria. Only in 1943 was a regular division — or rather, the remnants of an infantry division badly mauled at the front — stationed in Transnistria.

[69] Gheorghe Alexianu and Mihai Antonescu, *Roumanie*, Delagrave, Paris, 1933.

[70] Zierke, *op. cit.*; interview F; gh, "Transnistrien: Das Werk des Gouverneurs Alexianu," *Das Reich*, Berlin, August 1, 1943; Gerald Reitlinger, *The Final Solution*, Beechhurst, New York, 1953, p. 398; *Bukarester Tageblatt*, October 20, 1941; *The New York Times*, April 22, 1944.

[71] Carp, *op. cit.*, vol. 3 p. 18; *Der Deutsche in Transnistrien*, December 13, 1942; *Bukarester Tageblatt*, June 20, 1943.

In addition to his own secretariat, the Governor's staff consisted of a series of Directorates. The original Antonescu order had established Directorates in such fields as administration, transportation, agriculture, industry, education, religion, sanitation, and finance; by October 1942, their number had grown to 19, some with sizable staffs. Their functions expanded with the passage of time; thus, the Propaganda Directorate assumed responsibility for all censorship and also managed the piped radio system once it was restored.[72]

In the civil government there were, as a matter of policy, a considerable number of Bessarabians who knew the Russian language and were familiar with the cultural background and special problems of Transnistria. There were also ambitious young Romanians who had studied under Alexianu or his colleagues and obtained draft exemptions to serve in this way. In the hope of attracting "good people" — and making it possible for them to give up other jobs — Antonescu, in his first decree, provided that officials in Transnistria were to receive double the corresponding salary in Romania plus a subsistence allowance up to the basic salary. A Romanian civil servant transferred to Odessa would thus receive three times the pay he drew in Iași or Galați. A number of Transnistrian officials were Romanians who had been attracted by high pay.[73]

Transnistria was divided into thirteen districts (called, as were such districts in Romania, *județ*).[74] Each district was headed by a prefect, who had to be Romanian and was frequently an army officer. A sub-prefect, whose duties were largely advisory, was a local resident.[75] In Anan'ev, for instance, the prefect was a Romanian colonel, the sub-prefect a local Moldavian, who had been a tsarist officer and had at one time lived in Bessarabia.[76]

---

[72] Dr. B., "Wiederaufbau in Transnistrien," *Südost-Echo,* Vienna, vol. 20, no. 43, October 23, 1942; interview E; Walter Hoftmann, *Rumänien von heute*, Meiner, Leipzig, 1942, p. 26.

[73] Antonescu, *op. cit.;* Franz Riedl, "Aulbau am Dnjestr," *Berliner Börsen-Zeitung,* December 9, 1942.

[74] These were, roughly from north to south, Mogilev-Podol'ski, Tulchin, Jugastru (Iampol'), Balta, Rămnița (Rybnitsa), Golta, Dubosary, Anan'ev, Tiraspol, Berezovka, Odessa, Ovidiopol', Ochakov.

[75] Carp, *op. cit.*, vol. 3, map; "Transnistrien, Bezirke und Kreise," CRS, DHMR, 76152; Harold Laeuen, *Marschall Antonescu*, Essener Verlagsanstalt, Essen, 1943, pp. 169-171; *Relazioni Internazionali,* November 1, 1941, trans. in *Rumänisches Blut für das neue Europa*.

[76] *SD* Report 100.

The districts, in turn, were divided into rayons, or counties, as under the Soviets. Each of the 64 rayons of Transnistria had a rayon chief as a praetor, named by the prefect of his district. Most praetors were Romanian professional civil servants or officers; at their side, once again, were local praetors with advisory functions, usually former Soviet officials. In the towns, government was in the hands of an appointive mayor, known as *primar*, who (except for the two larger urban areas, Odessa and Tiraspol) was responsible to the rayon chief. By law both praetors and primars could be "natives," but almost all rayon chiefs were Romanians, while many of the mayors were former Soviet citizens. In all, Transnistria had two municipalities, fifteen townships, and 1261 rural communities.[77]

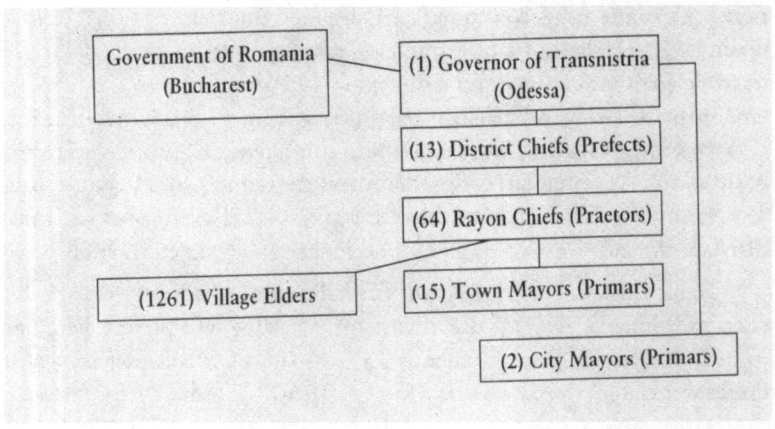

---

[77] Antonescu, *op. cit.;* "Provisorische Richtlinien... Beitrag zum Dekret-Gesetz Nr 1," CRS, AOK 11, 22409; Ihnen, *op. cit.;* Lemkin, *op. cit.*; pp. 239-240; *Bukarester Tageblatt*, August 20, 1943.

In addition to the government agencies enumerated above, there were, of course, gendarmerie units — at least one or two Romanian companies per judeţ, and the native police; there were also intelligence and political police (*Siguranţa*) personnel in Transnistria. Regular military units were still stationed there, though in considerably smaller numbers. The special economic exploitation staff is discussed in the next chapter. Transnistria had a regular inspection commission headed by Dr. Ilie Ţabrea; and on April 1, 1943, Antonescu named an *ad hoc* committee to make a 60-day investigation of the Transnistrian administration. A variety of smaller Romanian government and semi-government agencies had a lesser say in the activities of the province. („Friedliches Odessa," *Deutsche Ukraine-Zeitung*, January 10, 1943; "Provisorische Richtlinien,.. Beitrag zum Dekret-Gesetz Nr. 1," CRS, AOK 11, 22409; *Bukarester Tageblatt*, April 2, 1943; interview A; Major Bartsch, "Bericht über die Frontreise des Marschalls Antonescu," June, 1942, CRS, DKMR 27638/15; *Donauzeitung*, December 24, 1942).

The professional competence of this somewhat improvised but rather simply constructed administrative apparatus is a matter of some dispute. Apparently, there were some failures, just as there were cases of competence. The main problem, it seems, was to find suitable personnel for the lower levels.[78] Though perhaps not a completely impartial observer, a German officer who accompanied Antonescu on an inspection trip through Transnistria in mid-1942 reported:

> Most of the prefects are meritorious colonels and make a good impression. Most of the praetors seem to be usable. The overwhelming majority of mayors, especially in the small localities, on the other hand, are indolent, inexperienced Ukrainians of limited intelligence.[79]

A former high Romanian official who made frequent visits to Transnistria, however, found it most difficult to deal with the colonels and majors who headed the districts, whom he considered cocksure, stupid, and politically ignorant.[80]

Antonescu's original policy statement, cited above, was flexible enough to suit different schools of thought. Military commanders in the first days of the occupation had stressed that village elders were to be selected from among "the most decent and honest" residents. "The Romanian government," the proclamations blithely assert, "will treat the population with perfect humanity." For the moment, all laws — i.e., Soviet laws — were to stay in force unless specifically revoked or altered by the new regime.[81] In contrast to this relatively liberal policy, civil policy-makers adopted initially a colonial approach: Transnistria is to be exploited, not reconstructed — an approach that was bound to have both economic and political repercussions.[82]

By the end of 1941, the issue of how to treat Transnistria seems to have come to a head within Romanian circles, with one polar position maintained by pro-fascist politicians and propagandists, and the other, by a group of Bessarabians deeply steeped in Russian culture. The first group

---

[78] Ihnen, *op. cit.*

[79] Major Bartsch, "Bericht über die Frontreise des Marschalls Antonescu," June 1942, CRRS, DHMR 27638/15.

[80] Interview F.

[81] General Petre Dumitrescu, "Anweisung," August, 1941, CRS, AOK 11, 35774/6 (German translation from Romanian original).

[82] Ihnen, *op. cit.*

included Nichifor Crainic, the pro-fascist and pro-German Propaganda Minister, formerly a professor at the Bucharest theological seminary, and later a member of the German-sponsored commission to investigate the Katyn massacre. Professor Herşeni, Crainic's representative on the spot, who directed propaganda work in Transnistria, appears to have supported this group, which viewed Transnistria much as German officials viewed "the Slavic Hast."[83] The "Bessarabians" on the other hand, of whom there were a considerable number in the Transnistrian government, were largely men who had lived under Russian rule until the Revolution, some of them as tsarist officials and officers. Although usually without political sympathy for either tsarism or bolshevism, they frequently had considerable warm feeling for "the Russians" as such, spoke the language, though at times awkwardly after many years of disuse, and tended to the view that no pacification or lasting order could be established without enlisting the native population. To win the native population, the Romanians must give it a stake in the new order — material benefits, status, and creature comforts.[84]

Governor Alexianu occupied a middle position.[85] He sought to build up Transnistria and to convince the authorities in Bucharest to pour in funds and goods, perhaps, in part, to enhance his own power. But his attitude was basically patronizing, almost hostile, toward the native population; he widely proclaimed the need for radical re-education, for developing political understanding; though the peasants disliked them, he claimed that it was impossible to abolish collective farms; his formula, "freedom and labor" gave to the average citizen a freedom that was distinctly limited, and labor that was plentiful. Yet comparing his with extremist views and with German practice in the neighboring Ukraine, Alexianu was a moderate.

At times he would ascribe the relative peace and prosperity of his satrapy to the correctness of the "mollifiers"' approach.[86] His liberal tendencies were encouraged by the activities of individuals of some prominence in Romanian court circles. Countess Alexandria Cantacuzino, for

---

[83] Tverskoi; interview F.

[84] Tverskoi; interviews C and F.

[85] This may be well illustrated in his relative tolerance of Gherman Pântea, the Bessarabian mayor of Odessa, and his hostility to the Kiev-trained Bishop Vissarion, who advocated a more unselfish "pro-population" line. (See below, pp. 230-231).

[86] *Rumänisches Blut*, pp. 173-175; *Das Reich, op. cit.*; interview F; Tverskoi.

instance (whose family, Moldavian gently, had once been close to the Russian throne), now chaperoned girl-students from Odessa and "promoted cultural intercourse." As she declared publicly, "Whatever the future, no one will be able to deny that the Romanians, even in wartime, build places of culture and faith."[87] A certain pride in cultural accomplishments and economic plenty crept into the outlook of Romanian officialdom in Odessa. From about the spring of 1942 on, there was an inchoate but unmistakable effort to give special privileges to the native intelligentsia and to foster the rise of a collaborating, trustworthy elite.

Though by 1943 there was little enthusiasm in Romania itself for the new province and *"every* Romanian asked himself whether Transnistria was worth the sacrifices that continued to be made in the East," Romanian officials in Odessa were eager to demonstrate to visiting German newspapermen that the "mild" policies pursued in Transnistria yielded far better results than those followed in the Ukraine. The newsmen, at least some of them, were impressed.[88]

Odessa: The Primăria

The city of Odessa was at first placed under military government. When the Romanian army, accompanied by some German contingents, entered Odessa in mid-October, General Glogoșeanu, one of the ranking commanders, was appointed military commandant.[89] Within six days (as described elsewhere) his headquarters, a number of officers, and he himself were blown up. His successor was General Trestoreanu, Commanding General of the 13th Division.[90] Neither had had any special experience or interest in military government. Their orders struck the population as saber-rattling; it was not felt that the Romanians would enforce them, certainly not if there were mass disregard of them. That there should be so many regulations punishable by death seemed unfair and unreasonable — yet innumerable civilians already dangled from improvised gallows, lamp posts, and streetcar stops.[91]

---

[87] *Bukarester Tageblatt,* June 1, 1943; Manuilov, pp. 137-138.

[88] Hans-Joaehim Kausch, "Bericht über dire Reise nach der Ukraine...," June 26, 1943, document Occ E 4-11, YIVO, pp. 18-20.

[89] *Bukarester Tageblatt, October 22, 1941.*

[90] Carp, *op. cit.,* vol. 3, p. 149.

[91] Interviews A and C.

The need for a local government was obvious to all in these days of requisitions, senseless arrests, looting, and chaos. The problems, as one refugee recalls, ranged from where to get a piece of bread to how to regulate street traffic. The chaos of currencies, the transportation bottleneck, which prevented peasants from bringing their goods to the city, and, of course, the need to establish law and order in general made an effective government for Odessa imperative.[92]

The Romanians decided to give Odessa a government formally under the provincial government but administratively independent of it. They established a municipality or Primăria (the Romanian name, which came to be used by local residence as well) — headed by a mayor, who, together with several vice-mayors, formed the board of "city fathers." Under them was a structure of directorates reminiscent of those in the governor's office. There was at first no provision for the participation of residents, but with the general shift toward greater indigenous participation and responsibility, there were modifications that permitted Odessa residents to become heads of city directorates, even vice-mayors. The establishment of the municipality was announced on October 22, 1941, in the first issue of the semi-official city newspaper, *Odesskaia gazeta*, with pompous proclamations and appeals. By December 1941, the Primăria had begun to function in a more or less orderly fashion. Housed mainly in the old Stock Exchange building, specially and luxuriously repaired for it, its offices spread to other choice spots in the city, including the so-called Sailors' Palace *(Dvorets Moriaka)*.[93]

Gherman Pântea was appointed primar. A Bessarabian who knew Russian well, Pântea had studied at Odessa University, served as a captain in the tsarist army during World War I, become an ardent Moldavian patriot, and been active in the Bessarabian assembly — the *Sfatul Țării* — during the Civil War.[94] After two decades under the Romanians, he now returned as their lieutenant to Odessa. He is described by one observer as "a real little kulak, clever, covetous, not without brains." He would show up, unescorted and unheralded, at the city markets at 6:00 in the morning; passers-by, recognizing him, addressed him unceremoniously in the colloquial Russian form as "German Vasil'evich."[95] He was active, spoke

---

[92] Manuilov, pp. 56-58.

[93] Manuilov, pp. 62-66; Peterle, *op. cit.;* interview D.

[94] On the other hand, he was no important enough even to be mentioned in any of the standard studies of Bessarabia after World War I.

Russian, and understood the problems before him. Though not revered or admired, he was at least respected and widely accepted.

Not so some of his deputies. Of the five (at times, four) deputy mayors, two were local residents: Vladimir Cundert, a *Volksdeutscher* architect, who — quite competently, it seems — directed reconstruction in the city; and M. Zaevloshin, a Moldavian professor without special claims to fame. Neither appears to have had political influence. But the others, Elefterie Sinicliu, Vladimir Chiorescu, and K. Vidrașcu, were Romanians or Russian-speaking Bessarabians and enjoyed far greater prerogatives. The most important and most colorful was the young Vidrașcu, described as a flighty oversexed "lady's man," who knew how to look out for his own pleasures and interests. He had no inhibitions about using his official position for personal advantage, and arranged sumptuous parties with bands and lavish entertainment. Readily admitting that he was in Odessa to get rich, he was phenomenally brazen about accepting bribes — taking, for instance, a gold watch from a man seeking a two-month license to open a circus. He had to pass on licenses to open stores, theaters, and restaurants, and would often withhold authorization until "there was something in it" for him. People learned to include him, or one of his friends or relatives, as a stockholder, member, or beneficiary of proposed enterprises, to make sure of getting a permit. As will be seen, he was not alone in his venality — Chiorescu wound up buying a Bucharest hotel for several million lei after his sojourn in Odessa — but Vidrașcu's performance was more scandalous, dramatic, and unabashed than that of other officials.[96]

Under the Primăria there were some sixteen (the number fluctuated slightly) municipal directorates. In some fields, for example, education, broad directives issuing from the governor's corresponding directorate bound them; but other directorates had considerable leeway, except as limited by the Primăria itself. Decisions could be made by the mayor himself or by plenary meetings of the mayor, the deputies, and the heads of directorates. Some of the directors were Romanians, others, Odessa residents.

---

[95] Interview C; Tverskoi.

[96] Interviews A, C, and E; Document USSR-47; *Bukarester Tageblatt*, November 2, 1943.

[97] These included the directorates for Administration, Finance, Engineering and Technics, Culture and Education, Housing, Land, Inventory, Electric Power Stations, Transportation, Sanitation, Parks and Gardens, Viral Statistics, Water Supply, and Social Security. After a year, a separate Directorate of Religious Aliens was added.

Some are reported to have been reasonably honest and competent; one, at least, was an accomplished scoundrel.

The tasks of the various directorates were rather obvious. The Housing Directorate, among other things, registered vacant and abandoned apartments and assigned them to those who "deserved" a change of quarters. The Inventory Directorate, headed by a Moldavian resident of Odessa, registered all abandoned property, government stocks, and recovered loot — an activity of special and direct interest to Romanian officials. Small shops came under the functional directorate involved, such as Food or Engineering-Technical. Large plants were not taken over by the city; they remained directly under the Governor. The Land Directorate, under a local professor, started renting small *dachi* (country houses) on the peripheries of Odessa at low rents, to encourage truck farming and fruit growing there — these had not flourished under Soviet cooperatives but now proved attractive to the homeless and unemployed.[98]

Inevitably, the Romanian chiefs had to rely on local help. Every section had its translator and native aides. Much inevitably was taken over from Soviet administrative practice and organization, whether the Romanians wanted it or not: often native officials had served in the same capacity under Soviet rule. In the Directorate of Finance, on which some information is available, central financial control *(uchet)* and production planning followed the Soviet pattern: a central bookkeeping department, a department of taxation, another for the collection of fees, tariffs, and imposts, and finally a *smetno-biudzhetnyi* (estimates and budget) section, which corresponded to the old Soviet economic planning section. Having no capital of their own to start with, all enterprises had to submit advance estimates of their receipts and expenditures; in return, the directorate would give them paper advances; over-expenditures of a sizable amount were punishable.[99]

In the Primăria real power did not always reside in the men who formally held it, and in dealing with the Primăria much depended on personal pull, or "know-how." Considerable actual authority was wielded by a young, temperamental, capable Bessarabian girl, Cleopatra Consolarino. Smart and "activist" almost in the Soviet sense, she became Vidrașcu's right hand and often made the real decisions. Incidentally, she helped the

---

[98] Manuilov, pp. 67-81; Interviews A and D; Odessa, Serviciul de presă și propagandă a Municipiului Odesa, *Ein Jahr rumänische Vewaltung*, 1943, abstract in CRS, EAP 99/87.

[99] Manuilov, p. 72.

local theater procure substantial funds, mainly because she madly loved one of its dancers (she even had a brochure privately printed in his honor). A refugee novelist describes her under the name Dagmar — a woman who handled everything, applications for coffins, permits for school supplies, licenses for merry-go-rounds, requisitions for opera lights, even the inventory of the city museum. The official Soviet investigation, after the war, charged Cleopatra with active complicity in Romanian spoliation of Odessa, including the removal of art and property to Romania — charges which refugees are inclined to accept as well-grounded.[100]

There were others like Vidrașcu and Cleopatra in and around the Primăria. A few people worked hard — not so much from idealism as from self-interest. Many, while looking out for their own good, did their job. Others merely enriched themselves to the neglect of their official duties. Working hours, in Italian fashion, were from 8:00 to 12:00 and from 3:00 to 7:00; the afternoon shift tended to be purely perfunctory. Matters of urgency were often permitted to drag. Some city ordinances bordered on the ridiculous.[101] As one refugee lawyer stated, people were amazed to see that another system could be even more inefficient than the Soviet.[102]

Romanian prestige — and local pride and Odessa patriotism — tended to go up whenever high dignitaries visited the city. Rumors, some inspired, of visits by King Mihai or Queen Mother Elena, who for some reason enjoyed particular popularity, were frequent. Marshal Antonescu made visits in June 1942, March 1943, and again in June 1943. Alexianu periodically visited Antonescu and his advisors in Bucharest. But the *conducător*, as Antonescu was called, remained a remote figure. Though his portrait — next to King Mihai's and sometimes Adolf Hitler's — adorned most public establishments, he never achieved any popularity; not even the comprehensive decree of mid-June, 1943, which relaxed restrictions and met some of the aspirations of the citizenry, rendered him popular. A few Odessites noted favorably that he attended a

---

[100] Tverskoi; interview D; Ershov, *op. cit.*, p. 39.

[101] Kataev, in the first edition of his novel on wartime Odessa, reproduces the text of Order No. 88 by the mayor, dated April 6, 1943, strictly forbidding the sale and consumption in public of *semechki*, the favorite sunflower seeds, which used to be eaten — and spat out — all over Odessa. The line for first offenders was set at 10 to 100 marks, for repeaters from 50 to 500 marks. (Valentin Kataev. *Za vlast' sovetov.* Detizdat, Moscow, 1949, p. 502). The text of the decree is omitted from the later, revised edition.

[102] Interview A.

performance of the restored Odessa opera and that the opera thereafter had less trouble getting its budget approved.[103]

To the average citizen marshals and kings were fairy-tale figures, distant symbols of authority, even more distant than Soviet rulers had been. What was within his immediate experience was the Romanians' unpredictability and their stupendous proclivity to bribery, graft, and corruption. It did little good to recall that such practices were customary within Romania and other Balkan countries. Their impact on the Soviet citizen was further intensified by experiencing these same practices in areas of life unconnected with government and administration, as will be later discussed.

At times official reports would cautiously comment — as did the German consul general in early 1943 — that "subordinate organs occasionally incline to arbitrariness and corruption."[104] Other German observers were far more outspoken: "With the introduction of the Romanian administration one can now speak of the systematic plundering of the country, without any exaggeration."[105] Indeed, in mid-1943, a German journalist who visited the area wrote in a confidential report to the German Propaganda Ministry:

> Transnistria is being exploited by the Romanians to the highest degree, in part... to alleviate the food situation in Romania, which has become somewhat difficult, but above all for the personal enrichment of a clique which was already well off in Romania.[106]

If a German visitor perceived this, so certainly did the inhabitants of Transnistria.

Examples of corruption are too numerous to adduce; suffice it to cite two. The Soviet report of its postwar investigation in Odessa mentions one Romanian official, formerly a storekeeper, who wound up as owner of the Passage Hotel, the "Victoria" movie house, the restaurant "Karpaty," a printing press, several stores, and a soda water plant. The same report gives the testimony of a lawyer named Diakonov. Though Diakonov had collaborated with the Romanians, they charged him with concealing Jews. He bribed the commissioner handling the case to minimize the

---

[103] *Bukarester Tageblatt*, January 22, February 24, and June 21, 1943; interview C; *Molva*, No. 159, June 18, 1943, AA, reel 1273, frames 342476-79.

[104] German Consulate, Odessa, *op. cit.*

[105] SD Report 133, November 14, 1941.

[106] Kausch, "Bericht...," pp. 18-19.

charges; his family then bribed the procurator of the military court who heard the matter, and got a favorable verdict.[107]

In one of the few books on Transnistria available in English, Vladimir Petrov describes his experience in Odessa during his "retreat" from the Caucasus.

> In Transnistria, under wartime conditions, the possibility for Russians to avoid unpleasantnesses by paying bribes was definitely an advantage. After all, the appetite of the Romanians was a fairly modest one. When the Office of Public Safety held up permission for me and my friends to move to Odessa, I merely asked the captain in charge, "How much?" the looked at the ceiling and answered with a shrug, "One hundred marks." I was surprised. You could buy a pair of geese or six pounds of good salami at the market for 10 marks.

To a Soviet citizen, the situation was unbelievable, it was so unlike Soviet rule:

> It sounded like a joke when Aunt Shura told me about the time the Romanian military warehouse in Odessa had been robbed. The culprits were caught red-handed at the market, selling strips of parachute silk. They were tried by a military court and two of them were sentenced to death. However, their friends collected something like 5,000 marks and gave it to the military prosecutor. The next day the condemned men were free.[108]

The first American newsmen reached Odessa ten days after it was reoccupied in 1944. They spoke of the "one striking contrast" between Odessa and other areas — in Odessa "a background colored by complete corruption."[109]

Romanization

Other states had embarked on campaigns to "assimilate" the people of areas they had conquered, and Romania too decided to promote the "Romanization" of Transnistria. Since it could not make Romanians of the predominantly Slavic population of the area, "Romanization" consisted in

---

[107] Document USSR-47.

[108] Vladimir Petrov, *Retreat from Russia*, Yale University Press, New Haven, 1950, pp. 204-205.

[109] Richard E. Lauterbach, *These Are the Russians*, Harper & Bros., New York, 1945, p. 79.

fostering the Romanian (i.e., Moldavian) minority, teaching the language, spreading Romanian culture, and "demonstrating" Romania's historical claims to Transnistria.

This presupposed that Transnistria would be annexed or in some way integrated into *România Mare*. If it was to be treated as a spoil of war or a pawn for bargaining, it was absurd to try to Romanize it. Once in Romanian hands, however, Transnistria's appeal to at least a fringe of extreme nationalists and Romanian fascists was sufficient to bring about a Romanization campaign. Although this was perhaps not fully appreciated in Romania, this campaign was in direct conflict with the policy of another equally extremist group; this group, as will be seen, wanted to make Transnistria a dumping place for "undesirables" — Jews, gypsies, and other groups who were being exiled from Romania proper.

A standard device of the politician seeking to justify territorial claims is to rewrite the past. Romanian historiography was called in to help the hard-pressed regime. Historians like Academician Ştefan Ciobanu insisted that Transnistria had in the past been a real part of the Moldavian principality. Special monographs on the Romanian element in the history of the Odessa region were commissioned; it took some effort but it was shown that the Dacians had occupied the area in Roman days, that Romanian principalities had extended along the Black Sea coast, and that bishoprics of the Romanian church had at different times had jurisdiction cast as far as the Ingulets River. To show a continuity of Romanian influence took some strenuous "research," and the resulting studies were indeed peculiar products, with only useful facts presented and evidence often obviously distorted.[110] But they were judged admirable enough to publish — one of them even in Russian translation, on the first anniversary of the fall of Odessa.

The Romanian Scientific Institute was established in Tiraspol in late. Under the directorship of Professor Nicolae Smochină, who was described as long a student of Romanian-Slavic relations, the Institute prepared Romanian language texts and grammars, dictionaries, libraries of

---

[110] Alexandru Boldur. *Românii şi strămoşii lor în istoria Transnistriei*, rev. ed., Liga culturală, Iaşi, 1943; Nicolae M. Popp, *Transnistria: incercare de monografie regionale*, Dacia Traiana, Bucharest, 1943; Ernst Bauer, "Das rumänische Transnistrien," *Neue Ordnung*, Zagreb, No. 57, August 16, 1942; *Transnistria*, Bucharest, August-November, 1941, cited in *Ostland*, Vol. 20, No. 24, December 15, 1941, pp. 428-432; Karl H. Theil, "Rumänen jenseits des Dnjestr," *Völkischer Beobachter*, July 23, 1941, Iancu Nistor, *Aspeete geopolitice şi cultrale din Transnistria*, Dacia Traiana, Bucharest, 1942.

Romanian books and magazines, anything that helped spread the language among the "Transnistrians."[111] On the initiative of the Governor himself, a Moldavian Faculty was established at Odessa University in the winter of 1942, with a Romanian lady from Iași as dean, and a curriculum that was a humanities hodgepodge. Its students had an obviously privileged position — it was understood they would provide some of the future administrative cadres for the province — and they received special fellowships, dormitory facilities, and the like. In general, the Moldavian minority was transformed into an ethnic elite by the new regime.[112]

The most zealous "patriots" sought to justify the appropriation of Transnistria by emphasizing the number of Romanians farther east in the Soviet Union — even in the Northern Caucasus, and of course in the rest of the Ukraine. No one seriously "claimed" the areas on that account (though these happened to be areas where Romanian divisions were fighting). By special agreement with the Germans a "census" of so-called Romanians was taken throughout the occupied part of the U.S.S.R. The figures — which a high Romanian official now privately admits to have been "exaggerated" — alleged that there were nearly 1,200,000, even 1,800,000, Romanians in the Soviet Union, 782,000 in German-occupied parts of the Ukraine and the Russian Republic.[113] The way in which the census was conducted made putative Romanians conclude that its purpose was to have them transferred "back" to Romanian soil.[114]

In October 1942, the Romanian cabinet discussed the possibility of having these rediscovered compatriots moved (presumably by force, if

---

[111] *Bukarester Tageblatt,* July 9, 1943; Riedl, *op cit.;* Prof. S. Mehedinți, Institutul Științific Român transnistrian, "Dreptatea noastră," *Universul,* Bucharest, July 1, 1942. See also *Nation und Staat,* Vienna, vol. 14, 1941, p. 429, and vol. 15, 1942, p. 236.

[112] Interview D.

[113] *Romanisches Blut,* p 165; interview F; *Ostlond,* vol. 20, no 24, December 15, 1941.

A far more likely figure was that given by a Romanian daily in March, 1943. It reported that, as of the summer of 1942, 23,000 Moldavian families had been located in Soviet territory cast of the Bug (under German occupation). A group of these had been made to make records of their folk music "in order to preserve proof of the permanence of the Romanian element in the distant East" (*Universul,* March 15, 1943).

[114] The head of the registration commission, a demographer, Anton Golopenția, became head of the Romanian Statistical Directorate after the war, when its incumbent, Sabin Manuilă, a follower of Maniu, escaped abroad. Golopenția "disappeared" within a year; in about 1948, his wife was invited to identify his body at the Bucharest morgue. Romanian exiles have assumed that he met his death largely as a result of his wartime "registration" activities in the U.S.S.R., where he zealously converted Soviet citizens into Romanians.

need be) from the Ukraine to Transnistria, to make a more compact Romanian ethnic mass in the new eastern province. This, however, never took place.[115] An alternative way of Romanizing would have been a migration of Romanians from Romania to Transnistria. Businessmen and government employees went there, of course, but not to settle. Antonescu was reported privately to have spoken of using Transnistria to "solve" Romania's agrarian problem; land would be given to Romanian peasant settlers willing to migrate beyond the Dnestr.[116] Likewise in 1942, German censorship allowed the statement to be made that Romania planned to settle its own artisans and merchants in Transnistria.[117] But none of these plans for colonizing Transnistria was acted on.

The efforts to promote the Romanian language had a significant and widespread impact on the average Soviet citizen. Church services were frequently conducted in Romanian, much to the consternation of churchgoers; street signs and store marquees were often in Romanian as well as Russian; streets and squares were renamed to honor such figures as the legendary Michael the Brave, young King Mihai, and Antonescu; Romanian became the compulsory first foreign language in all Transnistrian schools; Romanian literature was imported to Transnistria, either in the original or in translation; and, in general, efforts of all sorts were made to impress the skeptical population with the high standards and accomplishments of Romanian culture.[118]

While knowledge of Romanian was often convenient, the average citizen of Transnistria regarded its study as a nuisance and an imposition, sometimes as an insult. Except among the most opportunist elements of the population, Romanization was met with passive resistance. Like other aspects of Romanian policy, Romanization had its ups and downs: little was done in the confusion of the first few months; it was pushed in 1942, a time of relative recovery and prosperity; from the spring of 1943 on, as the Axis military position deteriorated, Romanization was increasingly forgotten, though language instruction continued.

---

[115] Schechtman, *op cit.*, p. 179; *Neue Zürcher Zeitung*, October 23, 1942. See also A. Dol'nik, *Bessarabiia pod vlastiu ruuynskikh boiar*, Gospolitizdat, Moscow, 1945, pp. 171-172.

[116] Gheorghe, *op cit.*, p. 192.

[117] Alfred Sztuka, "Wirtschaftliche Grundlagen... Transnistriens," *Osteuropa-Jahrbuch*, Breslau, 1942, pp. 211-213.

[118] Peterle, *op cit.;* interviews A and C.

Reactions to the Romanization program varied. Hostility to church services in Romanian was well-nigh universal and often intense. Resentment of changes in street names was mild but symbolic. Schoolboys often learned Romanian very poorly, partly (teachers insist) out of a deliberate effort not to study it; girls generally knew it better, often because they went out with Romanian officers and men. Saleswomen in the open-air market twisted Romanian phrases to make fun of the occupiers. "Bună dimineața" (Good morning) rapidly became "Budemte meniat'sia" (Let's trade); other distortions followed the same pattern, and reflect the spirit of condescension in the popular attitude toward the conqueror.[119]

Attitudes toward the Romanians

Specific facets of popular attitudes and behavior will be discussed in subsequent chapters, but something should be said here about popular feeling in its more general aspects.[120]

There was, one refugee suggests, a small minority eager to work with the Romanians under virtually any conditions; there was another minority — its size cannot be exactly determined but it was probably larger — irrevocably opposed to collaboration. The bulk of the population had muted feelings: they were weary and politically indifferent, yet not without hope, particularly of attaining greater personal comfort and security. Relations with the Romanians were commonly conducted — as another defector puts it — "without excessive ideology." One made practical, day-to-day adjustments. The basic impulse, all sources agree, was to "survive," and if possible to "live comfortably" and "enjoy oneself." This meant "operating," manipulating, so as to get the most for oneself from the Romanians with the least trouble and embarrassment. There was no implicit endorsement of the new regime, but also no rejection of it. Expressions suggesting such clever maneuvering *(nalovchit'sia, ne vlipnut', khitrit')* recur time and again in the refugees' reconstruction of the era.[121]

Romanian behavior — that facet of it which the people could judge and assess on the basis of personal experience — was ill-calculated to win

---

[119] Ibid.

[120] Not surprisingly German reports commonly insist that the population preferred the Germans to the Romanians. While under certain conditions this may have been true, the consistent and insistent nature of such comments must be written off as unobjective.

[121] Interviews A, C, and E; Tverskoi; Manuilov, p. 71.

respect. It aroused apprehension and, among many, revulsion and indignation. After the more blatant atrocities and cruel abuses came to an end, other aspects of Romanian behavior came into greater prominence, especially the Romanian soldier's impoverishment and covetousness, and the ubiquitous graft. A German visitor observed that the people in Transnistria hardly viewed the Romanians as "conquerors" at all. By a curious psychological mechanism, the Transnistrians seemed to take pride in "generously" or "condescendingly" "forgiving" the Romanians for their abuses (all terms employed by refugees or found in contemporary reports). As a bitter German remarked in January 1942:

> The venality of the Romanians in all degrees and shades has already become known to the Odessites, so that their judgment of the Romanians is expressed in the term "gypsies." ...(they have for them) more scorn than hate.

The most perceptive of refugee informants consulted for this study gave "irony" as the quintessence of popular attitude toward the Romanians — slightly derogatory, slightly defensive, as if holding Romanian rule to be transitory and immature, but certainly not a fatal development.[122]

This disparaging judgment — and one can assume its prevalence after at least a few months of occupation — did not affect basic behavior. The people strove to adjust to the *status quo,* and to "make the most" of it. An informant recalls that people soon knew that you had to have a five or ten mark bill in your hand when you went to a Romanian agency to get something done. Some were at first reluctant to accept jobs from the Romanians, but many later did so for economic reasons, to satisfy their ambition, or out of a sense of social responsibility, for to some this seemed a way to help rebuild a normal life. One may speak of three distinct phases in the history of the attitudes of a mythical "average" resident: initially, he was suspicious and fearful; although he lived under difficult conditions, he was still hesitant to appear as an agent of the occupying power; from early 1942 on, a more "business-like" and less emotionally charged relationship with the authorities developed; he recognized the new order as a reality, and made the most of it; toward the end of the occupation a third phase

---

[122] Peterle, *op. cit.;* interview C; AA, "Ein Gewährsmann berichtet," December 31, 1942, forwarded to Pol XIII. AA, reel 5079, frames E 292536 ff; Sdf. von Berg to Sturmbannführer von Kuensberg, January 1942, "Lagebericht aus Odessa," AA, reel 2066, frames 448876-80; Mamukov, p. 7.

began, when the front returned, the Romanians yielded more and more authority to the Germans, material conditions worsened, and a spirit of panic and doom enveloped the "average" resident. The middle era, roughly from the spring of 1942 to mid-1943, was the high point of Romanian occupation.[123]

A substantial barrier separated the Romanians and the population throughout. The difference in language was in itself enough to prevent genuine identification. Social contact between residents and Romanians was generally limited to semi-official functions, love affairs, or contact that came about where Romanians were billeted in or near indigenous families. Romanian terror did not instill the utter horror Soviet terror had: Romanian bribery constituted a safety valve and helped make Romanian terror seem less monstrous, less ubiquitous, less insurmountable than its Soviet form.[124]

The people knew that they were substantially better off than they would have been under the Germans. Time and again they would point to the difference in material conditions or cultural opportunities between Odessa and Kiev. Travelers and refugees would confirm and perhaps even exaggerate these clichés. Toward the end of the era, there was genuine fear that the Romanians would turn Transnistria over to the Germans.[125]

The general direction of feeling was, however, toward increasing disillusionment and bitterness. Due in part to the very fact of foreign occupation, due perhaps in greater part to the change in military fortunes, it must be ascribed also to the behavior and policies of Transnistria's rulers.

---

[123] Manuilov, pp. 63, 86-88.

[124] Interviews B and E.

[125] Manuilov, p. 137; Peterle, *op. cit.;* "Ein Gewährsmann berichtet, *op. cit.*; interview D.

Chapter III

Social and Economic Trends

The Rural Areas

The Setting

Basically, Transnistria was an agrarian province. Except for Odessa it had no large towns; its residents were overwhelmingly of peasant stock; most of its land was used for agriculture; and the great majority of its population, as late as 1940, gained its livelihood from the land.[1] By far the largest crop was maize; wheat, barley, and rye were also of some importance. Potatoes and sugar beets played a smaller role. Sunflowers excelled in this region, and soybean cultivation was rapidly growing. Fruit, wine, and tobacco were among the more unusual cultures. A good many of the "industrial" installations of the province were geared to the processing or canning of produce, fruit, and fish. Before the war, agriculture had, of

---

[1] Seventy per cent of all the land in Transnistria was farmland (3,800,000 hectares); another 7 per cent (290,000 ha) was pasture. Forests covered only 5 per cent, and private plots, fruit and vineyards, and dwellings accounted for the rest (*Der Deutsche in Transnistrien*, Vol. 2, No. 19, May 16, 1943; "Transnistrien liefert bereits für Rumänien," *Krakauer Zeitung*, September 12, 1943). But it has been recently said that "the natural fertility of the soil in the province of Transnistria cannot be fully used because of the insufficiency of rainfall." The reason it always had "a large quantity of food available for delivery" was that it was not so densely populated as other parts of the Ukraine (Slavcho Zagorov et al. *The Agricultural Economy of the Danubian Countries*, Stanford University Press, Stanford, 1955, p. 261)

course, been organized along the standard Soviet lines: most of it in kolkhozes (collective farms) and some (especially cattle-breeding, experimental fruit and vegetable stations, and apiaries) in state farms.[2]

The German invasion had, as could be expected, wrought havoc with agriculture. Mobilization had already cut deep into the adult male age groups, which already had been proportionately smaller than female and younger groups. However, farm labor had ranked low on the scale of Soviet priorities for evacuation. The only ones, in addition to the draftees, to leave the farms were, by and large, managers and other officials, militia officers, and, occasionally, bookkeepers and agronomists. At least half the rural population remained.

Before their retreat, Soviet efforts had revolved around the evacuation or destruction of livestock and machinery. It has been estimated that at least half the area's cattle were being moved east. However, because of speed of the German advance and the deliberate slow-down tactic at times pursued by the kolkhoz personnel (often young farm boys, ten to twelve years of age), who reluctantly accompanied the eastward trek of livestock, many of the herds were overtaken by Axis troops, particularly on the western bank of the Bug River. Some cattle got across, some perished, but enough remained, and virtually all collectives whose livestock had been removed sent special "catchers," as soon as the Romanians or Germans arrived, to retrieve the herds.[3]

Machinery losses were more disastrous. Over half the mechanized equipment, including tractors, had either been evacuated or wrecked.

---

[2] Cf. Fritz Poppenberger, "Das Land am Ostufer des Dnjestrs," *Deutsche Ukraine-Zeitung,* September 12, 1942; and WA.B., "Transnistrien als Teil Rumäniens," *Münchner Neueste Nachrichten,* September 4/5, 1943.

[3] A census of animals conducted in Transnistria in December 1941, showed a drastic decline in the hog population (presumably because the Soviet authorities shot large numbers before leaving). The decline in sheep and oxen was less striking, yet also of some importance. Unfortunately, one source gives the December 1941, data in percentages of the July 1, 1935, census figures, while another gives some comparable absolute figures without indicating any trends between 1935 and 1941.
Horses: 78% of 1935 stock; or 205,000
Cattle: 72% or 375,000
Sheep: 73% or 278,000
Hogs: 35% or 180,000
(*Wirtschafcsdienst,* Hamburg, Vol. 27, 1942, p. 783; Florian Codrescu, "Transnistria," *Excelsior,* Bucharest, October 25, 1942). Considerable quantities of cattle and sheep were also delivered to the Romanian army or shipped westward across the Dnestr (Sec *Odessa v velikoi otechestvennoi voine,* hereafter cited as OVOV, Odessa, 1947-1953, Vol. 2, p. 57)

Because of the large-scale kind of agriculture in much of the area, mechanization was essential to successful and timely harvesting and plowing. Moreover, lack of transportation impeded the shipment of produce to grain elevators (and some of them had been wrecked). Lack of storage space in the village (due to the Soviet *zagot* collection system) produced immediate problems.

With much of the administration gone, with Soviet compulsions and controls removed, and confusion about the future plans and requirements of the new authorities rampant, there set in — at a crucial time of year for farm work — a period of uncertainty and disorganization that often had a paralyzing effect on the farmers' will or ability to work.

The Romanian authorities had no immediate wish to institute thorough-going changes in the agricultural system or property relations. Men like Alexianu argued that it was technically impossible to abolish collective farms; Romanian pressure for maximum output put a premium on maintaining the *status quo*. Reform would have entailed confusion and a slowdown of farm work. Any alternative system was assumed to be less authoritarian and less well geared to the collection of produce — it was felt simpler to collect from a few central points than from a large number of individual peasant households. The basic features of the kolkhoz were, therefore, retained, though some relaxations were introduced.[4] In this respect Romanian policy closely paralleled what was done in German-held areas of the U.S.S.R.

The Germans sought to retain a hand in the running of Transnistrian agriculture — to which, strictly speaking, they were in no wise entitled, but for which a precedent existed in the dispatch of German agricultural advisers to Bucovina and Bessarabia. It took direct intervention by German Ambassador Killinger with Antonescu to secure, on November 11, 1941, Romanian consent to this German interference, and one German agricultural adviser was assigned as a technical specialist to each judeţ and prefecture (i.e., 13 plus 64 men). This was less than the Germans had hoped for — they wanted to have at least one and perhaps two men in each rayon — but it gave them both insight and a measure of control. The German advisers periodically held conference among themselves. On their

---

[4] Alfred Sztuka, *op. cit.;* Karl Brandt et al., *Management of Agriculture...*, Stanford University Press, Stanford, 1953, p. 228; Ferdinando Chiarelli, in *La Voce d'Italia*, Rome, November 9, 1941, translated in *Rumänisches Blut für das neue Europa*, p. 173; "Transnistrien liefert bereits für Rumänien," *Krakauer Zeitung.* September 12, 1943.

performance and political impact, unfortunately, no information has come to light.[5]

It is exceedingly difficult to ascertain rural attitudes in Transnistria, because neither contemporary documents nor any first-hand informants could be found. From what material is available one gathers that, during the initial weeks of flux and chaos, Soviet peasant reactions in Transnistria were by and large identical with those expressed in German-held areas.[6] The Germans, like the Romanians, wanted to leave everything as it was and wanted the farmers to go on with their work, especially the work of harvesting. But the kolkhoz population often, apparently, took things into their own hands and began dividing collective property. Near Iampol', the Germans reported having succeeded in "re-establishing" the kolkhoz; it had been dissolved by its members as soon as the Red Army left. In the village of Ol'shanka, the first occupation troops found that grain, horses, cows, and flour bags had been divided among the members of the village; the two machines and six oxen continued to be collectively owned and the land had not been partitioned. In Dimitrashkovka, which had nearly 900 families, the village had spontaneously "assembled" and elected an elder *(starosta)* before the arrival of the German adviser. A German inspector found during an extensive trip through Transnistria in November, 1941, that "it is reported unanimously that the Romanian administration has not succeeded in preventing the dissolution of the collective in many villages."[7]

A Romanian expert and ex-Minister admitted in print that "the peasants desire a return to individual property and voluntarily renounce collectivism, yet paradoxically, because of the lack of inventory, one must for the time being maintain the norms established by the Bolshevik regime." Indeed, even in *Volksdeutsche* villages German officials who initially took

---

[5] Verbindungsstab der Deutschen Wehrmacht für Transnistrien, Abt. La, "Bericht über die Lage der Landwirtschaft in Transnistrien," January 31, 1942, CRS, Wi/ID, 2.1174; OKVR, Ihnen. "Tätigkeitsbericht für die Zeit vom 15.XI.-15.XII.," December 15, 1941, CRS, DHMR 76152; Vierjahresplan, Geschäftsgruppe Ernährung, Generalreferent Georg Reichart, "Bericht über den Stand der Erfassung landwirtschaftlicher Erzeugnisse und der Bestellungsarbeiten in Transdnjestrien...," November 15, 1941, CRS, Wi/ID 58; Killinger, wire to Auswärtiges Amt, Berlin, November 11, 1941, CRS, Wi/ID. 58.

[6] The author has sought to analyze the latter in an earlier paper (Alexander Dallin and Gerhard L. Weinberg, "The Peasantry as a Source of Soviet Vulnerability: Experiences in World War II," War Documentation Project, 1955).

[7] AOK 11, IV Wi, *op. cit.*; Reichart, *op. cit.*; Korück 553, "Ernteeinbringung," August 5, 1941, CRS, Korück 20383/7.

charge were constrained to rule that peasants be "forced to cooperate" in farm work, and to revive the old Bolshevik maxim that "he who does not work does not eat." The initial Romanian directive, as will be seen, demanded "collective harvesting," though it was admitted that "not every member of the kolkhoz could see this."[8]

The policy of maintaining the kolkhoz was pushed, and by the time the "pacification" of Transnistria was completed, the system was outwardly again in operation. The new collection and delivery system was, however, far less thorough and the controls instituted by the Romanians were inevitably far laxer than what had prevailed under Soviet rule. The peasants "got away" with far more than they had before, in such ways as falsifying reports, hiding grain, and evading work. Yet, outwardly the change was simply a new network that took the place of the defunct Soviet one.

Plus ça change

First arrangements were makeshift. In one case, 20 per cent of the harvested grain was given in August to farm members as an advance on their share, which was to be determined more fully at a later date; the balance was to be stored. In another, the Germans report, "the Romanians have determined that 25 per cent of the grain be turned over to the army and 75 per cent be left to the peasants" — this was considerably, even drastically, less than Soviet demands. (In this particular village, Romanian troops, apparently without official consent, sanctioned the partitioning of the collective farm by the peasants and even allowed individual harvesting by each household.) Probably because of some general directive, the most common plan was to divide the produce evenly between State and Farm — peasants were to deliver 50 per cent of the harvest to the authorities — at the time, the Romanian army — and keep the rest for themselves.[9]

A basic directive of Army General Dumitrescu to the local population in August, 1941, included the proviso that (1) farm work was obligatory for the rural population, and (2) half the harvest belonged to the

---

[8] Nicolae D. Cornățeanu, *L'organisation de l'agriculture roumaine en temps de guerre*, Bucharest, 1943, p. 57; "Schutzmassnahmen...," *op. cit.;* Fw. Hermann Maurer, "Erfahrungsund Tarigkeitsbericht," August 13-28, 1941, CRS, EAP 99/47.

[9] It seems that this system corresponded roughly to the practice common in this area before World War I, when the landed gentry left the peasant half the returns, provided he used his own horses, and one-third if he used the *pomeshchik's* horses.

kolkhoz, the other half to the state (army). The government pledged itself not to requisition without payment— a ludicrous promise in view of continual abuse and looting. It contained the first substantial alleviation of kolkhoz conditions:

> Agricultural labor may do farm work either as individuals or grouped in the collective farm. If (they prefer to work individually), kolkhoz property becomes the property of its members, who in return must deliver a certain share (directly) to the state (army).[10]

This directive was of symbolic rather than practical significance. Romanian enforcement was weak and sporadic; abuses were widespread among peasants and officials alike. In practice, the army took what it could. When confronted with "no-requisition-without-pay" proclamations and therefore compelled to adopt a more orderly process, the 50 per cent due the army was convened into a device for looting; one Romanian unit after another came around to collect the "fifty per cent" time and again. Since the Romanian army had no organized supply system and was told to live off the land, this behavior was understandable, but certainly not calculated to make the peasantry like the Romanians.[11]

Within a few weeks, however, a semblance of order was established, and the army moved on. A new agrarian system for Transnistria is defined in the first Antonescu decree, issued August 19. In it, the civil governor is ordered to assure harvesting and the storage of the harvest; to make inventories of collective and state farm property; to divide the harvest between state and population according to a fixed ratio; and to leave the cattle of the collective and state farms temporarily in the care of individual peasant families. Alexianu thereupon issued a proclamation according to which

> (1) the collective farms were to be maintained, and arbitrary partition was forbidden; (2) after deduction of seed reserves and payment (in grain) of service charges for the use of machinery, the grain was to be divided in equal parts between the peasants and the state.[12]

---

[10] Friedrich Theodor Prinz zu Savn und Wirtgenstein, "Bericht über meine Fahrt nach Russland in der Zeit vom 25.8.-1.9.1941," CRS, Wi/ID. 58; Wirtsehaftsstab Ost, Chefgruppe La, "Bericht/Aufttag von KVC Riecke," August 23, 1941, CRS, Wi/ID, 116; General Petre Dumitrescu, "Anweisung," August, 1941 (German trans. of Romanian original), CRS, AOK 11, 35774/6.

[11] SD Report 100; SD Report 133, November 14, 1941.

Some changes were made in Decree No. 55 of March 14, 1942: the collectives were renamed cooperatives and were divided into smaller "work communities." In effect, this made each former brigade (of about twenty families) a separate kolkhoz, with about 200 hectares of land. According to one writer:

> ...the main features of the kolkhoz form of agriculture prevailing there were retained but collectivization was relaxed by arranging the kolkhozv into work groups of ten farm families each. The dead and live inventories of each kolkhoz were divided and allocated to the work groups, which also received shares in the kolkhoz fields. In other words, the large kolkhozy of whole villages were broken up into small kolkhozy often farm families each.

This resembled German practice in some parts of the Ukraine, where five, eight, or ten households were jointly given land and equipment, though these units were not given formal juridical or administrative status. The Transnistrian system, a contemporary article explained, was "flexible," varying from area to area; this, one must assume, accounts for the different numbers of households included in the new small collectives. The writer quotes one village mayor as saying:

> It was necessary to work by a plan... in order to secure maximal yield. The whole community was divided into twelve groups, and each group was given a piece of land depending in size on the number of horses it had at its disposal. In addition, our community received 200 hectares for use from the neighboring Ukrainian village (which presumably lacked either manpower or machinery), so that we had to work an area of 1109 hectares with 75 horses. The area was fully plowed and sown...[13]

Decree No. 55 eliminated some of the formality and bureaucratic overhead. It abolished the *trudoden* system (bookkeeping "work days"), by which compensation was based on units determined by the time spent and the nature of the work done. It was replaced by a direct sharing of peasant households in the produce of the land they worked (now a smaller area than in the larger Soviet collective). While the abolition of the *trudodni*

---

[12] Antonescu, "Richtlinien zur Verwaltung der Provinz Transnistrien," August 19, 1941 (German trans. of Romanian original), CRS, AOK 11, 22409; Reichart, *op. cit.*

[13] Wirtschaftsstab Ost, "Monatsbericht," April, 1942, p. 23, CRS EAP 99/57; "Transnistrien liefert bereits für Rumänien," *Krakauer Zeitung*, September 12, 1943; Brandt, *op. cit.*, p. 228; *Der Deutsche in Transnistrien*, Vol. 1, No. 9, September 13, 1942, and Vol. 2, No. 29, July 25, 1943; *Neuer Tag*, Prague, May 17, 1942.

was clearly popular, difficulties arose over the "fair" division of land and the working out of sowing plans for each new share, since the quality of the soil and the crops to be planted had to be considered. The general principle that came to prevail was that greater performance warranted greater rewards.

Other changes equally popular with the Soviet peasant were getting the right freely to dispose of his "fifty per cent" of the harvest, to grow fruit and vegetables without restrictions, and to engage in unlimited small-scale cattle breeding. There is no evidence that the size of private plots increased, as they did in German-occupied areas. Contemporary observers point primarily to the larger share of harvest retained by the peasant as a major incentive to greater effort. Even after taxes,[14] the 1941-1942 delivery demands of the Romanians were smaller than those of the Soviets, and were, moreover, less efficiently collected. The consensus is that in 1942 the rural population of Transnistria was better off than before the war.[15]

Difficulties arose because a high proportion of the administrative and technical staffs had left; most kolkhoz chairmen were gone; of the 11,000 agronomists in Transnistria only 1,000 were on their jobs (though many more were assumed to be hiding within the province). The initial German instructions called for the continued employment of former kolkhoz directors, "since they naturally know the area best." The Romanians were loath to take such political chances; moreover, only a few of the managers remained, and because of peasant hostility, they could not always be left in office. New elders *(starosty)* were usually appointed or elected — generally by an informal process, which varied from village to village. The Romanians often preferred (and sometimes the peasants themselves advanced) a former victim of Soviet repression or a kulak; many who had been bookkeepers or agronomists under the Soviets shifted from specialized technical work to management and administration — there was a similar trend in urban industry. In general, however, the caliber of farm managers

---

[14] The various Soviet taxes were nominally replaced by a "single tax" on the land, amounting to 5 marks (i.e., 300 lei) per hectare, regardless of quality; half the tax was payable in kind, the other half in cash. There were also special levies: 1 per cent of the total harvest (before it was divided between government and peasant) went for social security, 10 per cent for fodder, and 10 per cent for administration of the cooperative. The household also had to sacrifice part of its harvest for the seed fund and to pay for the use of machinery. ("Die Aufbauarbeit in Transnistrien," *Frankfurter Zeitung,* November 12, 1942).

[15] *Krakauer Zeitung, op. cit.;* Sztuka, *op. cit.;* German Consulate, Odessa, dispatch, February 26, 1943; AA, reel 1273, frames 342512-15.

remained poor; in 1942 there were complaints that the unsatisfactory productivity of farms was due, at least in part, to the inadequacy of the new supervisors.[16] Unfortunately, because of lack of data, it is impossible to determine the importance of this and of other factors in accounting for the low productivity of agriculture.

Transportation remained a problem to the end; indeed, it had been a problem (though perhaps in milder form) for the Soviets. Most storage facilities for grain were located along rail lines, and the railroads were scarcely operating. Local elevators and barns were often insufficient to hold the harvest, and others that might have been used were inaccessible, because the Soviets had destroyed or evacuated so many vehicles. The harvesting itself was endangered by the removal or destruction of tractors and other mechanized equipment. The Machine Tractor Station (MTS) had been among the first rural installations to be evacuated. The tractor shortage, which at first sight seemed so acute, turned out to be less crucial than might be surmised. A good many tractors were repaired with spare parts found at reimagining depots or taken from wrecked vehicles; the local population apparently took considerable interest and pride in this work. The Romanians succeeded in reopening the Odessa GINAP agricultural machinery plant; this was operated by the Romanian Ford Company and was at least able to repair and keep up existing machinery. Several hundred tractors were bought abroad, primarily in Germany, by Alexianu's administration. All this helped overcome the shortage of mechanized equipment, and by mid-1943 some seventy tractor stations were again in operation.

Before the war, Soviet machine-tractor stations had been centers for the political control of the countryside; these tractor stations lost their political functions under the Romanians. Often owned by a nearby village, they continued to perform their economic functions. There were but few protests from the peasants against pooling tractors and other farm machinery; and the Romanians found the MTS useful and economical. What would have happened to them, especially with expanding private farming, must remain a matter of speculation.

The demands from other areas for farm machinery had some curious repercussions. In August 1941, Antonescu told the Germans he could not possibly spare Romanian tractors for Transnistria, as the restoration of Bessarabian and Bucovinian agriculture had priority. In late 1942 the tractor

---

[16] AOK 11, IV Wi, *op. cit.*; Sztuka, *op. cit.*; "Schutzmassnahmen...," *op. cit.*; VSt Transnistrie, Abr. la, *op. cit.*; *Krakauer Zeitung, op. cit.*; *Südostecho*, November 21, 1941.

shortage in Old Romania was apparently so severe that the authorities even withdrew 1,876 of the best tractors from Transnistria; inevitably the 1943 harvest there declined. At the same time, however, individual Romanian businessmen were shipping in agricultural machinery and offering it for sale to Transnistria. The conflict between these two policies was never reconciled. Actually, the shortage of tractors does not seem to have been too severe.[17] By the fall of 1942, new courses for tractor drivers were started in Odessa. In the last half-year of occupation (1943-1944) the situation improved further because the Germans, evacuating some of the eastern-most areas they had seized, shipped back agricultural equipment to Transnistria. But when the Germans retreated through Transnistria their evacuation of machinery was at least as ruthless as had been the Soviet; after reoccupation Moscow could rightly blame the Axis for the severe decline in mechanization on Transnistrian farms.[18]

Fuel might have been a serious problem. During the first months of the occupation, the shortage of fuel oil for agricultural machinery actually did severely curtail its use. In German-held areas, fuel continued scarce and a source of tension throughout the war. Transnistria, however, was fortunate in that Romania, of all the European countries, was relatively rich in oil and, once the transportation bottleneck was overcome, could supply without particular difficulty the rather considerable quantities needed for the operation of the Transnistrian economy (over 2,000 freight cars of 15 tons each, for the spring of 1942 alone).[19]

The Peasantry

The peasant population seems, as a whole, to have adjusted rather rapidly to the new conditions. The "New Order" probably affected them less than it did city-dwellers; and some of the changes it wrought appear

---

[17] German Legation, Bucharest, to Ha Pol IV b, September 15, 1941, AA, CRS, Wi/ID 2.1174; Brandt, *op. cit.*, p. 228; *Bukarester Tageblatt,* August 19, 1943; Tverskoi; SD Report 100; Prinrz Wittgenstein, *op. cit.;* AOK 11, IV Wi (summary report, no title), April 15, 1942, CRS, Wi/ID 2.580; *Krakauer Zeitung, op. cit.;* Reiehart, *op cit.;* VSt Transnistrien, Abt. La, *op. cit.; Der nahe Osten,* Istanbul, Vol. 13, No. 12, June 15, 1943, p. 281; OVOV, Vol. 2, pp. 62, 69.

[18] *Universul,* Bucharest, August 5, 1942; V. Gordienko, "Odesshchina nakanune uborki urozhaia," *Izvestiia,* Moscow, July 6, 1944; Berger to Himmler, October 22, 1943, CRS, EAP 161 b-12/335.

[19] SD Report 100; Fritz Zierke, "Jenseits des Dnjestr," *Völkischer Beobachter,* July 20, 1943; VSt Transnistrien, Abt. La, *op. cit.*

to have been in harmony with their aspirations. Even in the first weeks of occupation willingness to work was reported lair or better than before — a sharp contrast to what the Germans experienced farther north and east. When genuine incentives were offered or real improvement in economic conditions was apparent, the peasants worked with a will. No peasant informants have been located; the fact that well-informed urban informants had no knowledge of specific peasant grievances is itself an index to the relative absence of violent rural unrest. This certainly was not true of refugees from German-controlled areas of the U.S.S.R., where the kolkhoz issue was hotly fought and remained paramount.[20]

What the city-dweller saw was an upsurge of trade between town and country, and greater activity on the free market, to which the peasants would bring their own products. Even during the first weeks some peasants ventured to face the economic chaos and offered potatoes, flour, and bread, at first in barter for other products, but soon for cash. The peasants, by and large, sought textiles, shoes, and other consumer goods. They might accept silver and gold or metal ware. At times they would accept Soviet money, but then would charge considerably higher prices (rumor had it that the Germans would confiscate all rubles or exchange them for new legal tender). Until the monetary reform discussed below, however, the familiar ruble was accepted more readily than either marks or lei.

Soon peasants (often acting as middlemen for some of their neighbors, so that not every household had to sell its own produce) regularly brought goods to the markets, and returned with shirts or shoes or perhaps a shovel or sickle, even a hat or a watch.[21] As a refugee recalls,

> I had no difficulty getting on a train whose cars were marked "Zhmerinka to Odessa." After a while the train started. There were many passengers and everyone had an "agricultural-commercial" look. They were all carrying food. The car was piled high with bags and boxes, and with baskets containing chickens. In my compartment a man had a bag with a small pig which squealed throughout the entire journey. The closer we got to Odessa, the more people crowded into the car. Soon it became impossible to get out. Both platforms were stacked with goods. On one there were several kegs of wine, on the other a few live sheep.[22]

---

[20] Beauftragte des Chefs der SiPo u. SD, op. cit.; VSt Transnistrien, Abt. Ia, *op. cit.;* interviews A and B.

[21] Tverskoi; Manuilov, p. 56; Printz Wittgenstein, *op. cit.*

The standard of living of the peasantry went up at first as a result of the change of systems. Peasants were not only able to conceal some of the produce and appropriate some of the former kolkhoz property, but delivery norms were lower, the equivalent obtainable in consumer goods was higher, and collection was less efficient than under Soviet rule. In 1941-1942 the peasants were generally better off than just prior to the war. In 1943, however, the situation changed. It is well described in a summary report of the German consul general in Odessa:

> The situation of the collective farmers has deteriorated by comparison with last year. The collectives' deliveries in kind to the Romanians were at first somewhat lower than those collected by Bolsheviks. In addition, the Romanian organization for their collection was functioning far more poorly than the Soviet had and therefore the peasants could easily lie to the Romanians. In the meanwhile, the Romanian administration has improved the collection system and, in violation of earlier pledges, has felt obliged, in view of the military situation, to raise the delivery norms. The new quotas are particularly keenly felt in the delivery of sheep, hogs, and fowl. Not only the collective but the individual collective member must now also pay... Of late, the Romanians also go from house to house and confiscate without pay tobacco, wine, and eggs. Still something is left to the peasant, even if it isn't much. For what he has left he can charge much higher prices...

These higher prices were the result of an inflationary spiral that developed after Stalingrad. The German consul concluded that, as of late February 1943:

> Economically the peasants are dissatisfied because the Romanians demand high deliveries, often treat the peasants unfairly and arbitrarily and because the settlement of accounts with the kolkhozes often does not work out. However, politically they fear the return of the Soviets.[23]

Information from other sources on the whole confirms this view. The consensus is that even in 1943 the peasants were no worse off, and were still perhaps a little better off, than before the war.[24] But the basic features of the collective farm remained unchanged. A government decree had sanctioned the "departure" or separation of individual peasants from the

---

[22] Vladimir Petrov, *My Retreat from Russia*, Yale University Press, New Haven, 1950, p. 200.

[23] German Consulate, Odessa, *op. cit.*

kolkhoz, with land and cattle of their own. A number of peasants had established their own *otrub* (holding) — in substance, the revival of pre-collectivization holdings. This does not seem to have been a widespread practice — the scarcity of information about it suggests as much. But the peasants wanted more, and their pressure probably influenced Antonescu in mid-1943. Wishing to make a *grand geste* toward the Transnistrian peasantry, Antonescu decreed a reform which went further in the direction of private agriculture than anything permitted theretofore.[25] This decree, signed by him on June 15, 1943, at Vorontsov Palace in Odessa, and proclaimed as a token of Romanian appreciation for "disciplined and understanding" behavior by the population, provided, in Article I, for the assignment of land for cultivation by individual peasant households:

> (1) The Transnistrian farm land is turned over for individual cultivation to all residents who (a) have been working with special zeal on the land assigned them in "work brigades"; (b) who have delivered, through the village communities, their share of products from the livestock turned over to them, i.e., within the framework provided for the maintenance of the occupation army, for the pay of administrative expenditures, and for new investments; (c) who all through this time have evinced a correct behavior toward army and administration.
> (2) For the soil turned over for individual cultivation a yearly tariff in kind or in cash shall be paid, the sum to be determined according to the needs of the administration and the development of that region.
> (3) The residents are obliged... to plant crops communally according to the plans set by the agronomists.
> (4) The plot given each resident... shall be in accordance with his family and social burdens, the size of the community's land holdings, and the number of residents claiming to obtain parts of it...[26]

The decree was perhaps intentionally vague about whether private property was or was not being established. The impression given is that

---

[24] However, in August, 1943, the service charge for milling and other services was raised considerably, namely to 20 per cent on wheat and rye, and 15 per cent on other grains. Two months later it was raised to 40 per cent on wheat and rye, and 30 per cent on other grains (*Odesskaia gazeta*, No. 183, August 10, 1943; *Molva*, No. 260, October 16, 1943; OVOV, Vol.2, p. 17).

[25] It will be noted, however, that it came within two weeks of the German decree proclaiming (on paper) the establishment of private land property in occupied Russia.

land was merely being assigned for cultivation and exploitation, but was to remain subject to regulation; mandatory cropping plans were retained, but, unlike Soviet plans, were to be worked out locally by agricultural specialists. The decree was important more as a symbol than as a real departure in Transnistrian farming. The whole problem of the kolkhoz, so acute elsewhere in the U.S.S.R., somewhat managed to be subordinated to other issues in Transnistria, where parts of the collective system were maintained and others abolished or amended (see Chapter VIII).

The status of the sovkhozes (state farms) was even simpler. Here the problem of private ownership did not arise. Sovkhozes were transferred directly to Romanian state ownership, operating under the Agricultural Directorate as experimental and model farms, especially in cattle-breeding, vine and fruit growing. In the Lustdorf area, for instance, the wine-processing sovkhoz "Chervonnyi Khutor" had been preserved from evacuation by its agronomist; this agronomist became the farm's director under the new regime. While details on the operation of state farms are lacking, there do not seem to have been any abnormal tensions.[27]

---

[26] Tverskoi; *Molva*, Odessa, No. 159, June 18, 1943; German Consulate, Odessa, "Neue Innenpolitik in Transnistrien," June 21. 1943, AA reel 1273, frames 342476-81; Mamukov, p. 23. It is conceivable that the above text is not precise, as it results from multiple translation: the English is translated from a German version made from an official Russian text published as a translation of the Romanian decree.

[27] *Krakauer Zeitung*, op. cit.; *Der Deutsche in Transnistrien*, Vol. 1, No. 12, October 4, 1942; *Münchner Neueste Nachrichten*, op. cit.

For a survey of forestry in Transnistria, see *Bukarester Tageblatt*, March 9, 1943. On fishing, see Florin Andrei, "Die Fischerei in Transnistrien," *ibid.,* October 5, 1943. Fishing had been organized in collective and state farms, too. An informant who lived in a fishing village near Odessa for the first weeks following the siege recalls that at first there was a definite sense of relief that Soviet controls were over; as one colorful fisherman told him, "konchilsia bardak" — "the bordello is over." The fishermen's hopes for rapid improvement in their conditions were dashed, however, by the war damage to the hatcheries and the idleness of the nearby canning and processing plants, which had taken their catch off the fishermen's hands in the past. As a result, they were now often stuck with an excess supply, which in turn drove prices down. Inevitably disillusionment set in, caused largely by material conditions. The informant, who was not wholly conversant with the details, remembered that the fishermen sought the end of the collective but not of all cooperation. For instance, joint ownership and use of equipment and inventory, including nets and even boats, was accepted. Some individual fishermen became independent — *vydelilis'* — but most banded together in a form of cartel, or cooperative. (Interview E.) The Romanians, on their part, sponsored four new fishing preserves.

The Harvest

The measure of farm work is, of course, the harvest. Unfortunately, the available statistics on agricultural production are highly contradictory and incomplete; some of the errors and omissions in Romanian data were pointed out in contemporary German analyses. Of a potential 2.5 million hectares or so total crop land in Transnistria over 2 million were plowed in 1941, before the occupation. Only about 1,750,000 (or less) were harvested — more in the north than in the south. Some 90 per cent of the wheat acreage was harvested, but only 40 per cent of the harvest was threshed, the threshing of the rest being hopefully postponed until 1942. However, as the figures below indicate, the 1941 harvest was rather good, and the substantial share of it which went to the Romanians made a decisive difference to them in assuring the feeding of the armed forces. The planting in the fall of 1941 was, however, miserable. In some areas (e.g., Odessa) it amounted to 5 per cent of the acreage, at best (e.g., in Mogilev-Podol'ski) 20 per cent. The rain set in early and was intense. Fuel was lacking, particularly in districts distant from the Romanian border and from trunk rail lines. Disorganization was still extensive. The results were correspondingly poor.

In terms of acreage, things improved in the following year. In spring, the plan called for sowing on nearly 2 million hectares of crop land, and in 1943, nearly 2 1/4 million. Not quite so much was accomplished;[28] however, both total yield and, in a number of instances, yield per hectare went up again[29] in 1943 over the preceding year. While yield per acre remained nearly constant for such major crops as maize, sunflowers, and

---

[28] A report divides the cultivated area as follows:

Cereals — 1,537,762
Oleiferous — 93,285
Leguminous — 41,967
Tubers and root crops — 131,341
Textile plants — 230,850
(Florian Codrescu, "Transnistria," *Excelsior,* Bucharest, October 25, 1942)

[29] In terms of the goals which the authorities set themselves, the yield was rather good, and only a bit poorer than in the areas of Romania proper. As of June 30, 1942, for instance, the agricultural plan had been carried our as follows:

Bessarabia — 97.7%
Old Romania — 93.8%
Transnistria — 92.7%
(*Universul,* Bucharest, July 3, 1942)

beets, the manpower available to produce it was far less in 1942-1943 than before the war (in 1940), and there was also less farm machinery. The yield of wheat and rye declined; the reasons for this decline do not emerge from the source materials available. The most stupendous increase in yield was in potatoes — approximately twice as many were grown in 1942-1943 as in 1940-1941.

In general, crop yields were not fully satisfactory to either the local population or the authorities; both were convinced that, given more time and propitious conditions, the yield could be increased.[30] While exact comparisons are impossible, the data suggest that trends in Transnistria roughly paralleled those in German-occupied areas of the U.S.S.R., with perhaps a somewhat more significant increase in yield *per capita* of farm labor in Transnistria.

The Transnistrian experience of Soviet agriculture was too brief and too contradictory to permit of clear-cut conclusions. It confirmed that, as of 1941, there was among the Soviet peasantry widespread hostility to some of the salient features of the kolkhoz system. It emphasized the importance of incentives for peasant production and marketing — and also the possibility of improving both in a relatively short span of time. But it also indicated that other issues could take precedence over the solution of the agrarian problem.

Table 1: CROP STATISTICS[a] (in thousands of tons)

	Transnistria	
	1942	1942
Wheat	107	280
TOTAL NON-GRAIN CROPS	845	863
GRAND TOTAL	2,257	2,399

---

[30] Cornățeanu, *op cit.* p. 59; Richart, *op. cit.;* VSt Transnistrien, Abt. La, *op. cit.;* Romania, *Trei ani de guvernare,* Imprimeria Națională, 1943, Bucharest, p. 133; Major Bartsch, "Berichr über die Frontreise des Marschalls Antonescu," June, 1942, CRS, DHMR 27638/15; Ion Gheorghe, *Rumäniens Weg zum Satellitenstaat,* Welsernühl, Wels, 1952, p. 192; Mayor Jochim, "So arbeiten wir in Rosenfeld," *Der Deutsche in Transnistrien,* Vol. 1, No. 9, September 13, 1942; *Argus,* Bucharest, July 2, 1943.

Table 1: CROP STATISTICS[a] (in thousands of tons)

	Transnistria	
Rye	22	50
Parley	391	507
Oils	59	127
Maize	705	486
Other grain	128	86
AM. GRAIN	1,412	1,536
Pulses	30	60
Potatoes	421	625
Sugar beets	0	?
Rapeseed	1	?
Sunflower seed	187	178
Soybeans	9	0
TOTAL NON-GRAIN CROPS	845	863
GRAND TOTAL	2,257	2,399

a Based on Woermann, *Europoische Ernahrungswirtschaft in Zahlen*. Vol. 2, Berlin, 1944, cited in Karl Brandi et al., *Management of Agriculture...*, Stanford University Press, Stanford, 1953, pp. 217, 219.

Table 2: CROP YIELD IN TRANSNISTRIA[a]
(in kilograms per hectare; approximate)

	1940	1941	1942[b]	1942[c]	1943
Winter wheat	1,300	1,000	600	600	650
Summer wheat	900	800	600		
Winter rye	1,300	1,100	700	550	600
Summer barley	1,200	900	1,200	1,000	1,000
Oats	1,000	800	1,200	900	1,000
Maize	1.500	1,100	1,600	1,350	1,050

Table 2: CROP YIELD IN TRANSNISTRIA[a]
(in kilograms per hectare; approximate)

	1940	1941	1942[b]	1942[c]	1943
Sunflower seed	1,200	1,200	1,300	900	900
Potatoes	4,200	5,000	10,000	7,000	8,000

a. Based on Woermann, *op. cit.*; Alfred Sztuka, "Wirtsehaftliehe Grundlagen.,.," *Osteuropu-Juhrbuch 1942*, Breslau, p. 213; and Codrescu, *op cit.*

b. Figures as given in Sztuka. *op. cit.*; and Codrescu. *op cit.*

c. Figures computed by author on basis of Woermann, *op cit.*

The Urban Areas

Urban Society

An examination of the fate of Soviet urban society involves questions that lie at the core of this study: how did different socio-economic groups fare and adjust after the removal of Soviet controls and institutions; what groups, if any, displayed economic initiative; what forms did economic initiative take, and were enterprises successful; were there any changes in the relative status of socio-economic groups?

Only urban society in Odessa itself is here examined, and only in terms of its larger social groupings. Evidence on industrial labor is scarce; most of the information available pertains to professional and other white-collar classes, economic entrepreneurs, and political collaborators.

In marked contrast to German-held areas, there was little or no migration of urban residents from Odessa to the countryside, partly because of Romanian efforts to prevent it, but mainly because in Transnistria rural areas were no better off than cities. The standard of living in most German-held areas became suddenly higher in the country than in the cities, because food failed to reach the cities, consumer goods disappeared from them, and agricultural reforms increased rural productivity. Even during the first winter of Romanian rule, Odessa was better off than the kolkhozes; thereafter conditions in Odessa improved and there was certainly then no economic incentive to leave the city.[31]

---

[31] Interview A; "Agricultura sovietică in Transnistria," *Ogorul Românesc*, December 1, 1941, condensed in *Economia română*, Bucharest, Vol. 24, 1942, No, 1, p. 40.

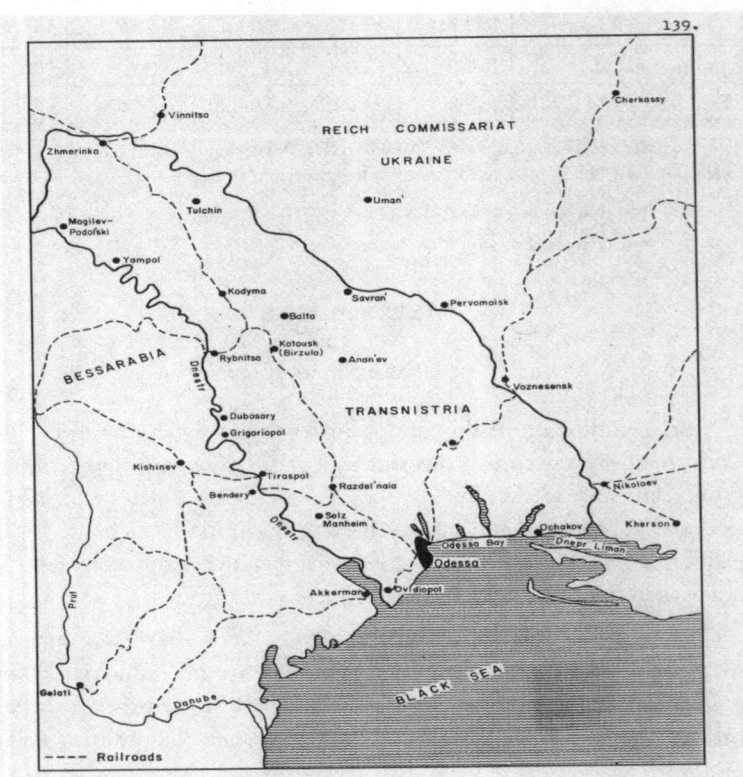

Map 2 -- Transnistria

The housing situation in Odessa affected all classes. There had been a dearth of adequate housing, but because of evacuations, flights, arrests, and exterminations there were now a number of vacancies. Some office buildings had been destroyed or badly damaged and some new agencies required space; but there was more and better office space available than previously.

The municipal Housing Directorate had charge of assigning such units. The Inventory Directorate was responsible for belongings and furniture found in abandoned apartments and houses; what was found was confiscated and no compensation made to owners. Because so much had been "appropriated" without official sanction during the first days of occupation, a special commission was established to appraise all equipment, and establish equitable procedures for the return of stolen property. All that happened was that the Romanians made off with the best of everything. Some furniture was stored in public warehouses, where it could be issued on official requisition or sold to individuals. Free apartments were assigned by the primăria as a political reward for collaboration. City and government employees received good dwellings which they could not have afforded under Soviet conditions at half the "nominal" rent; better housing was assumed to satisfy long unsatisfied "bourgeois" longings.

For the rest of the population, rent regulations made the apartment situation somewhat worse. Instead of the rather uniform and almost normal Soviet rents, a graduated system of rent payments was instituted; rents were now determined by the floor occupied, the quality of the apartment, its size, and the section of town in which it was located. Though not really onerous, rent became a greater item in the resident's budget than it had been. A number of people acquired, built, or shared private dwellings, e.g., in the suburbs, and there was some talk of cooperative housing projects (though no evidence of any having been built).[32]

Antonescu's decree of June 15, 1943, was intended as a major propaganda stroke and sought to depict the Romanian authorities as attuned to popular wishes. In it, urban complaints are mirrored. Article 6 was greeted with some genuine acclaim: "All urban residents... shall be entitled to a house with a garden or to an apartment." It was vague enough to permit the assumption that such property would be owned by the individual family. In practice, only Romanian citizens (including Russian émigrés) could acquire real estate. Actually, there was neither time nor inclination to

---

[32] Interviews A, C, and E; Manuilov, pp. 67-69.

implement it. Article 7 stipulated that the size of the house or apartment should depend on the size of the family and "the profession and the social necessities of life" of the owner. This would have perpetuated and institutionalized social inequality. It apparently represented a conscious effort to assure the intelligentsia, the collaborating white-collar groups, and the new economic elite, of the permanence of their privileged status. This provision, too, remained unenforced. Article 8 provided that former owners were to have priority on pre-revolutionary residential dwellings except when Romanian or Transnistrian staffs were using them; again, this was vague enough to arouse little opposition, as it did not specify whether there was or was not to be compensation; actually, compensation was made in at least a few cases.[33]

A fair amount of construction was undertaken under Transnistrian auspices. Many of the bigger and better dwellings were repaired. The façades on thoroughfares were repainted, surfaces were redone, gravel was spread around the public parks, and flower beds planted in the squares. Much of this, however, could be put under the rubric of conspicuous consumption — or waste; a minimum of work went into new construction and repair of workers' or other low-rent housing.[34]

The "New NEP"

Perhaps the most striking single phenomenon of the Transnistrian period was the upsurge of commercial activity. All social and age strata of the population, though in varying degree, participated in it. After the first few months of chaos and hardship, small restaurants and shops of all sorts burgeoned forth. Twenty years earlier the era of the New Economic Policy (NEP) had succeeded War Communism, and it is not amiss to call this a new NEP. An ethos of private retail trade became dominant but the framework of a state-controlled economy was retained; an acquisitive society emerged but many Bolshevik values, practices, and routines persisted.

Trade had entirely broken down when the Soviets left: stocks were depleted, stores had been raided or destroyed, the sale of agricultural products had been suspended, and cash was scarce.[35] In the early period of the

---

[33] Antonescu decree, June 15, 1943, *Molva,* No. 159, June 18, 1953. See also Chapter V of this study.

[34] Interview F.

[35] Sztuka, *op. cit.,* pp. 211-213; SD Report 100; Manuilov; pp. 70-72.

occupation these conditions were reflected in a mushrooming of so-called commissionary stores. These were substantially junk shops. Because most residents (especially the unemployed) were in great need of cash, store owners were able to get all kinds of things — from pianos, old samovars, and family silver to moth-eaten furs — at prices far below normal. The margin of profit from selling them to opulent residents was often considerable, especially as many of the "new rich" had no notion of what a fair price should be. Goods had sometimes been procured through looting, and their price therefore constituted pure profit. Sometimes — and this was their original purpose — commissionary stores would accept people's belongings and pocket a handsome "commission" for selling them.[36]

An author has given a description of a commissionary store:

A brand-new sign over the door, reading in French "Sevres." The two windows overcrowded with old china vases, watches, dishes, jewelry, a piece of silk, furs, icons, lamps, a microscope, musical instruments, old books… and inside, in semi-darkness, ancient furniture, a harpsichord, dresses, shoes…

Refugees recall that many women who had been "nothing but housewives" opened commissionary stores, a few even coming to own several of them.

The boom did not last long. Basically, the stores were a symptom of an unhealthy and unstable economy. By the fall of 1942, when the acute need for cash had passed, and stockpiles of goods abandoned by evacuees and Jews had been sold, the importance of these transactions declined; there was a considerable drop in the turnover of commissionary stores, and many were reorganized into shops of other kinds.[37]

Most enterprises were what sociologists call "tertian," or service, activities: restaurants and the Russian equivalent of snack bars, cafes, baths, laundries, hairdressers, hotels, shoe and watch repair shops, movies, theaters, and the like. There was a sudden rash of luncheonettes — the Romanian name, *bodega,* was soon taken over. Commonly, for instance, several women would join forces with a Romanian officer or a *Volksdentscher* resident as co-owners or lessees of a store or restaurant (on hotels,

---

[36] This was the usual role of the commissionary store in German-held areas, and suggests a poorer and more primitive economy (less cash in circulation, more barter) than in Odessa, where commissionary stores were a combination of second-hand store, pawn shop, and antique shop.

[37] Interviews C and E; Petr Ershov, "Strannyi konets," pp. 69 ff.

movies, and theaters, see Chapter V). Here and there a business would fall, but on the whole, they proved successful and, within limits, rewarding.[38]

It is interesting to speculate on why the overwhelming number of new enterprises were in the tertiary field.[39] The most plausible explanation is that it was the easiest field to enter. The government owned much of the manufacturing; raw materials were scarce; and many of the new "entrepreneurs" lacked manual or vocational skills; it was logical for them, therefore, to go into service activities. One might add another hypothesis. While some new enterprises produced necessities or near-necessities, many shops and service provided luxuries or at least unessential conveniences, by local standards. Possibly the stores selling Directoire style furniture, the restaurant with its gypsy violinist, and the merchant selling foreign silk stockings were all responding to deep-seated longings for "bourgeois" comforts and conveniences, and also to the general desire for normalcy, abundance, and conspicuous wealth.

There were, of course, some "productive" enterprises. Locksmiths, shoemakers, mechanics — men with individual skills, artisans[40] or technicians — opened their own shops. In the market a peasant sold vegetable oil (generally sunflower oil) which was bought in considerable quantities by German soldiers, who sent it to the Reich; next to this stand was a private cooperative[41] producing tin cans in which the oil could be shipped. Another *artel'*, or voluntary cooperative run on business principles, produced wicks for *primus* burners. A few former mechanics and smiths formed a workshop to produce cigarette lighters and nails. Bakeries and pastry shops were quite successful; several refugees claim that the *petits fours* and sweet rolls were better in Transnistria than anywhere else. Stands, booths, and kiosks of all descriptions and sizes dotted the major thoroughfares. Kataev in his novel published in Moscow after the war described (rather derisively, to be sure) a street scene in 1941-1942 Odessa:

---

[38] Manuilov, pp. 86ff; interviews C and E.

[39] Much of the business activity cannot be considered tertian; however, in the sense of having been non-essential. Until 1943, much of it was concerned with food processing or retailing.

[40] As indicated in another chapter, there was a severe shortage of artisans as a result of the removal of Jews to special reservations. Thus, in Anan'ev, 100 per cent of all glaziers and 80 per cent of all carpenters had been Jews.

[41] The Romanians frowned on the formation of large cooperatives, permitting only one Moldavian consumers' cooperative, but tolerated small cooperative workshops.

> Here and there fat women with huge earrings, hats, and mittens stood behind wooden counters (on the street) and sold homemade baked goods, homemade candles, Italian lemons, and some sort of jam in jars with multicolored labels.[42]

Elsewhere Kataev has his protagonist wire to the Soviet side a report on conditions in Odessa in the winter of 1941-1942. Naturally, this is supposed to be the dispatch of a trusted Communist, composed *post facto* by a Soviet author; yet even it reflects the economic hustle and bustle:

> One observes the activization of private trade. Many stands, tents, etc., have appeared; trade is conducted by "former people" (i.e., pre-revolutionary merchants, NEP men, etc.) who have come out of their holes. On Deribasovskaia (a main street) there are several commissionary stores, which make a sad impression. There is a flood of businessmen (from Romania), money changers, speculators...

Such was the "reactionary" life that sprang up a few short months after the Soviet authorities left.

According to Kataev and refugee informants, commercial activity had picked up by the spring of 1942.[43] In the course of that year, food was more abundant than in the difficult first months, and goods were "imported" in greater bulk. By December, a German visitor from Kiev commented admiringly on the good restaurants in Odessa — one could get appetizers, vodka, veal cutlets, and beefsteak — and in disbelief on the food stores full of sausages and hams.[44] And in 1943, foreign correspondents in Odessa would invariably comment on the number of snack bars, fur and jewelry stores, and cafes on and near the Deribasovskaia. A department store was opened on Deribasovskaia in late 1943. On the street, women and children would sell sweets and poppy rolls. "If one could afford it, one could live very well."[45]

---

[42] Interview E; Petrov, *My Retreat from Russia,* p. 206; Kataev, *op. cit.*, p. 204.

[43] Kataev. *op. cit.,* pp. 230, 386.

[44] In October, 1943, a new market hall was opened, having been rebuilt at the expense of the merchants and salesmen operating there. (Interviews A. E; Ia. Peterle, Odessa — stolitsa Transnistrii," *Novoe russkoe slovo,* New York, June 1, 1952; *Bukarester Tageblatt,* October 22, 1943).

[45] *Bukarester Tageblatt,* October 19, 1943; Ernst Bauer, "Odessa — die Stadt hinter der Eront," *Neue Ordnung,* Zagreb, November 2, 1943; AA, Pol XIII, Ein Gewährsmann meldet..." AA, reel 5079, frames E 292536ff

Not too surprisingly, in connection with this activity there was a good deal of speculation, abuse, and black marketing. Some engaged in fantastic exchanges of currency.[46] Peculiar characters suddenly began appearing on certain street corners — much as in the rest of "capitalist" Europe — offering to buy or sell gold, silver, rubles, even dollars and pounds sterling. Strictly speaking, there was no black market, as princes were relatively uncontrolled. However, certain imports and exports were concealed from public records — largely so as to circumvent official restrictions and avoid paying duty. In addition, a number of *bodegas* sold drugs, alcoholic beverages, and barbiturates "under the counter" without a license. Because of their very nature, not much is known about these transactions; none of the available sources could provide details. It may be worth noting, however, that, because they probably had had "practice" under the Soviets, many of the new "entrepreneurs" were able to conceal some of their operations from officials quite successfully.[47]

All evidence suggests amazing commercial activity, remarkable in scope and success.[48] Ingenuity, flexibility, initiative, and business acumen were displayed by many who had never had experience with "capitalist" enterprise or private trade. The figures on the number of enterprises differ widely — perhaps because of differences in the categories used — and range from a minimum of 1,500 private and 110 municipal stores in

---

[46] Cf. the following scene in Lvov: "I needed gold, in coins. 'We have Swiss francs, 20 franc pieces.' 'How much?' '1400 marks.' That was on the expensive side, but there was still a point in taking them. We could make a 30 per cent profit in Odessa." (Vladimir Petrov, *My Retreat from Russia,* Yale University Press, New Haven, 1950, p. 210.)

[47] Peterle, *op. cit.;* interviews A and C; Kataev, *op. cit.,* p. 230; Manuilov, p. 87.

[48] One should consider, in addition, the "foreign trade" conducted in Transnistria, much of it illicit, both by residents and others, especially Romanian merchants and officials. Serious obstacles to trade were the Transportation bottleneck and the wartime shortages in other European countries which reduced the scope of trade even after foreign representatives — such as a Finnish trade mission — visited Odessa. A number of Romanian tradesmen established themselves or branch offices in Odessa for months. Imports, especially from Italy and Germany, included lemons, oranges, candy, textiles, glassware; some coal was brought from the German-occupied Donets basin. The exports and imports, stringently regulated by the Romanians, were important as tokens rather than because of their actual scope or value. The most profitable operations probably remained officially unrecorded. All this, of course, took place in addition to official Romanian and German requisitions and sale of food delivered to the state by the Transnistrian authorities in Romania proper at a discount. Trade, and particularly foreign trade, activities were supervised by a central agency, the *Oficiul Central al Comerțului,* in Tiraspol, equivalent more or less to a government chamber of commerce. (I.G. Farben, "Transnistrien: Gebiet, Bevölkerung und Wirtschaft," 1942).

Odessa, reported in early 1942, to a maximum of 6,000 private shops, reported in early 1943.

Considering the special conditions under which this development took place, the available statistics are quite striking. As of June 30, 1942, 9,665 applications had been made for licenses for business or workshops by individuals or groups in Odessa. Of these, 7,465 had been investigated (many of the others were alternate applications or duplications), and a total of 3,536 licenses had been issued for retail trade and 926 for workshops. On June 30, 1942, 1,629 enterprises were actually functioning (in addition to municipal stores and government plants). In addition, there were seven public markets in operation, and two others about to open. The largest of these, Novyi Bazar, had 199 meat stands, 117 dairy stands, 12 municipal stores, 11 metal manufacturing and repair shops (mostly for containers and cans), and 7 snack bars; on the market square outside, there were 215 stands, including 50 selling vegetables. The other markets were smaller, but still had significant numbers of sellers.[49]

The Romanians did not create the economic activity in Odessa. They merely directed it. Though accepting state control, they sought to promote private economy. Pursuing a middle course, they avoided both full capitalism and full collectivism. One knowledgeable informant asserts that they gambled that the people would manage to secure food and other necessities if the physical and institutional framework for providing it was maintained or restored. The public markets, for example, were promptly re-opened. (This gamble turned out well; by the spring of 1942, there was no food shortage, and, by 1943, Odessa was living — by Soviet standards, and excepting a sizable underprivileged category — in relative plenty.) The Romanians encouraged trade and other private activities by abolishing maximum prices — permitting sellers (especially peasants) to charge any

---

[49] *Rumänischer Wirtschnfisspiegel*, Bucharest, Vol. 7 (1942), No. 16, p. 23; and E.I. Mamukov, "Rumynskaia okkupatsii Odessy i Transnistrii v 1941-1944 gg," (MS), Institute for the Study of the U.S.S.R., 1955, pp. 40-41; hereafter cited as Mamukov. The breakdown for actually operating enterprises in Odessa as of June 30, 1942, was as follows (cf. *Novoe Slovo*, No. 59, Berlin, July 22, 1942):

Food stores and *gastronomy* (179); cafés, snack bars, *bufety* (436); baked-goods shops (18); commissionary stores (54); department stores, haberdasheries (8); dairy shops (40) hotels and hostels (8); kiosks (35); commercial middlemen (6); sausage manufacture (8); bread bakeries (45); housing repair and construction (3); leather-goods manufacture (9); mechanics and locksmiths (110); blacksmiths (34); photographic shops and studios (15); electric repair shops (25); barbers and hairdressers (112); shoe manufacture and repair (17); railor5 (14); carpenters (12); others, miscellaneous (267).

price they wished for their products — and by granting a tax exemption for the entire first year to any new business licensed in Transnistria.

Licenses were required for the conduct of business. This gave the Primăria a chance to exercise control whenever desired. Even more important, licenses provided funds and gave officials a golden opportunity to promote their own interests. Even before the end of 1941, a small group in the Odessa primăria managed to make themselves co-owners of certain restaurants, to which they routed all official catering and entertainment. The section issuing licenses would often balk until bribed or otherwise "satisfied"; it became customary to make an official's wife or friend a co-owner or stockholder (*paishchik*) in an enterprise in order to secure a license.

All these "complications" became part of the routine; though strongly resented, they did not noticeably inhibit business activities. In fact, so profitable were Transnistrian enterprises that, in 1943, the authorities set up taxes and fees designed to "milk" them of three-quarters of their profits; this money was to be used for road construction and other public purposes. The comprehensive Antonescu decree of June 1943, confirmed freedom of trade (Article 14), subject to such regulation as might be subsequently issued, a rather meaningless pronouncement. Thus, on the whole, Romanian policy helped the growth of small-scale business and commerce, though not always in a fair and equitable manner.[50]

The only two Soviet writers, not Odessa residents, to publish abroad their impressions of wartime Transnistria both stress how important economic initiative was for the revival of the area. One calls it, a bit exaggeratedly, a miracle of free private initiative; the other says of the Romanians:

> The first, and perhaps most important thing they did was to grant everyone complete freedom of private initiative in trade and commerce... (As a result) the several city markets were overflowing with food at attractive prices, especially compared with the rest of occupied Russia...[51]

---

[50] Manuilov, p. 70; Tverskoi; *Bukarester Tageblatt,* November 2, 1943; interview A; Peterle, *op. cit.*; Sdf. von Berg, "Lagebericht aus Odessa," January, 1942, AA, reel 2066, frames 448876-80; *Molva, op. cit.*; Sztuka, op. cit.; gh, "Transnistrien: Das Werk des Gouverneurs Alexianu," *Das Reich,* Berlin, August 1, 1943.

[51] *Deutsche Ukraine-Zeitung,* January 10, 1943; Karl J. Müller, "Das Land zwischen Dnjestr und Bug," *ibid.*, July 26, 1942; interview E; Petrov, *op. cit.*, p. 203; Nikolai Fevr, *Sohusc voskhodit na zapade, Novoe slovo,* Buenos Aires, 1950, pp. 263-264.

The New Elite

The political and economic changes wrought by the substitution of Transnistrian for Soviet authorities brought in their wake a change in social stratification — partly planned by the new regime, but largely a spontaneous development reflecting organic processes in Soviet society.

One may appropriately speak of the emergence of a new privileged stratum in Odessa. It consisted of two distinct elements: (a) a kind of *non-veaux riches* who surged upward in a socially mobile society because of their "commercial" successes; and (b) an elite whose privileged position was based on political collaboration with the new authorities.[52]

The "commercial elite," a significant but not numerically large class, caught the spirit of the Romanian conqueror and applied to similar acquisitive ends their Soviet-bred experience. A few had been "failure";[53] many more had been *khoziaistvenniki* (supply managers, minor planning officials, subordinate administrative or other white-collar workers); others had no pertinent previous experience whatever. There were those who had training and experience antedating the Soviet era and those whose administrative-economic skills had been developed under the Five-Year Plans. Both proved equally capable of adjusting to and making the most of the new situation.

Not every storekeeper became a member of the new elite. The ordinary, small-scale businessman or woman did not; he was looked upon by his fellow-citizens with some respect and curiosity The commercial elite was made up of the few "overly successful," the "unhealthily wealthy" (terms used by refugee informants). They provoked the resentment of the mass, a resentment that is paradoxical, for the "commercial elite" had merely realized what most of the white-collar stratum would have liked to have achieved. The elite above all sought comfortable, abundant, secure "middle-class" living, and also the tokens and conspicuous consumption that are commonly associated in the West with wealth. A Ukrainian bookkeeper in two years became a rich "entrepreneur" thanks to a jewelry store

---

[52] The "managerial elite," to the extent that it existed, is described below in connection with industrial enterprises.

[53] Kataev paints a satirical portrait of a prototype of the new *zhulik* (swindler): a former NEP man, then a home-production artisan, then a superintendent of a housing project, who under the Romanians opened a commissionary store dealing in goods looted from the apartments of evacuees. (Valentin Kataev, *Za vlast' sovetov*, Moscow, 1949, p. 394).

he opened. An Armenian, before the war a storekeeper in a trust, got to own five shops. Now both owned large apartments; their ladies wore diamonds and gold; they gave expensive parties to which the "cream" of society — Romanian officials, officers, and leading collaborators — were invited; vodka and champagne were consumed in stupendous quantities; debauchery spread. Daughters of the elite would go out with Romanian officers; to study voice at the Conservatory was the fashion. At the opera, the ladies wore nail polish and huge rings on their fingers, and corsets under their finery. A refugee novelist has described an Odessa *nouveau riche* who had come to own two stores, a bakery, shares in a hotel, and various other undertakings. At a party he gave the mansion glittered with glassware; an orchestra played; huge chandeliers decorated each room; servants abounded, as did French perfume, Italian fruit, "classical" furniture, and rich *hors d'oeuvres*.[54]

Quite clearly, only a very few "arrived" sufficiently to afford such a life, and all accounts make quite obvious the people's awareness of the social injustice such a maldistribution of wealth constituted.

Popular responses to this new elite were divided. One response — which may conventionally be labeled "leftist" — rejected it as unjust, capitalist, unhealthy, immoral, or undignified. The other response — "rightist," one might say — rejected it but primarily out of frustration and envy, basically desiring to join the elevated and carefree set of the "successful" or their children, the Odessa version of a *jeunesse dorée*. Many of the potential exponents of the first may be assumed to have left eastward with the Soviets. The characteristic response was the second; the white-collar group that stayed generally itself strove for "bourgeois" comforts.

The "political elite" is a bit more elusive and more heterogeneous. Not every collaborator could be considered of the elite, and the motives of collaborators were various. The political elite, strictly speaking, included (f) a few top careerists out to make the most of the new situation, for instance, as heads of directorates, and (2) men who, like the editors of the dailies, one of the vice-mayors, or a few of the university deans, occupied responsible positions and were sought after by the authorities as well as by seekers of favors. Many of this latter class were tongue-in-cheek about the whole Transnistrian regime.

What strikes the analyst seeking to define the collaborator group more precisely is the great preponderance of males between forty and fifty

---

[54] Pererle, *op. cit.*; interviews A and C; Manuilov, p. 92; Ershov, pp. 69, 81, 91ff.

years of age. Perhaps this was because men younger than forty had to a large extent been evacuated or mobilized; of those who remained most were not qualified for responsible administrative or political jobs. Also, generally, pro-Communism appears to have been more deeply rooted in the younger age group; this was especially true at the university. Intellectuals above fifty, from a combination of motives, were apparently reluctant to embark on full-fledged collaboration. Some were just plain afraid. Others, were old enough to harbor no more ambition, preferring to sit it out. Also, these older men, who had received their training before the Revolution, gave evidence of feeling moral restraints and a Russian (not Soviet) patriotism, which militated against their working "for the foe."

What remained was the middle group — men in their forties. Some were "non-political" and would have operated under any regime that permitted them to pursue their work and improve standard of living; some had been frustrated in their hopes for promotion by Soviet conditions, and now relished the opportunities for advancement which opened up with the departure of Soviet incumbents and the establishment of a new regime. Implicit in their approach was a certain absence of ethical scruple — an amorality, rather than immorality, perhaps induced by Soviet life.[55] They were commonly rewarded both with higher positions — as professors, section heads in the administration, or managers — and higher living standards, because of getting priority in apartment assignments and the special low cost "governor's rations" to which all official personnel were entitled.[56]

Those members of the intelligentsia who refused to collaborate and were unable to profit from the commercial boom, were of course much worse off than before. There were such men, especially among the older intellectuals — for example, Kataev's prototype of the old Russian professor, Svetlovidov, or, in real life, Gotalov-Gottlieb. This venerable scholar had contributed to the original Russian edition of the Brockhaus encyclopedia, had later taught in Odessa, but refused to teach under the Romanians (it could not be ascertained whether he was of Jewish origin). There were other professors who refused to send their children to Transnistrian lyceums (see Chapter IV).

These were exceptions. To the average citizen they merely demonstrated that steadfastness in principles resulted in hardship and hazard. It

---

[55] It should be apparent that these are generalizations to which there are a number of individual exceptions.

was easy to rationalize that collaboration was a necessity, that it was not an endorsement of the new regime; some even argued that it was one's duty to take official positions so as to neutralize and counter-vail "the rascals."[57]

Industry, Management, and Labor

The Romanian approach to Soviet industry differed fundamentally from that of the Germans. There was no razing of industry, no "colonial" schemes, and no effort to export labor from Soviet territory to the mother country.[58] On the contrary, plans were made to repair damaged plants wherever the Soviet removal of equipment had not made this impossible. Smaller enterprises were often supervised by a directorate of the municipality or judeţ (e.g., the Engineering-Technical Directorate ran the stone quarries, the Food Directorate ran the processing and canning plants, etc.). The larger enterprises — plants or shops with over one hundred workers — remained in government hands. Refugees testify that the people (or at least the urban groups concerned) objected to denationalizing large plants and public utilities."[59]

One of the first projects organized by the Technical Directorate, in late 1941, was the resurfacing of Odessa's streets, the clearing of barri-

---

[56] For purposes of ration allocation, the category of officials included all university instructors and all lawyers who were members of the special "bureau," or union, of the Odessa *advokatura*. This bureau, with some 400 members, was officially connected with the primăria. Most lawyers did no law work since martial law remained in effect and most indigenous lawyers could not plead in Romanian before the courts-martial. This opened an opportunity for some Romanian lawyers to establish lucrative practices in Odessa. Most civil cases were decided by the prefects without benefit of judicial due process. Actually, by mid-1943 Soviet family, inheritance, and civil law was accepted in practice by the Romanians, though not formalized. (Interview A; Tverskoi; and gh, "Transnistrien: Das Work des Gouverneurs Alexianu," *Das Reich,* August 1, 1943). The indigenous members of the local police cannot be considered members of the elite, though they enjoyed considerable prerogatives in arbitrary conduct and immunity from prosecution for abuse and looting. It may be significant that the Russian who joined the indigenous police (like the Russian who worked for the Romanians as a censor or as a *Siguranţa* informant) was looked upon as something of a traitor. This was not at all the attitude toward other and "more innocuous" collaborators (Interviews B, C).

[57] Interviews A and C; Manuilov, pp. 62-65.

[58] As a matter of fact, when the German request for forced labor from Transnistria was turned down in the spring of 1942, the argument given was the need for manpower for industrial construction within Transnistria. (Gen Wi Ost, "Reisebericht... 8-16.6.42," CRS, Wi/ID 2.408).

[59] Tverskoi; Manuilov, pp. 67, 70; interview F; Mamukov, p. 23.

cades, wreckage, and debris, and the repair of the sewer system. These tasks were both necessary and possible; the repair of industrial facilities proved far more difficult. Few raw materials were found in Odessa and they were of little value. Invariably, the most important machines and tools had been evacuated; of what was left, the key parts were missing, wrecked, or hidden. Most plants, the Romanians and Germans found, could not easily be reopened.[60]

As a result, policies for the resumption of Transnistrian industry emphasized the smaller, especially processing, installations rather than heavy industry. During the first year of occupation, considerable headway was made. In mid-1942, a German officer inspecting the province found:

> ...industry everywhere under construction. Dairies, mills, soap factories are in operation. Along the coast fish is being canned. A good deal of caviar is being netted, and fishing is being furthered. The Ford plant in Odessa is in very good shape; it repairs tractors and captured trucks.

(Romanian Ford had been entrusted with the direction of a large Odessa agricultural machinery plant.) An article of the same period spoke of about one hundred plants in Odessa being back in operation; the items produced included canned foods, sausage, brushes, textiles, beer, vinegar, glass, soap, phosphate, scales, and cotton. By mid-1942, the Odessa tobacco factory was turning out one million cigarettes a day, which were either shipped to Romania or else sold throughout Transnistria in special government stores that also sold stamps and other government monopoly products such as salt and wine. In 1943, the tobacco crop was so good that the Romanian government bought 3.5 million kilograms (3.5 tons?) of tobacco in Transnistria.[61] The same picture of extensive reconstruction emerges from the statistics published by the Transnistrian government on the first anniversary of Odessa's capture (issued for use at a Transnistria exhibit in Bucharest).[62] These figures do not indicate the degree of

---

[60] Odessa. Serviciul de presă și propagandă a Municipiului Odesa, *Ein Jahr rumänische Verwaltung*, 1943, abstract in CRS, EAP 99/87; Wo Transnistrien "Tätigkeitsbericht," November 30, 1941, CRS, Wi/ID. 200; OKW Wi Rü Amt/Wi IVa, "Orientierung über die wehrwirtschaftliche Bedeutung der besezren russischen Gebiere, No. 5," July 28, 1941, CRS, Wi/ID. 196.

[61] Aufbau in Transnistrien," *Wirtschaftsdicust*, Hamburg, Vol. 27, 1942, p. 783; *Berliner Börsenzeitung*, December 28, 1943; *Rumänischer Wirtschaftsspiegel*, Bucharest, Vol. 7, 1942, No. 16, pp. 22-23; *Der neue Tag*, Prague, November 26, 1942, cited in *News Digest*, January, 1943.

destruction and repair, and the number of plants reopened, it should be remembered, is a most inadequate index of economic activity. Most or all of the huge plants remained closed or operated only in small sections: these were the ones that had been evacuated or wrecked, and these were the ones that had accounted for most of Odessa's industrial activity.[63]

Still reconstruction continued; Alexianu repeatedly stressed the need for higher output. By July 1943 — roughly the peak — 651 out of a total of 946 prewar factories in Transnistria were again in operation. The remainder stayed unrepaired.[64]

Transportation remained a separate and severe problem, as it had been under the Soviets. There was a shortage of freight cars and locomotives; the Dnestr bridges had been destroyed, and fuel shipments from Ploiești had to be routed over Lvov and Tiraspol. By November 1941, pontoon bridges were constructed but proved inadequate. As late as mid-1943 there were complaints that rail transport between Romania and Transnistria was unsatisfactory. It took 21 hours to travel the 600 kilome-

[62] Transnistrian Industry (Romanian Data) as of October 1942 (incomplete)

	Number of Enterprises Prior to War	Of these, undamaged in Oct., 1941	Total now in operation
Steam mills	409	40	351
Oil mills	101	12	88
Butter-churning	487	214	273
Dairies and fat-producing	43	1	41
Slaughterhouses	5	1	4
Sugar factories	19	0	12
Alcohol factories	7	0	7
Canning plants	10	0	5
Jam plants	19	5	14
Textile workshops	16	0	13
Soap and leather producing	44	3	33
Construction materials	61	4	42
Metal processing	61	2	27
Electric power plants	104	9	64
Paper and carton plants	8	0	4
Printing presses	27	0	19

("Die Aufbauarbeit in Transnistrien," *Frankfurter Zeitung,* November 10, 1942; and *Universul,* Bucharest, October 18, 1942.)

[63] hn, "Die Aufbauarbeit in Transnistrien," *Frankfurter Zeitung,* November 10, 1942; Major Bartsch, "Bericht über die Frontreise des Marschalls Antonescu," June, 1942, CRS, DHMR 27638/15; Sztuka, *op. cit.*

[64] *Bukarester Tageblatt,* January 22, 1943; Kausch, "Rumäniens Anteil: Der Aufbau in Transnistrien," *Deutsche Zeitung im Ostland,* Riga, August 17, 1943.

ter stretch from Bucharest to Odessa (through Iași and Chișinău). Under the Romanian-German convention of Tighina, the Germans shared in the administration and operation of the trunklines. Thus, they operated the Odessa-Lvov line, while the Romanians ran the Odessa-Birzula line. Freight rates charged on the railroad from Romania to Transnistria were raised in April 1943, to about three times what they were in Romania proper. Most of the workers on the railroads were the same as under the Soviets.

To speed transportation, a regular two-hour run was established by the Romanian airline, LARES, between Galați and Odessa. The Romanian Red Cross operated three buses daily between Nikolaev and Odessa; trucks, mostly, Wehrmacht vehicles, commonly covered the distance of 120 km, with wounded and furloughers, in three hours. After some intensive work, the first 100 kilometers of a new Tiraspol-Odessa highway were opened on October 17, 1943.

Only some 14 lines (over 100 kilometers) of the Odessa trolley and tram system were put back into operation. During the peak month of April, 1942, almost half a million persons were transported on streetcars, whereupon the Romanians raised the streetcar rate. Sometimes streetcars would run as much as several hours apart.

A colorful phenomenon in Odessa was the private *izvoshehik* (cab driver), who reappeared with his horse, cart, and other paraphernalia. Surprisingly, he would invariably own his own horse (though it remains a mystery how he acquired it), and a German observer found the horses better looking than those in Bucharest. For a fee and a sizable tip, the *izvoshchik* would take you to any part of town at a leisurely pace, but with comparatively little risk.

The port of Odessa was, of course, thoroughly demolished at the end of the siege. Detailed investigations revealed the need for extensive salvage and repair operations; the Germans undertook to assist in this, since they sought to use the harbor to ship oil to the Crimea and North Caucasus; about 10,000 tons of stones and wreckage were found in the port. Among the sunken ships was the 6,000 ton "Isla de Gran Canaria," a Spanish vessel which had been renamed "Pskov" at the end of the Spanish Civil War. Wharves and loading installations had been demolished and large stretches blown up. As late as mid-1943, the port made a sad impression on visiting newsmen. Some port facilities were put back into use, but not the breakwater or lighthouse.[65]

An obvious problem was the reorganization of industrial management. Except where Romanian officials were placed in charge (or where, as with the Ford Company, a plant was entrusted to a Romanian corporation), residents were recruited for managerial positions. Virtually all Soviet managers had left or disappeared — most of them, one may surmise, evacuated eastward before the Red Army's retreat. Where were new managers to be found? The evidence is most inadequate, but what there is suggests that specialists and technicians — engineers, bookkeepers, agronomists, planning officials, chiefs of individual shops — stepped into the shoes of departed managers. The directors of the Odessa electric power station, leather plant, brewer), and the port deep-freeze warehouse were all Soviet engineers. The same thing had happened in rural areas; technicians and agronomists moved up to become kolkhoz managers or directors of MTS.[66] For most this was a step up to a higher bracket, and presumably satisfying to their pent-up ambitions for promotion. Under Soviet conditions the technician had ranked far below the manager class in status and material rewards. In the selection of the new managers genuine skill or ability and the ability to ingratiate oneself both played a part — just as they had under Soviet rule.

There is unfortunately no information on the efficiency of these fresh recruits to managerial positions. Since most were put in charge of smaller operations, their tasks were not so stupendous as to be insuperable or altogether baffling. Those with exceptional ability or ambition had an opportunity to go into business for themselves.

As indicated earlier, the sources on the fate and attitudes of labor are particularly poor. Most workers in heavy industry and most skilled workers had either been evacuated or drafted by the Soviets, or had switched to other kinds of work.

---

[65] Ihnen, *op cit.*; Zierke, "Jenseits des Dnjestr," *op. cit.*, July 20, 1943; Kausch, *op. cit.*; Reichart, *op. cit.*; Karl J. Müller, *op. cit.*; Gen Wi Ost, "Reisebericht... 8.-16.6.42," CRS, Wi/ID 2.4008; *Bukarester Tageblatt,* January 13, June 10, October 1, 8, 22, 1943; German-Romanian railroad agreement, March 25, 1942, CRS, H 12/621; Hans Schumacher, "Im Gouvernement Transnistrien," *Deutsche Allgemeine Zeitung,* October 14, 1943; Friedrich Koepp, "An der Bugbrücke," *Revaler Zeitung,* Tallin, November 13, 1942; Kausch, "Bericht über die Reise," June 26, 1943, Occ E 4-11, YIVO, pp. 18-20; OKW/Wehrmachttrasportleirung Ost, "Hafenanlagen in Odessa," November 10, 1941, CRS Wi/ID 2.1199b; *Der nahe Osten,* Vol. 13, 1943, No. 1, p. 8, and No. 9, p. 206.

[66] Interviews A and C; Tverskoi; Manuilov; pp. 58-59.

In November, 1941, most industrial labor was unemployed: out of 20,000 peacetime workers in the seven major plants of Odessa, only 400 to 500 could be employed.[67] Oddly, two refugees report, a number of workers reported to their place of work after the Romanians arrived as if nothing had happened. For some time, chaos prevailed; salaries were not paid in money but in bread and other goods; only after the currency reform of late 1941 did cash payments begin, or rather cash payments against salaries due. Cash advances on wages owed varied from 25 to 100 marks, and no definite scale of wages and salaries was set. Gradually wage payments straightened out and by spring, 1942, became regular.[68]

All reports agree that labor was the worst off of all social classes. One gathers that anti-Soviet feeling was least intense, least widespread, and least articulate among workers. And in comparison with prewar conditions, labor fared worse than either intelligentsia or peasantry. At the time of Stalingrad when a severe inflation set in, prices on food, textiles, shoes, and fuel rose sharply.

> The ones who suffer from it (commented the German consul in Odessa) are those with fixed incomes, particularly the workers. The situation is aggravated by the war-conditioned lack of coal and other heating materials, which are now beyond reach for the workers, who under the Soviets regularly received their coal during the winter. Thus, the material condition of workers in Transnistria is today worse than under the Soviets.[69]

According to refugees, the hostility of labor toward the Romanians also arose from the Romanian policy of consciously fostering an elite of non-manual workers and perpetuating social inequality. Though not officially enunciated, this policy was reflected in the behavior of Romanian officials. They addressed workers as *gospodin* (Mister) rather than *grazhdanin* (Citizen), had them stand at attention when talking, and in general made sure to indicate the workers' inferiority in rights and status.[70]

---

[67] WO Transnistrien. *op cit.*

[68] Manuilov, pp. 58-59, 65; Tverskoi.
One source states that "average salaries at the start of occupation were 100 marks monthly and later rose to 200 and 300 marks," but fails to indicate either dates or level of occupation or skill involved (Richard E. Lauterbach, *These Are the Russians*, Harper & Brothers, New York, 1945, p. 85).

[69] A curious and perhaps unexpected development was the reported resentment of wage laborers against artisans, who could freely raise their prices — thus both increasing their own real income (something the workers could not do) and demanding a larger share of the workers' earnings for the same services.

At least on paper, an effort was belatedly made to rectify the situation in the Antonescu decree of June 1943.[71] Workers (both manual and white-collar) were to benefit from their efforts in three ways: (a) all branches exceeding their production plan were to receive 25 per cent of the surplus for distribution among the workers; (b) premiums in cash and in kind were to be issued in plants where, though no excess production was achieved, unusual efforts or exertion had been required; and (c) premiums were to be granted to workers in plants newly put into operation or restored to production.[72] But by then, it was too late to tip the scales and improve Odessa labor's estimate of the Romanians. The workers were worse off, and in 1943 the Romanians were losing. Here was one group which did look forward — though not wholeheartedly or with complete unanimity — to the Soviets' return.

Money, Prices, and Standards of Living

A good deal of contusion resulted from Romanian uncertainty about the kind of currency to be established in Transnistria. The Romanians seem to have made no preparations. The Germans had introduced the currency they used in all other occupied areas — special marks known as *Reichskreditkassenscheine* (known for short as RKKS), issued and exchangeable at special banks, traded for Reichsmarks when travelling to Germany and at least theoretically their equivalent. The Romanians brought with them regular Romanian lei. Marks, lei, and Soviet rubles thus circulated concurrently, the population preferring rubles and marks to lei. The Transnistrian government did not issue its own currency.[73] With the Soviet retreat, a scramble to get rid of rubles at maximum prices began (though some saved their rubles, "just in ease"). An official ratio among the currencies was established, with 1 RKKS equivalent to 10 rubles or 60 lei — a ratio similar to that introduced by the Germans elsewhere on occupied Soviet soil.[74]

---

[70] German Consulate, Odessa, dispatch, February 26, 1943, AA, reel 1273, frames 342512-15; interviews A and B, Ershov, *op cit.*, pp. 149-151.

[71] An earlier decree had raised the wages and salaries of certain categories, primarily technical personnel, by 35-40 per cent as of February 1, 1943 (VI. Borerskii, "Zhizn'v Odesse," *Novoe Slovo,* No. 22, Berlin, March 17, 1943).

[72] *Molva, op. cit.*

[73] Transnistria did, however, issue its own stamps *(Monatshefte für auswärtige Politik*, December, 1941, p. 1026).

The chaos continued for weeks. Apparently the Transnistrian authorities could not reach any decision. It was held undignified for a Romanian territory to have a German currency; yet Bucharest was intent on keeping a solid barrier between the Romanian and the Transnistrian economies, an end to which maintaining marks in Transnistria contributed. In September 1941, the Romanians actually began exchanging rubles for RKKS. Over 10,000 marks had been issued when, on orders from Antonescu, the entire exchange was halted. After six more weeks of procrastination (and probably disputes in Bucharest and some Romanian-German correspondence), it was finally, and rather ingloriously, decided to keep the marks. The RKKS became the sole legal tender. All over the province exchange points were opened which issued RKKS for rubles, up to a limit of 1,000 rubles per family. Larger sums (including Soviet government funds hidden or stolen by individuals in the final collapse) were exchanged through pull or bribes.

An impending disappearance of the ruble had been rumored for sufficiently long to make peasants who brought food to town prefer to receive other goods to rubles; if they accepted rubles, they charged considerably higher prices, but at least they got their "fair price." The workers and white-collar categories suffered most from the currency chaos. Even the Odessa Primăria paid no cash wages until the currency reform, issuing instead rations to its employees. When finally, in December 1941, the exchange took place, it was accompanied by considerable confusion. The primăria ordered the exchange at the rate of 20 (not 10) rubles to the mark. An admittedly hostile German observer has depicted the scene, but it agrees in essentials with other reports of it:

> In reality, only a fraction got to the exchanging, and this in spite of waiting in line in the frost from 6 a.m. to dusk. The queue of 200-300 persons in front of the exchange points is a daily occurrence. Before Christmas this business had to be stopped for lack of funds. Thus, the whole currency problem hangs in the air.

There was extensive abuse.

> ...Romanian guards as well as civilians are selling "coupons," i.e., sequential waiting numbers. Often exchanges are made (privately) at the rate of 1:40 and 1:50. In the Christmas shopping one ran into rates as high as 1:70 on the market.

---

[74] LIV. A.K., Ic, to AOK 11, Ic/AO, August 4, 1941, CRS LIV AK 15420/9; SD Report 100; *Bukarester Tageblatt,* October 20, 1941.

German soldiers who received their pay at the rate of 1:10 were of course deeply involved in black market valuta operations.[75] One form of abuse was finally made official. Shortage of funds led residents to sell valuables and gold. The Romanian government had its agents buy gold, first undercover and then publicly. In the end, the Finance Section of the Odessa Primăria openly purchased gold at the median market price, i.e., in effect legalizing the black-market price. People were surprised at how much gold there was around. At first, people sold their gold because they needed money, but gradually resentment against Romanian purchases grew and produced a drop in the number of transactions; another reason for this drop was monetary reform, which came just at this time.[76]

With rubles thus out of circulation and marks made legal tender, Romanian currency was left in an awkward position, made more so by official inconsistency. The use of lei was prohibited and their import into Transnistria severely punished. Though available on the black market (where "shady characters" traded even British and American valuta), it had declined in relative value by late 1942. The situation remained awkward. After the fall 1942, harvest Bucharest took a big step and legalized the lei, to help integrate the Romanian and Transnistrian economies (or at least such was the official explanation). The order proved to be a farce and the source of considerable confusion; by the end of 1942, death sentences were again put on the books for trade in lei, and there were no subsequent attempts to eliminate the RKKS.[77]

In the winter of 1943-1944, with the end of the occupation in sight, the RKKS in turn dropped in value. Instead of commanding 60 lei, it

---

[75] German Legation, Bucharest, *op cit.;* Manuilov, pp. 56-57, 64; Ershov. *op. cit.,* p. 75; Ihnen, *op.cit.;* Franz Riedl "Aufbau am Dnjestr," *Berliner Börsenzeitung,* December 9, 1942; Sdf.von Berg, "Lagebericht aus Odessa," January, 1942, AA, reel 2066, frames 448876-80.

[76] Manuilov, pp. 72-74.
The shortage of funds also led to the establishment of a municipal pawnshop in Odessa. The Finance Directorate instituted and directed it. It operated as a *lombard,* or mutual-aid project, issuing loans in return for articles left as collateral. The Primăria was persuaded to give credit to start it. Officially it was instituted as a good-will gesture; its former director states that some of the patriotic, liberal intelligentsia welcomed it as a device to keep objects of art and other goods out of Romanian hands. The total credit of the enterprise reached 600,000 marks; it made a total of nearly 20,000 grants (or loans). The director was a local resident, but the bookkeeper and interpreter assigned to him was a Romanian. The by-laws provided for monthly auctions of forfeited goods: actually, no auctions took place, and loans were often extended or renewed (Mikhail Manuilov, "Odessa during World War II" (MS in Russian), Research on the U.S.S.R., New York, 1952, pp. 74ff.; *Novoe slovo,* No. 78, September 29, 1943).

Social and Economic Trends 133

could now be Traded for ten or twelve. The Romanians did nothing to offset this except for their staff and for collaborators. Salaries and wages for Transnistrian employees were raised to enable them to procure more goods. In February-March 1944, rubles reappeared here and there, and people began to turn down paper money. Faith in money fluctuated with faith in the regime.[78]

Prices followed the ups and downs of political events. Since private trade existed alongside government and municipal enterprises, two sets of prices developed — not unlike the state and market prices under Soviet rule, and hence not a source of contusion to the Soviet citizen. While official prices were, by definition, regulated, free market prices were uncontrolled. The absence of maximum prices was considered an incentive to business. Market prices were supposed to be at least in the same general

---

[77] A contemporary document summarized the flow of money as follows:

Total of RKKS received by Romanian Ministry
of Finance from the Germans — 60,000,000 RKKS
Distributed as follows:
Transnistrian Government
expenditures — 27,000,000
Exchange of rubles — 15,000,000
Payment to troops on
active service — 18,000,000
          60,000,000
Funds procured through exchange of RKKS
for Romanian lei: 73,981,968 RKKS
          133,981,968 RKKS
RKKS procured by exchange of
currency and unused — 55,698,006
RKKS procured from German
authorities and used
in payment   60,000,000
          115,698,006
                           115,698,06 RKKS
Balance from exchange operations.   18,283,962 RKKS
(*Situația monetară in Transnistria la 10 martie 1943* (no author or source)).

[78] Riedl, *op. cit.;* interviews A, E; Q.W. Müller, op. cit.; *Frankfurter Zeitung, op. cit.;* VRR Klüber, "Leiwährung in Transnistrien," *Suedost-Echo,* Vol. 12, No. 51, December 18, 1942; Lemkin. *Axis Rule,* p. 240; *Der nahe Osten,* 1943, No. 9, p. 205.

In February 1943, a *Banca Transnistriei* was established as a central banking agency for the province to replace private sources of credit. Autonomous in operation, the bank had a branch in each județ and a representative in each rayon. It received savings deposits at 3 per cent and gave loans at 6 per cent *(Nachrichten für den Aussenhandel,* November 23, 1942; *Argus,* Bucharest, April 5, 1943). No other banks existed to absorb the surplus money in circulation and thus help stem the rise in prices.

order of magnitude as state prices, but a considerable gap developed between the two sets of prices. Since the issue of rations in state or municipal stores was restricted, other sellers naturally asked as much as they could without losing business. Thus (at an unspecified date, apparently in 1943) prices compared as follows:

1 kilogram of sugar, rationed: 3 RKKS

unrationed: 20 RKKS

1 kilogram of butter, state store: 6 RKKS

private store: 30 RKKS

Cigarettes, municipal store rations: 100 for 4 RKKS

unrationed, private: 20 for 1 RKKS

It is generally agreed that in the course of 1942 prices declined as the availability of goods increased. After the 1942 fall harvest they were at their lowest, and — a source of genuine relief to city-dwellers — there were no more food lines to wait in. In December 1942, a traveler described in amazement the ample supply of goods; on the free market he bought sausage at 8 and lard at 22 RKKS a kilogram. A lunch in a modest restaurant cost 3 or 4 RKKS, while in a good restaurant, including appetizer and vodka, it might run to 15 RKKS.[79]

From the winter of 1942-1943 on, prices rose sharply; as usual, when "crises" occurred, the peasants had responded with considerable sensitivity and speed to the changing political-military situation by withholding produce — thus driving prices higher. Moreover, winter weather prevented some of them from bringing their products to the city. Milk jumped to 3.50 RKKS a liter; butter rose to 55 RKKS on the open market; an egg now cost a mark.[80] Prices continued to rise as the situation deteriorated further, and (presumably late in the summer of 1943) butter cost 90, bacon 80, sugar 40, and bread 10 RKKS a kilogram. In the final days of the occupation, with all supplies cut off, a crazy inflation naturally set in, with a single loaf of bread being sold for 300 marks.[81]

What is striking is the normal, almost predictable "capitalist" behavior of price and currency fluctuations. The same concatenations that occasion

---

[79] *Bukarester Tageblatt,* November 2, 1943; Tverskoi; interviews A and B; AA, "Ein Gewährsman meldet," *op. cit.*

[80] According to a Romanian newspaper, sweets, though abundantly available, rose in price from about 5-6 marks to 14-18 marks, because the Transnistrian government auctioned sugar to the highest bidders. In part, this was merely a convenient pretext for raising prices. *(Argus,* Bucharest, December 11, 1942, cited in *News Digest,* London, January, 1943).

ups and downs in other economics — and in societies whose people were presumably enured to such experience — caused inflationary or deflationary trends in Transnistria. Given the general wartime situation, the fluctuation in prices was entirely "normal." The price changes tended, of course, to depress the standard of living of most residents, even when goods became more available. In the city, the toughest time was the first months and winter. Transportation shortages seriously curtailed food shipments; pharmaceuticals, kitchenware, and school equipment were in very short supply. The municipality established public canteens for all persons with more or less official status or connections, and food was issued, as has been seen, in lieu of wages. Needless to say, nothing was brought in from Romania to relieve the situation.

Improvement came, as noted in other fields, in the course of 1942, and, while prices climbed in 1943, so did the stocks of goods — food and other — available in Odessa. A refugee traveling from the North Caucasus who found himself in Zhmerinka, in Northern Transnistria, recalled later:

> ...There was something in Zhmerinka which distinguished it from all the other towns of Russia and the Ukraine under German occupation: an abundance of food in the market. Naturally no sanitary or hygienic standards could be applied to this market. But the food was out of all proportion to the population of Zhmerinka. There was fat, so rare in the Ukraine. There was butter, bacon, vegetable oil, meat — which we had almost forgotten existed: pork, chicken, goose — and many other things that made our eyes pop. Moreover, it was inexpensive. We bought a lot more than we needed, enough for a week...[82]

Gradually this food would be moved to Odessa or sold locally. Even in November 1943, when prices had risen beyond the purchasing power of many citizens, reports agree, "one could get anything" if one paid the price.[83]

It is true that consumer goods were less readily available than food grown within the province, and shortages in such things as textiles and

---

[81] German Consulate, Odessa, *op. cit.;* interview E; *The New York Times,* April 22, 1944; AOK 6, OQu/VII, "Abschlussbericht über die Verwaltung Südtransnistriens durch die Deutsche Wehrmacht," May 3, 1944, CRS, AOK 6, 59352/10; Lauterbach, *op. cit.,* p. 85.

[82] Odessa, Serviciul, *op. cit.;* Ihnen, *op. cit.;* Manuilov, p. 56; Petrov, *op. cit.,* p. 199.

[83] The rising cost of living spurred Alexianu in the spring of 1943 to grant a 50 per cent increase in salary for all employees of the Transnistrian government and subordinate public institutions. (*Curentul,* Bucharest, April 18, 1943; *Novoe Slovo,* Berlin, May 30, 1943).

shoes continued severe during the entire occupation.[84] With "contacts" and perhaps bargaining ability, however, one could usually find "everything," from French perfume to Italian citrus fruit. The problem was to have enough money. More money (and additional ration permits) could be had by holding several jobs. Having several jobs simultaneously was a widespread practice, especially among Odessa intellectuals — it was a practice not unknown to Soviet citizens though not one usually cherished by them.

Income, prices, and availability of goods fluctuated, but the general level was not drastically different from Soviet levels. The standard of living of the intelligentsia, by and large, did not change greatly. Some were decidedly better off; others lived more poorly. The "new elite," by definition, was a privileged group; so were the *Volksdeutsche*.[85] Workers tended to be a little worse off materially than they had been before the war, but the daily wage of 4-8 RKKS for an eight-hour day did permit them to make ends meet so long as rationed food, and especially bread, at relatively low prices, was available in sufficient quantities; the rural population, as discussed earlier, on the whole raised its standard of living at least in 1942-1943. Considering the low level at which the peasant had existed prior to the war, the improvement was by no means striking.[86]

In Odessa itself, many who had lived well before the war had left the city. Only a small minority of the city's population improved their standard of living, a minority important, however, for the political, economic, cultural, and administrative physiognomy of the city. For most residents, Romanian rule — considering that "this was war" — spelled no major change. The two major food crises were the first winter and the eve of the German retreat; the best periods followed the harvests of 1942 and 1943.

---

[84] *Bukarester Tageblatt*, November 2, 1943.

[85] The *Volksdeutsche* were to receive cigarettes, liquor, salt, and marches by official issue. The rations to which they were entitled exceeded those for the rest of the indigenous population, though no full ration tabulation has been found (*Deutsche Ukraine-Zeitung*, January 10, 1943; *Der Deutsche in Transnistrien*, No. 7, August 29, 1942). The most desirable category was the "governor's rations" (*gubernatorski paiok*), issued to most prominent collaborators, professors, and persons with official positions. Members of these privileged categories were often seen selling their "excess" on near-by black markets. (Interview G.)

[86] Sdf. von Berg, *op. cit.;* Reichart, *op. cit.;* Bauer, "Odessa — die Stadt hinter der Front," *Neue Orduung*, Zagreb, No. 121, November 28, 1943; O.K. Ananjew, "Lage in Ananjew" August 19, 1941, and O.K. II/939, "Einsatz in Beresowka," August 15, 1941, CRS, Korück 20383/10; Mamukov, p. 43.

As will be shown, changes in political attitude on the part of the population cannot be directly and immediately related to material well-being.

The Criminal Fringe

Mention must be made of the enormous increase in crime and near-criminal activities. Perhaps an inevitable consequence of war and of a change of control systems, crime of all kinds, from drunkenness to murder, increased. Informants who were by no means teetotalers recall in amazement the stupendous quantities consumed in Odessa, apparently in response to the uncertainties and hazards of the time. People drank everything from homemade *samogon* to Romanian *țuică* (plum brandy); bodegas would sell alcoholic beverages with or without permits; imported liquors could be secured for a price. Even intellectuals, a professor remembers, took to drinking far more than ever before. In Anan'ev, the mayor and two of his police officers had to be fired because they "exceeded their official functions" while under the influence of liquor.[87]

A more serious phenomenon has already been discussed: the staggering growth of graft, bribery and embezzlement. A product of the Romanians' ethical outlook and practice, of what Soviet life had taught about "maneuver," and of the breakdown of controls, it was a new way of life, a return — as Odessa residents put it — from the socialist economy to primitive accumulation. Denunciations, illegal trade operations, and similar practices have also been alluded to.[88]

These were indices to a general decline of morals, which inevitably led to a growth of criminality. Criminal elements, previously held in rein, now operated virtually unchecked. Odessa, a large port city with a rather dubious reputation, had perhaps more than the usual quota of such elements, and also many who were not strictly criminal but who operated on the fringes of illegality. Their number was increased considerably by the growth of unemployment. Intellectuals and farm workers were, for all intents and purposes, fully employed, but many industrial workers were unemployed. Certain others found themselves unemployed; some janitors and superintendents, for example, were replaced by informants of the Siguranța (just as they themselves had often served the NKVD). The

---

[87] O.K. Ananjew, *op. cit.*, August 24, 1951, CRS, Korück 20383/10; interviews A, C, and D; Kataev, *op. cit.*, pp. 199, 203.

[88] Peterle, *op. cit.*; Manuilov, pp. 55, 90, interview A.

youth was largely demoralized and undisciplined, as will be seen below; with school attendance no longer compulsory and many pressures on parents, hooliganism rapidly grew to menacing proportions — a trend intensified by the poor living conditions under which some (for instance, college students) were compelled to exist. Perhaps the feeling of insecurity was more intense among this younger group, which the new authorities neglected, which their elders often considered a "lost" generation, and which had never experienced anything but Soviet rule.[89]

Banditry became particularly bad during the last year or half-year of the occupation. The Romanians were weakening; the integrity of local property was of little concern to them; earlier curfew hours left malfeasants more time and opportunity; the greater activity of Soviet partisans made many tend to confuse partisan and criminal operations; and as time progressed, increasing numbers were led to "submerge" from public view into a peculiar criminal underground. Prom the summer of 1943 on, newspapers were hill of stories about convictions by the "Military Field Tribunal of the City of Odessa" for such offenses as concealing weapons, abetting criminals, and assault and battery. Women did not dare go on the street after nightfall. In October 1943, Alexianu ordered the arrest of all beggars for "re-education," in what amounted to a concentration camp. Even casual visitors noticed the yelling newspaper boys, beggars, and "precocious youngsters" of all sorts on streets like Deribasovskaia. The counterpart of the hooligans of the Soviet period, these actual or potential hoodlums (often among them boys who had been perfectly "good" until a year or two earlier) were an integral part of the city scene.

There were exceptions. For instance, an orphan whose father had been exiled and whose mother had vanished during the religious persecutions, rose from a teen-age *bezprizoruyi* (waif) to a "respectable" life. He became a shoeshine boy; working outside the German army hostel, he would get a mark for a shine (or 50 pfenning from "permanent" customers), and with this would buy bread and grapes. There was nothing "wrong" with the boy, nothing "reprehensible," though his future was bleak and his education and "social life" were inadequate.[90] Such instances were rare. Par more common was a deterioration into membership in the illegal, semi-criminal fringe.[91]

---

[89] See also WO Transnistrien, *op. cit.*; Manuilo, p. 106.

Social Change and Economic Initiative: Summing Up

Quite naturally, social mobility increased in Transnistria. Certain social strata were deliberately removed; the livelihood of still others (e.g., bureaucracy, heavy industry) disappeared. In the reshuffling a new elite and a new "cellar" of the social pyramid were created. Specific policies of the new authorities fostered the development of the elite, but essentially it was an organic outgrowth of the situation. There were in the elite people who had possessed status but lost it at the time at the Revolutions of 1917, or who, in the period of incomplete Soviet control, had constituted a kind of middle class of tradesmen, or who were members of the other outcast strata — kulaks, clergy, etc. There was another group, people reared under the Soviets, whose administrative and economic *stazh* (work experience) was limited to Communist conditions, and who had had no contact with a non-Communist world. The ability of "Soviet products" to achieve success may need stressing — most were not political appointees; they "arrived" thanks to their own economic initiative.

The evidence in Transnistria of initiative, particularly notable in trade, but also in skilled work, tellingly disproves the hypotheses of "inertness" in at least this area of Soviet life.[92]

One may speculate about why there are so many reports that conditions improved in wartime Odessa, for one thing, most refugee were

---

[90] Ein Besprisomi arbeiter sich herauf," *Bukarester Tageblatt,* October 14, 1943, "Stadt in Rauch und Flammen," *ibid.,* October 16, 1943; W.W, "Kommst Du auf die Deribas?" *ibid.,* October 19, 1943; Horaţiu Ionescu and Florin Andrei, "Aus Ruinen erhebt sich ein neues Odessa," *ibid.,* November 2, 1943; Alice Auerbach, "Mein Wicderschen mit Odessa," *ibid.,* November 5, 1943; "Poimka shaiki molodykh grabitelei," *Molva,* No. 130, May 12, 1943; Deutsche Akademie München, Lektorat Odessa, CRS, DAM 112.

[91] Time and again efforts were made to encourage charity to help the unemployed and indigent. The churches opened soup kitchens for the poor, and contributions from the newly-rich layer, through the churches, were publicized daily in the local newspapers. In July 1942, Pântea, the primar, made an appeal for contributions to help the poor. Its total yield was 132,867 marks, including a donation of 40,000 by the primăria, 25,000 netted by a municipal lottery, and 14,000 through collection boxes. (Mamukov, pp. 44, 51).

[92] This is reinforced by the evidence on the considerable sensitivity of the new economy, e.g., in price changes reflecting minor new impulses such as the arrival of German troops, events at the front, or the downfall of Mussolini.

The "inertness" hypothesis, advanced in various forms in the West by honest scholars as well as political propagandists, "explained" Russian or Soviet behavior in terms of passivity which prompts an acceptance of any authority or social and political environment and implies the absence or atrophy of individual initiative.

themselves members of the new elite (otherwise they probably neither could nor would have left). But four other factors come to mind.

(1) Because of the evacuation, army draft, and the transportation to Romania of the prisoners of war, there were fewer people to feed than in peacetime. More food was available per capita, and this helped avert a famine.

(2) Because of the political and military situation, Transnistria naturally exported less to other parts of Russia, and thus had more to consume locally.

(3) The reduction of the population, for the reasons enumerated above, and the removal of the Jews also helped cut the severe unemployment that would otherwise have set in.

(4) The standard of living and status of many improved because they shifted to a higher bracket, rather than as the result of changing standards within their old bracket. For instance, the wartime promotion of many technicians to managerial positions (which gave them official rations as well as prestige) constituted a unique advancement; it came about thanks to the great number of vacancies created by the departure of submergence of the Soviet managerial stratum.

All four considerations suggest that things would not have been nearly so good, even for relatively well-off groups, if the population of Odessa had not declined.

Chapter IV

Education, Culture, Church, and Press

There was a rather significant cultural revival, despite abnormal conditions. One reason for it was that a number of artists, teachers, musicians, and writers remained in Odessa. A larger percentage of them stayed than of others in public life, such as administrators or industrial leaders. Their remaining is to some extent an index to their political views — or in many cases to their lack of them; it also reflects the lesser urgency the Soviet authorities felt about their removal.

A second reason was that where theaters, schools, and printing presses were physically more or less intact, getting them functioning again was relatively simple and cheap, far easier, for example, than restoring production in a factory.

Romanian support of "culture" and education must be considered a third reason. They took pride in the revival of Odessa's opera, university, institutes, and theaters. Funds — particularly for the more conspicuous cultural pursuits (ballet received proportionately more than grammar schools) — were allocated with relative liberality and in striking contrast to German parsimony.

The relatively high value traditionally placed on artistic and intellectual endeavors in Odessa also helps explain the wartime cultural activity. Odessa had had a good opera and university, a number of other schools, and theaters. This is not to imply that other Soviet cities had no such interests, but one does have the impression that Odessa ranked "kul'tura" higher than, say, Magnitogorsk or Smolensk did.

The cultural revival was restricted almost exclusively to the city of Odessa. In rural areas, there seems not to have been nearly as much demand, and certainly very little was achieved. Though perhaps it exaggerated a bit, a German report of early September 1941, found in the hinterland "no cultural life and no cultural aspirations."[1] This was decidedly not true of Odessa itself. There, even before the end of 1941 — despite the hardships of the times — efforts had already been made to reopen the university, the cathedral, and the opera; and as late as the fall of 1943, the primar of Odessa was pointing to the cultural accomplishments of his administration as a major source of pride.[2]

There is perhaps another reason for Odessa's cultural revival. No contemporary accounts and no refugee informants spontaneously mentioned it, but in an atmosphere where alternative activities were distasteful, cultural activities were not only an escape; they gave one something to do of which one could be proud; they were perfectly respectable and socially useful; one was not constantly being forced to take sides for or against the occupation authorities (though of course, particularly in teaching, complete escape was not possible).

While cultural activities were diverse, honest informants have suggested that much of it was amateurish or pedestrian. Only a few endeavors — notably, the Odessa opera — were outstanding in quality of performance. The artistic shortcomings do not, however, reduce the symptomatic significance of this phenomenon, and a large part of the urban population welcomed the revival of cultural life.

Schools

The original Antonescu decree of August 19, 1941, had provided for the prompt reopening of elementary and trade schools and the lower grades of secondary schools; regarding higher grades, decisions were to be made at a later date.[3] On September 7, Governor Alexianu accordingly

---

[1] Beauftragte des Chefs der SiPo u. SD beim Bth. rüekw. H. Geb. Stid, "Tätigkeit," September 2, 1941, CRS, AOK 11, 35774/6.

[2] See, e.g., Dr. Ihnen, OKVR, "Tätigkeitsbericht für die Zeit vom 15.XI.-15. XII," December 15, 1941, CRS, DHMR 76152; interview C; gh, "Transnistrien," *Das Reich*, Berlin, August 1, 1943; Ionescu and Andrei, *op cit*.

ordered elementary schools to reopen October 1;[4] other schools soon followed. But only schools in the hinterland of Transnistria were affected; in the Odessa area, lighting was still in progress when the school year began.

An immediate issue was the language of instruction. The government plan originally allowed a choice of German, Romanian, or Russian, the three "co-equal" official languages of the province; soon Ukrainian and Bulgarian were added — the former for the peasant population, the latter primarily as a political sop to Romania's southern neighbor. Each village was to vote for the language it wished used for school instruction. In Ukrainian schools, German and Romanian were compulsory foreign languages; in Moldavian schools, German and Ukrainian.[5] The German schools were largely under the direct jurisdiction of the Reich.[6] Ukrainian was chosen as the basic language of instruction in 80 per cent of the schools in Transnistria; 11 per cent used Romanian (i.e., Moldavian), 5 per cent Russian (most of the urban areas), and 4 per cent German.[7]

Problems quickly arose about curriculum and texts. Religion was added to the curriculum of all schools as a compulsory subject — with results discussed below. The textbook problem was difficult; often pre-Soviet (1907-1914) books were used, but there were not enough of these; the only new textbooks printed were grammars and primers; many teachers did without texts, wearily dictating summaries to their pupils.[8] No attempt was made to re-introduce old pre-revolutionary orthography.[9]

By and large the system of instruction remained unchanged. The later Antonescu decree of June 15, 1943, formally provided (Article 12) for obligatory and free schooling in the mother tongue. What "tree" stood for — whether "unobstructed" or "tuition-less" — was never defined.[10] And it remained purely a paper provision. In actuality, a system emerged under which public and private schools co-existed. The public schools

---

[3] Antonescu, "Reichtlinien zur Verwaltung der Provinz 'Transnistrien,'" August 19, 1941.

[4] *Relazioni Internazionali,* November 1, 1941, cited in *Rumänisches Blut für das neue Odessa,* p, 93.

[5] Antonescu, *op. cit.;* "Friedliches Odessa," *Deutsche Ukraine-Zeitung,* Rovno, January 10, 1943; Chef der Si Po u. SD, IV A 1, "Ereignismeldung UdSSR Nr. 100," October 1, 1941 (also cited as SD Report 100), Riedl, "Aufbau am Dnjestr," *op. cit.*

[6] Maurer, *op. cit.; Der Deutsche in Transnistrien,* Vol. 1, No. 1, July 9, 1942.

[7] Walter Hoffmann, *Rumänien von heute,* Meiner, Leipzig, 1942, p. 27.

[8] Interview D.

[9] Interview E.

included elementary schools (one level for children 7 to 11, and a second for those from 12 to 16), secondary schools, now called (in Romanian style) "lyceums," and technical and trade schools. In Odessa schools for the deaf and for the retarded were also opened. This system, under the general supervision of the Directorate of Culture and Education, was again in operation by mid-1942. The governor's school directorate also sought to guide local education, but its directives tended to be generally ignored. Indeed, even local directives were ignored; conditions varied from school to school and many provisions (e.g., regarding textbooks, supplies, etc.) virtually could not be complied with.

The Odessa city budget was inadequate to provide for a complete school system, with all the maintenance expenses and salaries for teachers, service personnel, and a network of inspectors (mostly, former Soviet teachers). This was one of the principal reasons for the emergence of private schools. Groups of women teachers got together and set up lyceums, usually offering a pre-revolutionary curriculum.

Most of the teachers were women and older men — either former teachers or unemployed intellectuals who considered school-teaching an "honorable" occupation. Salaries were quite low — perhaps 200 to 300 marks a month for secondary and elementary-school teachers (as compared with 800 to 1200 marks for university professors). The city directorate had to confirm each teacher's license; while a few did not get their licenses confirmed on grounds of having been Communist Party members, there was no purge of educational personnel. If anything, pro-Soviet tendencies came to be more pronounced among students than among teachers.

School attendance was not compulsory. Herein lay the key to the dominant attitude toward elementary and secondary schooling of the school population itself. Just as the lack of schools had encouraged lack of discipline, hooliganism, and delinquency among teenagers, so the fact that one did not have to go to school encouraged absenteeism and breaches of discipline. "Escape from school," refugee teachers insist, was not a characteristic Soviet attitude but rather the product of conditions during the occupation. At times as many as half the class would be absent; teachers

---

[10] Antonescu, Decree of June 15, 1943, *Molva*, No. 159, June 18, 1943; German Consulate, Odessa, "Neue Innenpolitik in Transnistrien," June 21, 1943, AA reel 1273, frames 342476-81; "Zwei Jahre Transnistrien," *Krakauer Zeitung*, August 21, 1943.

suspected an organized system of alternation, by which perhaps a third of a class would be absent one day, and another third the next.

Discipline deteriorated partly because students paid tuition, and fees were necessary for the survival of all schools, private and public alike; more important, teachers were, for once, afraid of their students and feared conflicts with them. By and large, teachers tried to be "tactful," and to avoid clashes, rigidity, and "politics" in the classroom. However, pupils responded with more barbs, pranks, and bitter jokes. At root (one perceptive informant has suggested) was a strong "spirit of contradiction" *(dukh protivnrechiia);* students unconsciously looked upon the teacher as a symbol of authority and eagerly sought to "cut him down" to size.

The attitude toward studies was correspondingly superficial. Since there were few, if any, textbooks, students had to take extensive notes in class; older students could do this well (partly because they had had practice at it in the Soviet school system); but younger pupils could not take notes, so teachers had to write out summaries on the blackboard. Grades were generally mediocre, and worse for boys than for girls.

Parents were often reluctant to send their younger children to school. One would hear such comments as: "You know, these are such troubled times..." In worker families, children would at times be put to work rather than sent to school, or would be left at home to care for smaller children. Only those over twelve years old had a major and genuine incentive to attend school: school attendance meant exemption from forced labor. Those who attended trade schools also knew they might learn skills that would enable them to make a living. As a result, student interest in and identification with technical schools (for instance, for artisans, dental technicians, seamstresses) were far greater, and the proportion of students continuing their studies was correspondingly larger.

There was a general trend toward separate schools for boys and girls. In part this reflected Romanian influence, in part, the moralistic outlook of the new (or rather, very old) lyceum heads. Teachers assert that it was also the product of a general anti-coeducation feeling which, oddly enough, led during the war to greater segregation of the sexes in Soviet schools. There were sporadic parent-teachers assemblies and conferences, but these were commonly devoted to economic and technical problems, not to substantive policy. Russian history was virtually eliminated; a "general history" survey took its place. In this survey much attention was given to Romania's past. In general, "Romanization" was quite pronounced in the schools.

A few schools in Odessa maintained a high level of instruction. More often, schooling was mediocre or worse, because of poor attendance (hence poor pay) and poor discipline. The number of regular students registered in Odessa was considerably lower than what it should have been.[11]

Higher Education

Odessa had had, before the war, 18 institutes of higher learning and 29 advanced technical schools. Many of the specialists on faculties had been evacuated or drafted; much of the student body was gone; and much of the equipment had been destroyed, looted, or lost. Officially, the University — which had produced many men of note — was evacuated to Maikop, later to Bairam-Ali (Turkmen SSR); though it hardly functioned there, it did, in 1943, deprive the faculty members who stayed and worked under the Romanians of their titles and ranks.[12] The University was restored to operation and was the only university that functioned under the occupation; Romanians and local inhabitants were proud to point this out and to compare Odessa with Kiev, Minsk, and other occupied Soviet cities.

In December 1941 — less than two months after the city's capture — the plan to reopen the university was discussed in the embryonic Primăria and apparently forwarded to Bucharest for decision. At first, Pântea secured permission to sponsor a "corporation" (including all the former faculty members, Soviet and pre-Soviet), though not to resume

---

[11] It is impossible to estimate the numbers in different age groups, because of the absence of demographic data. However, the enrollment in the fall of 1942 of 6,687 pupils in elementary schools; 2,385 in secondary schools; and 933 in technical and trade schools in Odessa itself (with an estimated population of some 350,000) is considerably lower than it should have been, even allowing for the fact that many parents returned their children to school only during the following school year. According to semi-official data, the city of Odessa alone had, in 1942, 5 municipal elementary schools and 2 special ones; 1 secondary co-educational Moldavian school, one Ukrainian, and one Armenian secondary schools, plus boys and 9 girls municipal lyceums; there were also 11 trade schools. A year later, there were 8 boys' and 14 girls' lyceums, and some 50 elementary schools (including private ones). All of Transnistria was reported to have had some 250,000 pupils in school in the spring of 1942, distributed among 1,312 four-year village schools, 613 seven-year village schools, and 124 ten-year schools, plus a few lyceums. (Odesa, Serviciul de presă și propaganda a Municipiului Odesa, *Ein Jahr romänische Verwaltung*, extract in *Romänische Presseauszüge*, Vienna, May 15, 1943, CRS, EAP 99/87; interview A; and *Ostland*, Berlin, Vol. 24, No. 3, February 1, 1943, pp. 54-55.

[12] Document USSR-47; interview D; SD Report 100.

instruction.¹³ In January 1942, the old staff reconvened; only a few of those who had remained in Odessa refused to participate. The "academic corporation" prepared a plan for reopening the university; it included the restoration of the by-laws adopted after the 1905 Revolution; under these the university had autonomy and a system of elective deans and rectors. Bucharest soon approved the plan. A representative of the Governor, however, had to be given a place on the new council. The new rector was Professor Pavel Chasovnikov. A Russian surgeon, eminent as a practitioner, less outstanding as a scientist, he was widely respected, and had — and this is what was responsible for his selection — close ties, reputedly even distant blood ties, through his wife, with the Romanian court. To "balance" his appointment politically, the two pro-rectors were a *Volksdeutscher*, Schoettle, for liaison with the Germans, and a Russian, Potapenko, who — awkwardly enough — had tried to flee with the Soviets, had not made it, and had surreptitiously returned to Odessa.¹⁴

Some administrative reorganizations took place, generally annulling changes wrought in the Soviet period. A new law faculty was established, with Professor Zhilin — he had been persecuted by the Soviets but had survived as librarian of the history department — as dean of the law school. The law faculty then elected Professor Ivan Faas, a Russian of Swedish extraction who had taught at the university for many a year, as its administrative director. The Medical Institute, hitherto a separate institution, became the Medical School of the university. As before the Revolution, the Historical-Philological Faculty was re-established as a single school. Its first head was the famous Professor Boris Vasil'evich Varneke, author of the standard history of the Russian theater and of various other studies. A difficult man, supercilious and self-centered, Varneke soon clashed with his younger colleagues and was obliged to resign, though he continued as a professor. Thereupon, Professor Vladimir Feodorovich Lazurski, an old Tolstoyan who had been retired with a Soviet pension after proving unable to avoid political slips, was recalled and made dean. Later in 1942, additional faculties were restored (natural sciences, and pharmacy). The rector, pro-rectors, and deans of faculties — a total of twelve men — formed the "University Senate," which at least theoretically had full authority. A Bessarabian, Professor Moisev, was attached to it in a

---

¹³ The formal reopening of the University was announced as early as December 7, 1941 (E.g., *Völkischer Beobachter,* December 10, 1941).

¹⁴ Manuilov, p. 108, interviews A and D; Tverskoi.

semi-political advisory capacity; and Despotuli, a brother of the Odessa-born editor of the Nazi-financed *Novae slovo* in Berlin, became University Secretary in 1942, resuming his original name after a Soviet career as a tenor under the name of Kirsanov.

With a few exceptions, the caliber of men who headed up the revived university was high. Most had been prominent professors with genuine academic accomplishments to their credit. The entire university was Romanian-financed, but apparently government financing (whatever the regime) was considered inevitable and therefore accepted without much soul-searching.

The level and tone were, however, substantially lowered by two new departures.[15] In late 1942-early 1943, on Alexianu's initiative, a separate Moldavian faculty was added to train specialists, primarily to develop future administrators for Transnistria. As a result, the pace of Romanization was stepped up (the Romanian alphabet and idioms were introduced into the Moldavian language); the dean — a Romanian lady from Bessarabia — was appointed without faculty approval. Some of the students came from Bessarabia, others were Moldavians from Transnistria. They received generous fellowships and grants to pursue the mixed humanities program at the faculty; a specially equipped dormitory was built for them; they were visited by dignitaries, including Alexianu himself, and generally made to feel they constituted — in special favor, if not in academic accomplishment — an elite at the university.

The other new departure was the Institute for Anti-Communist Propaganda. Organized in April 1943, by Professor S. Panfil, the Romanian propaganda chief in Odessa, and headed by an old engineer, N. Iablonovski, it was an instrument of propaganda — conducted in primitive *agitprop* style. It prepared lectures on anti-Marxism and sought to train local teachers and editors as public speakers and political researchers; it also staged contests for anti-Bolshevik writings. Its success was small.[16]

The program of instruction varied from department to department, but generally the Soviet curriculum was retained. There were inevitable

---

[15] In addition to these two, the men who took over the direction of the Agricultural Institute (or "Faculty," as it was known) were both Romanians: Professor Tetradu was in charge, and Professor Victor Gimpu was deputy dean *(Novoe slovo,* No. 56, July 14, 1943).

[16] Interviews A, B, and D; AA, "Ein Gewährsmann berichtet"; "Poseshchenie Guvernarorom Transnistrii Prof. G. Aleksianu obshchezhitiia studentov i studentok moldovan," *Molva,* No. 130. May 12. 1943; "Ein Jahr Universität Odessa," *Bukarester Tageblatt,* March 2, 1943, and April 29, 1943; *Novoe slovo.* No. 92, 1943.

deletions in the field of Marxist theory, some changes in natural science argumentation, a reduction of history teaching (no first-rate historians were left, perhaps because in this field greater political loyalty was required and a more thorough screening — and purging — had taken place before the war), and the introduction of compulsory religious instruction. All students were expected to (but actually did not) learn Romanian. The university gave credit for courses taken in the Soviet period, so that students in their last years managed to get their diplomas under the Romanians. There was no commencement of students who had had their entire college training in "Transnistria": the occupation was too brief for that.[17]

In terms of material well-being, it is likely that both students and faculty were a bit worse off than under the Soviets — or at least those professors who had been regular instructors, and those students who had enjoyed scholarships, were. Yet, university professors netted 800 to 1200 marks a month — a considerable sum, and well above the average earnings of other white-collar workers in Transnistria. Their social prestige was also considerable, as the university was a source of general pride. A number of professors were taken on official visits to Bucharest, where they were received by government officials and "colleagues" in Romanian universities (some student groups were similarly chaperoned through Romania). Professors and students came from Bucharest and Iași to consult with specialists in Odessa or use the library facilities there. Some visiting professors arrived from Italy and Germany, and at least one sat as a visiting member on a board for a doctoral defense in Odessa.[18] Perhaps unavoidably, the university, as a token of "collaboration," had to exchange New Year's greetings with the rector of Bucharest University (who did reply); and in March 1943, Odessa University granted Alexianu an honorary doctorate.[19]

Except for the Moldavian students, most students had to fend for themselves in the absence of scholarships. It is interesting — and indicative of the privations non-Moldavian students had to undergo to attend the university — that a Romanian newspaper admitted that at least 800 Moldavian students could not attend the institute in the academic year 1942-1943 "because they had no clothes or means of subsistence."[20] Only in

---

[17] Interviews A and D; Tveiskoi.
[18] Interviews A, D and E; Peterle. *op cit.;* AA, "Ein Gewährsmann berichtet"
[19] *Bukarester Tageblatt,* January 10 and March 9, 1943.
[20] *Porunca Vremii,* cited in *Bukarester Tageblatt,* July 9, 1943.

1943 was an attempt made to have the university "adopt" indigent students. Because of this and other disruptive factors, the attendance at the university is impressive, particularly if one bears in mind that — by official admission — heating in the winter months was execrable and many buildings were (especially in the first year) in poor repair. However — as indicated earlier — attendance did provide a guaranty against forced labor conscription, at least until the summer of 1943; occasionally then groups of students were rounded up for farm work or other relatively short-term tasks. Many of the students had attended the university before the war; some new ones, especially girls, who sought to enter, were not admitted; in 1943, a small number of sons and daughters of Russian émigrés in Romania and Yugoslavia were enrolled. For reasons that cannot be determined — perhaps Communist Party or Komsomol membership, though former faculty members deny this — 358 students were barred the first term.

In the first academic year under Transnistrian auspices, the university, with a faculty of about 85, had a student body of 1,605: 1,040 girls and 565 boys.[21] In 1943, a rather higher number of students enrolled, but total enrollment dropped during the academic year due to a series of arrests and disappearances. As early as February of that year the German consul general reported, "I know for certain that Communist propaganda is being spread among the Russian students at the University." By the summer and fall the Romanians apprehended some students and a few researchers whom they claimed (and apparently with reason) to be partisans and Soviet agents.[22]

On the whole, the performance of the university was creditable. Other institutions of higher learning did not do so well. Perhaps the best was the huge Agricultural Institute — before the war, the central one for the entire Ukraine. The Romanians promoted its reopening, though only some 150 students attended. After it opened in May 1942, several affiliated institutes — on fishing and milling research — also reopened. In October 1942, the Tairov Institute, specializing in the analysis of wines, was reactivated.[23]

---

[21] *Bukarester Tageblatt*, March 2, 1943; interviews D and E; *Novoe slovo*, No. 12, February 10, 1943.
    The breakdown by departments was: Medicine — 816; Technology — 305; Philosophy and History — 249; Natural Science — 165; Agricultural Sciences — 151; Law — 72 (*Deutsche Nachrichten in Griechenland*, Athens, March 5, 1943, cited in *Newt Digest,* May, 1943).

[22] Interview D; Peterle, *op. cit.*; German Consulate, Odessa, "Neue Innenpolitik."

The Romanian Scientific Institute, set up in Tiraspol in 1941, has been mentioned. Its main accomplishment in the teaching field was the training of Romanian language instructors. In 1943, the Germans opened a branch office of the Deutsche Akademie München. Its "lectorate" in Odessa primarily taught the German language. The high number of pupils — some 1,100 — appears to have been due to the fact, however, that the Transnistrian Government had a commitment to the Germans to pay the tuition fees of any government employee who wished to study German; as a result, hundreds of clerks and railroad workers took courses, but these courses were soon suspended because of the general chaos of retreat.[24]

A musical conservatory reopened and functioned successfully, as will be seen below. Various other institutes existed but can hardly be said to have flourished — private efforts, particularly, dependent as they were on students' fees, often failed or restricted themselves to a few classes. And yet, considering wartime limitations even in "unoccupied" countries — say, Bucharest — and the stagnation of higher learning all over German-occupied areas of the Soviet Union, university life in Odessa must be considered to have been truly remarkable.

Press and Propaganda

The Germans had reason to complain, time and again, that Romanian propaganda was crude. The Romanians seemed indeed inept at inventing slogans to catch the popular fancy or finding themes capable of increasing the loyalty of the subjects to the new regime. Yet, though it lacked a systematic framework of theory or method, Romanian "psychological warfare" was far more successful than that of the Germans — not because it was subtle but because it recognized, at an early date, the axiom that doing things was far more persuasive than telling or promising things. The Germans did view Romanian efforts to step up cultural activities, concerts, schools, theaters, and the revival of the press as an "extraordinarily clever" *Tatpropaganda* (or "action propaganda," as distinguished from oral or printed propaganda).[25]

---

[23] Gen. WiStab Ost, "Reisebericht... 8 -16.6.42: Verhandlungsberichte," CRS, Wi/ID 2.408; Interview D; *Bukarester Tageblatt*, March 2, 1943; *Der Deutsche in Transnistrien*, No. 12, October 4, 1942.
[24] Deutsche Akademie München, Lektorat Odessa, CRS, DAM 112.

The revival of the press in Transnistria[26] was an important propaganda achievement. As early as August 1941, the Romanians began publication of an official organ entitled *Transnistria,* a weekly, it was printed in Bucharest and was written in Romanian. Unfortunately, no copies are available; citations and excerpts suggest that it consisted largely of official materials and decrees, with some propaganda material; there is no evidence that it continued beyond 1942. For the Romanian — or rather, Moldavian — population of Transnistria, a newspaper, *Glasul Nistrului,* was published in Tiraspol. However, in spite of a paper shortage, Russian-language newspapers were also authorized and supported (they were not in Bessarabia); no Ukrainian-language papers were allowed — the reason for this will be discussed later.[27]

Both in Odessa and the hinterland (in this ease, Anan'ev) there was at first a lack of newspapers and other sources of information. This encouraged rumor and gossip. Residents, accustomed to being saturated with Soviet propaganda and news media, felt a general sense of insecurity when newspapers were cut off. In practical terms, the absence of newspapers complicated the business of restoring orderly local government.[28] Before long, however, they began to appear in Odessa (and in a delayed fashion, in rural areas). There emerged three more or less permanent morning dailies; other publications — evening papers and magazines — were short-lived and financially unsuccessful. All papers, all other forms of publication, radio, and censorship itself were under the supervision of the directorate of culture (later, propaganda) of the governor's office. This directorate, under Professor Troian Herseni, a sociologist, was one of the few whose activities were not entirely autonomous to Transnistria: by Antonescu's initial decree of August 19, 1941, its directives were to be set by the Romanian Propaganda Ministry.[29] This meant that newspapers

---

[25] RMfdb0., Beauftragter bei der Heeresgruppe Süd, ro RMfdb0., FSr Pol: *"Abschrift* aus dem Bericht für den Monnr Dezember (1943) des Befehlshabers der Deutschen Truppen in Transnistrien," CRS, EAP 99/1184.

[26] The Germans' own propaganda effort in Transnistria consisted merely in the distribution of the regular DNB service to the Romanian authorities for use by the press. In addition, the *Volksdeutsche* population was serviced by a weekly *Der Deutsche in Transnistrien*, which, however, was recognized even by Germans as "utterly inadequate."

[27] Great Britain, Ministry of Economic Warfare, Basic Handbooks, *Rumania*, London, 1943, p. 5; SD Report 100.

[28] Manuilov, p. 59; interview E.

[29] Antonescu, "Richtlinien"

could not print anything overtly critical of the Romanians or Germans, that they had to follow a sordidly anti-Western and anti-Semitic line, were under censorship and subject to fines in case they violated the rather vague regulations.[30] And yet, in spite of all restrictions, the press in a mild way indicated something of the nature of public life and even certain political and moral differences among individuals and groups of residents.

The first paper to make its appearance was *Odessakaia Gazeta*. In substance it was and remained a mouthpiece of the Odessa Primăria and was looked upon as a semi-official organ. Initially under the supervision of a Romanian general, it appeared when Gherman Pântea was ready to announce his own appointment. The first issue, on October 22, 1941, pompously introduced the new order ("We, Gherman Pântea, in the name of King Mihai I, appointed Primar of the City of Odessa..."); this rubbed residents the wrong way. The readers were primarily connected with official affairs; it was the most strict and severe of the papers in tone and content, largely because it concentrated on the text of regulations and decrees. Edited by Dumitraşcu, formerly a teacher of the Moldavian and Russian languages, it was in effect a municipal organ; it had few editorials of basic significance. Its general tone was "official" enough, however, so that it was occasionally quoted even by the German press.[31]

By contrast, *Molva* was a far more professional newspaper in the "Western European" tradition, with — technically if not politically — high standards.[32] While *Odesskaia Gazeta* was sponsored by the Primăria, *Molva* leaned toward the Governor's office. Its circulation was consistently the largest of all Transnistrian papers, and available clippings (no complete files have been found) fully substantiate the view that it was, if not a good, at least an "interesting" paper. Its editor, M.N. Belkovski, was a Russian

---

[30] One refugee recalls how he wrote an article urging parents to send their children to school. The piece appeared the following day, with a paragraph added at the end in praise of Alexianu and thanking the government. (Mikhail Manuilov, "Odessa during World War II" (MS in Russian), Research Program on the U.S.S.R., New York, 1952, p. 100). Other instances of such changes by the editorial staff itself are known — they were often made to avoid possible "trouble" or to ward off official criticism, as discussed in the text below.

[31] Interview A; Manuilov, pp. 66, 99; interview D; Schumacher, "Im Gouvernment Transnistrien," *op. cit.*

[32] A Russian journalist touring the occupied areas on official business wrote, in an article published in Berlin, that *Molva* as well as *Odesskaia Gazeta* were the only newspapers he had encountered in all his meanderings through occupied territories which had "real" editorial staffs and offices of a professional type (Nikolai Fevr, "Odessa o odessity," *Novoe slovo*, No. 98, December 8, 1943).

journalist who until the Revolution had worked on Suvorin's famous *Nome vremia* in St. Petersburg; he had then gone into exile to Bessarabia, whence he now returned with professional know-how and official connections that helped him launch *Molva* on December 1, 1942. It appeared daily; its contents ranged from political news, literary pieces, and editorials, to local news, official announcements, and reports of crime. People who read it regularly insisted that on the whole it was interesting and good, except for its editorial line and a pronounced anti-Semitism. Occasionally, things would get through that were by implication anti-Axis (such as an article by a young instructor at the Agricultural Institute in praise of Timiriazev, the Russian scientist highly honored by the Soviets).

More often, however, it veered in the opposite direction.[33] For instance, Anatolii Maslennikov, a former Communist Party member and third-rate dramatist who wrote for kolkhoz theaters, escaped from the German-held part of the Ukraine to Transnistria and managed to get himself put on the staff *of Molva*. Soon he began a long series of *feuilletons* that were primarily virulently anti-Semitic; refugees agree that they provoked fairly unanimous hostility at least among the intelligentsia. When several contributors protested, Belkovski, the editor, readily agreed that the pieces were abominable but asserted that the authorities — and presumably, indirectly, the Germans — insisted, despite the objections of his own staff, that the articles appear. At least two former contributors to *Molva* agree that the incident led to a drop in the paper's circulation.[34]

It is significant that Maslennikov was a former Communist. Newspaper staffs included both pre-Soviet and Soviet journalists.[35] Few professional Soviet newsmen had remained in Odessa, but a new crop of journalists developed, mostly people who had been close to the writing field before the war. Curiously, Maslennikov was not the only "renegade" Party member. The third Odessa newspaper, *Odessa*, had as a key member of its staff a Komsomol activist, Zhdanovich.

Odessa, unlike the two other papers, was the epitome of "yellow journalism" — or what the Soviets call "boulevard journalism." It specialized

---

[33] Manuilov, p. 102; Peterle, *op. cit.*; interviews C and D; "Rumynskaia p'esa v russkom teatre *Molva*, October 5, 1943.

[34] Interviews C and K; Manuilov, p. 102.

[35] Of the four editors *Molva*, the editor-in-chief was an émigré; the literary and political editors were Soviet journalists; and the religious editor was a Russian priest from Romania (Interview K).

in local murder and rape stories, tabloid-type sensationalism of a non-political sort, lurid photographs, and sordid "exposés" of Soviet rule. Read primarily by the poorer sections — its circulation was highest in the workers' quarters of Odessa — the paper was significant primarily as a symptom of the times rather than because of any line it pursued. It can, perhaps, be regarded as expressing the general desire for normalcy, for "human interest," and for some "petty bourgeois" gratifications.[36]

In addition to these morning dailies, other papers sprang up, though they usually lasted only a short time; some were evening papers (which failed in part because the early curfew curtailed their sale), others were weeklies — under such titles as *Bulj, Dnestr,* or *Vechërka.*[37] There were occasional attempts to start journals and magazines, general-interest magazines like *Kolokol Nashi Dni* and *Mir;* a children's magazine, *Detskii Listok;* humorous papers, like *Smekh* and *Iumor;* and a theological journal. They were either crudely anti-Bolshevik, with indictments of "commissars" and accounts of personal experiences in labor camps, or else second-rate "creative" and often "sentimental" writing in magazines like "The White Lily." With a class of *nouveaux-riches,* Odessa even had its graphomaniacs who could (or whose husbands could) afford to finance the periodic publication of their "works."[38]

Only a few pamphlets were printed in Transnistria. Few books, save official ones, appeared; a slim volume of lyric poetry, published late in 1943, was an exception. As a rule, émigré publications, whether Russian or Ukrainian, were not admitted to Transnistria (though all informants knew instances of such materials arriving with travelers or through the mails).[39]

The radio sets confiscated by the Soviet authorities were never officially returned, though individuals who had retained them or had hidden receiving sets (or looted them) could use them with relatively little risk after the winter of 1941-1942; the piped Soviet-style radio broadcasts

---

[36] Interviews A. D and K.

[37] Other newspapers appeared in smaller localities of Transnistria (e.g., the Russian-language *Pribugskie Izvestiia* in Golta, the Transnistrian part of Pervomaisk). Another paper appeared in Balta. An attempt was also made to publish a Ukrainian newspaper in Odessa. Its editor, Ivan Polomarchuk, a Soviet newspaperman, was, however, arrested and apparently abused by the Romanian police after the appearance of the first issue (Interview H).

[38] Interviews A and D; Mamukov, p. 50.

[39] This did not prevent *Molva* from serializing Solonevich's *Rossia v kontslagere (Russia in the Concentration Camp).*

were, however, resumed in Odessa itself, as were loudspeaker announcements throughout the city.[40]

The Arts

The newly established Primăria sought to restore a modicum of cultural life — perhaps from genuine interest in it, perhaps as a token of good will, perhaps to divert popular attention from political shortcomings; one of its prime concerns was the Odessa opera. Famed for many years, often visited by noted foreign singers, it had assembled a first-rate orchestra, ballet, and staff of technicians. Most of them had not left Odessa during the evacuation. Reorganizing it took effort, but by December 7, 1941, it was announced that the Odessa opera was reactivated. Its new director was the aging tenor, V.A. Seliavin; its conductor — Nikolai Cherniatinskii. Performances were generally well attended, with a substantial sprinkling of Romanian and German guests; the foreign press gave particularly warm praise to the opera's bailer. On the whole, Soviet sets and choreography were retained for such standard items as *Boris*, *Onegin*, and *Carmen*. The Romanians seemed eager to help the opera (a desire spurred by the personal acquaintance of certain officers with ballerinas); after a visit by Antonescu, who enthusiastically applauded at the end, the opera had still fewer problems — to the point where Seliavin managed to keep his Jewish wife unharmed. Refugees confirm that the opera's performances were indeed excellent; as a professional critic put it, everything else in the city was by comparison second-rate.[41] It must be mentioned, however, that the opera authorities lent themselves to the performance during Lent of 1943 of the anti-Semitic musical play, "Tsar' iudeiskii."[42]

Odessa had likewise been a city of theaters — it had had twelve before the war. What helped their revival was that a considerable number of performers and technicians had remained in Odessa. Yet, in quality of performance, it was a new theatrical endeavor that ranked highest and attracted by far the greatest interest. This was the Theater of Russian Drama and Comedy, established by Vasilii Vronskii. Before the Revolution,

---

[40] Interviews A, C, D, and K; "Tse bulo pri rumanakh," *Chornomors'ka kanuna*, July 22, 1944; OVOV, Vol. 2, pp. 78-80.

[41] Clemens Markus, "Neues Schwarzmeer-Theater," *Bukavester Tageblatt*, July 25, 1943; Tverskoi; Manuilov, pp. 93*ff*; interview D; Gerhatt Herrmann, "Dornrös'chen Odessa," *Donauzeitung*, Belgrade, August 8, 1943; *Novoe Slovo*, No. 7, January 24, 1943.

[42] *Novoe Slovo*, No. 43, May 30, 1943.

Vronskii had been a young idol of the more "degenerate" Odessa theater-goers. He had begun his career in the Saburov theater of St. Petersburg, specializing in light erotic farces. His enemies later proclaimed that he had no concept of "scientific" drama and performance, that he played down "social significance" and had no understanding of, say, Stanislavsky or Meierhold. After 1917, Vronskii had left Russia and spent the inter-war years as a minor railway official in Romania. Though always elegant or even snobbish, he had of course aged considerably. Persons who saw him or knew him in wartime Odessa report that his seeming rejuvenation was incredible: with a rare spurt of energy, he gathered a team of performance, worked them and himself hard, and soon opened with a series of most successful plays, mostly revivals of the pre-revolutionary repertoire.

Vronskii had troubles, however, which came to a head in 1943. Some "ultra-patriots" among the Russian reactionaries accused him of pro-Soviet sympathies because, in 1940, he had considered remaining in Chișinău when the Red Army marched in. It was apparently also alleged that among his stagehands was a Jew, whom he had knowingly concealed. The crisis came when he put on a new play, *Bozhii Oduvan'chik*, by Pétr Pershin.[43] It portrayed a simple Russian woman, the innocent victim of abuse at the hands of the NKVD. Vronskii was arrested and accused of having made a barbed attack on the Romanian *Siguranța*, the secret police. During his six weeks in jail, he was repeatedly beaten; his mother-in-law, a successful store manager in Odessa, found Romanian lawyers with sufficient "pull" to take up his case and then, through bribes, to have him released.

Naturally, such incidents did not improve either morale or performance at the theater. Vronskii soon turned it over to a collective headed by one Zubov, who had financed much of the theater's activity.[44] Vronskii, who had many personal enemies, himself disappeared shortly before

---

[43] Pershin was a young newspaperman who had suddenly proved far more talented than his output under the Soviets would have led anyone to believe (though he soon became an outcast in the eyes of the Odessa intelligentsia because he took over the job of censor for the Romanian authorities).

[44] Zubov, at the end of the occupation, appears to have established some contact with the Soviet authorities or underground. He remained in Odessa when the Red Army returned; so did Mertsalova, a good actress, formally a Communist Party member, reportedly decent in personal and political behavior, and who refused to participate in political plays; so did Makkaveiskii, another good actor, who (unlike Mertsalova) has recently been mentioned in the Soviet press as again performing in Odessa.

the collapse. His huge staff had joined him not only for genuine artistic reasons, but also to avoid forced labor conscription; this was clearly understood and was mirrored in the low wages paid. Surviving Odessites still speak of Vronskii's incomparable performances during the war.[45]

Far inferior was the work of other theatrical groups. A local actor, Ancharov, opened an operetta. A group of actors, including refugees from Kiev and the Crimea, opened a "Romantic Theater." Another theater, directed by Evgenii Onipko, performed Ostrovsky and Lope de Vega. The Cultural Directorate of the government financed a children's theater, directed by R.M. Ranevskaia, whose production were adjudged amateurish but decidedly enjoyable. Most theaters were not government-financed; generally, they were organized by small groups of actors who yearned to show their talents or to profit from what seemed to be a real thirst for entertainment. As a result, there was a bevy of vaudeville-type "reviews," stage shows, "miniatures," and other performances of poor quality. Most such theaters closed after a few months.[46]

A Ukrainian dramatic theater opened in the old Sibiriakov (Stamerov) Theater. Under its manager, Bondarchuk, it produced several creditable plays, but the Romanians soon closed it down, apparently suspecting it of being a center of Ukrainian separatist sentiment. Another Ukrainian group that opened a theater was likewise forced to shut down in 1943. The Sibiriakov Theater became the new Romanian National Theater, staffed in part by actors brought in from Romania. A number of actors from Bucharest staged guest performances in Odessa. As part of the Romanization program, local theaters were encouraged to produce plays by Romanian writers, but few did. It is symptomatic, however, that when a Russian critic, writing in *Molva*, published a rather lukewarm review of a Romanian play staged, in Russian translation, by Vronskii's group, the paper was obliged a few days later to publish "a different opinion" — this one, by a Bessarabian, highly laudatory of author, translator, and performers. Both the original critical and the childish "rectification" were part of the Transnistrian scene.[47]

---

[45] Tverskoi; Manuilov, pp. 94-98; interviews C, D, and H; Peterle, *op. cit.*; *Novoe Slovo*, No. 66, August 18, 1943.

[46] Tverskoi; interview D; *Novoe Slovo*, No. 62, August 4, 1943.

[47] Document USSR-47; Peterle, *op. cit.*; Manuilov, p. 98; interview D; *Molva*, No. 130, May 12, 1943.

Movie houses were quite popular and well-attended. Some 23 were in operation in Odessa alone, and showed German and Italian films and newsreels largely. One refugee recalls that occasionally non-political American and prewar Soviet films were permitted. Movies were privately owned and were one of the most attractive areas of private initiative. For reasons that remain not entirely clear, Governor Alexianu, in August 1943, ordered the nationalization of movies, with full compensation to be made to private owners.[48] No informant had heard of the directive's having been implemented.[49]

The Conservatory was revived quite successfully. In late 1941, the Primăria gave it permission to reopen, and in March 1942, musical instruction began. In the summer, the Cultural Directorate of the government agreed to support its work, and a series of sections — piano, instruments, vocal, theory drama, choreography — were established; a choir and an orchestra were formed; and in the fall the Conservatory, under the directorship of Nikolai Cherniatinskii, a Soviet trumpet-player anxious to become a conductor, added its own elementary school and lyceum, with special emphasis on musical training. Its main star was Lydia Lipkovskaia, a Bessarabian-born singer who had been prima-donna of the Mariinski Opera in St. Petersburg. It had over 1,000 students. Some of its graduates worked at the opera; others gave concerts of their own. The Conservatory as such also sponsored over 75 public concerts. At times symphonic works would be preceded by a lecture on musical or literary subjects. It was accepted as both decent and clever to have programs weighted heavily with Russian national composers; a sample program might include Beethoven, Tchaikovsky, and Rachmaninoff — with the Russian composers considered a kind of patriotic gesture; the former dean of the Conservatory confirms that patriotic motives actually were behind this kind of programming.

The political-patriotic aspect was perhaps most apparent in the public concerts given by the choir of the Cossack units fighting with the German army, in 1943-1944. The last of three concerts was canceled by the Romanians, and apparently it took high-level pressure to have it restored.

---

[48] Possible reasons for the nationalization of movie houses by the Romanians were (1) conflicts among their owners, (2) evidence that at least one movie on Deribasovskaia had connections with the partisans, and (3) Romanian desire to use their receipts to replenish the government treasury.

[49] Manuilov, p. 99; interviews A and D; *Bukarester Tageblatt*, August 9, 1943; Mamukov, p. 49; *Novoe Slovo*, No. 12, February 10, 1943.

To alleviate the tension the cancellation had produced, Pântea personally attended the concert and made a large monetary gift to the Cossack choir. Finally, the local society of Russian veterans (mostly monarchists, as will be seen below) organized a benefit concert, whose program included the *1812 Overture* and Glinka's *Ivan Susanin* aria. According to an eyewitness, the entire audience rose when the *Marche Slave* was performed; allegedly the local authorities later reprimanded the head of the organization for the concert.[50]

This was the maximum of Romanian political intervention in the arts — of course the German and Romanian national anthems were performed, Nazi newsreels shown, and occasionally inept actors with political connections were given roles.[51] Many other things the Romanians did were politically neutral: eight city libraries, with a total of over 2 million volumes, were reopened to the public in 1943; and, after some delays and changes of exhibits, the standard museums of the city were likewise reopened.[52] The artists and painters of Odessa formed a society of their own — *Obshchestvo svubodnykh khudozhnikov* — which arranged exhibits of their works; later they opened a permanent *salon,* which sold their works and served partly as a social center for the free arts.[53]

To those with time and money, Odessa, even under the occupation, had plenty to offer in the way of entertainment and recreation. At least part of the population took pride in this revival; others took advantage of it to forget the seamy or disgusting sides of Transnistrian life. This was true only of Odessa itself; as has been suggested, rural areas did not display the same appetite for cultural activities, and certainly cultural opportunities in smaller urban and rural areas were incomparably poorer. The hinterland did not rate the "conspicuous consumption" in the arts that the Romanians indulged in the metropolis.[54]

---

[50] Tverskoi; Ershov, "Vozrozhdennaia konservatoriia," *Molva,* October 16, 1943; interview D; Manuilov, pp. 109-111; *Novoe Slovo,* Nos. 18 & 38, March 3 and May 12, 1943.

[51] With typical incongruity, the Romanians waited until September 1943, to issue an order forbidding the performance of musical works by Jewish and certain Soviet composers, such as Mendelssohn, Khachaturian, and Dunaevsky. Oddly enough, Shostakovich was not included in the ban. The approval of the censorship office had thenceforth to be secured for the public performance of compositions (OVOV, Vol. 2, p. 66).

[52] *Bukarester Tageblatt,* November 2, 1943; interview D.

[53] Mamukov, p. 51.

[54] See, e.g., Ihnen, *op. cit.*

The Romanians in Odessa were markedly attached to the "cultural world." Some became attached to individual actresses or ballerinas; others "attached" to themselves the equipment and property of the theaters when the time came to retreat behind the Dnestr. Cleopatra Consolarino, the Primăria's factotum, participated in the looting of the Ivanov Drama Theater in 1944. Costumes, shoes, and stage sets were removed to Romania; over 2,000 pianos were evacuated; many books from the city library wound up in Bucharest, Constanța, and Iași. Hundreds of paintings, much china, and many other objects of art were taken from Odessa museums by the Germans before the city was abandoned to the returning Red Army.[55]

With all its limitations, the artistic revival seems to have been truly impressive. Both Soviet citizens and émigrés helped bring it about; the quality of productions varied from excellent to poor, but the wide range in itself suggests how great the demand was in a large city such as Odessa, even under wartime occupation.

The Church

Particularly in the rural areas of Transnistria, there was ample evidence of strong popular attachment to the church, in spite of years of Soviet "militant godlessness." Even the German SD — not exactly a devout assembly — could not but report the existence of such feeling. In Anan'ev, for instances, the three churches promptly reopened when the Germans arrived; there had been no services since 1935; the first services were well attended; requests at once came in for *post facto* church marriages (somewhat difficult to perform because records, personnel, and equipment were lacking), and for baptisms (large numbers were baptized during the first weeks of occupation).

There was little equipment, even a shortage of candles, and, of course, few clerics. Some of this was remedied by the arrival of the armies of occupation. At first (until Berlin forbade it), the German army gave help — for instance, they restored a cathedral south of Tiraspol which had been converted into a barn, after they found peasants praying in it; according to an Italian paper, Alexianu decorated the German captain for this act. The Romanian army willingly lent its chaplains for local services — indeed, so eagerly, at times, that, in mid-August, a German corps commander reported that "Romanian propaganda units criss-crossing the

---

[55] Document USSR-47; interview D.

country were forcibly baptizing Ukrainian children." The fact that the Romanians, like the Russians and Ukrainians, were Eastern Orthodox[56] facilitated the giving of religious assistance. The reopening of churches was at times spontaneous as it also was under the Germans, but often accompanied by Romanian participation; at least initially this — as was hoped — tended to forge a certain bond of community in rural areas between the people and the authorities.[57]

In Odessa itself religious sentiment was by no means so pronounced. Nonetheless, as soon as the city fell to the Romanians a mass prayer was held on the square of *Nikolaevski sobor,* the old cathedral. One of the participants speaks of it as less an Orthodox religious manifestation than a communal, mass rally. Here, too, it took little time to restore a few churches at least and resume services.[58]

The organization of religious life was importantly influenced by Romanian policy. Antonescu's first decree of August 19, 1941, provided for the reopening of churches in Transnistria, and priests were enjoined to start at once "leading the population back to Christianity." Because of the shortage of priests and because the Romanians had specific missionary and Romanizing goals, a special body, the *Misiunea ortodoxa româna in Transnistria,* was appointed by Patriarch Nikodemus on behalf of the Romanian Holy Synod; it had the task of supervising religious activities generally and

---

[56] As for non-Orthodox denominations, the Lutherans in the Odessa area (largely ethnic Germans) were made charges of the Transylvanian church (Siebenbürger Evangelische Kirche), which sent a mission to Odessa, and which reopened a chapel (converted to a furniture store under Soviet rule) and cemetery. The first services, conducted by the four Lutheran missionaries, were well-attended; in a number of villages Lutheran sacristans (*Kuster*) were elected *(Kyrkor under karset,* No. 2, Lund, 1943, cited in *News Digest,* July, 1943).

The Catholic Church had no major outlet or channel for religious work in Transnistria, nor any sizable flock there. In contrast to the hostility between the Vatican and the German authorities, however, the Papal Nuncio in Bucharest, Mgr. Cassulo, visited Odessa and gave Alexianu a decoration on behalf of the Pope in recognition of his providing for the spiritual needs of the population and the prisoners of war in Transnistria (Transocean Radio, May 7, 1943). A Roman Catholic mission headed by Markus Glasser was established in Odessa with the sanction of the Romanians (*Pravoslavnaia Rus'* August 28, 1942).

[57] SD Report 100; LIY A.K., Ic, "Übergriffe," *op. cit.*; Mario Valaperta in *Il Regime Fascista,* November 30, 1941, reprinted in *Rumänisches Blut für das neue Europa,* pp. 177-179; Berrold Spuler, "Die orthodoxen Kitchen" *Internationale kirchliche Zeitschrift,* Berne, Vol. 32, 1942, p. 48; S. Simconov, "Pravoslavna misiia v Russiia," *Tsrkoven vestnik,* Sofia, February 20, 1942.

[58] Manuilov, pp. 132-133; interviews A and C; Friedrich Heyer, *Die orthodoxe Kirche in der Ukraine von 1917 bis 1945,* Rudolf Müller, Cologne, 1953, p. 171.

assigning the clergy to vacant posts. The Romanian press minced no words about how important "organizing Orthodoxy" in Russia was; in essence, the Romanians wished to substitute Romanian religious (and hence political) influence for Muscovite Orthodoxy.[59]

The Orthodox in Transnistria were therefore placed under the Romanian Patriarchate.[60] As early as September 1941, Iuliu Scriban was named to direct the mission as administrator of the Odessa eparchy; he was a man reputedly well-known in Romanian Ecumenical circles but rather unfamiliar with Russian affairs. An archbishopric of Tiraspol was established under Antal, formerly an army chaplain; Metropolitan Nicolae Bălan of Transylvania was active farther south.[61] In November 1942, Scriban was replaced (allegedly for corruption) by Archbishop Vissarion (Puiu), a rather fortunate choice. Though a Romanian, Vissarion had studied at the Kiev Theological Academy before the Revolution and spoke fluent Russian; he had been Bishop of Bel'tsy (Bessarabia), then Metropolitan of Cernăuți, and was known to have close contacts with the Anglican Church. In 1939, Vissarion had addressed an open letter to Stalin protesting the persecution of the clergy in the Soviet Union. (Since the end of World War II, he has been head of the Romanian exile church in Western Europe).

Vissarion appears to have enjoyed considerable popularity in Odessa, because of both his personality and his political stand. He insisted on close contact with the indigenous population and the working together of Romanian and native clergy; above all, he resisted the Romanization policy and the use of the church for this. Unlike most of his colleagues and subordinates, he favored a Church Slavonic liturgy and Russian services, and disapproved of the Romanian sermons, liturgy, and rites that others had introduced. On Christmas Eve 1943, after more than a year in

---

[59] Antonescu, "Richtlinien"; Heyer, *op cit.*, pp. 209-210; *Porunca Vremii*, September, *1941,* excerpt trans. into German, CRS, DW 44.

[60] No other Orthodox jurisdictions were permitted: neither the émigré churches, such as the Karlowae Synod, not the Ukrainian autocephalous church. Several priests of the latter church passed through Odessa in the winter of 1943-1944, during the retreat from the German-held parts of the Ukraine, and sought to conduct services in Odessa, but they were promptly debarred by the Romanian authorities, and continued their flight to Bulgaria.

[61] Heyer, *op. cit.,* pp. 209-211; *Rumänisches Blut für das neue Europa*, pp. 177-179; SD Report 100; interview K.

[62] Under Vissarion, the theological journal, *Transnistria Cristiană*, edited by Varlaam Kiritsa, and theretofore published in Romanian, began to appear in Russian as well.

Odessa, Vissarion was forced to retire to Bucharest. This was mainly due to Alexianu, for whom Vissarion represented a "pro-Russian extreme," and a group of pro-Romanization clergymen headed by young Archimandrite Antim, or Anthemios (Nica).[63] It was Antim who formally succeeded Vissarion as head of the Mission; this was paradoxical — for later Antim stayed in Romania and collaborated with the Communist regime, and Vissarion went abroad.[64]

Between 300 and 400 churches were reopened in Transnistria, and 617 clergymen (both Soviet and Romanian citizens) were assigned there. In early 1942, there were 84 missionaries and 150 native priests. By mid-1942, there were 411 clerics, and the number continued to increase. Because of language difficulties, only the Moldavian communities were fully taken care of — "imported" priests could most easily serve there. By mid-1942, the Mission began to allow Russians, who had to meet certain formal requirements, to take vows. The greatest shortage was in Ukrainian clergymen. In Odessa itself, about 25 out of 48 churches, which had once existed, were restored. Two monasteries in the Odessa area were modestly rebuilt, and were functioning when the nervous Romanian Mission fled in early 1944. Balta and Tulchin had their own bishoprics. In November 1942, a theological seminary was opened in Dubosary. A plan, announced in January 1942, to make Scriban, who was then head of the Mission, simultaneously dean of a new theological faculty at Odessa University was later abandoned, largely, it seems, because of German protests against systematic expansion of Christian teachings. Odessa had its own deanery; the first dean was a Romanian, but his successor was an indigenous priest. In the fall of 1942, the Primăria took church affairs out of the jurisdiction of the Culture and School Directorate and established instead a separate Directorate for Religious Affairs.[65]

---

[63] Vissarion's retirement was not officially enlarged upon. Rumor in church circles in Odessa had it that one reason for Alexianu's resentment against Vissarion was the latter's Easter sermon of 1943, which contrasted the piety of the rank-and-file (presumably Soviet and Romanian) with the lack of religious conviction or conduct among the Romanian administration and elite (Interview K).

[64] Manuilov, pp. 118-120; Heyer, *op. cit.,* pp. 210-211; interview D; Lauterbach, *op cit.,* pp. 83-84; *Douanzeiting,* November 21, 1942; *Bukarester Tageblatt,* February 18, 1943, March 3, 1943, and August 16, 1943 interview K; Spuler, *op. cit.,* Vol. 33, 1943, pp. 39-40.

[65] Heyer, *op cit.,* pp. 211-212; interview C; *Bukarester Tageblatt,* November 2, 1943; Mamukov, p. 44; Spuler, *op. cit.,* Vol. 32, 1942, pp. 48, 176-178; Spuler, Vol. 33, 1943, pp. 166-167; Spuler, Vol. 34, 1944, pp. 66-68.

Popular reactions to the church defy easy summary. Christmas, 1941, was apparently celebrated in many homes "as it used to be" — for the first time in many a year, though privations somewhat dampened the fervor; a group of children toured Odessa knocking on doors and singing *koliadki* their grandparents had taught them. There were festive Easter services in 1942, with Alexianu leading the procession to the cathedral. In connection with the Christmas celebrations in 1942, Alexianu had 218 prisoners of war released, ostensibly so that they might spend the holidays with their families. His announcement stressed the community of Russian and Romanian Orthodox sentiments. The Odessa municipality arranged a distribution of gifts to needy children at a Christmas tree erected at the stadium.[66]

And yet the situation was not as simple as it might seem. There were those who went to church, and those who didn't, but people's reasons for being in one or the other group were various. Among church-goers, there were unquestionably those with genuine faith; many of them were older people, many were women, but there were also some young people. Others attended services because it was the thing to do — a form of conspicuous behavior that suited well the attitudes of the *nouveau-riche* bourgeoisie. For some people the church was a symbol of anti-Bolshevism; one refugee felt that the rapid reconstruction of churches was widely accepted as a token of protest against the Soviet order. Still others, perhaps unaware of it themselves sought solace, comfort, and community, in a body that was both mysterious and familiar, both social and private — a spiritual womb in an era of insecurity and the symbol of a "just" life: the church recalled days which, if not better, had been at least somewhat more equitable.[67]

But there was also hostility or resentment toward the church. Some people, particularly among the young, objected to the church as an institution *per se*. More often, specific incidents had produced the negative feeling. Religious instruction had been made compulsory by the new regime, and while many parents appeared to acquiesce in this, pupils often

---

[66] Manuilov, pp. 134-136; Wirtschnftsoffizier Transnistrien, "Kriegstagebuch," 1942, p. 107, CRS Wi/ID. 202; *Novoe Slovo*, No. 7, January 24, 1943.

[67] Interview D; Manuilov, pp. 132-134.

Many churches also provided "extra-curricular" activities. Thus, "Lecture Halls of Christian Culture" were common. Amateur theatrical performances, lectures, soup kitchens, and orphanages were the most widespread forms of activity. (Interview K; *Novoe Slovo*, Berlin, No. 24, March 24, 1943).

resented it. Refugees relate that the teaching was done either by members of the Romanian Mission or by local residents with pre-revolutionary theological training. On the whole, it tended to be entirely dogmatic, and mainly a matter of memorizing long passages of the Bible or the catechism in Church Slavonic. Some of the teachers were poorly prepared to handle the subject. Soviet-trained high school and college students were at times incensed by the presentation or their Soviet puritanism affronted: two girls, embarrassed by a biblical tale told by the teacher, involving what by modern concepts would be incest, indignantly left the classroom exclaiming "What indecency!"[68]

Somewhat related to this was the rejection of the Romanian clergy by the population because of their perfume, their many-colored robes, lacquered shoes, and soft hats. "Old-timers" would remark: *Ne te sviashchenniki* — "they are not the right kind of priests." To the genuinely faithful this gawdiness in appearance was repulsive. Others, at first, thought it a hopeful sign. In private conversations (refugees relate), it was discussed whether this was not perhaps a portent of a secular attitude among a more highly educated clergy. These elements — largely liberal intellectuals — were disappointed to find (as one of them expressed it) that the clergy had remained "as archaic and immune to fresh winds" as ever. This feeling was intensified by the use of the church as a vehicle for spreading monarchism. In Romania itself the church was one of the mainstays of the throne and pro-monarchism was openly preached from the pulpit in Transnistria. The overwhelming majority of the population — and especially the intelligentsia — were alienated by this.

The Mission's Romanizing efforts helped cool others who had genuinely welcomed the religious revival. Many services were conducted in Romanian rather than Russian, and both the Ukrainian peasantry and the Russian city-dweller objected to this strenuously. The Romanian services were resented as (1) unintelligible, and (2) a national insult. Vissarion had sought to change this, but in vain. After his ouster, even broadcast services were in Romanian rather than Church Slavonic.[69] People remembered

---

[68] Interview A and D; Peterle, *op. cit.;* Heyer, *op. cit.;* pp. 210-211; gh, "Transnistrien," *Das Reich,* August 1, 1943.

[69] Every Saturday and Sunday, the evening service and liturgy was broadcast by piped radio from Znamenski Cathedral.

that the initial Romanian proclamations had promised each community the right freely to choose the language in which its religious services would be conducted.[70]

People at first regarded the reopening of churches as an improvement over Soviet conditions, but this feeling decreased in strength as news reached Odessa that the Soviets were introducing similar reforms. Acquaintance with the practices of the new church also led, as has been suggested, to a substantial diminution of zeal and approval. A refugee novelist who spent the war in Odessa has depicted this through the eyes of a "pure" young girl, the daughter of a priest killed by the NKVD, and brought up in a religious environment, but who now was much repelled by the reopened churches: there was no genuine faith among churchgoers; the selling of candles had become big business; priests became indecently drunk; others used the church to propagate political reaction and intolerance.[71] It did not rally and unite the people; it might have developed into a passive but firm "third force," but it did not.

City Life

On the whole, the church, geographically the center of most communities, failed to become in the same way its social center. Church life under the Romanians, at least in its scope, differed little from church life under the Germans. The other aspects of public life — operas and theaters, concerts, and circuses — exemplified a spirit strikingly different from that prevailing in German-occupied parts of the U.S.S.R. This difference is perhaps nowhere better illustrated than in the relatively insignificant things that made the "atmosphere" of the city. As early as November, 1941, the German Abwehr office in Romania commented, upon returning from Odessa:

> The impression which one gets as soon as one enters Odessa is utterly different from that which one has been accustomed to receiving upon entering any of the occupied cities of the East.[72]

If such a difference could be detected as early as 1941, it became far more pronounced in mid-1942 when life was somewhat more normal. Article after article in the German, Romanian, or foreign press commented

---

[70] Ibid.
[71] Ershov, "Strannyi konets," pp. 50-58.
[72] Abwehrstelle Rumänien, "Bericht über Wahrnehmungen in Odessa," November 4, 1941, CRS, DHMR 29222.

on the night life, the reopened cafes and hotels, and the milling crowds on such main arteries as the Deribasovskaia, restricted by nothing but the curfew. Time and again they spoke of "large, laughing, loud crowds" promenading after work. In the parks, older people might sit on benches to chat or listen to loudspeaker or band music; people would stroll up and down streets where jewelry and fur stores and snackbars had made their appearance. Newspaper boys, vendors of watermelons, sweets, poppy-seed *makovki* and *bubliki* (sweet pretzels), and beggars sought the attention of the crowds. There was a public lottery in the Alexandrovskii Park. There were soccer games between an Odessa team and a visiting team from Bucharest (unthinkable in the German-held areas). Pedestrians would be given handbills offering new bandages or promising to improve handwriting. Outwardly, much of the city had been fixed up; the key tourist attractions were in order (pre-revolutionary names had often been restored, though there were a few streets now named after Adolf Hitler, Antonescu, and King Mihai I); window panes brought in from Bucharest were used to repair the remaining damage; and visiting Romanians flocked to Odessa.[73] As even Kataev, the Soviet novelist, acknowledges in his account of the war years,

> Odessa became a *moderne* town, something like Nice, where some hoped to have a good time, others to establish commercial contacts, and still others to buy a *dacha* in the area of the Fontany (a suburb) or Lustdorf...[74]

As trade and speculation grew, there was a rapid mushrooming of *bodegas* — little restaurants. The major hotels, like the London and the Northern (*Severnaia*), reopened with bars, lounges, and restaurants. The famous Gambrinus restaurant reopened. And the restaurant of the *Severnaia* was remodeled as a *cabaret* by Pëtr Leshchenko, the famous singer of gypsy and folk songs, who lived in Bessarabia until the war. His appearances in Odessa earned him as much popularity there as his records had in

---

[73] Gustav Lang, "Transnistrien," *Deutsche Post aus dem Osten*, Berlin, Vol. 14, 1942, July, pp. 32-33; AA, "Ein Gewährsmann berichtet"; Peterle, *op. cit.*; *Bukarester Tageblatt*, October 19, 1943; interview A; "Zhittia v Odesi *Krakivski Visti*, Cracow, No. 77 (524), April 16, 1942; Müller, "Das Land zwischen Dnjestr und Bug," *op. cit.*; Bauer, "Odessa — die Stadt hinter der Front," *op. cit.*; Juan Manuel de la Aldea, "Odesa — la ciudad ha sido incorporada a nuestra civilizacion," *Arriba*, Madrid, December 5, 1943; Zierke, "Jenseits des Dnjestr," *op. cit.*; *Novoe Slovo*, No. 94, November 25, 1942, and Nos. 22 and 97, March 17 and December 5, 1943.

[74] Kataev, *op. cit.*, p. 306.

the West, and his restaurant became a popular hangout.⁷⁵ Like the *Severnaia*, some hotels, restaurants, and stores were not locally owned: they belonged to individuals or groups of Romanians or Russian émigrés, many of them from Bessarabia. But local residents were also involved in similar — and similarly lucrative — "decadent," or "petty bourgeois" enterprises. This is the picture as citizens of Odessa recounted it to visiting newsmen after Soviet recapture:

> Little wineshops and sidewalk cafés opened, selling fine French champagnes and Dutch cocoa. Romanian restaurant proprietors introduced "lotto" and other mass gambling games. Romanian officers imported silk stockings and pretty trinkets. Shares were sold in imaginary corporations. Uspenskaya Street was renamed for Antonescu, and Karl Marx Ulitsa became Adolf Hitler Street.⁷⁶

It took a lot of gold to make all this glitter. While the strolling and bench-sitting were free, restaurants and night clubs became so expensive as to be beyond the reach of many residents. The curfew hour restricted activities; it was first 4 p.m., later 6, and gradually extended to 11 p.m.; in the winter of 1943-1944, the hour began being pushed forward once more.

Odessa was fortunate in matters of health.⁷⁷ Though pharmacies, sanitariums, and resorts had been looted and all but destroyed, and the best doctors and pharmacists had either left with the Soviets or, if Jews, had soon been eliminated, sanitary conditions were apparently rather good. The Primăria's Directorate for Health and Social Services, under a Romanian *docent*, Popescu-Buzău, established a separate hospital for contagious diseases, took over the facilities of the University Clinic and other sanitary installations, and restored ambulance service, mobile health inspection units, a special sanitation police, pharmacies, and delousing units. In July 1942, a German hospital was opened. Actually, before the end of the year Odessa's medical services (in particular, those of the University Medical Faculty) were so good that the city had no epidemics at all.

---

⁷⁵ Manuilov, pp. 88-89; Tverskoi; interview A.

⁷⁶ Laurerbach, *op. cit.*, p. 82.

⁷⁷ A minor phenomenon is the striking decline of sports activities in Transnistria. Except for the sport club "Victoria," which existed from early 1942 on, and which toured Bessarabia (*Novoe slovo,* No. 16, February 24, 1943), there is no evidence of sports activity or interest. The scarcity of adult males doubtless contributed to this, as did the general accent on more rewarding business. Also, few "sporting types" remained and the values associated with the Soviet collective "physical culture" were no longer highly regarded.

Presumably, the greater availability of foodstuffs helped prevent the epidemics that afflicted German-held areas. Odessa's health facilities were so well-known that Germans and indigenous employees from Nikolaev were sent there for treatment (though it took weeks to obtain entry and exit permits).[78]

The health of the countryside was not quite so good. Antonescu's initial order had assured a good level of health through local funds and local doctors, but it took more than an order to achieve this. A German army doctor who investigated children in a randomly selected village found lung tuberculosis widespread and some malaria; of the 1,705 pupils under 16 that he examined, as many as 134 had trachoma; in general, children were not getting enough milk — not because there was none but because government delivery requirements were too high. Even so, a modicum of medical service was supplied, and he felt that severe mass illness could successfully be avoided.[79]

As is perhaps inevitable under such conditions, venereal disease, which had been rare in Odessa, rose rapidly after the Romanians arrived. It seems to be fairly well agreed that local girls did not associate extensively with the soldiers of the occupation, though a number of "marriages" took place between Romanian officials and local girls — a police prefect married an actress, a colonel married a salesgirl, a Romanian businessman married the daughter of a local professor. Indeed, Romanians and Germans at times complained about the unresponsiveness of Odessa girls. The Romanians "solved" the problem by establishing houses of prostitution.[80] Some local residents claim not to have known about these; others had heard of them, but had not seen proof of their existence. The Soviets made much of the issue: during the war Ilia Ehrenburg ranted about the fact (if it was fact) that "on Antonescu Street, Madame Bardonescu (had) opened a swish bordello for Romanian aristocrats"; and after the war, the Soviet

---

[78] SD Report 100; interview A and D; Tara, April 14, 1943; Bfh. H.Geb. B, Abr. VII, "Lagebericht vom 10. Oktober 1942," Document 051-PS: *Der Deutsche in Transnistrien*, No. 1, July 9, 1942; Mamukov, p. 48.

[79] Antonescu, "Richtlinien"; 6 Kp./Lehrnegt. Brandenburg, z.b.V. 800, Truppenarzt, "Erfahrung und Tarigkeitsbericht," August 26, 1941, CRS, EAP 99/47.

[80] A former Red Army man admits that, even before the war, the public park in Odessa "had played a big role in the life of the Odessan garrison: it took care of the army's sexual problem. Prostitution, officially forbidden and according to official statistics nonexistent, flourished in Odessa. In this very park, the Soviet daughters of Corinth made 'free' love for a meager 5 rubles..." (Fred Virski, *My Life in the Red Army*, Macmillan, New York, 1949, p. 132).

Extraordinary Commission accused Vidrașcu, among others, of owning a brothel.[81] The one piece of documentary evidence in the Soviet collection of materials on the Romanian occupation is a license of the Primăria, signed by Vidrașcu, granting the lease of a second-floor apartment in the Spartak Hotel on a major thoroughfare of Odessa "for the purpose of opening a house of encounter" for Romanian and German military personnel.[82] The Romanians seem to have been anxious to keep the very existence of brothels secret, apparently aware — and quite correctly — of the keen sensitivity of the local population to them.

High art and debauchery, footlights and gutter, were all part of wartime Odessa. For the "Transnistrians" it was fortunate that a large part of the "cultural world" had remained in the city. The demand for cultural activities, for news, and for entertainment proved more deep-seated than had perhaps been realized. There seemed to be a deeply engrained desire to live normally and enjoyably, and to substitute relaxation for wars and plans and fronts and rations. Despite all the ugliness that accompanied it — from political censorship to prostitution — the cultural revival, in the broadest sense, was easier to effect and was more genuine than Odessa's economic revival (which, though frenetic, was hardly sound) or its political revival (which, though intense, was hardly extensive).

---

[81] Interviews A, C, and E; I. Ehrenburg, *Voina,* Vol. 3, OGIZ, Moscow, 1944, pp. 66-67.

[82] OVOV, Vol. 2, p. 18.

Chapter V

Politics: Attitudes, Ideas, and Action

Major Trends of Attitudes and Behavior

It is appropriate to place the discussion of Transnistria's political life after the discussion of its economic and cultural pursuits. It was much less important. The reasons for this can be identified. At first the problems of existing at all — in view of all the shortages — made any systematic attention to government organization or to political programs or theories unlikely. Only in a minority did the very chaos engendered by the change of authorities seem to have prompted a desire for political action. This may be attributed, in part, to the long years of Soviet rule; most citizens — especially, the younger ones — found themselves politically confused — they were unaccustomed to thinking in terms of political alternatives.

Moreover, the Romanians provided another compelling reason for political inactivity. Their earliest directives forbade all manifestations of political activity. Because of the police, censorship, and the limitations imposed on contact with the world abroad, it was nearly impossible to voice or try out political ideas in free discussion or to gain facts and ideas from intensive contact with foreign groups or publications. But in Odessa there was little inclination even to try such things. To questions that implied a political outlook the ordinary citizen would make the counter-query "What's in it for me?" or "What's the use?" The occupying authorities also felt that fear of Soviet retaliation in case the Red Army returned

— a feeling widespread both in the summer of 1941 and in the last year of the occupation — inhibited the expression of political sentiments.¹

Public interest and behavior were directed in the opposite direction. Most people in Odessa — and on this refugee and contemporary German reports concur — preferred to forget about politics; their attitude was "We want to live," (and live comfortably, securely, and pleasantly). Another report pointed out that, when Romanian propaganda took up the theme "Enjoy yourself," it rode the crest of the popular wave and became effective.² In a way this *was* a political program, but it was not perceived as that. The dominant view was "Po-dal'she of politiki": away as far as possible from politics. In deliberately steering clear of political "involvement," the majority appears to have been motivated principally by fear, fear both of Soviet and of Axis action: politics, they had learned at a bitter price, was a risks and unrewarding business.³

There was in Odessa, it is true, a small group of intellectuals who wasted no time in hailing the new order. A few self-styled activities got signatures of local citizens to a pompous address which was handed to the authorities. Some did so out of "careerist" motives; others were sincere in their support. The son of a rich merchant, who had lost all his possessions in 1918, went around among university professors urging them to back the "Christian" Romanians against the Bolsheviks and to express their willingness to collaborate. There were a number of signatures, but most of those approached declined to sign — either from fear or, as informants insist, from a sense that such an appeal was "indecent." A number signed out of political naiveté and within a few months came to regret the support they had given; among these was Professor Varneke, the theater specialist. The address was printed with all signatures, in the first issue of *Odesskaia Gazeta*.⁴ This kind of effort was, however, quite exceptional.⁵ There exists, of course, a basic difficulty in gauging political attitudes, both at the time and, even more, at present, years after events. As has been pointed out in other studies of Soviet behavior, and has been found true of Soviet behavior under the German occupation, there was a remarkable

---

¹ General Petre Dumitrescu, "Anweisung," August, 1941 (German trans. from Romanian original), CRS, AOK 11, 35774/6; Manuilov, p. 57; interview D; O.K. Ananjew, *op. cit.*, August 24, 1941, CRS, Korück 20383/10.

² Tverskoi, Beauftragter bei der Hecresgruppend Süd, Maj. O.W. Müller, to RMfdb0, Führungasstab Politik, February 2, 1944, CRS, EAP 99/1184.

³ Interview C.

⁴ Interview D; Ershov, "Strannyi konets," p. 34.

gap between attitude and behavior.⁶ The rather well-informed German consul general in Odessa complained, in early 1943, in discussing the existence of pro-Soviet sentiments in the population: "The faces don't betray it, and the words cannot be believed."⁷ Indeed, the basic *ustanovka* (attitude), discussed among residents of Odessa, was that one must "operate" and pretend — in effect, stay out of trouble, and by hook or crook make the most or best of the situation; there was little concern over arriving at a correspondence of pretense and substance, and for the morals of personal behavior.⁸ The political allegiance of the population — overt or genuine — was inevitably affected by external events. The course of the war itself was of tremendous importance, for many a citizen felt that truth (or at least safety) was on the side of the stronger battalions. Such an attitude was nowise tantamount to inertia; people who could make choices made them, and not always along the line of least resistance. In the fall of 1941, public respect for Soviet authority had broken down. At least the overt tokens of allegiance were transferred to the new order by the major social strata with a minimum of soul-searching. This happened mainly because Soviet controls and authority seemed to have collapsed so completely, and because it was generally felt that the Romanian occupation — unlike the German (though even here feelings were mixed) — was a transitory phenomenon that could not possibly be permanent — it was an aberration of history and one had to accept it as one accepted and adjusted to droughts, wars, and pestilence.

The overwhelming majority were willing, in the fall of 1941, to wait and see what another regime had to offer and to make the best of it. One is tempted to maintain that most of the intelligentsia — the evidence on urban workers is too inadequate for one to hazard any guess — were pre-

---

⁵ It might be noted that it was not the lack of "potential politicians" in Odessa that made for the lack of political *activity*. An absence of people suited by background, experience, or personal qualities to assume political initiative has at times been adduced to explain the dearth of autonomous politics under the German occupation. The instance of Transnistria suggests that the presence of such personnel may well be necessary, but surely is not in itself enough to produce an active political life.

⁶ On this point, see Alexander Dallin and Sylvia Gilliam, "Some Aspects of the German Occupation of Soviet Territory in World War II," Russian Research Center, Harvard University, 1954.

⁷ German Consulate, Odessa, dispatch, February 26, 1943, AA, reel 1273, frames 342512-15.

⁸ Interview C.

pared to make a genuine break and effect a lasting divorce from the Soviet cause. This did not mean they endorsed the Romanian regime.

The first reaction to the Romanians, as has been seen, was cool if not hostile. Changes in Transnistrian attitudes fall into three distinct periods: (1) the initial months of shortages and terror, strangeness and privation; (2) the middle period, roughly the year 1942 and part of 1943, when economic life and civil government were more stabilized and there was greater plenty and greater security — a time when the relationship between victors and vanquished was closer; and (3) the final months, almost the entire last year of the occupation, in which the Romanians' weakness and corruption reached new extremes, the military situation turned against them, relations deteriorated, and everything favored the people's divorcing themselves from their temporary masters.

Political activity was minimal not only in the first period but also in the second. Only the final phase seems to have witnessed an upsurge of political life. The most acceptable explanation of this seems to be that toward the end Romanian controls weakened to a point where they permitted what they had earlier barred. Probably there also had to be a time-lag, a relative stabilization of day-to-day life and economic conditions before some segments of the population moved to the next, and more sophisticated, stage: a search for political answers. A parallel development took place in German-held areas of the U.S.S.R. The rising tide of patriotism or nationalism which engulfed Soviet-held areas of the U.S.S.R. — whatever its motivations and limits — could not but constitute a challenge and evoke certain echoes in Transnistria. Many in Odessa were aware of relaxations on the Soviet side; rumors of even more far-reaching reform circulated frequently; and the heightened political interest in 1943 represented, as it were, the question, addressed to the Romanian authorities, "Can you match this?"

That political activity came to the surface in 1943 must not lead one to assume that there were no political attitudes earlier. They were revealed in tell-tale ways. In the fall of 1941, there were some instances of local residents denouncing pro-Soviet saboteurs to the Germans and Romanians, though at times (a German report stated) "initially only under pressure." While (as will be seen in the following chapter) Soviet partisans had virtually no popular support, commonly residents would not think of turning them in, so long as they personally were not threatened by failing to do so. Nor would the people turn in escapees from the Red Army who had failed to register with the Transnistrian authorities, or escapees from Romanian prisoner-of-war camps. Curiously, even collaborators who accepted the new order and benefited from it would indignantly balk at the idea of turning in their fellow-citizens — *svoikh* — to the authorities — *oni*.[9]

Collaboration was thus not necessarily an index to attitudes. Yet it appears to have been true during the first period — though not during the second — that fear of Soviet retaliation and fear of an unknown new regime combined to deter many intellectuals from seeking or accepting positions in the administration. Though refusal out of fear of consequences did not necessarily imply political hostility, there were cases where it was an element: at least two teachers refused to work "for the Romanians" as a matter of principle, even though they thereby risked their personal well-being. Cases of people refusing, not all work, but to teach a particular "absurd" thesis or to carry out a specific "revolting" ordinance, became more numerous, and some were fined or ousted from jobs. Refusal to collaborate for obviously political reasons, was rare among all groups so long as the Romanians were in full control. It is a curious indication of the political horse-sense of the population that refusal to work with the Germans was far more widespread and emphatic. In May 1942, for instance, the German Economic Mission in Odessa tried to talk some Russian specialists at the hydrometeorological institute into working for the Reich. To their surprise they found that "willingness to enter into German service is very small." And when, in the spring of 1944, the Germans wrested the administration of Odessa from the Romanians just before the final collapse, the popular antagonism was so striking as to frighten the Wehrmacht authorities: the city seemed to have died out overnight; stores closed down; supplies were no longer for sale; and people became uncommunicative. Part of this was due, no doubt, to the imminence of the Soviet return, but it also reflected the almost universal judgment that the Germans were far more brutal and hostile than the Romanians: whenever Romanians and Germans were compared, the Transnistrian population congratulated itself on having the Romanians.[10]

Political factors entered the thinking of that section of the intelligentsia that helped restore a modicum of government. During the era of "stabilization," some institutional framework was felt necessary as a matter of

---

[9] 50. Inf. Div., Ic, "Tatigkeitsbericht," September 6, 1941, CRS, 50 ID 16110/11; RSHA, "Eecignismeldungen UdSSR," Nr. 117, October 18, 1941; interview B.

[10] Manuilov, pp. 62, 140; interview D; Wirtschaftsoffizier Transnistrien, "Kriegstagebuch," *op. cit.*

"order" — one needed some *ustroistvo* (institutions) to know what one could do and what one could not, a system of government that would make it clear who had what authority and who was responsible for what. In large measure, participation in Transnistrian government represented not a political judgment but a search for security and order. The specific political structure elicited considerable discussion, but it excited little passion and investigation. People accepted the fact that "some authority" was inevitable; since the whole system seemed so transitory it mattered little just what the rules were as long as they were reasonably consistent and fair.[11]

The 1942-1943 era of relative comfort and security produced a minimum of political activity; it seemed to extend little beyond the publication of interminable memoirs of former labor camp inmates or anti-Bolshevik editorials of an orthodox, pro-Axis variety. Whatever else there was took place beneath the surface. Yet, apparently a deterioration of faith in the new system set in, or continued. One informant has seriously suggested that the intelligentsia in Odessa increasingly had the feeling that "it had made the Russians into conquerors and the Romanians into... victims"; this convenient (and not entirely untrue) rationale depended on the Romanians behaving as victims; their failure to do so tended to intensify discontent. The greatest impetus to a reassessment of allegiance, however, was the military about-face. The echo of Stalingrad reverberated throughout Odessa. German repots speak rather openly of general panic in the city, reflected in the drastic rise of prices on the market, the preparations some officials made to evacuate their families and belongings westward, and the beginnings of attempts by some residents to "whitewash" themselves by cooperating with the few Soviet agents and partisans around Odessa. It is here that the third, final stage began.[12]

After Stalingrad "no one in his right mind" believed that the Romanians would be able to hold Transnistria indefinitely. Soon the government began making concessions with the intent of binding the population more closely to the Romanian chariot. As is frequently the case, however, concessions merely whetted appetites and, taken as an indication that the authorities were "on the skids," provoked further alienation. Reports of Soviet victories and reforms meanwhile filtered through, and many who

---

[11] Interview E; Manuilov, pp. 84-85.
[12] German Consulate, Odessa, dispatch, February 26, 1943; Deutsche Akademie München, Lektorat Odessa, CRS, file DAM 112.

had high hopes for the future of Transnistria now looked forward to the Soviet's return as a "lesser evil." Many, it is true, did not take an anti-Romanian stand because Soviet rule was even more unpalatable to them, particularly if they had been drawn into the whirlpool of collaboration. The tragedy, from the point of view of the "liberal intelligentsia," was the absence of any third course of third force. The only choice was between Axis and Soviets.

Even those, however, who would not act or take sides against the Romanians — and probably they were in the majority — felt a certain alienation that transformed what had been latent resistance into more overt opposition. In schools, students vied with each other to demonstrate their politically-determined orneriness. In private conversations many who had never admired the Bolshevik order now suddenly found that under Soviet rule the absence of social distinction between white-collar and manual workers had really been an appealing though unnoticed fact. In the country, peasants watching the planes go over would again speak of the Red Air Force as *svoi* — "our" planes — as they would not have two years earlier. And when, in late 1943, the Transnistrian administration began to ask for the names of employees wishing to be evacuated in case of crisis, the majority even of collaborators (though most exposed to Soviet persecution) refused to sign up. In people's eyes, Romanian rule suddenly became a symbol of futility, obsolescence, and injustice, and the Red Army appeared in moments of wishful thinking as the People under Arms, protagonists of a national crusade, and bearers of a new and appealing message.[13]

Not every citizen of Transnistria underwent such a metamorphosis of opinion. A minority of collaborators — primarily white-collar workers — (perhaps rationalizing self-interest) were determined to stick to the regime that employed them; others did not want to believe that the Red Army could ever return and sought solace in rumors of secret weapons and British landings.

The basic pattern, however, appears to have been substantially the same for all social and age groups: after the first cooling in 1941, a certain relaxation and accommodation, and then a new alienation. As suggested earlier, pro-Communists seemed to be most numerous among the youngest, and collaborators most numerous in the age group between 40 and 50; the oldest group, at least of intellectuals, tended to be most reserved

---

[13] Peterle, *op. cit.*; interviews A, D, and E.

and, perhaps animated by Russian nationalist sentiments and more rigid standards of morality, refused to engage in "wanton collaboration." The spirit of alienation seems to have struck the workers earliest — not so much for political as for economic reasons — and the peasantry last and least — perhaps for a combination of political and economic reasons. Pro-Soviet nostalgia in general appears to have been distinctly weaker in the countryside than in the city.

The Communists

An issue on which the ordinary citizen was forced to make a personal political choice was presented by the Communist who remained behind. Some Communist Party members and ex-officials had managed to survive. It is true that the Party brass had been evacuated and that officials of rayon committees and primary organizations who stayed went underground. Yet there were some people who concealed their Communist past and some who had been, or claimed to have been, no more than nominal Communists.[14]

There were, of course, some denunciations of Communists to the new authorities — inspired by political zeal, a desire to ingratiate oneself with the police, or a wish to settle old accounts. By and large, however, rank-and-file Party members were left alone. Non-Party members were hesitant about hiring them — partly from fear of the Romanians, and partly from fear of running into Soviet agents among them; but there was no mass hostility toward individual Communist Party members, or members of the Komsomol.[15]

Romanian policy toward the Communists was rather ambiguous. Once the initial wave of terror subsided, it did not go so far as to exterminate them, as the Nazis at times suggested. A number of former Communist Party members even worked in various official capacities under the new regime. All Communists, including Komsomol members, were required to register (and stay registered in case of movements); they had to check once a week with the local police *uchastok* (precinct); and they

---

[14] Initially, the occupying authorities seem to have missed many Communists. The Germans, for instance, actually believed that in Anan'ev, a town of over 5,000, there had been only 30 Party members and that all of them had fled. Likewise, they believed, initially, that all Bolsheviks had left Tiraspol.

[15] Interviews A, C, and E.

were formally barred from employment in government or municipal enterprises — but this was not stringently enforced. A few "active" Communists were put in jail, but, except for agents and partisans, prosecution of them was almost nil. The extent to which they continued in the open without any special onus and the extent to which they were anxious to profess their change of heart are best illustrated by the Party organization, 42 men strong, of the Odessa trolley line workers. In 1942, the group volunteered (on whose initiative is unknown) to repair the crosses on the Odessa churches when the latter were reopened; for this the former Party cell received an expression of gratitude from the Romanian church authorities.

The Romanians began liberalizing their policy toward party members in the summer of 1943. Antonescu's decree of June 15, 1943, removed some restrictions. One summer Sunday, the commandant of the Odessa military district, General Gheorghiu, had ex-Communists and others convene at a mass rally on Kulikovo Pole, and announced their release. No longer were they subjected to any registration procedures or job discrimination. The move, it is unanimously reported, made a distinctly favorable impression on the population. Interestingly enough, there is no evidence that a single one of those thus unleashed joined the Red partisans.

There were, no doubt, men and woman in Odessa who considered themselves Communists throughout. There were those who heatedly defended dialectical materialism over the kitchen table and fervently prayed in church on Sunday. There were those who simply could not free themselves from the ways of reasoning and responding that had become so habitual over a period of years. But the tenacity of doctrine, *per se,* was surprisingly small. Practical experience rather than theory guided and determined action and allegiance. And if evidence is needed to prove the ability of the Soviet population to discriminate, to accept some things and reject others, a striking demonstration of it is seen in the spree of destructiveness right after the Soviets left: it is reported that almost everywhere statues of Lenin remained standing while those of Stalin were knocked down.[16]

---

[16] Interview A, B, and C; Tverskoi.

Ersatz Politics

In the absence of opportunities for overt political activity, political opinions and attitudes manifested themselves indirectly in what may be called an *Ersatz* politics. Rumors were one such substitute, and while their tenor and content seem impossible to reconstruct at this date, those who were there concur in stressing their great frequency, their relative reliability, and their ability to mirror crucial issues of the day — at times merely reflecting the thirst for and the desire to transmit news; at other times suggesting slogans or formulas for "solving" problems.[17] Almost in the same category are political jokes which seemed to flourish from mid-1942 on, largely at the expense of the Romanians.[18] This may have been a complex compensation mechanism that permitted the "occupied" to feel superior to the victors. It is interesting to note, however, that no political jokes have ever been reported from the entire German-occupied area of the U.S.S.R. There, the dominant atmosphere was too inauspicious for humor.[19]

As has been suggested, cultural activity — be it as teachers, newspapermen, or as actors — was a form of, or rather a surrogate for, political activity, for many intellectuals.[20] The university's request to be governed by the by-laws that gave it autonomy was symbolic and fraught with political implications (see above, Chapter IV). The very concentration of intellectual endeavor in cultural pursuits, broadly viewed, was due, in some measure, to the political fields being closed. "Cultural" work was personally honorable, useful, and socially respectable; through the press, the classroom, or on the stage one could help perpetuate Russian culture, values, and traditions.

The church, too, was a form of political expression. It was used, it is true, primarily by the spokesmen of monarchism; the extent to which the monarchists monopolized the church repelled some of the "liberal intelligentsia" and made them desist from church attendance altogether. In some

---

[17] SD Report 100; interview C.

[18] The more widespread among them were distinctly derogatory of Romanian culture and accomplishment. They included the apocryphal statement attributed to Nicholas I, who, when told of the Romanian nation, is said to have replied: "A nation? I thought it was a profession." Quips like "a people with pass-keys and violins" (the words rhyme in Russian) were also popular.

[19] Manuilov, p. 57; interviews A and E.

[20] Peterle, *op. cit.*

ways, however, the church represented a generalized anti-Bolshevism, and did not require or suggest more specific political ideas. For some, more than any other of the permitted institutions, the church provided the best symbol of a Russia purified of Bolshevism.[21]

Neither of the two émigré movements that had some support in other occupied areas — the Ukrainian Nationalists and the Russian Solidarists, discussed below — made much headway in Odessa. Once again, many who backed them seemed to be searching for a political solution not too closely identified with either Romanians or Soviets. This quest for "third solutions" produced one project that was unique to Odessa. As early as January 1942, a German SS officer, who wanted the Reich to take over Transnistria from the Romanians, reported that it had been rumored that Antonescu would give Odessa to the Germans "as a Christmas present," and that people were discussing the possibility of making Odessa a "Free City" — like a Hanseatic city or, in recent times, Danzig.

This idea had a history. Odessa had been made a free port in the early 19th century, largely to attract foreign trade. During the Civil War, the idea was revived by Ukrainian nationalists who, faced with anti-separatist sentiment in Odessa, promoted the Free City idea as a compromise: at least the port would not then be an independent Russian enclave in the Ukraine. In 1942, the idea again gained currency, especially among white-collar workers who had feelings of guilt about working for the Romanians. It provided a way of avoiding Romanian and German as well as Soviet control. It appealed to the romantic, to local patriots, and to those who felt guilty about their lack of Soviet patriotism. Not seriously considered by the Romanians at any time, the idea remained alive, and at least one informant — rather given to enthusiastic espousals —insists that, in 1942, it would have "received a majority vote" if freely voted upon in Odessa.[22]

Program for Tomorrow

None of the published sources and none of the informants suggest that there was anything vaguely resembling an articulate political party or program evolved in Transnistria. In some measure, to be sure, this was because the Romanians prohibited political activity Yet, even in private

---

[21] Manuilov, p. 132; interview D.
[22] Sdf. von Berg, "Lagebericht aus Odessa," January, 1942; interviews B and E.

conversations, according to informants, the intelligentsia — perhaps the most likely locus for an embryonic movement or formulation of goals — apparently did not discuss anything that could be called a program. It is true that most of the intelligentsia remaining in Odessa were specialists in fields other than the social sciences and had no direct experience in government or systematic training in political theory except for dialectical materialism. This was not peculiar to Odessa; under Soviet conditions, whenever Communist leadership was removed there would inevitably be a shortage of people experienced in the field of government.

There is no indication of what kind of future Russia the people hoped to see. The only available evidence — save the peasants' demands for agricultural reforms, discussed elsewhere — comes from a few members of the university who *post facto* sought to abstract some of the dominant concepts "in the air" which, they felt, would have been accepted by most of the intelligentsia. It is easier to identify the areas of rejection than concepts positively espoused. Rather clearly, terror of any sort — Soviet or non-Soviet — was rejected. As a political system, fascism-had exceedingly few advocates. Monarchism — whether in the old tsarist garb or a constitutional form — was considered virtually unthinkable, "impossible," except by some older individuals. "Capitalism" had assumed a sufficiently negative coloration in the course of years, and its establishment seemed economically so impossible, given the Soviet legacy, that well-nigh nobody would have accepted it or even propounded it as the basis of the new order. Only two positive concepts seem to have had real currency: the idea of popular sovereignty and the concept of parliamentary government. Beyond that, the political image becomes blurred and divided."[23]

There seemed so exit widespread satisfaction with the renewed contact (however abnormal the means by which it was achieved) with the "West." All informants and some contemporary sources express gratification about it and point to it with pride."[24] Consulates, trade ties, mail, trips, university exchanges, guest performers — all this seemed to put Odessa back on the map, seemed to show that it had rejoined the human race. This anti-isolationism was apparently pronounced in all occupied territory (perhaps more pronounced in Odessa than in less cosmopolitan cit-

---

[23] Manuilov, pp. 69-70; interviews A, B, and E.
[24] Some of this, it is true, may well have been due to the fact that such sentiments were being communicated to "Westerners."

ies), and gave rise to the expression, cited independently by several informants, that *zapakhlo zapadom* — "one could again smell the West."

Such a feeling did not prelude the rise of some Soviet or Russian patriotism. What is surprising, however, is how little patriotism there was, less than anywhere else in the U.S.S.R. — both Soviet and German-held. No adequate explanation can be advanced. It is only a suggestion, but perhaps the reason is that, in both Soviet and German-occupied areas, patriotism was a lubricant, an incentive, a rationale for action against a foe: the objective situation, with iron logic, invited a fight. Not so in Transnistria; here the climate of public life was far more neutral, more denatured, more reconciled; here the people seemed tired of banners, slogans, and political emotions, and seemed to prefer a comfortable and secure life. Perhaps one other hypothesis should be added: the unusually strong "local patriotism" and feeling among Odessites of being an in-group displaced and partly obviated the all-Soviet patriotism which emerged elsewhere. Such an argument, however, can easily be overstressed, and the virtual absence of tangible patriotism in Odessa must remain something of a mystery. Only in the last half year or so of the occupation does any evidence of Soviet (or Russian) patriotism appear in conversations and political anticipation.

A consistent attitude toward state property or state management is equally difficult to uncover. On the one hand, there seems to have been no hostility toward government ownership of heavy industry, public utilities, and other large economic enterprises; on the other, there was distinct opposition to state direction of agriculture (particularly in the form of kolkhozes) and to state monopoly in retail trade and other forms of business, as discussed in another chapter. Thus, the drive for personal profits from economic activity seemed to co-exist with another set of values that accepted government ownership, particularly of "greater," "heavier" branches of the economy, as more equitable. A positive image of the successful businessman, the individual entrepreneur or storekeeper using his talents, now unshackled from Soviet restrictions, developed, but it coexisted with Soviet stereotypes — reinforced by experiences under Transnistrian rule — of capitalist abuse, corruption, and injustice. One might suggest that the occupation was too short to permit the crystallization of any real formula; the interim concept, if there was a dominant one, was probably that of a mixed economy.[25]

---

[25] Interviews A, C, and E.

Finally, one should mention, as a fringe kind of political concept, the peculiarly strong sensitivity of the people to injuries to the individual's dignity — a sensitivity equally strong in German-occupied areas. Soviet rule had apparently sensitized Soviet citizens to react strongly to corporal punishment and other forms of personal humiliation and abuse. Soviet indoctrination about the dignity of man had been accepted and was turned against abuses perpetrated by the Soviet regime itself. The same sensitivity inspired some of the Russian resentment of Romanian abuses and terror; it also contributed to the high value placed on the "individual" by the Russians under non-Soviet conditions, when a different hierarchy of values began to appear.

None of this, however, adds up to a political program. The emergence of some conventional political activity came only as a concomitant of the weakening of Romanian rule and the appearance of Russian émigré representatives.

Émigré politics

In politics a disproportionate influence was wielded by two numerically small categories: the so-called *byvshie liudi* ("former people," who had status or wealth before 1917) and the returning émigrés. Their influence was due, one suspects, to the fact that they were more articulate in formulating their views, that they remembered concretely actual alternatives to Bolshevism, and that they were now politically more secure than the rest of the population; they could therefore in leisure and safety better afford to devote time and effort to political activity. Moreover, many were professional anti-Communists and as such far more sensitized to political concepts and nuances and far more likely to have their favorite brand of patented reforms than average Soviet citizens. The "former people" tended to dig up genuine or spurious old titles of nobility, awards and decorations dating back to the tsarist era, and other claims to status and distinction. The Romanians seemed to honor these claims; probably because they regarded the "formers" as politically more reliable, they gave them certain privileges in securing apartments, employment, and pensions.[26]

The returning old émigrés were few in number. They were mostly Russians who had gone abroad and settled in Bessarabia, or other parts of Romania, or in Bulgaria and now desired to "return home" or, in some

---

[26] Manuilov, pp. 84-85; interview E.

instances, to profit from their linguistic and other skills. The Russian emigration in the Balkans, and particularly in Romania, was a mixed lot. While some had resisted Romanization, many had changed their outlook, language, even their names. By and large, the Romanians had suppressed Russian schools, church, and cultural activities within their borders. And among those who were legally permitted to enter Transnistria were, perhaps by an unavoidable process of selection, a great many whose cultural or political standards were none too high and who were apologists for fascism; most of the rest were politically rather reticent.

It is not surprising that they by and large evoked hostility in the local population — more than the Bessarabian influx did. They seemed to have "learned nothing and forgotten nothing"; those who had once belonged to the privileged classes now sought to reclaim their former factories or land or dwellings; they bitterly disappointed those residents of Odessa who had looked to them for political guidance; "for a long time we, having lived thirty years under Communist tyranny, had the conviction that our émigré compatriots... represented a powerful force in the free countries." It was a shock to learn they did not, and that their political positions were the subject of controversy; "this... stopped some of us from assuming a clear-cut political position."

There were exceptions. Artists were welcomed back with genuine pleasure: they had something to give and demanded nothing unfair in return. Vronskii, Lipkovskaia were in this category; so was Pëtr Leshchenko, the night-club singer, who enjoyed considerable popularity. Nor did the hostility extend to the children of old émigrés who returned to study in Odessa; in the country, there was a sense of quiet, dignified pride in their having returned. But mostly there was disappointment and hostility. The refugee novelist P. Ershov, in later reconstructing Transnistrian life, picked as his prototype of the émigré the schoolmate of his hero: a lazy *barin* (lord), he makes a decidedly poor impression on the Odessa residents who once knew him; his snobbery, his self-advertising, and his utter lack of a sense of social justice and "equality" arouse the indignation of the younger set.

Some émigrés, of course, were personally quite well-liked. Some baffled the local residents by their effrontery and the shameless way they promoted their own interests, either by their own efforts or with the support of the authorities (usually gained through some well-placed bribes). Some émigrés demanding their property back were rebuffed by the primăria, and Odessites apparently fully backed the primăria. In mid-1943, the new

Antonescu decree sanctioned the return of houses to their former owners; a few émigrés had deeds or other proof and managed to have their homes restored to them. Thanks to pull and bribery, the daughter of a rich merchant, who had meanwhile died, got back a seven-story apartment house her father had owned until 1917; she even managed (a mere six months before the retreat) to sell it to a Romanian. Such operations evoked more of bewilderment and wonderment than enmity. The restoration of landed estates and industrial facilities caused resentment, but the return of living quarters of commercial sites was accepted.[27]

It was inevitable that the right wing of the Russian emigration tended to have something of a monopoly. Middle-of-the-road and leftist refugee groups had scarcely any following in Eastern and Central Europe; and those few who lived in Axis Europe (for instance, Prague or Paris) had no way of publicizing their views or contacting their fellow-citizens on occupied soil. The first refugees to reach Odessa were — and local residents guessed this with a curiously keen instinct — often agents of the Gestapo and SD or the Romanian Siguranța. A few agents claimed an affiliation with émigré political groupings, but this was often purely nominal.[28] One Savchenko, for instance, claimed to be an old army captain, and pretended to be working to create a Russian "youth movement"; he turned out to be recruiting personnel for a German intelligence organization. Though some individuals undoubtedly worked with him, the urban youth, which he aimed at, rejected him.[29]

Though apparently not until 1943, refugees representing General Abramov, the head of the Bulgarian branch of the ROVS *(Russki obshchevoinski soiuz)*, a rather extensive military organization of "White" Army veterans (repeatedly the target of Soviet infiltration) made some *bona fide* contacts with Odessa residents. The contacts, however, appear to have been sporadic and for information only.

A bit more substantial were the endeavors of the NTS, the organization of Russian Solidarists. A younger, more "activist" group, the NTS had a fascist-corporate ideology and a number of capable members; it sought to enlist in its ranks those with official positions — mayors, chiefs

---

[27] Manuilov, pp. 59-62, 112; interviews A, B, and E; Ershov, *op. cit.*, p. 41.

[28] Though without conclusive evidence, it appears that at least a few individuals who ostensibly were working for émigré groupings of the right and Axis intelligence agencies were NKVD agents or informants.

[29] Manuilov, pp. 114-118.

of police, editors, or interpreters — in the occupied parts of the U.S.S.R. To most residents of Transnistria — as elsewhere in the U.S.S.R. — NTS was entirely unknown. Only a select few, generally leading collaborators or university professors, were approached by them and contact was made through personal acquaintances. In mid-1943 Nikolai Fevr, a journalist on the staff of the Berlin *Novoe Slovo* and an NTS member, visited Odessa for nearly two months (unfortunately his memoirs on this period have never been published). Popular in some intellectual circles, he spent some time recruiting adherents. However, his official position called for circumspection, particularly since the rift between the German officials and the nationalistic NTS was growing.[30] Two NTS men, apparently from Yugoslavia (where the NTS had had its center), approached a certain professor in the fall of 1943 in a spirit of romantic subversiveness. The professor recalls that he had never previously heard of them and that they seemed immature — half-childish, half-fanatical. They asked for his help in staging a mass rally — which was never held — and in distributing brochures.

In late 1943, a small youth delegation came to Odessa — either from Yugoslavia or Bulgaria; it was impossible to determine which. The Russian émigrés, or children of émigrés, who made it up called themselves *vladimirovtsy* — it has been impossible to trace or identify them further, but the name suggests a Monarchy-cum-Orthodoxy orientation. One refugee from Odessa, who was then "in the know" on primăria affairs, writes:

> According to my information, this entire group was recruited by the Gestapo (probably not strictly correct, but used as a generic term for German intelligence organs) for surveillance and agents' work in occupied territory. Strange as it may seem, this... (group) established contact with the few NTS members who resided in Odessa.

It is even alleged that a number of the group, Verbitski, now dead, was specially charged by the NTS to expose anti-NTS Russians even by means of provocation — an allegation which, however, cannot be verified.[31]

---

[30] The NTS had initially cooperated with the Nazi authorities. However, in 1943-1944, the SS and other anti-NTS elements in Berlin brought about a suspension of collaboration and the temporary arrest of NTS leaders. For details, see Boris L. Dvinov, *Polities of the Russian Emigration*, Document P-768, The RAND Corporation, 1955; and U.S. Department of State, External Research Staff, Series 3, No. 76, NTS — *The Russian Solidarist Movement*, Washington, 1951.

[31] *Ibid.;* interviews A, D, and E.

The *vladimirovtsy* are nowhere else mentioned and were unknown to other informants. It seems possible that the author confused them with a group elsewhere reported as *petrovtsy*, known formally as the *Organizatsii molodiozhi intent Petra Velikogo*, the Peter the Great Youth Organization associated with ROVS. If so, this is probably the very group of some twenty-two men who were the subject of considerable émigré controversy because of their chief, Captain Klavdii Aleksandrovich Foss. Foss was Abramov's aide in Sofia. In the pre-war ROVS he was part of the so-called "Inner Line," the medium and object of a widespread Soviet infiltration move; in late 1938, Abramov's son, whom Foss had apparently recruited, was proved to be a Soviet agent. During the war Foss and his group moved from Sofia to Nikolaev, where they worked for a German intelligence agency — apparently naval intelligence, though this cannot be established with certainty.[32]

The efforts of another group of old émigrés, the so-called *Schutzkorps* (guard corps) had some tangible results. The *Schutzkorps* was a military organization, consisting of three, later five, regiments of old émigrés resident in Yugoslavia; in 1941, it volunteered to help the Germans liberate Russia from Bolshevism. On the whole they were a rather reactionary lot, intrigue-ridden, composed mostly of men in their fifties and sixties. The Germans initially sanctioned the use of the corps for guard service; later made an anti-partisan combat unit, it was repeatedly thrown into action against the Serbian guerrillas.[33] In 1943, it became a regular formation of the Wehrmacht and allowed to extend its recruitment to other countries, including Romania. As a by-product of this permission, in December 1943, the *Schutzkorps* opened a recruitment bureau in Odessa; the former Café Libman, a popular and centrally-located spot, was assigned to the bureau and the old Russian (tsarist) tricolor flag was displayed in its windows.

The flag and the way the office appeared aroused considerable interest in town. This was, after all, the first endeavor of this sort, and the only in Soviet territory. But curiosity almost at once turned to hostility. The office lasted only a few months and in that short time had several chairmen, who were relieved one after another. One of its "chiefs of staff" was Sr. Lt. Zalevsky, a typical old-guard professional military man with mono-

---

[32] Mamukov, p. 56; Boris Nikolaevski, "Vnutrennaia liniin i kap. K.A Foss," *Novoe russkoe slovo*, April 16, 1950, and Ivan Solonevich, letter to the Editor, *ibid.*, May, 1950.

[33] For background information on the *Scutzkorps,* see chapter XXVII in Alexander Dallin, *German Rule in Russia, 1941-1945* (London: MacMillan, 1957; rev. ed. 1981).

cle and stick, who "dealt with volunteers as tsarist officers had with their valets." Odessa officials helped get Zalevsky recalled.

The *Schutzkorps* recruiters seemed to be offering a third solution, a way of avoiding both the Bolsheviks, who were just then advancing at a menacing pace, and the Germans. Informants agree that those who enlisted did so only because they had completely failed in Odessa — there were relatively few of these — or because they feared the returning Soviets. Since the corps took only volunteers with no next of kin, men with families and belongings could not use the *Schutzkorps* as a way of getting to Yugoslavia. Still, a few did join, though apparently none of them out of genuine conviction. Their experience with the *Schutzkorps* proved execrable; the old White officers looked on the "Soviet scum" with disdain and scorn. A few volunteers tied from Serbia back to Odessa.[34] Vladimir Petrov, a refugee who passed through Odessa on his way westward, describes in his memoirs his encounter at the Odessa "Recruiting Post for Russian Volunteers" with an official who, a year earlier, had been chief of police under the Germans in the North Caucasus.

> "Is the recruiting successful here?" (Petrov asked)
>
> "Well, not too much so — ten or fifteen men a week. Life is good in Odessa, so that there aren't many people who want to go and fight. The ones who volunteer are usually those who for some reason have to get out of Odessa quickly. For instance, criminal elements, thieves, sometimes bandits, or simply homeless refugees."
>
> "Do you think they'll thank you for that type of volunteers?" I asked him.
>
> He waved his hand. "I don't give a damn. I'm not looking for any medals for this work. My job is to take everyone who is willing and send them to Belgrade. Usually about half of them desert on the way, but that's outside of my responsibility..."[35]

For all classes in Odessa, the Recruitment Office seemed a confirmation of the stereotypes about how reactionary and moribund the emigration was.

It was apparently not that they were "Whites" of the Civil War that made the *Schutzkorps* seem undesirable — the only resident political organization of any consequence was composed of veterans of the campaigns of 1918-1921.[36] This was the OBCh or OBVCh *(Obshebestvo Byvshikh*

---

[34] Interviews A and D; Manuilov, pp. 128-129; *Bukarester Tageblatt,* July 25, 1943.
[35] Petrov, *Retreat from Russia,* p. 208.

Voinskikh Chinov) or more simply Veterans' Society, formed through the efforts of Nikolai Lukich Pustovoitov, a professional soldier who had been a colonel in the Tsarist army but had spent the entire Soviet period in Odessa (partly in hiding). Pustovoitov was not the ignorant, pompous, narrow-minded martinet kind of professional soldier; he apparently befriended a number of individuals in "Transnistrian society." He persuaded the Romanians to authorize his organization as a mutual-aid society — anyone who had belonged to any of the earlier (presumably Tsarist and "White") armies could join. According to the only informant really familiar with its work — though perhaps too favorable to it because of his own close association with it and with Pustovoitov — the society also engaged in other activities, such as establishing an orphanage[37] and financing the St. Magdalena Church in Odessa. Civilians became lay members, so to speak "sympathizers," and a women's auxiliary was set up, which helped invalids and prisoners of war in the Odessa area and was active in church work; the Society earned the benevolence and backing of Metropolitan Vissarion.

Some people who might have supported the OBVCh kept away from it because it had reputedly attracted the attention and interest of the Abwehr and Siguranţa; it was thought that they recruited agents from among the OBVCh's military membership, though the extent of their activities is not known; apparently the civilian arm was not involved in this way.

OBVCh had, in addition to its philanthropic character, a certain political significance. The Bulgarian branch of ROVS sent in a good deal of propaganda material, including primarily monarchist publications such as the wartime appeal of Grand Duke Vladimir Kirillovich, pretender to the Russian throne. It appears that this material was received "very coolly," except by a few old-timers. The monarchist spirit of the OBVCh, at first rather pronounced (thanks to the background of its membership and Romanian support), declined as the increasing influx of civilians, especially in the latter part of 1943, strengthened the liberal wing. What finally

---

[36] One cannot affirm that it was the sole such group. There may well have been informal, quasi-political associations, workers' circles, and other organizations. However, except for the Soviet partisans, it is the only one which any of the live informants or published sources refer to.

[37] The opening of the orphanage was publicized at the time *(Novoe Slovo,* No. 18, March 3, 1943).

tipped the balance against the restorationists was the news of Vlasov's so-called Smolensk Manifesto.[38]

This manifesto called for an anti-Stalin movement composed of Soviet citizens and was led by Lt. Gen. Andrei A. Vlasov, who had been captured by the Germans in July 1942. That the manifesto was published indicates that this particular "political warfare" notion had been accepted by at least some German military and propaganda circles. The Vlasov movement gained some momentum in 1943, but was soon put on ice. The members and supporters of the movement (and its military arm, the so-called ROA) never seem to have realized the full extent and nature of German control and direction of at least its overt manifestations. In Odessa, the Vlasov movement was unknown until at least the late spring of 1943. It remained less well known there than in most urban centers of occupied Russia. The Romanians occasionally mentioned it in their domestic press, but they were loath to foster any Russian national sentiment that had an institutional framework, lest the native population make greater demands and seek to become more independent. News of the Vlasov movement did get in: relevant items occasionally appeared in the local press; at times, copies of Russian émigré newspapers arrived from Paris, Berlin, Belgrade, or Riga; and at times visitors to Odessa "spread the word." In mid-1943, the German leadership clamped down on the Vlasov movement, and news of it ceased — much to the bewilderment of those interested in it, in Odessa as elsewhere in occupied areas. Pustovoitov, one of those who had shown considerable interest in it, then applied for permission to send a five-man delegation to Vlasov. The Romanians failed to reply to his request, and so dragged out the decision that he decided to send three men anyway. Through informants within his own organization, one suspects, the Germans learned of his intention and intervened to prevent the trip. When Count Eristov, then on the staff of the Vlasovite military arm, ROA, passed through Odessa on the way from the Crimea to Berlin, he promised to "establish liaison" between them and Vlasov's "headquarters." But nothing developed from this momentary contact. Finally, when the *Schutzkorps* opened offices in Odessa, some pro-Vlasovites — generally, the anti-monarchist, nationalist Russian intelligentsia, including some of the older men — got the OBVCh to apply to the Primăria for permission to recruit replacements for the ROA. Their demand was rejected but they were allowed to collect contributions. In

---

[38] Manuilov, pp. 117-121.

early 1944, the establishment of a *Fond Osvobozhdeniia (Liberation Fund)* was announced. One informant active in its formation states — though his statement was not substantiated by others — that 40,000 marks were collected on the first day alone, a sum which so scared the Romanian authorities that they ordered the account closed and the collection suspended.[39]

In scope political activity connected with émigré groups was thus rather modest, though its potential was in some instances relatively vast. The actual membership of quasi-political groups was limited primarily or exclusively to white-collar workers and the new elite — a fact which may reflect the social selectivity of the informants but which more probably indicates the hiatus in Odessa society between white-collar and manual workers. Politics may have been no less important to manual workers, but it was more inaccessible, more unintelligible, and as something to get involved in, more pointless.

The Nationality Question

In Odessa, Russian, Ukrainian, Jewish, and other ethnic groups were mingled, but evidence of national friction and feuds in strikingly absent. Jews were officially subjected to special discrimination and Germans and Moldavians were officially elevated in status. But this was the product of occupation policy rather than of popular sentiment.

In Odessa itself, the Ukrainians — that is, those who spoke Ukrainian at home and considered themselves Ukrainians — were only a small fraction, variously estimated at from 5 to 20 per cent of the population; those who understood and spoke Ukrainian were considerably more numerous. In the hinterland, the proportion varied from place to place; some areas along the Bug were solidly Ukrainian; others had a Ukrainian majority, with Russian and other (German, Moldavian) minorities; in parts of what was formerly the Moldavian S.S.R. there were few Ukrainians. All the evidence suggests an absence of Ukrainian chauvinism and separatism. Refugee informants,[40] and contemporary reports agree on this. As early as September 2, 1941, the German SD reported from Transnistria, "in the territories examined, one must note that among the Ukrainians

---

[39] *Ibid.*, pp. 129-131; interview D; Petrov, *op. cit.*, p. 207.
[40] It is probably revealing that the author's attempts to find a refugee informant from Odessa who was a Ukrainian nationalist failed, in spite of attempts to get in touch with various Ukrainian groups and individuals in New York, Munich, and Canada.

there is no striving for political independence."[41] A few weeks later it stated more generally:

> It is striking that among all three ethnic groups (in the Transnistrian countryside) — the Ukrainians, Moldavians, and Germans — the distinctive ethnic character is still expressed only in the language. All other forms of national expression have almost completely died out after 23 years of Bolshevik rule. Popular songs and dances are present in scarcely discoverable remains. National dress and nationally-tinged spinning or weaving have completely disappeared...[42]

A German officer, around the turn of the year, reported that in Odessa itself the people thought of themselves and their fellow-residents not in terms of ethnic categories but as part of a local community.[43] A German correspondent in 1942 was permitted to state in print that in Transnistria "the nationality question... is not of primary urgency (*vordringlich*).[44]

If there was no nationality problem at first, inter-stimulation of Romanian (and also German) policy and the endeavors of Galician nationalists created one. Officially, Romanian policy called for ethnic and linguistic equality of Moldavians, *Volksdeutsche*, and Russians — or, in the hinterland, Ukrainians.[45] In practice, the Moldavians became an elite; the Germans were given a privileged position to which the Romanians had to reconcile themselves; the Russians occupied a middle position; the Ukrainians were the object of somewhat greater discrimination than urban Russian groups; and Jews were the bottom of the ethnic pyramid.

Romanian enmity toward the Ukrainians had a history. Conflicts between Ukrainians and Moldavians as individuals were less significant in this than the conflicts that arose between Ukrainian and Romanian nationalists on political issues: suffice it to point to Bessarabia and Bukovina as territory contested and claimed by both groups. In the Second World War, Romanian expansionists were afraid that the Ukrainian nationalists would come to challenge their monopoly of power. Most Ukrainians rated no

---

[41] Beauftagte des Chefs der SiPo..., "Tatigkeir," September 2, 1941.
[42] SD Report 100.
[43] Berg, *op. cit.*
[44] Gerhard Christoph, "Bessarabien und Transnistrien," *Volk und Reich*, Berlin, Vol. 18, 1942, pp. 99-103. See also Manuilov, pp. 104-105, 241.
[45] See "Friedliches Odessa," *Deutsche Ukraine-Zeitung*, January 10, 1943.

special consideration because they were peasants, and the small urban Ukrainian intelligentsia in Transnistria was viewed with constant suspicion by the authorities.

The Ukrainian nationalist émigrés, on their part, provided some genuine basis for Romanian hostility. A few Ukrainian military formations attached to the German 11th Army crossed through Romania into northern Transnistria. Whatever the motives of their German sponsors, the Ukrainian political groups supporting the move had in mind the establishment of a separate Ukrainian state (though necessarily under German auspices) and of Ukrainian municipalities and governmental units on a local and regional level.[46] Odessa was an obvious target for infiltration. Mstislav Chubai, a Ukrainian nationalist, in his memoirs, says that the group to which he was attached had been assigned by the Galician nationalist leadership the task of establishing in Odessa a temporary oblast' government. If driven out by Romanian or German action, they were to remain in Odessa as an organized underground. "Initially," he is forced to admit, the population looked upon them as German agents. The absence of Ukrainian separatism he attributes to Odessa's status as a "stronghold of Russification." A few surviving members of the SVU (the "Union for the "Liberation of the Ukraine"), which had been almost exterminated by the Soviets some ten years earlier, joined the nationalist nucleus of Chubai's men, but otherwise the Galician enterprise was a failure.[47]

The national consciousness of the Ukrainian population was, however, stirred by Romanian behavior. Memoirs abound in details of clashes and alleged abuses.[48] A German army corps reported that Romanians were forcibly baptizing Ukrainian children in the countryside, and telling the population to learn Romanian as the country would be Romanized.[49] The Ukrainian theater in Odessa, licensed sometime in 1942, under the direction of a competent veteran, Bondarchuk, was not allowed to function for long. Bondarchuk was arrested as a separatist and the theater dissolved. Whether or not the charge was justified cannot be determined. It need not have been, for another Ukrainian theater, opened in 1943,

---

[46] For details on Operation "Roland," see John A. Armstrong, *Ukrainian Nationalism, 1939-1945*. Columbia University Press, New York, 1955.

[47] Mstislav Z. Chubai, *Reid orhanizatoriv OUN Vid Popradu po Chorne More*, Cicero, Munich, 1952, pp. 52-54; Manuilov, pp. 104-105; Interviews A and D.

[48] E.g., Chubai, *op. cit.*, pp. 55-61.

[49] LIV. A.K., Ic, "Übergriffe."

proved equally short-lived because of the withdrawal of the primăria's permit.[50]

The semi-official account by Mykola Lebed', a key figure in the movement, admits that the UPA *(Ukrains'ka Povstans'ka Armyia,* or Ukrainian Insurgent Army) had little success in enlisting support. On October 14, 1943, the Siguranţa arrested several UPA members near or in Odessa along with a number of innocents suspected of Ukrainian nationalist agitation. After two weeks — Lebed' alleges, and there is no independent substantiation of the story — all were freed, and the Romanians offered to negotiate with the nationalists. The ensuing talks, he states, were soon broken off by the UPA's political arm because (1) the Romanians would not "recognize" Bucovina and Bessarabia as part of the Ukraine, and (2) the Romanians were found to be subject to German dictation — something the nationalist leaders had once themselves experienced but since escaped. By the end of 1943, he insists, "the first small units of the UPA" were established in Transnistria, particularly along the Dnestr River. They had a few minor skirmishes with Romanian gendarmerie near Zhmerinka but they never amounted to an armed force. This indeed seems to have been all the nationalists managed to do in this area.[51]

The conclusion that the Ukrainian nationalists had no success or influence in Transnistria is inescapable. Among the reasons for this failure is, of course, the traditional absence of national friction or Ukrainian nationalism in Odessa province. In addition, the terrain — there were no forests — was not propitious to the formation of rural partisan. The differences in the occupation policy of the Germans and the Romanians also helps explain their failure. Nationalism, well-nigh non-existent in 1941 in German-held territory also, grew in the subsequent couple of years, in part, because no other native political movements were permitted and, in part, because of the widespread popular hostility to both Soviet and German regimes; the feeling of "a plague on both your houses" took (at least for some tens of thousands) the form of espousing Ukrainian separatism as a third solution. In Transnistria, Romanian rule simply did not invite such a drastic "third solution." It is significant that, in Odessa, Ukrainian separatism seems to have gained some minimal support only in the final few months, when Germans began replacing Romanians as masters of the province.[52]

---

[50] Interviews A, D, and H.
[51] Mykola Lebed, *UPA,* Vol. 1: *Germany,* UHVR, 1946, pp. 54-55.

The Ethnic Elite

Romanian, German, and Italian residents inevitably constituted an elite under the Transnistrian order.[53] The Italian colony in Odessa was rather small. Its members were, on the whole, well assimilated and did not evince the same condescension and superciliousness which the other two Axis minorities displayed. They had no economic or territorial claims that they sought to have vindicated; and they continued to live as before, backed whenever necessary by the Italian consul in Odessa, a former journalist, Maurilio Coppini. Coppini, in the Italian consular service before the war, knew Russia and spoke the language, and seems to have been generally popular with the local residents, with whom he maintained some social contact. He backed Badoglio and was forced to leave hurriedly in the late summer of 1943. "Italian Odessa" — exposed to the competing pressures of Italian fascist indoctrination and local values — split into pro-Badoglio and pro-Mussolini factions, but unfortunately details are not known.[54]

The Moldavians also became a privileged group. To the Germans, they would "specifically insist" that they were "not Romanians," that they felt closer to the Ukrainians than to the Romanians.[55] Even the Romanian press — or at least its more moderate organs — admitted that the Moldavians had no "conscious" Romanian nationalism.[56] But, if the Transnistrian authorities wanted to give them a particularly privileged position, most Moldavians felt it would be foolish not to let them. They became more immune from punishment, privileged in the allocation of goods and in securing positions, politically less subject to terror, and in other unmistakable ways elevated in status.[57] Their fellow-citizens of non-Moldavian

---

[52] See Beaufrtagter bei der Heeresgruppe Süd, *op. cit.*

[53] A number of Bulgarians resident in Odessa and especially other parts of the Ukraine were "repatriated" (most of them had never been in Bulgaria) in early 1944, at the request of Sofia and with the consent of Berlin and Bucharest. Other minorities in Transnistria, such as Greeks, Tatars, and Armenians, were not subjected to any special discrimination by the Romanians.

[54] Manuilov, pp. 142-149.

[55] SD Report 100.

[56] "Transnistrien und die Rumänen," *Ostland,* Vol. 20, No. 24, December 15, 1941, pp. 428-432. See also "Die Rumänen in Transnistrien," *Südost-Echo,* Vol. 12, 1942, No. 45, November 6, 1942; *Rivista di studi politivi internazionali,* Florence, Vol. 15, No. 3, July, 1948, p. 92; and chapter II above.

stock took another attitude toward this metamorphosis: refugee informants agree that previously there had been no ill feeling against Moldavians, but that now most of the population became hostile, partly out of envy and partly out of indignation about the unfair advantage the Moldavians enjoyed.[58]

The *Volksdeutsche* in Transnistria occupied a very different position. Clustered in villages in different parts of the Odessa area, they were rather well-assimilated and generally spoke Russian to each other (even the Germans had to acknowledge this) or a peculiar Russified jargon of Bavarian, Palatinate, or some other regional German vernacular which their forefathers had brought with them. These ethnic Germans had been the subject of extensive study in the Reich.[59] On principle, Berlin claimed them, as it claimed all Germans abroad. It was hard to determine how many *Volksdeutsche* there were; in a census taken under the Romanians, when the benefits involved in claiming the status were well-known, some 125,000 declared themselves Germans; German claims went as high as 185,000. In Odessa itself only some 7,500 Germans were left, with women in considerable preponderance.[60] Most *Volksdeutsche* resided in a few rural areas.

Some of their settlements experienced German occupation before the area was transferred to Romanian hands. A part of the famous Brandenburg Regiment (which had basically intelligence tasks) occupied the German villages along the Kuchurgan River and around Gross-Liebental near Odessa.[61] Though the Germans claimed that "many" residents were glad to see them, they had to report that there had been Communists among the German colonists, that many *Volksdeutsche* wanted no part of the new order, and that general standards of health, education, and cultural aspiration, let alone national consciousness, left much to be desired. Nonethe-

---

[57] For instance, 24,860 Moldavian families in Transnistria were supported at the expense of the state during the last quarter of 1942. (*Porunca Vremii*, February 21, 1943).

[58] Interviews B and D; "Poscshchenie Guvernatorom Transnistrii Prof. G. Aleksianu obshchezhirtiia studenrov moldavan," *Molva*, No. 130, May 12, 1943.

[59] *Der Deutsche in Transnistrien*, No. 5, August 16, 1942, and No. 11, September 27, 1942.

[60] Himmler conference, February, 1942, NG-1118; "Bericht des SS-Sonder-kommandos der VoMi über den Stand der Erfassungsarbeiten," March 15, 1942, CRS, EAP 1618-12/213. Gerhard Wolfrum, "Deutsche Aufbauarbeit in Transnistrien," in *Deutsche Arbeit* (Berlin, December, 1942, p. 371) reports that the 124,892 who registered *as Volksdeutsche* included non-German wives and windows of ethnic Germans.

[61] For a detailed report, see "Schutzmassnahmen...," *op. cit.*

less, the official German approach was to make fellow-nationals (*Volksgenossen*) "again" aware of their "true" ethnic affiliation. The Germans began a thorough administrative reorganization that involved the revival of the pre-Bolshevik system of village government; bringing in the harvest; installing guards and securing property; setting up price controls for food and other critical items; "elimination of suspect *(belastete)* elements"; compilation of vital statistics and basic data; revival of medical and social services and the church. The widespread raids of marauding Romanian soldiers resulted in frequent German protests. On August 15, the Commanding General of the German 11th Army proclaimed that the *Volksdeutsche* were under his protection; Romanian chiefs of police near the German villages were at once informed of this and some tightening of discipline resulted. After a couple of weeks, however, German units were moved out of Transnistria;[62] they left behind a modicum of government and order, and an atmosphere in which "privileges" for ethnic Germans were taken for granted.

The Romanians who took over made no such distinctions. They automatically confiscated grain and cattle and they looted in German villages just as they did in other villages. By early September, a German report caustically (and wistfully) stated: "Since the introduction of Romanian administration one may speak without exaggeration of the systematic plunder of the country." Other Germans reported — in this instance truthfully, it would seem — that the *Volksdeutsche* greeted the Romanians with apprehension and regret.[63] The German authorities soon started negotiations with their Romanian allies about the status of these compatriots-to-be. The *a priori* formula that the Reich had jurisdiction over all Germans everywhere had been honored by Romania when she permitted the removal of Germans from Bessarabia and Dobrudja. The Reich now wanted back some of the sovereignty it had ceded to Romania: in substance it asked for extraterritoriality for the German colonies. This was a demand difficult for Antonescu to refuse, yet most irksome to grant. The German negotiations were conducted by both the Foreign Office and the military, though the administrator of the ethnic Germans was to be the

---

[62] In the ease of Gross-Liehental, the occupation took place only on September 16, as that area had originally been part of the Odessa defensive perimeter. The Germans found the standard of living and education, despite far more extensive war damage, to be much better there than in the Kuchurgan area, apparently because it was so close to Odessa itself.

[63] Verhalten der Rumänen im Gebier Transnistrien," SD Report 133, November 14, 1941; Prinz zu Savn und Wittgenstein, "Bericht über meine Fahrt nach Russland."

Sonderkommando "R" of *Volksdeutsche Mittelstelle* (or VoMi), the resettlement and servicing agency of the SS. Of the many moves involved in persuading Bucharest, suffice it to cite the preparatory German conversations with Alexianu and with an ex-Minister, Cornățeanu, both of whom were to present the Reich's arguments to Antonescu. On November 10, 1941, the Nazi ambassador, Killinger, was to take up the problem officially. Basic agreement was reached on November 14, 1941, with Antonescu unwilling or unable to object. Talks aiming at a more detailed agreement implementing the terms were conducted in Transnistria between Alexianu's staff and the VoMi chief, Oberführer (Colonel) Hoffmeyer. The result was that the VoMi was given a completely free hand in *Volksdeutsche* villages; a network of eighteen districts *(Bereiche)* was established, with an SS officer as commandant *(Bereichskommando-Führer)*. Over them were the praetors of the four predominantly German rayons (Landau, Hoffnungstal, Selz, and Gross-Liebental); new praetors were to be appointed and were to be *Volksdeutsche* citizens of Old Romania. The Transnistrian authorities recognized the local government and police that had been set up in the German settlements and, in effect, agreed to keep out as much as they could.[64]

This agreement did not settle all outstanding issues, and new ones accumulated as time passed. In the first months of 1942, the VoMi had a special team conduct a census of ethnic Germans; all over the age of 14 were given certificates to take the place of Russian passports; the certificate entitled the bearer to German protection. The Romanians were somewhat dismayed by this. Another source of tension was the question of whether ethnic Germans were liable to military service, and if so, whether they should serve in the German army, the Romanian army, or the local police force.[65]

In general, however, the Germans paid little attention to the Romanians. In June, 1942, the Jewish theater in Odessa was reopened as the "Deutsches Haus." Without consultation the VoMi began a newspaper in Odessa, *Der Deutsche in Transnistrien*. On a low informational and political level, this weekly was widely circulated among the *Volksdeutsche* but,

---

[64] Reichart, "Bericht", Ihnen, *op. cit.;* Verbindungsstab der Deutschen Wehrmacht für Transnistrien, Abt. La, "Bericht über Lage der Landwirtschaft in Transnistrien," January 31, 1942, CRS, Wi/ID 2.1174; *Der Deutsche in Transnistrien,* No. 17, November 8, 1942; Wolfrum, *op. cit.*

[65] Berichr des SS-Sonderkommandos," *op. cit.;* VoMi to RFSS, March 6, 1942, CRS, EAP 161b-12/167.

according to a German admission, far from satisfied their hunger for news and printed matter.[66]

In the summer of 1942, a new agreement was negotiated between Hoftmeyer and Alexianu. It confirmed the VoMi's authority to publish a newspaper; it approved the formation of the *Selbstschutz*, a *Volksdentsche* militia for men above 18, which had already been established to maintain order locally, and to handle paratroopers, partisans, and others. Such a force had been implied in the earlier agreement; but some Romanian prefects had asked the militia to turn in their arms, a demand curtly rejected by the Germans. *De facto* seizures of land by the *Volksdentsche* communities — they apparently had taken advantage of their stronger and more organized status to appropriate the land and harvest of adjacent villages — were "formalized." Alexianu promised to release Germans convicted for possessing private radios, and, in exchange for agricultural produce, agreed to supply the ethnic Germans with cigarettes, spirits, salt, and matches. Rather one-sided in its terms, the agreement was signed by Alexianu on August 14 and by Hoftmeyer on August 30, 1942.[67]

The ethnic Germans had been far from happy both under the Soviets and during the initial phase of the occupation. In rural areas, the SD asserted in November 1941, many *Volksdentsche* felt they had been better off under the Soviets than under the Romanians, who were still living off the land in an indiscriminate fashion.[68] Before the end of the year, however, the *Volksdeutsche*'s condition improved — this was due in some measure to the superior organization and discipline imposed by the VoMi and other German units, but largely to the special advantages they were accorded. German villages were freed from the necessity of delivering cattle and grain to the Romanians; they were protected from looting; they were allocated German war booty — Soviet horses, tractors, and machines; their fuel problem was taken care of by the authorities; and their ration quotas were higher than those of the neighboring Ukrainians.[69] Inevitably their privileges caused resentment among non-Germans;

---

[66] *Der Deutsche in Transnistrien*, No. 1, July 9, 1942; Beauftragter bei der Heeresgruppe Süd, *op. cit.*

[67] VoMi, Einheir Feldpost 10528, "Rundanweisung Nr. 67," September 9, 1942, N0-5561. See also *Der Deutsche in Transnistrien*, No. 2, July 26, 1942.

[68] "Verhalten der Rumänen," *op. cit.*

[69] VSt Transnistrien, Abt. La, *op. cit.*

the *Volksdeutsche* were themselves aware of it, but entirely unwilling to give up their special status on that account.

The visiting VoMi head, Lorenz, was struck by the improvement when he toured Transnistria in mid-summer 1942. He reported to Himmler that, in administration, economic utilization, private incentive, the food supply, and status in general, the *Volksdeutsche* were "in every respect a model." He urged Himmler to make a trip to see for himself. Even Gottlob Berger, the chief of the SS administrative headquarters in Berlin, noted the contrast between the ethnic Germans in the German-held Ukraine and in Transnistria; at the Führer's headquarters it was asserted that in the Ukraine things were "dead," in Transnistria, "burgeoning life has emerged, in 1942 the number of births has risen substantially, and the economic revival is unmistakable."[70]

German help from then on was minor: once raised to the status of a rural elite, the colonists, though subsisting in semi-isolation, continued rather well off. In 1943, a survey showed them as decidedly better off than other farmers, largely because of the tax exemption they enjoyed. German effort now concentrated on the introduction of home industry and new skills; much of the weaving and spinning equipment confiscated by the Germans in Belgium and Northern France was to be shipped to Transnistria for their use.[71] However, the course of the war forestalled such transfers. The question that loomed above everything else was the transfer of the Germans themselves.

Berlin had never taken a clear-cut position on the future of the *Volksdeutsche* in Transnistria. It sought to have all Germans under its sovereignty; but, as in Italy, it was loath to press for major resettlement from the territory of its allies, especially in wartime. An internal report by the army units initially in charge of the Kuchurgan area reflected a widespread sentiment that "future life and construction were possible only under German sovereignty," and that "many (of the colonists) look forward to resettlement."[72] Whether or not this was wishful thinking, certainly in Berlin there was a school of thought favoring this. A representative of the Four-

---

[70] Berger, "Besprechung im Führerhauptquartier," August 17, 194, N0-2703; Lorenz to RFSS, July 10, 1942, CRS, EAP 161*b-12/193*. See also *Der Deutsche in Transnistrien*, No. 3, August 2, 1942.

[71] German Consulate, Odessa, *op. cit.;* "Heimindustrie in Transnistrien," 1943, CRS, 161b-12/193.

[72] "Schiutzmassnahmen...," *op. cit.*

Year Plan who toured the area in November 1941, reported that former German owners expropriated by the Bolshevik Revolution now sought to reclaim their holdings. Prince Wittgenstein had personally gone to inspect a village formerly a possession of his family. Such men justified their claims as being in the interest of Germany: in German held areas of Russia no private property was being re-established, but it would be well to register all German claims in Transnistria with the Romanians — "should Transnistria remain with Romania, these former German properties would revert into German hands."[73] However, it was clearly premature to do anything about this, and there were, from the Nazi viewpoint, strong objections to reinstating pre-1917 owners. More appealing, though just as chimeric, was a plan connected with the Germanization of the Crimea. The Slavic population of the Crimea and eventually the Tatars were to be moved out; the SS (which handled the planning) looked for "replacements" and stumbled upon the idea of transferring the 140,000 Transnistrian Germans to the Crimea — without their property.[74] The plan was approved in principle, but its execution was postponed. The atmosphere of the times is well reflected in Himmler's comment, in January 1943, at the time of Stalingrad:

> I too am of the opinion that the Transnistrian Germans cannot be transferred before the end of the year. Perhaps, in view of the conditions in Transnistria and the necessity of keeping up the war potential there, it will be possible to transfer them only the year after next.[75]

Such long-range plans were obviously frustrated by the course of the war. The general trend of migration was westward, rather than eastward, even before the tide of war changed. In 1942, a number of *Volksdeutsche* from the Ukraine voluntarily migrated to Transnistria. In Transnistria meanwhile, a consolidation of villages had taken place: the VoMi forcibly moved all ethnic German families living singly in scattered villages among Russians and Ukrainians into consolidated *Volksdeutsche* settlements. More than 200 communities were "emptied" of their few German residents; these Germans were consolidated in 228 villages (and the city of Odessa). This act at last turned the ethnic Germans against their SS overlords in a decisive fashion, in spite of the material advantages they enjoyed.[76]

---

[73] Reiehart, *op. cit.*; Prinz zu Sayn und Wittgenstein, *op. cit.*

[74] Himmler Conference, *op. cit.*

[75] Himmler to HSSPF Russland-Süd, SSPF Krim and RKfdFdV, January 20, NO-2209.

As the Red Army approached Transnistria, the German authorities concentrated their evacuation efforts on the *Volksdeutsche* the VoMi was, after all, expert in the moving of millions. Young men were encouraged to volunteer for the *Waffen-SS* — apparently some did, though they retained their hostility to the anti-Christian tenets of the SS. Others were evacuated wholesale; the cluster of villages around Alexanderstadt and Kronau was removed in late October 1943, going first to Romania and Galicia, then on to Eastern Germany. Almost all the *Volksdeutsche* who remained behind, though oppressed by the reports of lack of care, shelter, and food for the evacuees, felt that they had no choice. The Soviet Union had abolished the Volga-German ASSR early in the war and exiled its population; German residents of the U.S.S.R. seemed to have been proscribed, liquidated, or moved into utter isolation. Thus, when the Soviet onslaught came early in 1944, virtually all of the 135,000 *Volksdeutsche* left their homesteads in Transnistria and moved westward — some succumbed on the way, but most reached Austria or the German-annexed provinces of Western Poland.[77]

The *Volksdeutsche* were a problem primarily to the Soviet regime and to the Nazis. To the residents themselves — both German and non-German — it had not been much of an issue; it only became one because of the policies of the authorities. Rather obviously, the privileges enjoyed by German colonists aroused the resentment of their neighbors, who did not happen to be of German descent but who worked just as hard, or even harder, who had to pay considerably higher taxes, and who enjoyed far less security and had a lower standard of living. The creation of an ethnic elite proved economically possible, but only at the price of arousing profound antagonism in the rest of the population.

The Ethnic Dumping-Ground

Transnistria seemed a convenient dumping-ground to "purifiers" who sought to cleanse Romania of "alien" elements. The gypsies, traditionally a part of the Romanian countryside, were to be ousted; and not

---

[76] Bth. H. Geb. B, Abr. VII, "Lagebericht," October 10, 1942, 051-PS; Koepp, "An der Bugbrücke," *Revaler Zeitung*, November 13, 1942; *Der Deutsche in Transnistrien*, No. 17, November 8, 1942.

[77] Evacuation report from Alexanderstadt and Kronau, October 21, 1943, CRS, EAP 99/47; Beauftragter bei der Heeresgruppe Süd, *op. cit.;* Office of Strategic Services, R&A, No. 2611, "Population Movements of Black-Sea Germans," November 13, 1944, p. 6.

only were Jews to be eliminated from Romanian social and economic life, they were, according to some fanatics, to be moved wholesale into Transnistria.

With the gypsies, the process was relatively simple. With a minimal application of force, it seems, all nomad gypsies (just what the criterion was remains unclear) were, by October 1942, reported to have been exiled, or transplanted, to Transnistria. By implication, the decree had given them a "last chance" to settle and prove themselves law-abiding constructive citizens.[78] Little was heard about them thereafter; perhaps Governor Alexianu's decree of October 1943, converting the army barracks at Birzula into a concentration camp for the re-education of beggars, vagabonds, and nomads was aimed at them.[79]

By the large, the Jewish population of Romania was not involved in the Transnistrian situation, though discrimination and abuse continued. Anti-Semitism had been strong in Romania for a number of years; since 1938, under the Goga regime, "direct action" had been tolerated, even to the point of pogroms. Political fanatics sought the ouster of the Jews or, in Nazi fashion, their liquidation; other circles strove merely for the elimination of Jewish competition and control in Romania's economic life. Even under Antonescu, however, anti-Semitism, though for a while flagrant and open, never assumed Nazi extremes; paradoxically, during the last year or so of his regime, it abated considerably — partly reflecting the growing alienation between Antonescu and the anti-Jewish legionnaires (who[80] had enjoyed German protection), partly revealing Bucharest's preparations for a separate peace.

Even more difficult, and more tragic, was the fate of the Jews in Transnistria itself and of those in Bessarabia and Northern Bucovina, the provinces reannexed to Romania as a result of the Eastern campaign. Of all aspects of the Transnistrian experience, the fate of the Jews has received the most systematic study, and the source materials (though much of it is in Romanian, Yiddish, Hebrew, and Hungarian) are considerably more copious than on other issues. Because of this, and because the significance

---

[78] "Romänien ohne Zigeuner," *Krakauer Zeitung*, October 23, 1942.
[79] *Bukarester Zeitung, October 15, 1943.*
[80] The Yiddish Scientific Institute (YIVO) has a special section on Transnistria in its monumental bibliography project on the late fate of the Jews in World War II now in progress. It can be currently consulted at the YIVO library in New York.

of the question for the present paper is marginal, a relatively condensed account will suffice.[81]

Prewar Transnistria had probably about 300,000 Jews; of these, more than half lived in the city of Odessa. It is commonly estimated that about two-thirds of this number were evacuated eastward before the Red Army abandoned the area; these estimates seem, if anything, a bit too high.[82] Most evacuees were people in official positions or the professions; few, if any, of the poor left.[83] Several refugees confirm that there was a widespread feeling among the Jewish residents who remained that "the Germans can't be so bad" — "I remember them from the First World War" — and that, although there might be some discrimination, the Jews would surely not be exterminated. Soviet silence about German anti-Jewish activities during the Nazi-Soviet Pact and also during the war — a silence which has been commented upon by others in various connections — helped make the Jewish population insufficiently aware of the particular danger they faced (and it was also uncertain whether Odessa would fall to the Germans or to the Romanians) and thus helped doom them.[84]

Their earliest experience of the occupation was not exactly comforting. From the start the Romanians used Jews to clear rubble; columns of them could be seen daily, along with war prisoners, in the Odessa streets. Romania's anti-Semitism, though intense and widespread, was generally neither animal nor systematic. During the first weeks, it is true, *Einsatzgruppe "D"* of the Nazi SD operated in Transnistria, and engaged in the same random wholesale liquidations that it had conducted elsewhere in the occupied East. Nor did the German army itself hesitate to retaliate

---

[81] The most thorough study is Mathias Carp, *Cartea neagră: suferinţele evreilor din România,* SOCEC, Bucharest, 1947. Two good English summaries, though each containing errors, are: Joseph B. Schechtman, "The Transnistria Reservation," *YIVO Annual of Jewish Social Science,* New York, Vol. 8, 1953, pp. 178-196, and Gerald Reitlinger, *The Final Solution,* Beechhurst, New York, 1953. For a dramatic account, see Curzio Malaparte, *Kaputt,* Dutton, New York, 1946.

[82] It is, of course, dangerous to arrive at the figure by deducting the number of Jews registered under the Romanians from the prewar figure. Many Jew's concealed their racial or religious affiliation. Even after the ghetto was established, one informant guesses, there must have been over 10,000 Jews living illegally in Odessa. Moreover, the category of Karaims (Tatars by race, though Jews by faith), who were not subject to persecution, mysteriously grew to several thousand in Transnistria — obviously a convenient cloak for Jewish residents (Interview A).

[83] Schechtman, *op cit.,* p. 180; Reitlinger, *op. cit.,* pp. 239-240.

[84] Interview A; Peterle, *op cit.*

for sabotage or subversion, real or presumed, by Jews (as in the case of Kodyma, cited earlier); it also instituted the customary yellow stars and other external stigmata that set the Jewish population apart, preparatory to its physical segregation.[85]

However, the Germans' stay was brief, and did not affect the area of major Jewish residence near the Black Sea. This was the Romanians' chore. Their approach was at first ambivalent. The troops looted indiscriminately anyway and did not need a special moral justification, as had the Germans, to appropriate the goods of Jews. Anti-Jewish feeling was common among the soldiers but not necessarily virulent, and was often much subordinated to other emotions and aspirations.[86] The blowing up of the NKVD building by a Soviet agent, the week after Odessa fell, precipitated the first draconic "retaliation." Actually, there is no conclusive evidence that Jews inspired it (though the Romanians claimed that the Great Synagogue was a headquarters of resistance) or even participated in anti-Axis acts. But after the explosion long columns of men and women were led down the streets to the port and to the suburbs, and were shot summarily by the hundreds. By October 23, there were over 5,000 victims of retaliatory terror, mostly Jews; and by the end of the month, there were over 20,000 dead.[87]

This sudden and rather panicky response was succeeded by an order, on November 7, 1941, ordering all male Jews from 18 to 50 years of age to report to the city jail within 48 hours. On November 11, came Alexianu's Ordinance No. 23, providing for the establishment of ghettoes and concentration camps in Transnistria. The order, an analyst correctly suggests, made of the province "a gigantic penal colony." The Jews in each community were set up, in effect, as a closed colony; they could not leave without permission, on pain of being shot. Group leaders were appointed to be responsible for every twenty residents. New wage scales were set

---

[85] *Rumänisches Blut....* p. 175; Beauftragter des Chefs der SiPo..., *op. cit.;* O.K. Ananjew, *op. cit.*

[86] Curiously, the Romanians insisted to their German allies that they *were* anti-Semitic. Allegations that they were really not (advanced, for instance, by Heydrich, Himmler's right-hand man) were rebutted, citing the Romanian pogrom in Iași after its reoccupation, and other details. The Romanian envoy in Berlin likewise explained to the foreign office that such German claims were erroneous (Killinger to Auswärtiges Amt, September 1, 1941, and Erdmannsdorff, memorandum, October 15, 1941, Document NG-3989).

[87] Petr Ershov, "Odesskaia tragediia," *Biulleten' odesskovo zemlinchestvn,* New York, 1953, No.6; Peterle, *op. cit.;* Reitlinger, *op. cit.,* p. 240; Carp, *op. cit.,* Vol. 3, p. 199.

providing for lower compensation for Jewish labor. A Russian refugee from Odessa recalls the catastrophe:

> In November the formation of ghettoes was proclaimed. Now there began suicides; physicians, jurists, teachers drowned or hanged themselves, leaving behind brief tragic notes. A few went insane. Those being chased into the ghettoes marched as in a funeral procession from their homesteads to their new residences (Dal'nik, Slobodka, etc.). Whole families, from the gray-haired grandfather on down, walked with solemn, stony faces into the unknown, into suffering. Little children silently staggered along, not understanding what went on. And then... then some wound up in some barns in Dal'nik, which were put on fire at night. The people tried to break out, jump out of the windows: they were shot, they burned alive. Many thousands died. In the coldest days of December and especially January (1942), they began to transfer the Jews on cold freight cars from Odessa-Sortirovochnaia to Berezovka Rayon. The people froze to death in the cold cars, and at the destination they were lifted out like planks and buried in mass graves...[88]

Berezovka became one of the centers in which Jews from Odessa were resettled. Odessa, with a prewar Jewish population (officially) of about 175,000, in 1943 had only 54 Jews living there legally — all in a small ghetto operating as a government workshop. Conditions in ghettoes ranged from execrable to tolerable. Health and sanitary standards were exceedingly low, and epidemics and mortality were high. Intellectuals suffered from enforced idleness. Little communication or contact with the outside world was permitted, though the Romanians could be bribed to allow an occasional food parcel to arrive, to let an inmate sell a ring or diamond, and certainly to desist from physical annihilation.[89]

A curious side-story pertained to a Romanian attempt to push some 70,000 Jews from Transnistria into the neighboring German-controlled Ukraine. In February 1942, the Rosenberg Ministry and Foreign Office in Berlin were notified that the first 10,000 or so had actually been shoved across the Bug "illegally" in the area of Voznesensk. Berlin promptly asked the transfer to be stopped, if only because of the danger of typhoid epidemics. The SS "specialist" on Jewish affairs, Eichmann, notified the Foreign Office in April that, while Berlin approved of the Romanian effort to

---

[88] Carp, *op. cit.,* Vol. 3, p. 200; OVOV, Vol. 2, p. 7; Schechtman, *op. cit.,* p. 180.
[89] Schechtman, pp. 182-184; Carp, *op. cit.*

get rid of the Jews, this particular operation was dangerous, chaotic, uncoordinated, and hence objectionable. If the Romanians failed to stop the transfer, the SD was to be free to shoot the Jews. By mid-May 1942, the problem was over; the Romanians had complied. As the German official in Nikolaev reported, by then many of the evacuees had died, while some of the others were shipped back to the Odessa area.[90]

Romanian "laxity" (a term which can be used only with considerable reservations in this particular context) provoked Nazi reprimands. A minor reason for Romanian "indulgences" was that some branches of the economy in Transnistria would have been paralyzed if all Jewish artisans had been barred from work. More important, bribery — even of convinced anti-Semites — and personal sympathy did produce numerous exceptions to the overwhelming tragedy taking place. The property of evacuated and killed Jews was looted or formally reassigned to others. Even marble tombstones were removed from the Odessa Jewish cemetery. The Hoffmeyer-Alexianu agreement of August 1942, permitted ethnic Germans in Odessa to occupy the apartments of "departed" Jews, against payment for furniture to the Romanian authorities. In October 1942, it was announced that a mixed Romanian-German commission would check, inventory, and reassign Jewish property confiscated or looted in Odessa. Oddly enough, however, some indigenous Jews were employed by the Odessa police and other official agencies and Romanian Jews were given temporary permits quite legally to visit Odessa, for purposes of trade.[91]

The attitude of the Odessa population toward these events cannot be easily summarized. It would be erroneous to deny the existence of anti-Semitism. It would be equally false to attribute to non-Jews any general jubilation over the Jews' fate — a fate that decimated their numbers to a point where, in September 1943, there were officially only some 32,000 of Transnistria's Jews left alive.[92] Contemporary documents speak of the help the Ukrainian auxiliary police — which was full of unscrupulous opportunists — gave the authorities in the persecution of Jews; refugees

---

[90] Reitlinger, op. cit., pp. 401-402; AA, Luther, memorandum, February 11, 1942, RSHA IV B 4a (Eichmann) to AA, April 14, 1942, and AA (Rademacher) memorandum, May 12, 1942, NG-4817; RMfdb0., D III (Bräutigam) to AA, March 11, 1942, 3319-PS, *Trial of the Major War Criminals,* Vol, 32, pp. 183-184.

[91] SD Report 100; interviews B and E; Berg, *op. cit.;* Prost, *op. cit.,* p. 163, *Der Deutsche in Transnistrien,* No. 12, October 4, 1942; VoMi "Rondanweisung," *op. cit.*

[92] Schechtman, *op. cit.,* p. 191.

report a flood of denunciations (both truthful and false) of Jews to the new regime; as indicated above, groups of youngsters had voiced anti-Jewish slogans even before the Soviet order collapsed.[93] The semi-criminal fringe of the population was responsible for much of this. Some of it stemmed from enmity, some of it from a desire to ingratiate oneself, and other personal considerations. Anti-Semitism was apparently least active in intellectual circles (evidence on rural life is too scant to permit inferences). Some of the freshly-baked white-collar collaborators, however, in their initial zeal readily subscribed to appeals which indicted the Jews as germ-carriers or even progenitors of Bolshevism.

On the other side of the ledger must be placed the numerous examples of concealment and help offered to individual Jews by non-Jewish residents of Transnistria. The first German intelligence report after the capture of Odessa unequivocally indicates that "during the first days the population... proceeded toward the Jews with relative loyalty." The official Soviet postwar investigation of conditions in Transnistria contains the store of a lawyer the Siguranța prosecuted in the summer of 1942 for hiding Jews. A refugee writes:

> One must say, to the credit of the remaining population, that there were courageous people in town and county, who helped the (Jewish) survivors for long periods of time; and this at a time when punishment for such help was severe... Objectivity requires one to note that the broad masses experienced these days (the extermination of the Jews) with a sense of shame, horror, and despair, and this helped determine their attitude toward the occupying authorities.

At times, to be sure, there was a self-concerned element in their horror. When a woman on an Odessa streetcar joked about the anti-Jewish measures, one day in 1942, another woman loudly responded: "What are you rejoicing about? Today it's they, and tomorrow it'll be we." Yet there was more to it. As earlier noted, the viciously anti-Semitic series of articles in *Molva* prompted a decline in its circulation. Several theatrical managers and directors were known to have Jews among their personnel; the wife of Seliavin, the opera director, was Jewish; and one of the accusations leveled against Vronskii, it has been seen, was that he concealed Jews in his theater. Refugees report that individual Jews managed to stay for months in

---

[93] Interviews A and C; O.K. Snigerewka, "Lage," October 5, 1941, CRS, Korück 20383/10.

the city on various tasks, without being denounced to the authorities, though usually fear led their Gentile acquaintances to stay away from them in private and in public.[94]

The most dramatic act was the transfer of Jews from Bessarabia and Bucovina to Transnistria. In line with the view of Transnistria as a "dumping-ground," the Romanian government decided on the wholesale removal of the Jewish population from the re-annexed provinces by force — this decision came at a time when Jews resident in Romania proper, though they suffered from discriminations, were free not only to engage in business but to go to Odessa. As early as August 1941, the SD reported, rich Jews were given a chance to buy themselves free (i.e., bribe officials); the rest were chased across the Dnestr into Transnistria — then still German-held. The Germans refused to accept them. In the words of the SD report, they were

> ...chased back and forth until they dropped... Old men and women lay along the road at short distances from each other... Up to the blocking of the Dnestr bridges the Romanians drove about 35,000 Jews into the area east of the Dnestr, which was a German sphere until August 28, 1941. As earlier reported, some 37,500 Jews were taken back to Romanian soil at Mogilev-Podol'ski and Iampol'...[95]

The wholesale migration from Bucovina and Bessarabia began in October 1941, and involved well over 110,000 persons. Inevitably, organizing them and housing and feeding them in Transnistria raised severe problems, and there were epidemics. The evacuees suffered untold hardships; some 28,000, quartered in ethnic German villages, were simply liquidated. Of the more than 110,000 known evacuees, only some 77,000 were alive in March 1943; by September 1943, their number had dropped to 50,000.[96] By August 1942, when the transfer was almost complete, Bucharest announced that eventually "all Romanian Jews will be deported to Russia," presumably hoping that some could be dumped east of Transnistria, in German-held soil. Individuals from Bucharest and other urban areas were now likewise exiled to Transnistria, of course with-

---

[94] Abwehrstelle Rumänien, "Bericht über Wahrnehmungen in Odessa," November 4, 1941, CRS, DHMR 29222; Document USSR-47; Peterle, *op. cit.;* Manuilov, p. 68; interviews A, C, and D.

[95] Beauftragter des Chefs der SiPo u.SD, "Bericht... Besatzungstruppen," September 2, 1941.

[96] The district of Mogilev had more than half the survivors, and Balta a quarter of them. The districts of Odessa and Berezovka had fewer than 1 per cent each.

out their belongings. Illegal return to Romania was punishable by death. Conditions were miserable — partly from policy, but more often from the carelessness of lower-level Romanian officials responsible for the evacuees. The mortality rate soared. There were many thousands of orphans.[97]

Yet the amazing thing was the inconsistency of Romanian policy. In January 1942, Bucharest sanctioned a central agency for the evacuees. In mid-1942, the agency called for an inquiry by the International Red Cross. Official Bucharest at first reneged, but it did authorize the dispatch of a committee from Romania to investigate the condition of the Jews. Meanwhile foreign agencies had been given at least some information. The investigating committee was received by Alexianu and given a chance to inspect the major Jewish communities, to gather statistics, and to talk to Jewish residents. Its report was made available to the World Jewish Congress. The Red Cross, in Geneva, became interested in the evacuees' fate and in 1943 began to dispatch some food to help them.

A reversal in Romanian policy on the Jews came about gradually. In 1942, the Queen Mother and the Romanian Orthodox Church apparently applied pressure on Mihai Antonescu to relax the anti-Semitic course. As the estrangement between the Conducător and Legionnaires became more complete, his zeal for anti-Jewish action decreased. After Stalingrad, when Bucharest started thinking more and more concretely about a separate peace, such a relaxation was deemed a "good-will" token toward the Allies. In 1943, the evacuees were decidedly better off; mortality and epidemics declined; the birth rate even increased. Toward the end of 1943, as the Red Army rapidly approached the borders of Transnistria, the whole problem of the Jewish exiles had to be reconsidered.[98] In November, it was discussed by the Romanian cabinet: it turned out that no one knew just how many people were involved. Antonescu, the stenographic minutes of the

---

[97] Reitlinger, *op. cit.,* pp. 394-399; Schechtman, *op. cit.,* pp. 180-191; Carp, *op. cit.,* Vol. 3, p. 438; Lemkin, *op. cit.,* pp. 240, 565; *Hitler's Europe,* p. 616; Ihnen, *op. cit.*; *Krakauer Zeitung,* August 13, 1942; NG-4817; 3319-PS.

[98] In May, 1943, German Ambassador von Killinger had wired Berlin from Bucharest that the International Red Cross had inquired whether Antonescu would support the emigration of Jews from Transnistria on ships supplied by the Red Cross. Antonescu, Killinger reported, who feels "the concentration of Jews in Transnistria is undesirable and who definitely wants to be rid of the Jews, is said to have replied that... a new (and favorable) situation obtained if Red Cross, and not Romanian, shipping were involved." Berlin instructed Killinger to try to keep the Romanians from letting the Jews go; Germany would "take them off their hands," ostensibly so they could be used as labor in the East (Auswärtiges Amt, Inland II (von Thadden), "Vortragsnotiz," June 1, 1943, Document NG-3987).

session indicate, opposed German pressure for the Jews' extermination. Now, to prevent their falling into Soviet hands, he agreed to re-admit them to Romania (except for Communists among them). The following month, a delegate of the Swiss Red Cross, Charles Kolb, was received by Mihai Antonescu and given permission to tour Transnistria for ten days. Unfortunately, his report on conditions is not available, but it produced a Romanian retreat. In January 1944, the Romanians made a "compensation agreement" with the Jewish community in Bucharest. One of its provisions allowed Jewish exiles to return if they paid for their own railroad ticket and a high fee for a valid passport. Actually, only few managed to be repatriated; a few hundred more were shipped off to Palestine; the Joint Distribution Committee and the Jewish Agency for Palestine were allowed to care for the remainder. Bucharest had completely reversed its policy.[99]

The whole problem of evacuees affected the native Transnistrian community but little. The average resident had only a hazy idea of what was going on. He was, however, aware that here was another instance of mass discrimination and that his homeland was being made the "compost heap" of the Greater Romania. Such a realization could not but instill fear and revulsion.

Appendix: Forced Labor in Transnistria

Of all the measures adopted under German occupation, probably the most destructive of popular allegiance was the forced labor system. From the spring of 1942 to the end of the occupation, literally millions of men and women were forcibly conscripted and moved to the Reich to work under conditions that were materially and morally abominable.[100] The residents of Transnistria knew of the atrocities and the fate of these forced laborers. Somehow, the Soviet-bred grapevine operated; some escapees from the German-held areas gave details; and Soviet propaganda, for once, needed to exaggerate little to instill genuine terror in the population.[101]

The population of Odessa could not but indulge in some self-congratulation that it had escaped this experience; outside Transnistria the

---

[99] Schechtman, *op. cit.,* pp. 184, 187-196; Reitlinger, op. cit., pp. 401-409; "Auszug aus dem Stenogramm über die Sitzung des Ministerrates vom 17. November 1943," YIVO, Occ E5a-5; AA, Inland II, "Vortragsnotiz," June 1, 1943, NG-3987.

[100] For a discussion, see chapter XX in Dallin, *German Rule in Russia, 1941-1945.*

[101] Manuilov, p. 106.

only escape was into partisan-held territory. It is true that there were hazards even in Transnistria. Without the consent of the Romanian authorities, the German liaison officer of the economic staff in Odessa had started recruiting for labor work in Germany. As soon as this was brought to the attention of the Transnistrian authorities, Governor Alexianu protested to the Germans and forbade further recruitment, even ostensibly voluntary recruitment; he did, however, permit the 800 men and women already conscripted to depart for the Reich. When Major General Nagel of *Wirtschaftsstab Ost* (the German staff in charge of economic exploitation) visited Odessa on an inspection tour in June 1942, the situation was regularized and in effect forced labor recruitment was killed: Nagel upbraided the officer involved for acting without the consent of the Romanians; henceforth, it was agreed with the Governor's office, recruitment would be only oral; no German publicity for it was to be permitted; and since no separate recruitment offices were to be set up, the forced labor draft — or whatever volunteering for it might occur — would be handled through the German consulate general just then being established. For all intents and purposes, this was the end of the *Ostarbeiter* program in Transnistria.[102]

Another type of forced labor for the Germans was in effect for a brief period during the harvest season of 1942. To relieve the shortage of manpower in the German-held Ukraine, the Germans requested workers, and 40,000 Transnistrian residents were placed at the disposal of the *Reichskommissariat* Ukraine to help with the harvest. What their fate was cannot be determined; presumably they returned home after completing their task.[103] There is no indication that this gesture, which yielded the Romanians nothing, was ever repeated.

The Romanians had their own equivalent of forced labor. It was not as brutal, as forcible, and as catastrophic as the German, but it was real enough. On November 26, 1941 (just as the Germans were about to decree that compulsory labor would be required of all able-bodied residents in their occupied areas), Alexianu issued an order compelling all residents from 16 to 60 years of age to spend up to a maximum of sixty work days a year on tasks set by the regime.[104] In practice it was not as universal

---

[102] Gen Wi Ost, "Reisebericht... 8.-16.6.42," and Rue IVc, memorandum, June 3, 1942, CRS, Wi/ID 2.408.

[103] Vierjahresplan, GB. Arb., "Einsatz von Ostarbeitern aus Transnistrien im Reich," October 29, 1942, NG-1298.

as it appeared on paper. Not only did school attendance and government work provide exemption (as discussed earlier), but bribery to get immunity from forced labor was institutionalized. An official tariff was set: 20 marks a day for men and 15 marks a day for women (plus an initial administrative fee of 25 marks) was considered equivalent to — and a legitimate substitute for — compulsory labor. Evasion by paying the fee was extensively resorted to; an official German report reveals that the Directorate of Labor made 8,000 marks in a single day from this source.[105]

In October 1942, the Romanians announced plans to establish a Transnistrian "labor army," which was to give all males over 20 years of age one year of training; Jews were to be exempted. Presumably it was to involve semi-military instruction and would increase the physical fitness of the trainees, who were to receive dark brown uniforms. Actually, the plan remained pretty much on paper.[106]

There were compulsory labor contingents in Transnistria, engaged to a large extent in repairing war damage and restoring to operation facilities ranging from trolleys to industrial plants. In the fall of 1943, with shortages becoming more severe, the Romanians revoked the general exemption for students; at that time girls were sent in considerable numbers for a week's harvest work to the country — and, according to one of their instructors, returned rather satisfied, tanned, and none the worse for the experience.[107]

In the last months of the occupation when the Germans took direct charge of the province, they reported no difficulty in finding labor where they needed it for last-minute defense and construction work throughout the hinterland. Only in the city of Odessa itself were there problems. "The

---

[104] The stipulations of this decree, too, reflected the attempt to legislate social inequality. While "plain people" were theoretically obliged to contribute sixty days of work, certain classes of white-collar workers, managers, and entrepreneurs were given smaller loads, varying from eighteen to forty-eight days, according to the putative social status or importance or their position (U.S. Legation Stockholm, Despatch No. 2332, "Conditions in Transnistria in the first half of 1943, as reflected in the German-controlled press," October 20, 1943, OSS Document 52850).

[105] OVOV, Vol. 2, pp. 8-9; Ihnen, *op. cit.*; interview A; Tverskoi; gh, "Transnitrien," *Das Reich*, August 1, 1943; *Frankfurter Zeitung*. December 1, 1941.

[106] *Curentul*, Bucharest, October 1, 1942, reported by Havas, October 3, 1942.

[107] Interviews C and E. Individual instances of similar practices were reported as early as June, 1942 (cf. *Molva*, No. 178, July 11, 1942).

labor force was secured with the assistance of military administration officials installed at the prefecture..." They did not have the "requisite security forces," they admitted, "to engage in measures of compulsion."[108]

Some managed to get out of doing such service for the Germans; others did not. The last-minute effort forcibly to evacuate labor, and especially specialists, westward through Romania — an effort begun by the Germans weeks after it was impossible to assure decent conditions — met with an exceedingly mixed response. The overwhelming majority of workers preferred to stay where they were and take their chances with the Soviet regime.

The intensity and ever-presence of feeling about forced labor under the Germans, and its near-absence under the Romanians, goes a long way to explain the difference in public temper and allegiance between the German-held U.S.S.R. and Transnistria.

---

[108] AOK 6, AWiFü, "Lagebericht," April 23, 1944, CRS, Wi/ID 2.361; H. Gr. A, Wi-Abt, "Lagebericht für den Monat February 1944," March 1, 1944, and H.Gr. Südukraine, Wi-Abr, "Beitrag zum Monatsbericht," April 10, 1944, CRS, Wi/ID.201.

Another experience, which later turned out to have left a profoundly hostile impact on the population, was the transshipment, in the winter of 1943-1944, of children recruited for labor battalions in the Reich. The children were brought from the German-occupied Ukraine westward by way of Odessa (Richard E. Lauterbach, *These Are the Russians,* Harper & Brothers, 1945, p. 87).

Chapter VI

Moscow's Long Arm

The Opportunities

With the departure of the Soviet authorities from Odessa and the collapse of military resistance, "Soviet power" vanished from Transnistria. Most stalwart Communists had been evacuated with their agencies, plants, or army units. Institutions and symbols of allegiance disappeared; only intangibles remained: memories, hopes, and fears. These, intermingled with new impressions and attitudes, soon gave birth to distortions of memory, upsurges of hope, fits of terror, all fertilized by an abundance of rumors. Some rumors, some reactions were implanted or spread by Soviet agents; but many more were communicated by those who were themselves utterly unaware of doing so. Much of the reversal of opinions and attitudes from the fall of 1941 to the spring of 1944 was spontaneous; it came about as a natural consequence of personal experiences and the impact of military and political events. But Moscow, in an effort to speed and intensify these processes, sought to play the part of history's midwife, ready, if need be, to perform drastic surgery to assure the victory of the cause.

For this the Soviet authorities needed active, reliable adherents in Transnistria. Because of the evacuation of many faithful followers, the studied passivity and submergence of others, and the genuine defection of still others, the establishment of trustworthy cadres even for partisan warfare, agent's work, and intelligence operations in Transnistria was difficult.¹ Partisans and agents were of three categories: (1) stay-behinds who had been so designated in advance of the Soviet retreat; (2) military stragglers and civilians selected by the stay-behinds to augment their own contingents; and (3) men and women sent into Transnistria from the outside.

Unfortunately, the evidence on this whole complex of problems is highly inadequate. Romanian records are not available, and Soviet accounts are notoriously untrustworthy on this subject. Few Soviet memoirs or semi-historical works on Transnistria and the partisan movement there have appeared, perhaps because there was very little (in terms of numbers involved and accomplishment) to write about.

Here and there small partisan groups began to operate even while military operations were in progress, primarily for military purposes and at the behest of the Red Army. On September 28, 1941, while the siege of Odessa was in progress, the Romanians uncovered a five-man team in Alexandrovka and captured its head, Grigori Kutsov. The group, trained by a lieutenant and politruk (Army "political assistant") in Ovidiopol', had been sent into the Gross-Liebental area to determine artillery installations and report their location to Red Army units on the east bank of the Sukhoi Liman, to make attacks on enemy troops, particularly on German soldiers, to cur telephone wires, and the like — primarily reconnaissance and intelligence tasks, which were to be performed in civilian clothes. All five men probably either belonged to the militia in Ovidiopol' or had been recruited into the local destruction detachment.² The German report on Kutsov's capture states that "it is noteworthy that the population gave no support whatever to the partisan group."³

Others had tasks of a more permanent or political character. It is hard to say what was behind such instances as the reported arrest, two days after the Romanians arrived, of a 68-year-old woman who was caught just as she was ostensibly about to blow up the Odessa public market hall.⁴ From the first, the Romanians were warned by anti-Soviet elements that the Red Army or NKVD had, before leaving, mined a number of key

---

[1] The behavior and treatment of former Communists who remained "on the surface" in Transnistria are discussed in Chapters III and V.

[2] In addition to Kutsov, the group consisted of a *Volksadeutscher*, Albert Georg Diehl; a Jew, Isaak Likhtengaus; a Russian with the pseudonym of Pius, presumably the political officer; and a Ukrainian sergeant from Ovidiopol', Kretsenko.

[3] Chefb SiPo u. SD, "Ereignismeldungen UdSSR Nr. 117," October 18, 1941; *ibid.*, Nr. 136," November 21, 1941.

[4] *Bukarester Tageblatt*, October 22, 1941.

buildings. Reportedly the opera house was mined, but an employee familiar with the wiring had led detonation specialists to where they could disconnect the mines before they went off — this story recurs several times but without conclusive confirmation.[5]

Both to the residents of Odessa and to the occupying authorities, the first — and, as it turned out, the last — major shock and panic-engendering experience was the explosion of the Odessa NKVD. The story is best related by the official report submitted confidentially by the German intelligence branch office in Romania, which dispatched an officer to investigate the occurrence:

> Until October 22 (1941), the entire military life of (Romanian-held) Odessa took place on Engels Street. The Romanian komman-datura was established there in the building of the NKVD administration. Under the Bolsheviks the neighboring houses were inhabited exclusively by privileged individuals. From the first moment of the city's occupation, the Romanian intelligence service had informed the command that captured materials warranted warnings that all the buildings on Engels Street had been mined. On Tuesday, October 21, the building of the Romanian kommandatura was momentarily evacuated on the basis of an alarming rumor. About 3:30 p.m. on October 22, two Communists reportedly again appeared with warnings that the building would be blown up within the next half hour. Not enough attention was paid to this report. At 5:50, the building actually blew up... Up to the time of my departure, 46 corpses had been found, including 21 officers; a further number is expected...
>
> There is no doubt that the explosion was set off long-distance by electrical (?) means. In the morning of October 23, a complete telephone installation was found under the bed of a Jew in the immediate vicinity of the blown-up building; the telephone apparently led to NKVD men hiding in the catacombs; its owner stated that the direction of partisan activities came from the catacombs.[6]

The explosion was apparently believed due not to booby-traps but to delayed-action "bombs" (i.e., mines).[7] That such devices were left behind

---

[5] Interview B; Poppenberger, "Das Land am Ostufer des Dnjestrs," *op. cit.* See also Luigi Cuecco in *Corriere della Sera*, October 21, 1941.

[6] Abwehrstelle Rumänien, "Bericht über Wahrnehmungen in Odessa," November 4, 1941, CRS, DHMR 29222.

The catacombs will be discussed below.

was confirmed by a later *Abwehr* report on the discovery, in the port of Odessa, of an explosive charge in a cellar:

> Two wires stuck out of the cemented cellar floor, leading to the electric wiring system, which however was not connected. Upon removal of a cement layer about 5 cm. thick, 20 to 25 kg. of toluol (TNT) was found connected with the electric priming device as well as an ignition system responding to pressure. The latter would have been set off upon application of 60 to 70 kg. of weight on top of the cement layer, i.e., if accidentally a man had stood on top of it.[8]

It appears more likely, however, that the NKVD building explosion was set off by Soviet agents left behind in the city. Such is also the version circulated by Moscow, though in a much-embroidered and rather impossible form. Kataev, in his hotel of wartime Odessa, has his hero Druzhinin (patterned after Badaev, a partisan leader described below) set off the explosion from a concealed position miles away, in the Shevchenko Park. Subsequent Soviet accounts attributed the explosion to "partisans." Other official publications add the further fiction that the blast took place during a banquet at which the Germans were turning over the administration of Transnistria to the Romanians; according to this version, six generals, the police prefect, and 57 soldiers were killed.[9] Actually, in the number of casualties this was fairly close. Romanian records show that those killed included General Gl. Glogoianu, the original city commandant, 16 officers, 35 soldiers, and 9 civilian officials. Four German naval officers and two interpreters were among the victims. The building was completely wrecked, and glass was shattered within several blocks of the building.[10]

It goes without saying that the explosion was the major topic of conversation in Odessa. If it was meant to be a reminder of the continued presence of Soviet eyes and ears, it was indeed successful. This and subsequent acts of sabotage[11] caused enough nervousness so that Romanian officers stayed away from the opening performance of the Odessa opera

---

[7] Paul Leverkuhn, *German Military Intelligence*, Weidenfeld and Nicolson, London, 1954, p. 62.

[8] OKW/Ausland/Abwehr, "Russland — Verminung von Gebäuden in Odessa," April 17, 1942, CRS, 227 ID 21496/4.

[9] Kataev, *op. cit.*, p. 217; Borisov, *op. cit.*, p. 52; V.M. Kononenko, *Chernomortsy v boiakh za osvobozhdenie Kryma i Odessy*, Voenizdat, Moscow, 1954, p. 32.

[10] Carp, *Transnistria*, Vol. 3, p. 199; Abwehrstelle Rumänien, *op. cit.*; Manuilov, p. 40; Ihnen, *op. cit.*

two months later. The same jitteriness spread to civilians, however; if the blast was meant to rally the people of Odessa to the Soviet cause, it backfired miserably: residents looked on the explosion as pointless and as disrupting the modicum of order that was being established; and it provoked a most cruel and indiscriminate retaliation, the mass murder by the Romanians of innocent civilians. It was this incident that led to the first wave of public hangings and the first mass extermination of Jews; its consequence was a total of over 20,000 victims! And for the future, 200 hostages were to be shot for *every* officer killed, and 100 for every soldier. Such a result, deliberately provoked, made no sense if the Soviets hoped to enlist the help of civilians or looked forward to an early return (the whole scorched-earth policy suggested that they did not). It made sense only if they sought to promote and intensity an "inevitable" conflict between the people and their "temporary occupiers."[12]

The Odessa Catacombs

Even as far back as the Turkish days, Odessa was built over an intricate network of passageways and underground mines tunneled into the spongy rock that served as building material for the city. At one time pirates, later contraband smugglers, had found shelter in these low corridors. Individual foes of the Soviet regime, as well as persons sought as criminals, were said to have taken refuge there in the thirties. Estimated to be over 200 kilometers in length (though much of it not high enough to walk through), the catacombs were known to have over 160 exits — some of them leading into cellars of old patrician houses in the city, others into water wells, still others into suburban fields and cemeteries. No precise map of the system existed, and few dared to go into the catacombs without a trustworthy guide.

It was natural to leave here, in the *very* heart of the enemy's area, an active underground with supplies, arms, food, and radio communication with Soviet headquarters — close enough to strike out and gather intelligence, yet relatively secure. This plan was particularly appealing as the terrain of most of Transnistria was in no sense suspicious to partisan warfare,

---

[11] These reportedly included the burning down of a number of buildings in the center of town, such as the famous Café Fankoni, the former building of the Credit Lyonnais, the Petrokokino store on Grecheskaia, and others in the area of Deribasovskaia, Lanzheron, and Sadovaia (Manuilov, pp. 42-43).

[12] Carp, *loc. cit.;* Abwehrstelle Rumänien, *op. cit.;* Manuilov, p. 42; Ihnen, *op. cit.*

being neither swampy nor woody (except in the north and northwest). Thus, the Odessa catacombs became the headquarters of the local partisans, or more correctly, stay-behind agents; different groups hid there, sometimes unknown to each other; agents who had to disappear from the "surface" found refuge there; and at least sporadic contact was maintained between the catacombs and higher headquarters on the Soviet side of the front.

The exploits and tragedies of the catacomb dwellers are the stuff of which drama is made, and it is not surprising that the only realistic account should have been written by a prominent Soviet author, Valentin Kataev, in the form of a novel, on the basis of research on the spot after the war. Although it adhered to the official ethic, Kataev's novel proved to be so "realistic" that it attracted the ire of the party authorities and was rewritten to order. The first, unrevised edition provides the best available information on the catacombs — in spite of a good deal of "dramatic effect," exaggeration, and the excessive steadfastness and loyalty of his protagonists. His account, due exceptions made, tallies generally with stories from refugees and with what little there is in German and Romanian wartime sources.[13]

The story of the catacomb underground[14] starts shortly before the evacuation of the city. The party oblast committee selected a few men, probably those active in the destruction battalions, to represent the obkom on the spot and to direct small underground groups, one for each rayon of the city and its environs. It is likely that the local NKVD participated in the decision-making, and almost certainly each team included at least one representative or agent of the State Security system.[15] The nucleus often included one or two women, who functioned as cook, nurse, supply-keeper, and sometimes radio operator. Most of the people in underground groups were members of the party or, if youngsters, brought along as messengers or for other tasks, of the Komsomol or Pioneers. Though apparently against great odds, in view of the secrecy of their task and the last

---

[13] Kataev inspected the Odessa catacombs soon after their recapture, and shortly thereafter published a preliminary, factual account, "Katakomby," in the Odessa almanac, *Geroicheskaia Odessa* (1945). Clearly, this experience inspired the subsequent writing of *For Soviet Power!* The 1945 account (as reprinted in OVOV, Vol. 2, pp. 214-230) shows that some of the passages for which Kataev was harshly attacked a few years later (for instance, the song of the partisans in the catacombs) were historical, rather than invented by the author.

[14] The following is based on Kataev, *op. cit.;* OVOV, Vol. 2, pp. xii, 168-169, 242; Manuilov, p. 44; and Abwehrstelle Rumänien, *op. cit.*

minute chaos, each group leader was enabled to secure considerable stores of equipment, arms, food, and a variety of items ranging from candles and batteries, radio tubes and matches, to typewriter ribbons and darning needles. No one, however, expected the underground denizens to stay in the catacombs for more than a few weeks or months; at least, plans did not call for a longer stay.

The human problems of adjustment to underground life are of little relevance to the present study. The composition of the groups is of some interest. The model of Kataev's hero, the group leader of a suburban rayon, was S.F. Lazarev, the first secretary; one of his aides was reportedly second secretary of another raikom, ordered by the obkom to stay; a third was an old Bolshevik and Party instructor; a fourth, deputy chairman of the rayon soviet. The obkom appears as the organizing unit but as having evacuated — an impression which more recent Soviet accounts seek to "correct," by implying the obkom went underground too.

At first the catacomb dwellers were rather idle: they listened to Moscow radio; they reported by wireless to the obkom (at the time located, it would seem, in Sevastopol) every five days about political events, intelligence gathered, and general morale in Odessa; they sporadically were in contact with operatives "above ground," who acted as part-time agents or informants of the underground. As time went on, it became clear that not all was well with the underground. Not only were there inevitable shortages — some of them critical; not only had the sojourn dragged out far longer than anticipated, but the occupation authorities were making determined attempts to track them down. Many Romanian attempts were unsuccessful, but occasionally they would make a real "catch." Most inter-

---

[15] In addition, the NKVD left some of its own personnel in Odessa, e.g., the head of its Operative Section, Aizenberg; a Civil War partisan, Vasilii Vorakov, and (according to the Germans), a procurator, Belousov, who had worked in Kiev until the outbreak of war. Supposedly some NKVD personnel received special training before being returned to Odessa or else pretended to have been evacuated. Thus (a German document claimed) the head of the Central Prison in Odessa, Fedor Kuz'mich Fedorov, was sent to Balaklava in July 1941, to attend a special training course (presumably organized by the NKVD) and returned to Odessa in October with the mission of opening a commissionary store when the Germans arrived as a cover for agent's work. Another, Miaskovski, director of cold storage at the Odessa meat *kombinat*, was ordered to stay in Odessa under his real name, pretend to be disillusioned with the Soviet regime, and not to deny his former Party membership — while actually sabotaging the meat industry (German records, primarily HGr. Süd, Ic/AO, Bavarian Military Archives, Munich, cited in D.I. Karov, "Sovetskoe podpol'noe i partizanskoe dvizhenie v Odesse i Odesskoi oblasti v voinu 1941-45 gg." (MS), Institute for the Study of the U.S.S.R., Munich, 1955, pp. 7, 10-11).

esting in this connection is the report of the German commandant, who was invited to attend a briefing of the Romanian police prefecture at the end of January 1942. After the arrest of members of the underground, the picture pieced together by the police was this:

> A senior Russian officer, Kuznetsov (perhaps Lazarev's cover-name), who remained in Odessa and hid in the catacombs after the departure of the Red Army, was charged with (the direction of) the terrorist movement in Odessa and environs. K. leads two groups: one, which works above ground in the city, with the primary task of finding out the location, strength, leaders, billets, equipment, etc. of allied (i.e. Axis) units. The other is located underground.... Of the surface group, 18 men have already been arrested by the Romanian security service, including two women who were in close touch with Kuznetsov.
>
> The underground group had radio contact with Moscow and Sevastopol or an unknown point at the frontline of the south front. The underground is estimated at from 30 to 40 men and may possess supplies for up to a year, including uniforms of the Soviet, German, and Romanian armies...
>
> The "surface" group was arrested in the night of December 3-4 (1941).

The document proceeds to detail the communication channels between the two groups: the women operatives in the city customarily transmitted and picked up messages through a narrow tube connecting the underground passages with the outside world; messages were written on narrow strips of paper and inserted into cigarette paper tubes. This particular group was restricted to one section of the catacomb labyrinth, as apparently the Romanians had walled off several sections; in each section, however, units continued to operate. Once the Romanians sought to enter the catacombs, but were met with machine-pistol (i.e., sub-machine gun) fire and suffered several casualties.

The particular value to the Romanians of the catch described above — besides the elimination of some 18 agents — was the seizure of correspondence between Kuznetsov and his "surface men" and also the fact that one of the girl agents, after she had been caught by the Romanian police, continued to dispatch fake messages to Kuznetsov. In his directions, Kuznetsov ordered the formation of ten-man teams to carry out terrorist attacks, explosions, and assassinations of German and Romanian officers; other instructions called for the distribution of leaflets and other propaganda. Actually, one exchange of letters took place between Kuznetsov and his girl agent in the physical presence of Romanian and German intelligence personnel — on February 5, 1942, when the underground still was not aware of the fraud being perpetrated on them.[16] Here is the text of the 20th and 21st letters sent to the girl Eugenia by Kuznetsov (re-translated from the German translation, which has some obvious and sometimes identifiable errors):

(1) Good day, Pëtr (Eugenia's cover-name)! I am worried about you and have waited impatiently for five days. What goes on in the city? This is not the first time that there is terror and horror; one should no longer be amazed at it, as these outbursts are quite natural and proper for the fascist beasts and their followers. In don't understand why they rave and rant like this. Our troops are applying considerable pressure, especially on the south front under the leadership of Comrade Timoshenko. Accordingly, the Germans are retreating. On January 29, for instance, we recaptured Lozovaia station and have encircled Kharkov; we are now 25 km. from Kharkov and move in the direction of Dnepropetrovsk. See why these musicians (i.e., Romanians) got wild and why they smell funeral incense?

I recommend that all contagious people (literally lepers, i.e., probably agents exposed by the Romanians) be identified so that they can be gotten rid of the easier later on. This does not mean that they should be spared now: they should be promptly killed as long as this is still possible — provided you don't get caught yourselves.

I recommend that you show all three channel openings (exits?) to all men to prevent any possible confusion. The Germans have been seizing all men from 15 to 55 years for defense work. They perish from excessive work, cold, and hunger. Here this could also happen. In such a situation, you should not get caught with your mouths wide open, but should immediately come and join me, if possible as a group... (February 5, 1942).

(2) I am very much depressed about the case of Alexander and worried about K. I have already given the necessary instructions. All those who are under suspicion (of being agents, in the eyes of the Romanian authorities) should immediately come down to me, at the risk of having to kill the guards, should they disturb us. I recommend that Fedor Mo. come down to me, too, since he is being

---

[16] Oblr. Demdl, "Besprechung am 31.1.42 auf der Kgl. Rum. Polizeipräfektur in Odessa," and "partisanenbekämpfung in Odessa, Vorgang am 5.2.1942," CRS, DHMR, 29221/1.

kept (under surveillance) as a suspect, and should our troops approach, he would surely be shot. Help the wife of K. with the goods and possessions of those who come down to us. They should all come down in rags and sell all they can... (February 5, 1942).

Kuznetsov himself, however, and his staff were not caught. Apparently he either pretended to believe in, for morale purposes, or read into the messages he received the prospect of an early Soviet landing near Odessa. The agents arrested in January-February 1942, claimed to have considered it imminent, and felt that the partisans would constitute an organized force in the enemy's rear, and would coordinate their activities with the airborne and seaborne landing units. Even the Germans gave some credence to the reports,[17] though one must consider the existence of such a plan exceedingly unlikely. Only the timing makes sense: this was the moment when the Soviet winter counter-offensive was at its peak, the Red Army had landed near Feodosia and was in the process of clearing the Crimea. It is likely, however, that some agents had been given this story by Kuznetsov to make them more loyal, and to make the Romanians, if they apprehended the agents, panic more readily.

Actually, of course, no landing took place; after a few months, the Germans and Romanians occupied all the Crimea, and in May the last besieged Black Sea port, Sevastopol, fell to the Axis. The Germans apparently captured at Sevastopol personnel or records that permitted them to expose further agents in the Odessa area. Just what occurred is not known, but Kataev admitted in his first edition (significantly, the statement was omitted from the revised edition):

> The farther the German army advanced to the east, the more difficult it became (for the Odessa partisans) to operate... The enemy's intelligence began a systematic, relentless struggle with the Soviet partisans. The fall of Sevastopol inflicted a terrible blow on Druzhinin's organization. In the course of several days three combat groups of fives (five men each) "fell through," and 14 agents were arrested.[18]

Yet the remaining men continued underground, some dying in the catacombs from malnutrition, malaria, or other diseases. Because of the

---

[17] See also Verbindungsstab der Deutschen Wehrmacht in Transnistrien, "Auszug aus Merkblatt über Verhalten in Odessa," February 1942, CRS, DHMR. 29221/1. The discovery of some partisans and agents was publicized (cf. *Deutsche Bug-Zeitung*, No. 3, March 21, 1942).

[18] Kataev, *op. cit.*, p. 345.

relative failure and inactivity of their own organization, it is alleged, the underground leadership, at some time in the first half of 1942, made contact with the local criminal underground to establish a form of cooperation and "mutual aid." From mid-1942 on, too, the partisans in the catacombs apparently had sufficient contact with the Golovanevsk forest partisans in the north (in the triangle formed by the Bug and Siniukhina Rivers) to send a few men at a time on "vacation" there, partly to restore their health, partly to give them a breather from the underground existence. Allegedly the Germans captured a few such vacationers, and this helped them — though nowise crucially — to fight the catacomb dwellers. Curiously, the entire vacation system is not mentioned by Kataev or any other Soviet source, presumably as undignified and detracting from the martyrdom of the underground.[19]

Now and then the Romanians would choose a catacomb exit, almost at random, and wall it off; then they would, in cooperation with a German technician, use gas — primarily tear gas but at the end also poison gases — but did not venture down. The work of the "partisans" seems to have shifted more and more to the northwestern suburbs of the city — Krivaia Balka, Usatovo, and Kuial'nik — where peasant women lent them some support. Though not very active, and none too successful in demolition and assassination attempts, the group survived.

After April 1942, the underground began to concentrate on leaflet appeals (many of them handwritten) to special categories of targets, e.g., railroad workers, longshoremen, and the like. Contemporary *Abwehr* information also indicates that an officer sent in from the Central Staff of the Partisan Movement in the Ukraine (the regional sub-command of the over-all partisan "brain," operating under Khrushchev's nominal supervision) directed a concentration of efforts (about mid-1942, perhaps a few months later) on the disruption of German transportation and communication as well as a stepping up of propaganda work. Both these lines are believable since they coincide with directives issued at about the same time to partisan forces operating in Belorussia and the RSFSR, presumably in accordance with decisions adopted in Moscow.

Efforts to disrupt the railroad lines around Odessa failed; sabotage in the port area consisted in nasty but not fatal jobs such as switching freight cars on wrong sidings, affixing wrong labels to boxes, piercing truck tires,

---

[19] Karov, "Sovetskoe podpol'noc i partizanskoe dvizhenie v Odesse i Odesskoi oblasti v voinu 1941-45 gg.," MS, Institute for the Study of the U.S.S.R., Munich, 1955, pp. 24, 32.

and adding sugar to gasoline. Indeed, the activity of the partisans was so limited that it has been suggested that perhaps there was a Soviet decision to have the Odessa underground lie low in the period between late 1942 and late 1943, so as to avoid annihilation and attracting Axis interest, while continuing clandestine information-gathering and propaganda work. This hypothesis cannot be fully dismissed, though all proof is lacking. In April 1944, the Odessa partisans admitted that "nothing much was done about organized resistance in Odessa until after the tremendous German debacle at Stalingrad."[20] Even then failure marked the movement. As an exceptional Soviet account admitted after the war,

> Severe blows were inflicted on the Odessa underground. In March 1943, a failure occurred in the work of the underground obkom. A substantial part of oblast and rayon underground leaders and members were arrested.[21]

Still, in July 1943, the German consul in Odessa had evidence to confirm that (according to Romanian intelligence) "Major Kutuzov" (sic: Kuznetsov) with some eighty to one hundred men was still in the catacombs. Indeed, they held out to the very end.[22]

The Transnistrian Partisans

Transnistria was poor partisan territory: poor geographically, poor in popular support, and poor in partisan organization, supply, and liaison. Even compared with the modest activity of adjacent areas, Transnistria had few and small partisan teams. Mostly these were small groups, formed at the initiative of one or several stalwarts; they operated for only a short time (or remained inactive) in a narrowly circumscribed locale; they often had no contact with other guerrillas or higher headquarters, and were often soon destroyed or apprehended. Although sometimes made up of genuine heroes, the groups were generally quite ineffective. These were martyrs rather than fighters, and there were not many of them. But in a much more real sense than the Odessa underground they were partisans: guerrillas rather than agents.

---

[20] Ia. Shrernshtein, "Nepokorennyi port," *Ogni Chernomoria*, Odessa, 1949, reprinted in OVOV, Vol. 2, p. 242.

[21] Ibid.

[22] Karov, *op. cit.*, pp. 23-27, 29, 46; Lauterbach, *op. cit.*, p. 86.

A few such groups existed in the more distant suburbs of Odessa. One was a contingent of sailors who had somehow remained behind; and another consisted of workers from the local electric power station and one of the minor plants. Here and there individual stragglers from the Red Army, after hiding for a while, found their way to these units, though the overwhelming majority of former soldiers preferred to settle legitimately once the initial fury and terror had passed. These partisan units were generally small; some had a radio receiver and a typewriter; one or two may have had a printing press. Occasionally they might engage in some small-scale "diversionary act," but they concentrated rather on word-of-mouth propaganda among the population and the periodic dissemination of leaflets and typed bulletins. These groups were active enough to warrant mention by the Romanian press; a series of articles began appearing in July 1942, on the work of "Communist terror bands in Transnistria," claiming that over fifty men had recently been liquidated.[23]

Actually, farther north, throughout most of the expanse of the province, there was scarcely any partisan warfare at all. At first (German and Romanian reports concur on this) the area was even quieter than the vicinity of Odessa. There was some small-scale activity in the Dubosary area, apparently caused by a group of partisans consisting of Soviet railroad workers. The only other significant group, in the Savransk-Golovanevsk area, operated under the name of "Burevestnik" (Stormy Petrel); it was apparently left behind by the Pervomaisk party organization, which had withdrawn into the Savransk forests. When it proved to be a total failure, the ex-secretary of the Pervomaisk gorkom, Nikolai Kostiuk, was sent back in from the Soviet side, in the fall of 1942, to try and unite the scattered remnants of partisan and opposition groups in the whole area west of the Bug around Pervomaisk; he became commissar of the "Burevestnik" unit, whose membership never exceeded sixty, until the winter of 1943-1944 when Soviet reinforcements were flown in.[24]

The only other group in the north — in the absence of more successful or sizeable units, it has become the object of official Soviet

---

[23] Borisov, *op. cit.*, p. 54; interview D; *Der Deutsche in Transnistrien*, No. 2, July 26, 1942; Kononenko, *op. cit.*, pp. 32-33.

[24] From August 1943 on, thanks to the support of the Fourth Ukrainian Front, "Burevestnik" was enlarged and reorganized with I.A. Kukharenko as commander and V.E. Nesterenko as commissar. Both were Ukrainians flown in from the Soviet side. By November 1943, the enlarged formation allegedly had 200 members, and thereafter it grew even more rapidly as the Soviets drew near (OVOV, Vol. 2, pp. 173-175).

hagiography — was "Partizanskaia Iskra" (Partisan Spark). A 36-year-old Ukrainian village school director, Vladimir Morhunenko, organized this group in Krimy, west of Pervomaisk. He had been left behind for this purpose by the party, which he had but recently joined. It consisted of some twenty school boys and girls, and had some of the trappings of a conspiratorial game (members signed the oath of allegiance in their own blood, and subjected new members to all sorts of queer "tests"). Its work was brief and primitive: posting handwritten leaflets in the village, listening to broadcasts from Moscow on a stolen school radio, sinking a few rowboats in the Kodyma River, and dumping gasoline out of metal containers at a near-by MTS. Morhunenko succeeded in establishing, or maintaining, contact with the Pervomaisk group, but what could he do? The Soviet version claims that one of the boys, a good and active student, who now proved "over-eager" to attack Germans and Romanians, was a "traitor" (and was promptly shot by the partisans). When the partisans decided to try a large-scale operation — the laying of mines on the railroad leading to Pervomaisk (this was at the time of Stalingrad, and the assignment was apparently to prevent supplies and reinforcements from moving east) — they were encountered by a well-prepared Romanian force and captured. Among the ninety-odd persons arrested were virtually all the members of "Partizanskaia Iskra." Over thirty of them (including Morhunenko), the Soviet version claims, were shot by the Romanians in February 1943, after a "futile" inquiry.[25]

In comparison with the major partisan concentrations elsewhere in Russia, all these groups were trifling. This was true even of the one group whose leader had been made Hero of the Soviet Union. This was the unit operating both in and out of Odessa under Captain Vladimir Alexandrovich Molodtsov (known under the cover name of Pavel Vladimirovich Badaev). They had men in the catacombs as well as in hideouts in the suburbs. Better organized and more enterprising than others, this group dared more — and was more easily infiltrated. In early February 1942, Badaev spent a night in the apartment of one of his team members, Boiko-Fedorovich, who, it turned out, had been recruited by Romanian counter-intelligence. Within two days, all sixteen "urban" members of the group had been arrested. The Soviets later claimed — after the award of high decora-

---

[25] Ihnen, *op. cit.;* OVOV, Vol. 2, pp. 40-52, 173-180, 194; V.M. Senkevich, *Sovetskaia Moldavia v bor'be protiv fashistsktkh zakhvatchikov,* OGIZ, Moscow, 1944, pp. 58-63; Borisov, *op. cit.,* pp. 57-58; A. Prisiazhnuk *et al.,* "Partizanskaia Iskra," *Pravda Ukrainy,* Kiev, May 7-8, 1955.

tions to Badaev and one of his young helpers — that twelve of the group (the other four were not tried — conceivably because they all worked with the Romanians) stubbornly refused to divulge any information, even under torture. On July 3, 1942, the Odessa dailies announced that they had been court-martialed, sentenced to death, and executed.

Kataev, who mentioned Badaev in a postscript of acknowledgments, patterned his hero, Druzhinin, after him. Hence a few further details may be added to his portrait. According to Kataev, he had been a lieutenant, later captain, of State Security, originally assigned to the border troops west of Odessa. Subsequent Soviet efforts to attribute to his group various railroad explosions and other demolitions in the city may or may not be correct, for Kataev recognized that it was a matter of policy to ascribe to Badaev varied and widely scattered acts of sabotage and subversion, so as to raise his prestige, confuse the Romanians, and instill terror.[26]

All the evidence about one more partisan group comes from postwar Soviet accounts. A small unit was formed by S.I. Drozdov, a Communist engineer, in Il'ichevski rayon; it did almost nothing until April 1943, when an escaped Communist prisoner of war, Ovcharenko, took charge of its political work (whether or not he had been sent in from another partisan group or from the Soviet side cannot be determined). He fused the group with other ephemeral units. By the end of the year — so postwar accounts claim — the formation, now the Stalin Brigade, had some 200 members and published a newspaper, *Za schast'e rodiny* (*For the Happiness of the Homeland*), on its underground printing press. Supplies and personnel were evidently sent in to it from the Soviet side, and it owed its growth and survival in large measure to aid from the 3rd and 4th Ukrainian Fronts.[27]

Unfortunately, this is all that can be established.[28] Even complete information from both the Soviet and the Romanian sides, though it might add interesting details, probably would not materially alter the general picture of a very modest partisan movement in Transnistria.

---

[26] Al. Shneider, "Ero bylo v Odesse," *Bol'shevistskoe znamia*, Odessa, February 2, 1945; Borisov, *op. cit.*, pp. 55-56; Kataev, *op. cit.*, pp. 214, 227, 554; OVOV, Vol. 2, pp. 21, 39-40, 210.

[27] OVOV, Vol. 2, pp. xii, 155. 169-171, 245.

[28] The issues of an Odessa daily for January 1945, which contain further details on the above groups, are not available.

The Partisans and the People

Still, the city population was aware of the partisans' existence. This in itself was an accomplishment, for unconsciously many citizens after the tide of battle turned, seemed to adapt their behavior to the expected standards of the Soviet authorities; perhaps some refrained from collaborating simply out of fear of the ever-present eye of the partisans. One might add, as a sample, what a fairly knowledgeable refugee knew about partisan and agent work in wartime Odessa — not because he was unique but because he may be assumed to have been typical. He knew, of course, of the explosions in the center of town. He had heard of the catacombs and of Romanian attempts to catch partisans there; for a while, like others in Odessa, he actually believed that the partisans had been exterminated — so quiet were they or so demoralized. But new small raids on city supplies or army stocks convinced him and others of the partisans' survival. Rumors had it that an emissary "from Moscow" had even managed to arrive and join the small underground group — this detail, incidentally, is missing in Kataev's first edition but is included in the revised version, apparently to inflate the role played by the Soviet high command in the direction of the partisans' work. The Romanians seem to have announced the capture of the group, including the representative from Moscow — but it was apparently a false report.

The same refugee had one personal encounter with a person he claims was an agent of the NKVD. He later found out that this man, A.M. Ion, had been a *seksot* (secret informant) of the Odessa section of the NKVD before the war and had purposely "surrendered" to the Romanian army several weeks before the fall of the city, and had given it intelligence, which proved to be correct. When the Romanian army entered Odessa, he managed to get a trusted position, and arranged, for instance, for the billeting of a Romanian general; later, he worked closely as an informant or investigator for the Siguranţa. The refugee's attention had been drawn to Ion, who lived in the same apartment house as he did, because of his aplomb and the authoritative tone with which lie — after all, a Soviet citizen — treated all around him. After a long time the refugee learned that a Romanian officer quartered in the building was shadowing Ion, whom the Romanians themselves had begun to suspect. A number of anti-Communists were denounced as Soviet agents by Ion and mistreated by him when under arrest or investigation. Finally, he sought to trap the Romanians, by enticing them to a partisan unit, which was prepared to give the occupiers battle; but the Romanians brought Ion himself along, and in the ensuing skirmish he was killed.[29]

Such an encounter with an agent was apparently quite typical. By and large, the effect of an encounter was a double one: it instilled fear of the Soviets, and it augmented the hate against them. Other factors, however, by 1943, outweighed for many such fear and hate. In an upsurge of genuine patriotism and anti-Romanian feeling, or in anticipation of the Red Army's return and the consequent need to "whitewash" oneself, or for such reasons as blackmail or material need, a number of Odessa residents joined the underground in the last year and especially half-year of the occupation. Some of these had been Communists all along but had tried to "sit it out." Others, especially university and high school students, were new recruits: the spirit of opposition and resentment among them has been described elsewhere, and each wave of Romanian arrests in their midst — particularly in the fall of 1943 — produced a further defection to the "underground." Several younger faculty members at the university were involved, and the feeling remained that, is spite of arrests, there was an active "cell" in operation there.[30] The actual accomplishment of academic cells was trifling; it consisted generally in spreading propaganda and, rarely, committing some symbolic act such as raising the red flag over a public building before dawn.[31] Probably the greatest effect of this activity was the sense of insecurity it produced both in the university faculty and the Romanian authorities. As a partisan leader told a touring American newspaperman soon after the recapture of Odessa, "Perhaps more than anything else, we constituted a psychological threat."

By 1943, attempts to reinforce the partisans from the outside multiplied. These reflect the continuing Soviet preoccupation with the partisan movement, the stabilization and augmentation of Soviet authority, and the anticipated advance of the Red Army, for whom the partisans could constitute "a second front" behind the enemy lines. At the same time, the scope and nature of such attempts in Transnistria, as compared with those farther north — say, in the Briansk or Bobruisk areas — strongly suggest that the Central Staff of the Partisan Movement had little faith in the

---

[29] Manuilov, pp. 44-54.

[30] Interviews C and D; Peterle, *op. cit.*

[31] In July 1943 (Soviet accounts allege), the Romanians shot 22 students, mostly teenagers (some innocently implicated), for listening to Soviet radio broadcasts. Apparently, their execution led to some actual protests to Pântea ("Dvadtsat dva," *Chornomors'ka Komuna*, Odessa, December 24, 1944. See also OVOV, Vol. 2, p. 255).

power or ability of the Transnistria partisans. In mid-1943, the German consulate reported from Odessa a bit optimistically that for months there had been no evidence that the local partisans existed; there had been nothing but some minor sabotage on the railroad lines. Around May 1, however, a group of 150 to 200 men had tried to cross over the Bug from the German-held Ukraine into Transnistria. Repelled at Pervomaisk, they tried again at Voznesensk, but were beaten off; sixty-four of the men, who proved to be part of a partisan unit, were captured by the Romanians.[32] Unfortunately nothing about their affiliation and task has come to light. Perhaps they belonged to the larger group under Vasily Andreev, a partisan officer who, after a stint in the Briansk woods, was ordered to move to Moldavia, as Kovpak was sent into Galicia. Andreev's efforts were on a smaller scale and accomplished less; most of his surviving men seem to have operated in the northern part of the Moldavian S.S.R., both on the Bessarabian side of the Dnestr and, to a small extent, in Transnistria. Neither of the two major "roving" bands of Soviet partisans operating in the Ukraine — under Kovpak and Naumov — reached Transnistria. Subsequent Soviet accounts, however, sought to credit both units with stimulating partisan activity around Odessa. Thus, a Communist organizer, who admittedly had remained inactive since 1941, established contact with the bands passing to the north in the spring of 1943 and formed a small partisan unit, "Yuzhnyi," in the Golovanevsk forests.[33]

Activity was stepped up in anticipation of the Red Army's return. Now the task of partisans and agents was specifically geared to military purposes; their long-range political functions disappeared. Even earlier, small groups of Soviet parachutists had been reported in the Transnistrian countryside. In the summer of 1942, a team which had landed with hand grenades, submachine guns, a radio set, and money was exterminated after a four-hour battle with a *Volksdeutsche* militia detachment.[34] More groups and supplies were flown in from August 1943, on. In September 1943, a girl partisan and a woman radio operator were parachuted near Odessa and promptly apprehended. Convicted only of illegal entry into Transnistria, they received two-year sentences. Soviet accounts allege that they later escaped and transmitted information about activity in Odessa harbor.

---

[32] German Consulate, Odessa, to AA, Berlin, July 31, 1943, AA reel 1273, frames 342473-94.

[33] OVOV, Vol 2, pp. xi, 167-168.

[34] E.g., *Der Deutsche in Transnistrien*, No. 2, July 26, 1943; OVOV, Vol. 2, pp. 173-175, 188-192, 242.

Others undoubtedly evaded detection. Especially in the winter of 1943-1944, such landings multiplied. German *Abwehr* reports claimed that

> ...according to statements by the Mizin partisan group, the partisan headquarters at Melitopol' sent seven groups of parachutists into the provinces of Moldavia, Odessa, and Nikolaev, in order to organize the local partisans.[35]

The most interesting attempt was that of the group headed by V.D. Avdeev (known under the cover-name of Chernomorski), and including mine-laying and guerrilla specialists. Dispatched by the fourth Ukrainian Front by order of the Ukrainian Staff of the Partisan Movement (nominally headed by Khrushchev, actually run by Communist Party Secretary Demian Korotchenko and Timofei Strokach, at present Minister of the Interior of the Ukraine), the group was dropped by air on the outskirts of Osipovka on January 16, 1944. Several of its members successfully got into Odessa, contacted Drozdov's Stalin Brigade there, and made preparations for an armed uprising that was to coincide with the Soviet army's approach to the city. However, Avdeev's trail was uncovered by a provocateur among the partisans, and the Romanian (and perhaps German) police managed to corner him. Rather than be apprehended, Avdeev, on March 2, committed suicide.

Actually, the work of his and similar groups may well have borne some fruit. In the final weeks of the occupation, the partisans apparently did give the Red Army some military information by radio and in other ways helped confuse the Germans in their final defense of Odessa.[36] However, the Soviet picture of partisan accomplishments even in this period seems heavily overdrawn.[37]

The very paucity of detail, of memoirs, and of postwar documents on the Soviet side suggests the absence of any substantial accomplishments — except martyrdom — to exploit models for emulation or (at least overt)

---

[35] Abwehrtruppe 320, "Tatigkeitsbericht... February 1944," March 1, 1944, CRS, AOK 6,50808/4.

[36] In late March 1944, however, a major explosion took place in the Krivaia Balka catacombs, apparently due to the partisans' careless preparation for "surfacing" when the Red Army approached. The Germans thoroughly investigated the occurrence and, fearful of a rising, tried in vain to enter the catacombs with the help of poison gas *(Abwehr* report, cited by Karov, *op. cit*, pp. 12, 49).

[37] Borisov, *op cit.*, pp. 63-64; Kononcnko, *op. cit.*, p. 33; Lauterbach, *op. cit.*, pp. 87-89; OVOV, Vol. 2, pp. xiii, 41-42, 199-200. See also Armstrong, *op. cit.*, for a discussion of the partisan movement.

study. The volume published by the Odessa oblast committee on the Second World War makes this clear even while seeking to inflate the partisans' record.[38]

Though evidence is sadly lacking, it can be inferred that the people gave the partisans little support until at least mid-1943; only where personal contact was established (for instance, between individual partisans in the catacombs and the peasant women near one of the suburban exits) and where human compassion overrode political considerations did they get support. Because there were not the brutalities and forced labor draft of a German occupation, only an infinitesimal number of Transnistrians joined the partisans.[39] The unfavorable terrain helps explain this. But Romanian policy was decidedly one of the factors accounting for the small scale of partisan activities and successes.

---

[38] OVOV, Vol. 2, pp. 160*ff.*

[39] A refugee author asserts, without any proof whatsoever, that Odessa was used by the Soviet intelligence service during the war for channeling agents into the Balkans and Western Europe. While this is conceivable, there is nothing to demonstrate it, and the particular paper in question abounds in factual errors (D.I. Karov, *op. cit.,* pp. 37-46).

Because of the very nature of the problem, no evidence is available on Allied intelligence activities in Transnistria. The only possible clue refers to Juan Manuel de la Aldea, a Spanish newsman who was press attaché at the Spanish embassy in Bucharest. As part of his functions, he visited Odessa during the war and published an article on it (see Bibliography, below). A German report transmitted through the consul in Basel in December 1942, claimed to know that de la Aldea was actually (though perhaps unwittingly) having his reports transmitted to British agents in Switzerland (Consulate Basel to AA, December 23, 1942, AA reel 244, frames 160904-05).

Chapter VII

The Last Phase

Between Battlefield and Round-Table

By the summer of 1943, the military trend was unmistakable. After the calamity at Stalingrad, the German army was unable to recover the initiative for any length of time. Its counter-offensive was rapidly exhausted; its remaining positions in the North Caucasus were abandoned; and the Red Army gradually unleashed, from the Orel front down to the Black Sea, a series of blows which carried it all the way from Kharkov to Kiev. It was clear that, barring a miracle, the German retreat would continue; the remnants of the Romanian and Italian forces, badly mauled in the east, retreated to the safety of the rear areas. Transnistria, so undisturbed by military events for two years, began to feel the increasing proximity of the front and the presence of prisoners, wounded, and soldiers on leave.

It was a matter of strategy for Axis forces to hold Transnistria, or at least its southern part, as long as possible. Odessa was an essential transfer point in supplying the increasingly isolated German and Romanian forces in the Crimea. Retaining it in Axis hands kept the Soviet forces farther away from the Ploieşti oilfields and, generally, from Romanian territory.[1] The attitude of the Romanians had, however, changed considerably. Their enthusiasm for the war had considerably abated as early as the siege of

---

[1] V.M. Kononenko, *Chernomortsy v boiakh za osvohozhdenie Kryma I Odessy*, Voenizdat, Moscow, 1954, chapter I.

Odessa, because of the heavy casualties they suffered; the defeat before Stalingrad had intensified their doubts and complaints; and the international situation was such as to galvanize into actions the Romanian political factions who sought to approach the Allies — either Britain and the United States, or the Soviet Union — with the aim of negotiating a separate peace.[2]

Relations between Romania and Germany became exacerbated, just at the time that Italy defected from the Nazi fold, after Badoglio's coup. Even physical clashes between German, Italian, and Romanian troops became commonplace, especially in *étappe* cities such as Odessa, where soldiers could easily find relaxations and inebriation. The citizens of Transnistria had before their eyes the visible evidence of an increasingly disintegrating Romanian power.[3] Yet Bucharest did not readily yield to German pressure on all points. Indeed, it was in the final months of 1943 that a bitter exchange developed between Antonescu and Hitler. It was prompted by the deteriorating military situation and the German expectation of retreating into Transnistria; evacuated agricultural equipment and inventory would reach the province even earlier.[4] On October 25, Hitler sent Antonescu an imploring, strongly-worded appeal. In addition to requesting early and heavy Romanian participation in the eastern campaign, he asked

> that the necessary utilization of Transnistria as rear area of Army Groups A and South not be impeded by some formalistic-juridical or economic objections and difficulties... The question how many troops and supplies, cattle and grain reserves can be located in Transnistria, and how the payment can be settled etc., should not even be raised, let alone negotiated... May I request your approval that the direction of railroads in Transnistria be transferred to German hands...[5]

---

[2] For a summary of these negotiations, see *Hitler's Europe*; for an extensive discussion, see Hillgruber, *op. cit.*

[3] A notorious incident involving German and Italian troops and Romanian police in an Odessa café was reported by three different informants (Cf. Manuilov, pp. 137-140; interview C; Peterle, *op. cit*).

[4] On October 22, 1943, Gottlob Berger notified Himmler: "Today such shocking reports about the threatening situation in the Ukraine arrived from the Reich Commissar and from (agricultural chief) Körner that Rosenberg has requested the Führer to secure Marshal Antonescu's consent for us to bring agricultural machinery, cattle, and grain into Transnistria with our own escorts..." (Berger to Himmler, October 22, 1943, CRS, EAP 161b.12/335).

Two weeks later, Hoffmeyer (who had meanwhile been promoted to SS general and in effect supervised the agricultural evacuation program) complained to Field Marshal von Kleist, commander of the Army Group that was retreating toward Transnistria:

> On orders from Bucharest transmitted by the Governor, the Romanian agencies have for about six weeks been conducting a systematic evacuation of Transnistria, which has extended not only to the removal of industrial installations and machines but of late also to agriculture. Systematically all horses are being withdrawn; the MTS are already closed; oil and grain mills are crated and await shipment... so that further conduct of economic activity becomes impossible.

Since Transnistria was becoming increasingly important as an agricultural surplus area, Hoffmeyer urged Kleist to "do something" — probably hoping that he would intervene with the Romanian military.[6] But to no avail.

On November 15, Antonescu's reply went off to Hitler — characteristically, in Romanian. He refused to increase the number of Romanian troops and supplies at the front; he welcomed the absence of German troops from Romania (since the consequences of their stay there in 1941 "could be felt for a long time" afterwards); and he asked Hitler to reconsider the question of transferring the railroads; the lines had been running to everyone's satisfaction under Romanian management. He agreed that it was necessary to consider Transnistria a "war zone" and that problems related to it could not be approached "in the spirit of a banker." But that was all.[7]

Berlin finally consented to leave the railroads with the Romanians, but refused to re-open the whole problem of Transnistria's status. To strengthen the German position, particularly *vis-à-vis* Alexianu, the High Command on November 25 created the post of "Commander of German Troops in Transnistria," and appointed to it the general in charge of Army Group "A" Rear Area, Lt. General Auleb. He took over the functions of the liaison office in Odessa and at the same time became territorial commander. By unilateral action, Berlin was moving in to control Transnistria.[8]

---

[5] Hitler to Antonescu, October 25, 1943, USSR-240; excerpts in Hillgruber, *op. cit.*, p. 176, and *Trial of the Major War Criminals*, Vol. 7, pp. 318ff.

[6] Hoffmeyer to Kleist, November 9, 1943, CRS, Wi/ID 2.419.

[7] Antonescu to Hitler, November 25, 1943, USSR-239; excerpts in Hillgruber, pp. 176-177.

Meanwhile the situation had become critical. As early as September 26, informants claimed to know that

> Wives of Romanian government employees are being evacuated from Odessa and Transnistria. German troops are to replace Romanian occupation troops in Transnistria. The Germans are pressing Antonescu to hand over the administration of Transnistria to the Germans.

And a week later, sources in Bucharest reported that the Romanian government had ordered the evacuation of materiel and a number of men from Odessa. Three hundred railway cars were dispatched there to bring back officials and archives.[9] Another month, and the situation became more serious still.

> The withdrawal in the area of Army Groups "A" and South (wrote a German observer) provoked strong unrest in Transnistria in November 1943. The Romanian administration sought to save what it could. The families of officials, cattle, horses, and vehicles, machines, factories, and objects of art were "secured" by removing them to Romania. At the beginning of December the temporary consolidation at the front and a strong word from Marshal Antonescu stopped this plunder. But there was no calming down of the population.[10]

Further retreats were expected, and people spoke in terms of an impending crisis. German "hospital bases" were established at several points in the Odessa area. German supplies were moved in but, commented a German army report, "since the Romanian Governor Alexianu makes difficulties about the quartering of German supply services, we shall have to help ourselves..." By the turn of the year, a refugee recalls, German troops had begun to pass through Odessa on their way westward, their morale depressed and their fighting zeal exhausted; the troops themselves ironically and sadly jested about their "elastic defenses." Rumors began to fly that the Germans, dissatisfied with their ally, would take over the administration of Transnistria.[11]

---

[8] Hillgruber, p. 177; OKW/WFSt/Qu.View.1 (Keitel), "Befehl für die Einsetzung des Befehlshabers der deutschen Truppen in Transnistrien," November 25, 1943, CRS, DHMR and EAP 99/72.

[9] OSS Documents 47308 and OB5630.

[10] Beauftragter bei der Heeresgruppe Süd to RMfdb0., Führungssrab Politik, February 2, 1944, CRS, EAP 99/1184.

In the city, meanwhile, uncertainty was spreading. The Romanian forces and the local police were scarcely able to maintain "law and order." A German visitor to Odessa from Bucharest reported in mid-December:

> ...the panic which had lasted some time has considerably diminished, but the city is overcrowded with German and Romanian staffs... After the outbreak of darkness, no lady would dare go out by herself because of the prevalent insecurity.

Banditry was on the increase, and hooliganism reached new extremes.[12]

The insecurity was compounded by the resumption of Soviet air raids. In 1942 and 1943, there had been practically none. Late in 1943, the planes began to reappear, more often on reconnaissance than on bombing missions. Anti-aircraft installations, partly German-manned, were strengthened. And a full hit by a single Soviet plane on a workers' project in the suburbs added to the atmosphere of fear.[13] The political orientation had clearly changed. A university professor recalls that his students spoke of the planes overhead as "ours" — something that would have been impossible in 1942. Especially the younger set looked forward to the Romanians' collapse; and when schools began registering those who would wish to be evacuated in case of crisis, the numbers who signed up were trivial. Even Soviet wartime songs and ditties got somehow into circulation — in all likelihood through the radio, rather than through the underground. It was such developments that led, in late 1943, to the arrest of many university students and some younger faculty members on charges of pro-Soviet activity.[14]

---

[11] Peterle, *op cit.;* Leit. San.-Offiz. DHMR, "Monatlicher Lageberiche," October 15, 1943, CRS, DHMR; H Gr.A, HWiFu, "Kriegstagebuch." 1943-1944, CRS, Wi/ID 2419.

No such plan seems actually to have existed. Rosenberg, after seeing Hitler about the problem of German supplies moving to and through Transnistria on November 17, 1943, noted that "some of the Germans active there seem to consider themselves, as it were, forerunners of a German administration. I have forbidden this, but I wanted to ask the Führer whether the problem of Transnistria might become acute for us. The Führer replied in the negative..." (Rosenberg). "Vermerk Über Besprechung im Führerhauptquartier am 16./17.11.1943," Document 039-PS.

[12] Deursche Akademie München, *op. cit.*; interview D.

[13] Manuilov, p. 141; Peterle, *op. cit.*

[14] Interview C; Manuilov, p. 150.

This was an additional reason for the orders of October-November, 1943, closing schools and preparing for the *university's* evacuation westward from Transnistria. See OVOV, Vol. 2, pp. 67-68.

The Romanians themselves made a "gesture"; they too obviously anticipated having to deal with the Soviets in the near future. About February 1944, a Soviet plane crash-landed off Odessa. Only the pilot's corpse was rescued; his papers identified him as a twice-decorated Hero of the Soviet Union. Much to the Romanians' amazement he was found to have been wearing a cross on his chest. The next day the local press carried an official communiqué of the incident and announced that the flier would be given a public Orthodox burial. The funeral attracted a great crowd; the Germans stayed away from it. On the whole, popular response to the Romanian gesture was favorable; there was considerable debate about whether the cross signified a genuine change in conditions in the Soviet Union, and also about what the Romanians were seeking to accomplish by this sudden and unusual move, which contrasted so with their behavior on other occasions.[15]

There is no doubt that, as events moved toward a climax, the population of Transnistria — except a small but growing minority irrevocably committed to the Soviet cause — clung almost hysterically to the Romanians in their distrust and fear of the Germans. Numerous incidents reveal the difference in attitude toward the two Axis states. Some involved simple chance encounters; others were calculated political gestures. Perhaps the most dramatic though entirely ludicrous came when the rumor spread that Queen Helena of Romania was on a shopping tour in Odessa. Several Odessa "society ladies" came upon a group of Romanian "nobles" in a store, and, genuflection and all, approached one they assumed to be the queen. "Little Mother, for God's sake," they appealed, "do not forsake us and abandon us to the Germans!" To the embarrassment of both parties, the lady turned out to be no queen at all; the incident was widely reported not only in Odessa but in Bucharest and in Berlin.[16]

Such outbursts were especially characteristic of those who had acquired a vested interest in the *status quo* — a certain universe of middle-class conveniences and phantom security. While the ladies appealed, their husbands (one may assume) were preparing to evacuate their funds and belongings. By the turn of the year, Odessa was beginning to die out. The evacuation of goods and of some of the people; the closing of stores, theaters, restaurants; arrests and disappearances — all these were tokens that the end of Transnistria was in sight.

---

[15] Manuilov, pp. 141ff.; interview A.
[16] Peterle, *op. cit.;* interview C.

Military Government

By January 1944, the Soviet army was advancing westward through the right-bank Ukraine. The Romanian authorities now decided to face reality. Civil government in Transnistria was bound soon to become a sham. The first major admission that a new situation existed was the replacement of Governor Alexianu on February 1, 1944, by a military governor, Lt. General Potopeanu, formerly Romanian Economy Minister, the name Transnistria dropped out of use, and the authorities were increasingly referred to as "Military Government between Dnestr and Bug."[17] The full story of Alexianu's removal remains to be unraveled, but his rule had come to an end.

During the following six weeks, the military situation deteriorated further. In February, the Red Army crossed the Bug and advanced into Northern Transnistria, seizing Bel'tsy and advancing on toward Romanian soil. The Third Ukrainian Front was converging on the Black Sea area, facing the German Sixth Army which was in charge of its defense. Inevitably, German influence increased in what remained of Transnistria; the Romanians were frenetically engaged in saving their skins, their belongings, and what goods they could by hook and by crook get their hands on — a most undignified repetition of their earlier plunder, which did nothing to endear them to their erstwhile subjects. As early as January, the Transnistrian authorities ordered the praetors to honor German requests for forced-labor contingents.[18] An informal agreement between the Germans and Romanian authorities stipulated that, in case of a continued Soviet advance, the German military government would replace the Romanians; at the same time, Antonescu ordered his officials not to abandon their posts in panic unless the Germans were retreating too.[19] In various ways, German pressure grew until, in mid-March, when the struggle for the Odessa area was obviously only weeks away, Romanian rule was entirely superseded by German military government. On March 16, 1944, what remained of Transnistria became a German area of military opera-

---

[17] Hillgruber, *op. cit.*, p. 177; DNB, February 4,1944, reported in *News Digest*, London, February 7, 1944, No. 1363, p. 19.

[18] AOK 8, AWiFü, "Zehntagemeldung," January 21, 1944, CRS, Wi/ID 2.587.

[19] OKH/GenStdH/GenQu., "Monatsbericht Ost Januar 1944," February 21, 1944 (Army Group "A"), Document EC-107, p. 9.

tions; German military government took over what functions Potopeanu still retained at the end of his brief interregnum.

The German order, rather elegantly, stipulated that the "assumption of administration is intended as a transitory measure." In a queer *post mortem* acknowledgment of what had never been formalized, it stated that "The area taken over will continue to be considered a part of the Romanian state." Interesting because it indicates the Germans' realization of the difference between their policy and Romanian policy was the stipulation that "The principle, hitherto adhered to (in Transnistria), of *generous* treatment must be maintained and respected even by all subordinate agencies."[20] On the whole, the Germans sought to retain most of the native administration; obviously this was no time for a basic reorganization.[21] In front areas, the army corps replaced civil administration altogether; farther back, civil administration continued to function under the supervision of regular German rear area echelons, namely, Sixth Army Rear Area command, field and city komendaturas; in the northern part of Transnistria, the remaining German-held area, around Golta (west of Pervomaisk), went to the Eighth Army operating there.

The city of Odessa was likewise subjected to an administrative reorganization. Gherman Pântea and his followers had sought safety farther west. The Germans appointed a military government officer, *Verwaltungsrat* Noruschat, as "Plenipotentiary" for the city. As mayor they named — as late as March 24 — an engineer who had collaborated with them farther east as mayor of Stalino, Ivan Petushkov; information on him and his activities is scant. (Curiously enough, even well-placed refugees who were still in Odessa knew or recall little about this final phase of the city's non-Soviet experience).[22] The structure of city government, or what remained of it, stayed unaltered, but Romanian directors were replaced by their Russian underlings — even that late, this apparently tickled the ego of the Russian officials. The new city administration had only a short time to go

---

[20] Hillgruber, *op. cit.*, p. 183; AOK 6, OQu/Qu 2, "Übernahme der Verwaltung in Transnistrien," March 20, 1944, CRS, AOK 6, 59352/8; AOK 6, OQu, "KTB-Beirrag," March 26, 1944, CRS, AOK 6, 59352/7.

[21] Both for the Germans' plan and for their estimate of the situation as it existed, the instructions issued for the military government organs on March 20, 1944 are of some interest. Their text is reproduced in the Appendix to this study.

[22] AOK 6, Ia/OQu, "R-, L-, Z-Massnahmen im Grossraum Odessa," March 26, 1944, CRS, AOK 6, 59352/7; AOK 6, AWiFü, "Lagebericht," April 23, 1944, CRS, Wi/ID 2.361; *The New York Times*, April 22; Lauterbach, *op. cit.*, p. 87.

and few things to do. The Germans, skeptical of victory and verging on despair, were rather conciliatory about internal affairs; they even entrusted a German army seal to the city "fathers," to be used at their own discretion for the issuance of safe-conduct certificates.[23] City government, however, rapidly became a sham.

Odessa was being cut off, and there was already talk that it might once again be besieged.[24] By late March, the Red Army was poised on the eastern bank of the Bug, about to cross the river in a drive for Odessa. For the Germans and Romanians, the problem uppermost was evacuation and destruction — just as it had been for the Soviets in the summer of 1941. For the population, the question was whether to go or to remain.

"Evacuation" is scarcely a suitable term to apply to the Romanian removal of property, which was conducted both on an individual and on an "institutionalized" basis. Even refugees otherwise rather kindly disposed to the Romanians recall with shivers and disbelief the way things were taken to Romania. Soviet accusations against Alexianu's men provide much factually correct information on this arbitrary spoliation (though the charge that more than half the cattle and three-fourths of the horses were driven off seems a bit exaggerated and may have been a convenient excuse for lagging Soviet harvests after reoccupation). The equipment removed included trolley cars and rails; the seats of the Odessa opera; the underground cable of an electric trunk line; thousands of pianos and pieces of furniture; theatrical costumes; parts of public libraries; even plain closets and desks; and any objects of art that could be found.[25] All this was removed by any available conveyance — and hurriedly, since on April 1 the railroads passed from Romanian to German hands; hundreds of trucks and carts crowded the roads to Iași and Constanța — only the minimum carried strictly "military" loads; most were filled with plunder.[26]

---

[23] Manuilov, pp. 152-155.

[24] The German Naval High Command insisted that Odessa "must remain in our possession" because of its importance for the supply of German forces in southern Russia and the Crimea (Bemerkungen des Ob.d.M., "Über die Bedeuning von Odessa für die Kriegsführung im Südosten," March, 1944, CRS, OKW/104).

[25] An American scholar, then Balkan specialist in the Office of Strategic Services, recalls that "in the fall of 1944, I myself saw some of the Odessa trolleys running on the streets of Timisoara in the Banat, with their Russian markings still not painted our" (Robert Lee Wolff, *The Balkans in Our Time*, Harvard University Press, Cambridge, 1956, p. 235).

[26] Document USSR-47; V. Gordienko, "Odesshchina nakanune uborki urozhaia," *Izvestiia*, July 6, 1944; Manuilov, pp. 152-153.

The Germans had problems, of course; this was their first experience operating "in the sovereign territory of another, allied state and in the presence of a purely private economy." The actual transfer of economic installations to the Germans took place only shortly before Odessa was abandoned, but the stocks of supplies were substantial.[27] They remained on the spot, because evacuation soon became impossible and, as will be seen, was forbidden for political reasons. Politically, the Germans did little to arouse the population, except for one interesting operation. North of Odessa, in a largely Ukrainian-populated countryside, they embarked on a systematic promotion of separatist "Bandera propaganda." It was assumed that this would (a) be more palatable than outright German propaganda, and (b) still tend in an anti-Soviet direction:

> "Z" (i.e., *Zersetzung*, or sedition) tasks camouflaged as Bandera[28] propaganda (wrote the German intelligence unit there): (1) struggle against all occupiers, with stress on the struggle against Moscow; (2) appeal to active collaboration by the Ukrainian population, hoarding of food, passive resistance by all toilers in factories and kolkhozes; (3) appeal to determined struggle against Russian imperialism, desertion, small-scale sabotage, and formation of partisan bands (when the Red Army returns). In the rear area, dropping of leaflets camouflaged as Bandera propaganda with directions for small-scale sabotage. Rumor propaganda and agitation in the rear area, primarily with female agents...[29]

The effect of such moves, one suspects, must have been quite trivial. By and large, judgments had crystallized far too much to be affected by a bit of propaganda. What could still be affected was the decision whether or not to stay. The major political "line" was:

> Await quietly the arrival of "our men," that they are now "different" from what they had been, that they bring a new order, because the war had taught the authorities many things and changed policy. And how many people — and this included gray-haired ones — believed this and genuinely rejoiced!

This line was propagated probably both by Soviet agents and — to a far-reaching extent — also by individuals sincerely believing it. The major reasons why the overwhelming majority of the residents stayed in Odessa

---

[27] Bericht über die Durchführung de Z-Massnahmen in Gross-Odessa, Tiraspol und Beljajewka," April 18, 1944, CRS, Wi/ID 2.361.

[28] Stepan Bandera was the leader of a quasi-fascist Ukrainian nationalist organization.

[29] Abwehrtrup 20-1, "Tätigkeitsbericht," March 1, 1944, CRS, AOK 6, 50808/4.

(those farther north had virtually no opportunity to leave) were, however, fear, inertia, and faith in survival. To choose an unknown foreign world, alien in customs and language, never seen or tried, itself on the verge of collapse, required strong determination, especially when the physical process of evacuation had become difficult.[30] A German report found that "the population would rather suffer Bolshevik reprisals than leave their homes." It goes on to say "the Soviets' return is not desired; however, the partisans receive support from fear of subsequent repercussions."[31] The stage was set for the last act.

By late March, there were still supplies enough to feed the city for three or four weeks; the Germans had all sorts of plans for new ration cards and the distribution of foodstuffs.[32] This mattered little, for everyone had taken to hoarding; early in April some stocks were distributed to residents free, just as the Soviet had opened some warehouses rather than have them fall into German hands. Otherwise, the city had "died." With the Germans' assumption of authority and the expected Soviet arrival, overnight most stores and *bodegas* closed down; speculators and *nouveauxriches* hurried to remove their belongings; and a few who had profited from the occupation went literally underground, hoping to secure forgiveness; the partisans displayed a little more initiative in printing and posting leaflets.[33]

The evacuation of civilians from Odessa had to be strictly regulated because there were few ways to leave. The Romanians had an "evacuation point" which issued a total of about 8,000 entry permits into Romania, primarily to engineers and other specialists, intellectuals, and artists. A part of the equipment and most of the staff of the opera and of the leading theaters were moved wholesale to Timişoara, in Western Romania, where many were interned after the *coup d'état* in Romania the following summer; others were forcibly taken to Vienna by the Germans. The Germans Army Group "A" decided on March 23 that the evacuation of Transnistria was forbidden, primarily to avoid panic and defeatism, but also because it would have been impossible to carry out. The Sixth Army, it is true,

---

[30] Peterle, *op. cit.*; interview E.
[31] OKH/Gen.StdH, *op. cit.*, pp. 5,8.
[32] AOK 6, Qu. 2, "Übernahme..."; AOK 6, Armeeintendant, "Abfindung von einheimischen Arbeitskräften, die bei deutschen Dienststellen in Transnistrien beschäftigt werden," April 23, 1944, CRS, AOK 6, 59352/7.
[33] Manuilov, p. 140; interview E; Kataev. *op. cit.*, pp. 506ff.

objected to this, fearing that too many adult males and too many supplies would then fall into Soviet hands, but no basic reversal took place. However, special categories of evacuees, including the remaining ethnic Germans and some specialists, were shipped out; in the way it was done it is impossible to distinguish voluntary and compulsory removal. Finally, Odessa was cut off; the last departures took place — as they had from the beleaguered city in October 1941 — by sea, this time to Sulina, at the mouth of the Danube.[34]

On March 28, the Red Army took Nikolaev and the next day crossed the lower Bug in force. On April 5, Razdel'naia fell, and there with the Odessa-Tiraspol highway was cut. The last issue of *Molva* appeared on the 8th. On the 10th, after a brief but bitter fight, the Red Army re-entered Odessa. On April 12, Tiraspol was occupied, and four days later all Transnistria was again in Soviet hands.

During the final days, the Germans concentrated on destruction, since evacuation was impossible. Port installations, some industrial facilities, and transportation junctions were blown up; the electric power plant, various mills, stores of bread, sugar, and other foods were destroyed. Of Odessa's population, scarcely 200,000 remained; many had hidden in the vicinity; some had sought safety in the countryside; and some had left westward with the Romanians and Germans.[35]

The days of Transnistria were over.

Again in Soviet Hands

The population of Odessa met the returning Red Army with a combination of hope and fear. A young man from Odessa, who was drafted soon after, told his German captors:

> The behavior of the Odessa intelligentsia in the face of the alternating political situation was rather passive... Only those most compromised had left; the bulk of the residents had stayed. People feared Soviet repressions, but there was no other way out.[36]

---

[34] Manuilov, pp. 127, 152-154; Peterle, *op. cit.;* interview D; AOK 6, "Abfindung..."; H.Gr.A., Wi.-Abr., "Lagebericht," March 1, 1944, CRS, Wi/ID 201.
[35] Borisov, *op. cit.*, pp. 63-72; AOK 6, AwiFü, "Lagebericht."
[36] OKH/GenStdH/FHO (IIIa), "Kgf.-Vernehmung," February 18, 1945, CRS, H3/690, pp. 245-246.

It was precisely this absence of alternatives, mixed with a measure of patriotism, wishful thinking, and nostalgia, that induced even some "collaborators to stay. The director of the Inventory Directorate of the Primăria, Molov, remained; so did Professor Lozurski, head of the Faculty of Literature at the University, who had argued for some months that the Soviets had changed ("Oni uzhe ne te-zhe"). Most Russian actors stayed in Odessa. Diakonov, one of the leading lawyers who had actively worked with the Romanians, not only remained, but testified profusely before the Soviet investigating commission.[37]

The old Soviet atmosphere retuned promptly as controls were reimposed, reconstruction began, and arrests and the draft were resumed.[38] Within a few days of its recapture, a few plants were opened in Odessa; the Soviet authorities began collecting and soliciting funds among the workers of the port and the tobacco factory. On April 23, a mass rally was held in the center of town, at which Nikita Khrushchev and Marshal Malinovski (commander of the Third Ukrainian Front, which had taken Odessa) appealed for speedy reconstruction. Repair and reconstruction "brigades" were organized to help restore apartment houses, hospitals, and schools "voluntarily" after working hours. Though the authorities initially sought to impede the refugees' return by withholding passes and transport certificates, gradually some of them began to filter back to Odessa. The greatest impetus to reconstruction came after total victory in 1945. By the fall of that year, most of the schools, the opera, theaters, and the university were open once again. There were long delays in getting the electric power station going. The October Revolution plant was at least partly back in operation after May 1945. The January Uprising factory had also resumed production of oil-pumping equipment and cranes, while at the Marty plant, shipbuilding was slowly beginning again.[39]

---

[37] Document USSR-47.

[38] A few days after the reoccupation of Odessa, a Soviet newspaperman wrote:
...Beyond Sabaneyev Bridge is an extraordinary chaos of pianos with smashed keyboards and torn-out pedals. The Germans set fire to the charming colonnaded Stolarsky music-school, pillaged the class rooms... On Deribas Street, the façades of buildings grown shabby during the occupation are covered with cheap Romanian signs. What did the Romanians sell in Odessa? The property of the people of Odessa... All Odessa wants to be given something to do. At the first news that military commissariats have set up, everyone comes rushing. Our car gets stuck in Komsomolskaya Street. It is impossible to get through. The entire street is blocked with people waiting to enlist... (Evgeny Krieger, "Odessa's Night and Morning," *Soviet War News,* No. 841, April 24, 1944).

In the very first days after the Red Army's entry into the city, the age groups from 1894 to 1929 were ordered drafted; mobilization, which was apparently stretched out over several months, helped not only to increase the army's manpower but also helped the authorities apprehend "suspect" males.[40] The inevitable arrests began. Unfortunately, no reliable data are available. It is known that policemen who had served under the Transnistrian authorities were arrested. It is understood that a considerable number of collaborators received sentences of from five to ten years. Professor Chasovnikov, who had gone to Bucharest and, thanks to his contacts there, assumed Romanian citizenship, was extradited and tried in Odessa; rumors about his fate differ too greatly to be reliable. Other fugitives from Odessa were caught in Timişoara; after the *coup* in mid-1944, Soviet prisoners of war, who "liberated" themselves, helped arrest some of the refugees who had remained there. Apparently, individual fates were determined by a variety of considerations. Of the leading actors, to judge by the Soviet press, Makkaveiski is again acting and is favorably reported on, while Mertsalova, who had never engaged in politics, seems to have disappeared. Professor Varneke, who had enjoyed considerable prestige in prewar Russia, seems to have fallen from grace: the first edition of the Great Soviet Encyclopedia had devoted a long article to him; the second, postwar, edition fails altogether to mention him.[41]

With the evacuees' return, here, as elsewhere in the U.S.S.R., residents divided into two fairly hostile camps: evacuees and stay-behinds.[42] The government generally backed the evacuees as the more active and more loyal elements. Their attempts to reclaim apartments, furniture, and other goods abandoned four or five years earlier (and which meanwhile might have been resold several times) often ran into stalwart opposition. Court action was often required to settle disputes. A new question in standard Soviet forms was whether or not the individual had lived under the

---

[39] Borisov, *op. cit.*, pp. 74-75; V. Kurbatov, "V Odesse," *Krasnaia Zvezda*, November 16, 1945; anonymous, "Odessa: Poslevoennyi period" (MS), 1952.

[40] It is interesting that a random sampling of German prisoner-of-war interrogations for the winter of 1944-1945 revealed at least one young deserter from Odessa who gave as the reason for his desertion his experiences under the Romanians.

[41] OKH/GenStdH/GenQu., *op. cit.*; OKH/GenStdH/FHO (IIIa), *op. cit.*, pp. 228-229; Manuilov, p. 153; interviews D and E.

[42] Frequently a by-product of this division was a growth of anti-Semitism among those elements who had stayed on the spot; virtually all surviving and returning Jews (uniformly deprived of all previous possessions) invoked, or sought to invoke, official help to recover what remained of their former goods.

occupation. As late as 1950, a postwar escapee reported that students were refused admission to a mechanics' school in Odessa because, as children, they had lived under the Romanians.

Yet, gradually, the experience of the war receded and discrimination abated. Housing, it is true, was hard to obtain: priority went to public and industrial construction. The standard of living was lower than before the war, at least for a number of years. In spite of official attempts to combat it, speculation once again thrived in Odessa. In 1951, visitors could see orphans and beggars walking the streets. On the whole, however, by 1951, Odessa had resumed its life as a major Soviet city.[43]

* * *

How the Soviet authorities treated the Transnistrian experience lends support by indirection to the interpretation of the impact of Romania rule advanced in this paper. What is left unsaid is as significant as what is made explicit. During the war, the Soviet press had glorified the defenders of the city and portrayed the siege as a major military and political feat. Over 400 of its "heroes" were decorated, and by decree of December 22, 1942, a special medal "For the Defense of Odessa" was instituted. Odessa has customarily ranked the special gun salute reserved for "hero-cities." About the Romanians, however, the Soviet wartime press was strikingly silent. Now and then there would be brief mention of partisan warfare in the Odessa area or the Moldavian S.S.R., but little real news about what went on in Transnistria. After the area's recapture, it was convenient to blame agricultural and industrial difficulties (and not without reason) on the destruction wrought by the retreating enemy. Only rarely did the Soviet press give a detailed picture of Romanian-held Odessa, as Ilia Ehrenburg did in 1944. In the customary amalgam of truth and untruth, he made bitter fun of the "Daco-Romanian" claims to Russian territory. The accomplishments of the pioneers of "Greater Romania," he wrote, were limited to the opening of swish bordellos in Odessa. "In Odessa University, semi-literate violinists... give lectures on the grandeur of the Daco-Romanians, while Romanian gendarmes use gas against the Odessa residents hiding in the

---

[43] "Odessa: Poslevoennyi period."

catacombs."⁴⁴ Compared with the ferocious and documented accounts of German atrocities, these were mild and toothless charges.

In 1944, it was possible for several foreign newspapermen, including *New York Times* correspondent WH. Lawrence, and Richard E. Lauterbach, to visit Odessa within a week of its recapture to gather information on Romania rule, and to interview men such as Dean Vasili of Uspenski Cathedral. Bearing in mind the treatment accorded the Nazis by the Soviet press in 1944, it seems remarkable that censorship passed Lawrence's dispatch, which did little more than say that the Romanians had put silk stockings up for sale in Odessa and that in general "the Romanians had been somewhat loose and lax administrators, open to bribery and corruption."⁴⁵ The same "non-totalitarian" picture was implicit in the lengthy official report of the Soviet Extraordinary Commission released on June 13, 1944. Compared with its reports on other areas — separate reports were produced on every German or Romanian held area — this was a strikingly weak document. Its main lines of attack were on (a) corruption; (b) destruction and plunder by the Romanians, and German destruction before they left in April, 1944; (c) atrocities. Interestingly, in the latter category not the least indication is given that the overwhelming number of the victims were Jews; on the contrary the document took considerable pains to give non-Jewish names of a few sample victims as if to reinforce the reader's impression that all Soviet citizens were exposed to murder and abomination. The report claims, though without a conclusive breakdown, that a total of 200,000 persons perished in Transnistria — a figure none too meaningful unless it is known whether prisoners, Bessarabian Jews, and other categories are included.⁴⁶

Both this and other Soviet reports named various Romanian and German generals and officers sought as war criminals. In May 1945, several of these, including General Trestorianu, the Odessa commandant, were tried in Bucharest by the Romanian authorities. Antonescu, Alexianu, and other leading Romanian officials were sentenced to death and executed after a secret trial.⁴⁷

---

⁴⁴ I. Ehrenburg, *Voina*, Vol. 3: *1943-44,* OGIZ, Moscow, 1944, pp. 66-67; Gordienko, *op. cit.*

⁴⁵ *The New York Times,* April 22, 1944 (dispatch filed April 16, 1944). See also Lauterbach, *op. cit.,* pp. 79-89.

⁴⁶ Document USSR-47.

⁴⁷ *Bol'shevistskoe znamia*, Odessa, May 18, 1945; *Izvestiia*, January 11 and 18, 1946.

Soon after the war, the Odessa oblast' authorities set up a "Commission for the History of the Fatherland War." In 1947, it published the first volume of a series, devoted to the period from June 22 to October 16, 1941. The second volume, covering the period of occupation, appeared two years later, and a third in 1953. Interestingly enough, their publication was scarcely publicized; volumes II and III are apparently far less readily available than the first; and they are not mentioned as a source in any of the subsequent books and articles on the subject (such as the second edition of the *Great Soviet Encyclopedia* or the Borisov pamphlet). The second volume is a collection of factual, though propagandistically selected documents, and the keen reader can gather between the lines the limited success and support the Bolshevik organization enjoyed in Transnistria. Still, the volume is helpful to the analyst; moreover, it contains excerpts from other books and magazines not otherwise available. The third volume has not been located abroad.

Soviet authorities had publicly to face the problem of how to treat Transnistria after the publication of Valentin Kataev's novel, *For Soviet Power!*, in 1949. As mentioned earlier, the first version of this book, though typically Soviet, revealed something of the shortcomings, the diversity of views, the relative inactivity, and the small scope of the partisan movement in Transnistria. In February 1950, a leading Soviet writer-critic, in a lengthy article that merits close study, sharply attacked Kataev;[48] he clearly had official support and encouragement. The upshot was an extensive revision by Kataev. A few significant changes may be mentioned. The underground group's leader emerges as far more authoritative, and the dealings between the Party Secretary and the members appear more formal; now the underground group keeps records, adopts resolutions, conducts "meetings." They are much more aware of their objectives, and their preparations are better planned and less chaotic than in the earlier version. The group's operations now seem much more extensive and ambitious, and also more coordinated with other groups. Several new characters appear, including especially a Comrade Vasili, the commander of a parachutist team, who comes "from Moscow" — introduced in an obvious effort to stress the omniscient wisdom and centralized direction emanating from the Kremlin and extending as far as the Odessa catacombs. Moreover, the partisans apprehended by the Romanians now kill

---

[48] Mikhail Bubennov, "O novom romane Valentina Kataeva," *Oktiabr'*, Moscow, February, 1950, pp. 3-19.

the "traitor" who has infiltrated the group and exposed it to the authorities. The entire book has acquired a far heavier Soviet impress, and much of the charming spontaneity of the earlier version has been replaced by the conventions typical of Soviet fiction.[49]

For "patriotic" as well as dramatic reasons, even Kataev exaggerated the role of the partisans. Overemphasis on the partisans and the great role assigned to the party in virtually all postwar partisan memoirs characterizes other and more recent Soviet articles and books on the war years in Transnistria — in general, there are fewer of them than on other critical areas. A certain awkwardness in the treatment of the whole problem persists. Since 1953, several "factual" pamphlets, largely on the military aspects of the campaign and siege, have appeared in Moscow.[50] It perhaps reveals the "new spirit" that the latest article, published in Kiev in May 1955, stresses Romanian abuses that were both real and genuinely important in determining popular attitudes: "Every enemy soldier could enter a house as if it was his own, and could appropriate whatever he liked. The occupant's boot trampled the native (*rodnoi*) soil and... human dignity."[51]

---

[49] Kataev, *Za vlast' sovetov*, Moscow, 1949 (1st ed.), and 1953 (revised ed.).
[50] See Borisov, Kononenko, and K.V. Penzing, *op. cit.*
[51] *Pravda Ukrainy*, May 7, 1955.

Chapter VIII

Some Conclusions and Implications

The Romanian occupation of Transnistria between October 1941 and March 1944 is often cited by Soviet refugees who lived under German rule as a foreign occupation that was considerably "better" than the German. It is this that in part prompted the present study. As might well have been expected, the picture of sweetness and light in wartime Odessa proves to be overdrawn. Nonetheless, the Transnistria experience was significant and, in many respects, unique.

Both in their policy and their practice the Romanians were considerably more lax than the Germans. Romanian rule lacked much of the extremism, racism, superciliousness, and rigidity of German rule. In day-to-day relations, it was far more indifferent to political consequences, but the average Romanian soldier manifested a considerably greater acquisitive spirit than did the German. In that the Transnistrian regime looked on Transnistria as an opportunity for positive Romanian colonization and its citizens as potential citizens of the mother-state, it was very unlike the Germans.

The Romanians, in consequence, were not reluctant, like the Germans, about investing capital in the economy and particularly in cultural projects. Romanian laxity and comparative benevolence — due in part to the (perhaps subconscious) respect which Odessa enjoyed among many Romanians as a cultural and economic metropolis — produced an atmosphere of bribery and speculation. More important, the absence of both

Soviet controls and Nazi authority gave rise to a society which was more nearly a microcosm of a free Russia than that of any other Soviet city. Odessa enjoyed opportunities for self-expression greater than it had possessed for many a year and surely much greater than any other Axis-occupied parts of the U.S.S.R. had.

To what extent can the experience of Odessa be considered typical or indicative for the rest of the Soviet Union? It must be granted that evidence on rural Transnistria is scant and perhaps inadequate for meaningful generalization. Certain general statements can be made about the city of Odessa, provided, however, certain variables are kept in mind. It should be remembered that these were war years, and that war discourages certain marginal "non-essential" activities — in social, intellectual, and political life — and tends to impose a measure of austerity. In demographic composition, wartime Odessa was atypical: the number of adult males was considerably smaller than in peacetime — due largely to mobilization into the army and evacuation eastward. The evacuation also introduced a selective factor by primarily removing the pro-Soviet element of bureaucracy, Party members, and economic management, as well as a considerable number of industrial workers, foremen, and, of ethnic groups, a substantial percentage of the Jewish population. The result was a particularly acute shortage of men with administrative know-how; the intelligentsia as a whole was less significantly affected.

One may argue that Odessa was at no time a typical Soviet city. More than most other cities, it had had its own specific cultural and social reputation and routine, its own jargon, and perhaps its own values. This was truer before 1930; the trend in the Soviet era had been towards standardization, and, in 1941, Odessa was in the process of being assimilated and was approaching the Soviet urban norm. Certain of its peculiar characteristics, however, persisted, and these, it may be posited, intensified the Romanian-bred proclivity for shady dealings. Odessa was perhaps a little more cosmopolitan than most Russian cities; the nationality question also was apparently — though it is hard to prove this — less acute there than elsewhere in the Ukraine. With these exceptions, the responses of the residents of Odessa may by and large be assumed to have been the same as those of other Soviet urban citizens.

It is convenient to divide the Romanian occupation into three periods: the first months, in the winter of 1941-1942, when the general uncertainty and economic chaos produced a certain crisis and near-stalemate, though signs of economic and slight cultural change were already being manifested; the major period of the occupation, from the spring? of 1942 to the summer of 1943, when both the economy and artistic and social life underwent substantial changes and gained a certain new *élan* though accompanied by distinctly unsavory business practices and the prevalence of graft; and the final phase, in late 1943 and early 1944, of Axis military setbacks and the concomitant economic and political crisis in which most inhabitants looked forward to the return of the Soviet authorities and shaped their own behavior accordingly, in which prices rose as goods became scarce, and the Germans finally took over military government from the crumbling Romanian administration.

The economic, cultural, and political activities of the native population have been examined. The galvanization of economic life was most substantial and began earliest; that of cultural activities was easiest to accomplish and remarkable but was, by its very nature, limited; autonomous political activity was least and came last, though often supplemented by or sublimated into forms which may be labeled *Ersatz* political action. That there was so little political activity of a conventional sort does not necessarily indicate a lack of interest in public affairs. To a large extent, it is attributable to people's preoccupation with more immediate and personal concerns, to lack of experience in making political choices, to the restrictions imposed by the new authoritarian regime, and to the ubiquitous sense of fear that lingered even after the Soviet forces left.

There was considerably less reason for fear in economic pursuits, and many who would not or dared not give public expression to their political views and desires (insofar as they were capable of articulating them) had little or no hesitation about engaging in private business enterprises. The economic upsurge — if not in productivity, at least in individual participation and involvement in it — was unmistakable enough to warrant labeling it a "New NKP"; and it disproves, at least in this sphere, the hypothesis of an "inert" Soviet population.

Indeed, the occupation bared how deep-seated the quest for personal advantage was; most city-dwellers were willing and able to display initiative in order to secure it. They shaped a new way of life which was typically that of an acquisitive society.

The "inertness" hypothesis is further disproved by the high degree of sensitivity with which economic life responded to external impulses. Prices fluctuated to take into account changes in weather, supply routes, competing imports, the arrival of soldiers on leave, and other variables; currency exchange reflected not only supply and demand but also military developments and political trends. And it is surely not an "inert" society that reacted as Odessa did to such events as the battle of Stalingrad:

> The people had entirely lost their heads (the German consul cabled home from Odessa in February 1943). The peasants sold what they had, in order to procure horses and carts. In the cities all cash was exchanged into foodstuffs. This contributed in turn to a substantial rise in prices. For days, the foodstores in Odessa were sold out. Many Russians spoke of suicide if the Bolsheviks should return...

Actually, in the year before the Soviet return many changed their minds, and there were few suicides and relatively few attempts to escape in the spring of 1944. This very ability to make political choices and to change one's mind politically further invalidates the "inertness" theory. Moreover, the evidence indicates that political choice was not a function of material well-being. Undoubtedly, their lack of an adequate subsistence level helped push many workers and some intellectuals into opposition to the Transnistrian authorities; and unquestionably the high standard of living attained by some of the "new elite" helped anchor their loyalties on the Romanian side. Yet there are too many instances at variance with this to accept it as the general rule; while material security may often have been a necessary prerequisite, it was certainly not sufficient in itself to produce allegiance.

Although displaying economic activity and a distinct hostility to certain facets of Soviet life, the population manifested unwittingly a considerable residue of the Bolshevik ethic and its patterns of behavior. Unfortunately, it is almost impossible to assess *post facto* these facets, particularly on the basis of such source materials as have been available for the present paper.

The turbulent siege and occupation, with the population movements accompanying them, naturally increased social mobility, particularly in an upward direction. Most significant perhaps was the emergence of a "new elite" — which developed partly as a result of Romanian policy but which was largely a natural outgrowth, and which secured for itself privileges in economic and social status. A small group within this elite were political figures accepted or appointed by the Romanians; a larger group, the new managers of economic enterprises and other administrative-supervisory personnel; the greatest contingent were those engaged in "commercial capitalism" — both legitimate and shady — and who had been especially successful.

The political collaborators came primarily from the intelligentsia (in the broad Russian sense of the word); they included people who had been Soviet-trained as well as those with pre-Soviet experience. Men in the age bracket between forty and fifty predominated; the younger age groups were either not in Odessa or were afraid; the older ones lacked incentives for collaboration and were at times held back by greater moral scruples than the Soviet-bred generation.[1] The economic "entrepreneurs" came from all walks of life, both men and women, laborers and professors, both pre-Soviet and Soviet-trained; perhaps predominating were men whose previous work had prepared them for such tasks: NKP men, store-keepers, and those who had white-collar positions in the Soviet economy. The managerial elite came almost entirely from the technician class; they had had similar work in the Soviet period and when their superiors left moved upward from the level of specialists to that of managers; this satisfied both their ego and their wish for greater economic reward.

The extent to which previously frustrated ambitions were now satisfied cannot be measured. Virtually all social strata sought "normalcy," security, and abundance; these fundamentally "middle-class" aspirations stemmed both from Soviet-generated values and from a hostile reaction to certain facets of Soviet life. In refugee discussions of this period, labels such as *obyvatel'skie* and *meshchanskie* (philistine) recur with striking frequency as if to underscore this desire for more comfortable living; those who could afford it sought conspicuous wealth and consumption as well as comfort. Indeed, black-marketeers, brass bands in the public squares, cafe life, and retail stores, a re-opened university and opera, lipsticks and corsets, were all expressions of this feeling. More than once visiting Germans characterized the prevailing spirit of Odessa as "Enjoy yourself' — or perhaps "Enrich yourself."

All these were manifestations of what may be called the "rightist" response to the Soviet regime. There was also a "leftist" reaction, equally diffuse though much less pronounced. It objected not only to the corruption and social inequality of the Romanian-instituted system, but also to the Soviet regime's similar shortcomings. The "leftists" rejected Soviet rule precisely because it was not as Communist as they wished it. A small

---

[1] It is interesting to note in this connection that, with one single exception (Lazarev, born 1895), the Communist underground and partisan leaders in and around Odessa belonged to a slightly younger group. While the political collaborators were often born between 1890 and 1905. the Communists often had been born between 1900 and 1917 (e.g., Gorbel' 1905, Drozdov 1905, Morgunenko 1905, Kostiuk 1907, Badaev 1910).

minority of society, the "leftists" were to be found both among the intelligentsia (for instance at the university) and in the workers' quarters.[2]

Most of the population attached no onus to "collaboration." There was at first some fear and a wait-and-see attitude, but no moral condemnation of collaborators by fellow-citizens, except of those in certain specific pursuits. Police personnel, informants, and censors, for instance, were decidedly frowned on (even by other collaborators) for their "indecent" or "treacherous" activities. The Romanians made rather strenuous efforts to get the allegiance of the population, but though residents accepted collaborators, they did not accept their new masters. Patriotism and especially local pride seem to have been strong even where anti-Bolshevism was intense.

Two rather complex problems remain to be clarified.

(1) It has been commonly posited — and the present writer fully agrees — that the opposition to the collective farm, either *in toto* or to some of its salient features, is a real "Achilles heel" of the Soviet system. This view is reinforced by the mass of evidence showing a spontaneous partition of collectives, or parts of them, when Soviet controls broke down during the war; where the kolkhoz system remained substantially intact, the kolkhoz generally became a source of popular grievances and contributed in varying degrees to the disillusionment of the rural population with the German order.[3]

Oddly enough, however, widespread rural acceptance of the Romanian alternative was not preceded or accompanied by a liquidation of the kolkhoz system. Some changes were introduced, but the basic institution was scarcely altered. In this instance, in other words, a satisfaction of anti-kolkhoz grievances was not a prerequisite for loyalty. The following explanations seem to carry the most weight:

(a) Even though the kolkhoz system was formally retained, the spirit in which it was operated was different. The Romanians did not enforce

---

[2] One may assume that there was a larger proportion of "leftists" than "rightists" among the personnel evacuated and absent from Odessa: the "leftists" were more often the younger generation and more often among the official and other categories entitled to evacuation. They often had a better understanding — and a stronger *a priori* rejection — of Nazism; and they tended to accept the Soviet regime as the "lesser evil" so long as the war lasted.

[3] The author has sought to examine some of these problems in an earlier paper, "The Peasantry as a Source of Soviet Vulnerability in World War II," War Documentation Project, 1955.

kolkhoz regulations as the Soviets had, and this tended to make the peasant less sensitive about the collective.[4]

(b) The retention of the system seemed less important than the fact that (1) deliveries to the state were somewhat reduced — this tended to raise the peasants' standard of living, and that (2) the removal of restraints on trade and prices encouraged trade and various deals that enabled the rural folk to secure more products — necessary consumer goods as well as "luxuries" — than they had under Soviet conditions.

(c) The above factors dulled the immediacy and urgency of anti-kolkhoz sentiments, and other aspects of the Romanian occupation, such as the restoration of church life, tended to give the Romanians a positive halo — at least in 1942 and part of 1943. All of this made the peasantry accept the new regime even though the collectives were as yet unabolished.

This does not invalidate the hypothesis that anti-kolkhoz sentiment was widespread; there is certainly no evidence from Transnistria that the collectives were popular or that people wanted to keep them. It does indicate, however, that under certain circumstances — and theoretically these can occur under Soviet as well as non-Soviet rule — desire for rural change can be so submerged or suppressed even among anti-kolkhoz that a regime wedded to the perpetuation, in one form or another, of the collective farms is still accepted.

(2) Another seeming paradox arises in connection with the thesis that Soviet citizens have a particularly keen sensitivity to symbols of individual and group dignity, personal abuse, physical and moral humiliation. This implies that judgments about a political system are more importantly influenced by personal, day-to-day contacts and experiences than by abstractions, slogans, and ideologies (though this is not to deny the role of abstractions). Yet, in Transnistria, the new system was accepted in spite of extensive abuse, looting, rape, and a general atmosphere of insecurity and unpredictability. The actions of individual (and generally poorly disciplined) Romanian officials or soldiers could not be predicted, and their ubiquitous graft and avarice did nothing to enhance their standing in the

---

[4] A nationalist Ukrainian peasant boy, who defected to the West after the war, commented that the *kolkhoz* population during the war fared best under the Romanians, for in spite of condescension and abuse, there was less looting, lower taxes, and more self-government (Harvard University Refugee Interview Project, B6, No. 314).

residents' eyes. The paradox may perhaps be explained in the following manner.

The average resident of Transnistria had considerably more contact with the occupying authorities than did the Soviet citizen in German territory; this was particularly true in urban areas, but even elsewhere Romanian officialdom was proportionately more numerous and visible than, say, the Germans in backwoods villages around Briansk, Polotsk, or Pskov. In German-held areas the few contacts with the Germans were often of a "negative" sort — compulsory commandeering of grain, punitive anti-partisan operations, forced-labor conscription, and the like; in Transnistria, because of the greater frequency of contacts, "negative" experiences were a smaller proportion of the total.

But the difference in number of contacts does not seem to explain the difference in attitude toward the Germans and the Romanians. One may argue with some justification that the abusive, arbitrary acts of the Romanians constituted only a part, and perhaps none too significant a part, of the total of impressions; other milder, and at times more benevolent, experiences counterbalancing these went into the formation of the total judgement on the new order. Refugees and Germans alike frequently assert that in Odessa the people did not hate the occupying power — as they often did in German-held areas, especially toward the end of the occupation; instead, they regarded the Romanians "with contempt and almost pity." Psychologically perhaps a natural and useful defense, this condescension on the part of the occupied toward their occupier helped establish a *modus vivendi*; the occupied did not feel nearly so "inferior" as they did in German-occupied territory. The basic difference in the approach of the Romanians and the Germans lies at the root of the difference in the way their rule was regarded.

Thus, although individual, personal experience with the new order, and particularly impressions of abuse and humiliation, played a considerable part in Transnistria as elsewhere in Soviet territory, it was not the controlling element in determining popular attitudes toward the occupying authorities.

At the start, most residents were willing to accept the new system and make the most of it; gradually disillusioned, most were at the end willing once again to accept the Soviet system. The growth of hostility toward the Transnistrian regime, especially pronounced in 1943-1944, was due to several major causes: general war-weariness and a desire to "get it over with"; the contagious upsurge of patriotism and the widespread belief that the Soviet government had reformed and been liberalized during the war, the actual turn of the tide on the battlefield; fear of Soviet persecution for collaboration with the enemy, which prompted a rationalizing of anti-Romanian attitudes; and the deterioration of economic conditions in Odessa. And, of course, in time, *any* military or foreign occupation is bound to become onerous and unpopular.

When all this is said, however, the contrast with conditions in the German-held areas of the U.S.S.R. strongly suggests that there is a distinct functional relationship between the type of occupation policy and conduct, on the one hand, and response of the subject population, on the other. Viewed in terms of the judgment, attitude, and perhaps behavior of the Soviet population, it does seem to have mattered a good deal *how* the occupying power conducted itself. In the period of 1941-1945, the citizens of the U.S.S.R. (as exemplified by the Transnistrian sample) were neither so firmly wedded to the Soviet cause as to endorse it unquestioningly and irrevocably, nor so blindly hostile to it as to accept any alternative without further inquiry and experience. The way the balance tipped in any given situation — holding external factors such as military events constant — depended greatly on the purposes, methods, and attitudes of the alternative regime.

Without a doubt, the Romanian system in Transnistria was far more popular than was the German. Germans and neutral observers, Soviet refugees, and of course the Romanians themselves repeatedly stress that in Odessa conditions were better than in German-held areas — higher living standards and a climate of greater relaxation and security. This was significant, as, in the last analysis, economic and political life in wartime Odessa was in many ways unhealthy and abortive (cultural life tended to be more genuine and of higher quality). Even so, this Transnistrian experience, at least in its middle span and at least for large segments of the population, involved certain markedly welcome changes over either Soviet or German rule.

It is difficult to say just what factors were crucial in making Transnistrian rule seem to the people preferable to a German occupation. In all likelihood it was a combination of positive and negative elements. The absence of German forced-labor conscription and certain other forms of terror and duress, for instance, played a considerable part, so did the greater economic plenty, the greater leeway given the resident population in business and in cultural and educational pursuits, and the greater opportunity for self-expression enjoyed under the Romanians.

Soviet reactions reflect the preference for Transnistrian rule over German rule. The partisan movement in the area was ephemeral as compared with that in the "classical" areas of Belorussia and the R.S.F.S.R. The Soviet authorities were hard-pressed to find effective accusations against the Romanian authorities there. The contrived and relatively shallow nature of most of their charges (except for the spoliation of Soviet installations, objects of art, and private property) in itself attests to this fact.

Transnistria was no viable body politic. Virtually no one regarded it as such. Yet it demonstrated that the Soviet population was capable of operating in a non-Soviet environment and under a non-Soviet regime; and that it was willing, under certain circumstances, to adjust to a non-Soviet system once the latter appeared to be more or less solidly entrenched, and once it promised to satisfy at least some of the aspirations which Soviet rule had failed to satisfy. It demonstrated that the Soviet population knew, within limits, what it wanted, that it was capable of choosing, and that it chose that which promised it a squarer deal.

It must be borne in mind, however, that the material well-being and prestige of some of those well off under Transnistrian auspices would not have been so great had not a significant segment of the population been removed — a consideration which, is it true, might have been counterbalanced and neutralized, if factories and other evacuated or destroyed equipment had remained in operation. The emergence of a new elite, also, produced a curious operational dilemma for the occupying power: the granting of privileges anchored the loyalty of the elite more solidly; yet the very formation of an elite by these methods tended to antagonize the rest of the population. The Romanians never coped with this problem, just as they never adequately coped with the problems of the long-range political evolution of Soviet society. Transnistria was a short-term experiment. For a variety of reasons, its lessons are limited. The implications, nonetheless, remain.

Summary

As a result of the German invasion of the Soviet Union in June 1941, the Odessa region found itself in the throes of mobilization, reorganization, and evacuation. Later, from mid-August to mid-October 1941, it was under siege by Romanian forces. Finally, from October 16, 1941, to April 10, 1944, it lived under Romanian occupation.

At the outbreak of war, the local state and party authorities in Odessa apparently moved swiftly and even, after recovering from the initial shock, efficiently to carry out the first major "war measures" passed down from Moscow and Kiev. There is little evidence of initiative on the part of local officials so long as the channels for the transmission of orders from above remained intact. There are suggestions that the local officials were afraid to improvise and awkward in devising *ad hoc* emergency measures. This was true mainly in political and administrative matters.

Individual initiative was more apparent in two other areas: technical and logistic ingenuity were apparent in the handling of production and transportation under emergency conditions, and some local initiative was forthcoming in proposing military moves. The prime example of the latter was the suggestion by an Odessa naval officer in August 1941, that Odessa should be held rather than abandoned.

Plans for mobilization, establishment of "destruction battalions" (in theory convertible into partisan units, though in fact largely thrown into combat), and civil defense measures had been prepared in advance or were easily organized according to standard patterns. A number of other problems, such as evacuation of personnel and installations, provision of food for the city and its hinterland, and emergency mass enrollment into the so-called *opolchenie,* were apparently handled without much skill. Some of these tasks, such as the evacuation, were accomplished incompletely and behind schedule. Others, for example civilian conscription, were something of a failure, probably because of the intrinsic difficulty of the tasks rather than the failings of key individuals.

Most Red Army and Navy personnel and a few party officials kept their "administrative nerve" better than managers of economic enterprises or some of the state and city officials. Many of the latter were ill-prepared to cope with such unexpected and gigantic responsibilities and were prone, on convenient pretexts, to evacuate themselves and their families. Moreover, the progressive breakdown of overland contact with Odessa and the disruption of the military chain of command intensified the confusion, and under the siege, fostered a sense of futility among local officials.

Party organizations generally operated more smoothly and continuously than state and soviet organs, so that responsibility for decision-making shifted informally to *obkoms* and *gorkoms,* as it may have done less conspicuously in peacetime.

At this time of crisis, the multiplicity of peacetime authorities clustered into two groups: the military (army and navy) and the political (party and NKVD). In the organization of the evacuation, the two acted jointly: the army and navy assumed responsibility for military personnel and equipment, and the party took charge of the withdrawal of civilian personnel and industrial facilities. On the other hand, the three major military decisions — to hold Odessa under siege, to stage a relief operation at Dofinovka, and to abandon Odessa — were all made by the military alone (in this case the Soviet High Command, the *stavka)* and were transmitted to Odessa from the outside. The first of these, however, and perhaps also the others, stemmed from local suggestions. In mid-August 1941, the commander of the Odessa Naval Base took it upon himself to suspend the evacuation and urge the Black Sea Fleet to prepare to hold out under siege, a suggestion favorably passed on by the *stavka.*

The lull scope of NKVD and police activities cannot be gauged from the available evidence, but they seem to have dovetailed with party operations, as in the establishment of underground units, control of industrial production, supervision of fire-fighting after air raids, and apprehension of "panic-makers" and "saboteurs."

In order to coordinate emergency measures during the defense of Odessa and to secure a maximum of cooperation among the increasingly autonomous branches of local authority, a network of small administrative committees was established, consisting typically of one representative each from party, state, and police (NKVD), and sometimes army. Such three- or four-man committees were left in charge of *rayony* and towns when the regular authorities had been evacuated or had dispersed. The effectiveness of these committees depended on the individual members. They seem to have functioned with a measure of success. On the whole, orders issued by the various Soviet authorities both before and during the siege were given the same kind of perfunctory or superficial obedience that Soviet decrees had commanded before the war. Sometimes orders were obeyed overzealously, as after the appeal to expose enemy spies and agents; at other times, they were followed with extreme reluctance, as in the rationing of water, the destruction of certain supplies, and the mining of certain buildings — all matters which affected the individual citizen. It appears certain that the number of individuals failing to obey regulations — dodging mobilization, circumventing official evacuation, violating ration decrees — was substantially greater than in "normal" times. To some extent, the breakdown of Soviet authority and prestige was a concomitant of the deteriorating military and political position, for it stemmed from the belief that an early change of regimes would bring impunity for lawbreakers.

The most chaotic administrative operation, perhaps, was the evacuation of men and materiel. This was due in large measure to the absence of previous experience or preparation, as well as to contradictory directives and concepts of priority. The same difficulties afflicted the shift to underground work when the surrender of Odessa became imminent, and these were further complicated by the need to operate surreptitiously in order to avoid denunciation for "defeatism" by those zealots who did not publicly admit the possibility of surrender to the Germans.

Soviet sources are misleading on the part played by the party and the Komsomol, whose rank-and-file members clearly fell short of the achievements attributed to them after the war. Apparently, party officials consciously established priorities in indoctrination. Acknowledging that they could not maintain under crisis conditions and with reduced personnel the "monolithic" control of peacetime, the authorities (probably at the *oblast* level) chose to concentrate on a few matters, such as the security of the port and the morale and loyalty of its key personnel.

The Odessa experience suggests that the breakdown of Soviet prestige need not necessarily entail a collapse of Soviet control in fields where the party decides that its maintenance is crucial. The processes of government, conditioned by the increasing proximity of the front lines, were carried on as long as the authorities made a point of carrying them on. Though abnormally slow and complicated, they were not disrupted significantly by popular discontent or even disloyalty. Life under Soviet conditions, both before and after the war, appears to have been marked by a wide divergence between popular feelings and overt behavior. During the siege, the many degrees of defeatism and disgruntlement had little direct bearing on behavior or on the persistence of Soviet rule.

Yet the war and the siege had a profound impact on the people's morale. Nervousness, rumor-mongering, hoarding of supplies, anticipation of Soviet defeat, resentment of evacuation of the privileged, lack of news, and sleepless nights from air attacks contributed to a sense of insecurity. With the passage of time, many of the more reliable citizens were evacuated or mobilized. There is no evidence of a fanatical determination to hold the city. The man in the street had become broadly indifferent or latently hostile to the Soviet system. Yet he continued to report for work and fulfill his duties, at once hoping for and fearing the imminent change.

Explicit political initiative, aside from the official Bolshevik variety, remained virtually nonexistent until the capture of Odessa in October 1941. This surface passivity stemmed partly from the many years of outward obedience to authority and partly from a sense that the prescription for survival was silence. Moreover, those age and social groups which might have taken political action were the very ones most likely to have been evacuated: army officers, factory managers, Soviet officials. Widespread expectation of Soviet defeat and vague talk of a new, non-Soviet order mingled, often incoherently, with Russian or Soviet patriotism in such a way as to confuse the average citizen and persuade him anew that the best policy was one of watchful waiting.

The increasing hardships of life left the citizen little leisure for political ideas or action and turned his attention to hoarding, black-marketeering, and speculation, activities which the weakened Soviet controls could no longer thwart. The peak of this kind of lawless individualism was the rash of looting which broke out in Odessa during the confused days of the withdrawal of Soviet troops and the arrival of the Romanians. The looters were by no means only professional thieves or criminals. Most of the town reportedly participated in the chaotic "appropriation" of government property and of goods from the apartments of evacuees.

Soviet administration during the siege was impeded less by popular discontent than by wartime dislocations, inexperience, inability to cope with novel situations, and fear of assuming responsibility not formally delegated from above. This is not to minimize the extent of popular discontent, which grew as the siege dragged on, presaging the end of Soviet rule. A substantial part of Odessa's residents, expecting a complete collapse of the Red Army, were prepared to accept an alternative to Soviet rule, and this fact goes far to explain the strikingly small support which, during the Romanian occupation, the people tendered the Soviet partisans and underground.

The partisan organization itself was less effective than in most other parts of the occupied U.S.S.R. Only toward the end of the war, when systematic military support from the Soviet side was given the small partisan nuclei, and when many citizens joined the bands to whitewash themselves in anticipation of the Red Army's return, was it of any significance. Apart from popular discontent with Soviet rule, the main reason for the partisans' failure to attract more support was the relatively mild occupation policy of the Romanians in the Odessa area, which they renamed the province of Transnistria. One can establish a district correlation between the toughness of occupation policy and the support received by the partisans from the population. Transnistria and the Northern Caucasus, where occupation policy was least oppressive, stand out as areas of failure for the Soviet partisan movement.

The Romanian-occupied territory of Transnistria contrasted sharply with the German-ruled areas of the U.S.S.R. Some Romanians wanted their country to annex Transnistria and turn it into a Romanian province. Others argued that Romania had no need, no capital, and no manpower to acquire *Lebensraum* in the East. In any event, it was not to become a colonial area, for the Romanian regime, plagued with other problems, regarded Transnistria simply as a bargaining counter for the postwar return of Transylvania from Hungary to Romania.

Romanian occupation policy, both in intent and in implementation, was much laxer than that of the Germans. Romanian conduct lacked the extremism, the dogmatism, and to some extent the superciliousness of the

Nazis. In day-to-day relations the authorities exhibited indifference to the long-range political consequences of their actions, while the annexationist minority among the occupiers treated the former Soviet citizens much as they did their fellow-Romanians.

While Romanian policy and conduct in Transnistria were not uniformly lax, the local inhabitant enjoyed enough freedom to display their abilities and interests, and generally to demonstrate how a large urban Soviet population could operate under a measure of autonomy. The absence of both Soviet and Nazi controls made of Transnistria a microcosm of a "free Russia." Although Odessa was not in all ways a typical Soviet city, the lessons of its wartime experience are nonetheless significant and valid.

The Romanian occupation may be divided into three periods: the winter of 1941-1942, when economic chaos, privation, and fear combined to produce a mood of crisis; the major period, from the spring of 1942 to the summer of 1943, which witnessed substantially increasing activity in economic, cultural, and social life; and the final phase, in late 1943 and early 1944, when the setbacks of the Axis powers led most of the inhabitants to adjust their activities to the expected return of the Soviet authorities.

In the middle period, the galvanization of economic life was the earliest and the most substantial sign of indigenous activity. Initiative in the field of cultural, educational, and religious affairs was considerable. Autonomous political activity was the last to appear, the least pronounced, and was often supplemented by or sublimated into forms that have been referred to as *Ersatz* politics. The limited evidence of conventional political action does not imply an innate lack of interest in public affairs, but rather a preoccupation with more pressing, personal concerns, a lack of political experience, and inhibitions lingering from the past.

On the economic side, the occupation revealed among the people a deep-seated quest for personal advantage, and the necessary ingenuity to secure it; in brief, the will to evolve toward a typically "acquisitive" society. Connected with this was the emergence of a new elite with a materially and socially privileged position. Some of its members were appointees of the new regime; others were the new managers of old enterprises; but the greatest number were adventitious captains of "commercial capitalism," legitimate as well as shady.

Summary 271

While the political collaborators were predominantly "intellectuals" of both pre-Soviet and Soviet vintage (with men between the ages of 35 and 50 predominating), the new entrepreneurs came from all walks of life and included men and women with previous experience of business: storekeepers, white-collar Soviet economic personnel, and NEP men. The new managerial elite consisted almost entirely of technicians who had replaced their former directors after the latter were evacuated.

There was a segment of the population, especially among university circles and some of the skilled workers, that strove to provide an ideal or moral basis for the new order of society. Its aspirations never crystallized clearly, for it never acquired a medium of public expression. The views of these people conflicted violently with Romanian practice in that they opposed both corruption and social inequality.

The bulk of the population were opportunists, but their patriotism was too strong for wholesale identification with the Romanians. On the other hand, not until 1943 was there any considerable revulsion against the occupiers. The typical evolution was from initial accommodation, through gradual disillusionment, to ultimate hostility. Several factors were responsible: general war-weariness; an upsurge of patriotism; a wide spread belief that the Soviet regime had been reformed and liberalized during the war; the reversal of fortunes on the battlefield; deterioration of material conditions in Odessa toward the end of the occupation; and a sense that the Romanians, who were after all foreign and somewhat supercilious, had not satisfied and would not satisfy the desire for security and stability.

The growth of hostility against the Romanians, however, should not be allowed to obscure the contrast between Transnistria and the German-held areas of the U.S.S.R. The relative success of the Romanians supports the thesis that the specific nature of occupation policy and behavior mattered a good deal in determining the response of the subject population.

The Odessa case confirms the suspicion that many citizens of the U.S.S.R. were neither so firmly wedded to the Soviet cause in World War II as to endorse it unquestioningly, nor so blindly hostile to it as to accept another form of government without inquiry and experience. Whether, given a choice between forms of government, the Soviet people will take one side or the other must depend to an appreciable extent on the purposes, methods, and attitudes of the alternative regime. With all its limitations and abuses, the Transnistrian experiment rapidly gained popular confidence through higher living standards and an atmosphere of greater relaxation. The absence of terror and forced labor, and greater opportunities for self-expression, both economic and cultural, go far to explain the overwhelming popular preference for Romanian over German rule.

The story of Transnistria demonstrates that Soviet people can effectively operate in a non-Soviet environment, under an anti-Soviet regime. Under certain conditions, the bulk of those in one southern area were willing to adjust to and make the most of an environment more favorable to individual initiative than the Soviet system.

Appendix

Order No. 1
(Source: CRS, AOK 11, 22409/79)

(Translation)

To the Destruction Battalion in Komintern Rayon of Odessa Oblast, July 2, 1941

Art. 1. On the basis of Order No. 247 of the NKVD of Odessa Oblast, dated June 25, 1941, I assume the tasks of commander of the destruction battalion in Komintern Rayon. As my Deputy for Political Affairs, I appoint Comrade Maksiuk.

Art. 2. I appoint as chief of operative work at the headquarters of the destruction battalion, with the title of chief of staff, Comrade Komanov, I.I. As adjutant of the staff, I appoint Comrade Danidov.

Art. 3. The destruction battalion is to be established in company strength, consisting of three platoons and two separate platoons, for which purpose the following officers are appointed:

		Deputy for Political Affairs:
Company commander:	Comrade Manzhos	Comrade Kozishkurt
CO 1st Platoon:	Com. Vesnenko, N.	Com. Ishtovenko
Co 2d Platoon:	Com. Posidelski	Com. Belavski
Co 3d Platoon:	Com. Strelets	Com. Tsibulka
Co 4th Sep. Platoon:	Com. Stepanov	Com. Shevchenko
Co 5th Sep. Platoon:	Com. Garnoshenko	Com. Chavra

Art. 4. All platoon leaders shall immediately assume their positions.

Art. 5. The company commander, Com. Manzhos, and the other platoon leaders, are to select, no later than by July 3, those persons who possess sufficient military knowledge to be made squad leaders, so as to have at least four squad leaders to each platoon, and each squad with no fewer than nine men. The roster of men assigned as squad leaders is to be submitted for my confirmation.

Art. 6. I make the several platoon leaders individually responsible for the composition and condition of their platoon. Company Commander, Com. Manzhos, is personally responsible for the state of the company. In all instances of violation of discipline, internal disorder, and unrest, he is to apply the severest measures of disciplinary punishment, in accordance with regulations. He is to report all such instances to me.

Art. 7. The chief of staff of the destruction battalion, Com. Romanov, is entrusted by me with the direction of operative work:

(1) elaboration of training plan;

(2) determination of alarm system;

(3) establishment of internal details for the battalion;

(4) elaboration of a practical plan for tactical training, to include an attack in inhabited localities ad mine fields. Fixed days are to be set for the conduct of tactical exercises.

Art. 8. My deputy for political affairs, Com. Maksiuk, is to work out a program for political activities for the entire battalion. The implementation thereof is to be assigned to the political officers within the framework of the battalion. The direction of political work lies in the hands of Comrade Maksiuk.

This order is to be made known to the entire battalion.

Commander of the Destruction Battalion
(Izverezhnik)

Enclosure: Top Secret

T/O of Destruction Battalion

1. Btn CO — 1
2. Dep. for Pol. Affairs — 1
3. Chief of Staff— 1
4. Staff Adjutant— 1

5. Company commander — 1 officer for 100 riflemen
6. Platoon leader — 1 officer for 30-35 riflemen
7. Squad leader — 1 officer for 9-10 men
8. Chief of Ammunition Supply — 1
9. Supply (clothing) NCO — 1

Instructions Issued to German Military Government Organs, March 20, 1944[2] (Translation)

(1) *General Administration*

(a) The center of gravity of the administration is the rayon. The Romanian praetors (rayon chiefs) are to remain in office for the time being. All higher Romanian administrative agencies (district, sector, etc.) disappear. The indigenous mayors remain in office subject to screening.

(b) Only those branches of administration are to be continued which contribute to the maintenance of security and order as well as those essential for the supply of troops and population.

(c) Romanian administrative law remains in effect unless specifically altered by order of German administrative agencies.

(d) Schools are to be closed only where the buildings are needed for billeting of troops.

(e) The organization of Christian churches remains unaltered.

(f) The financial administration is to be pursued within the framework of the current budget on the rayon level. The Bank of Transnistria remains in the country and will be taken over by competent German officers. The rayons continue to be able to dispose of their accounts. Salaries continue to be paid; those for March have already been paid by the Romanian administration... As receipts from taxes are not expected to suffice, the levying of a capital tax and credit with the Bank of Transnistria are contemplated.

(g) Postal, telegram and telephone service for the civilian population is not to be continued.

(2) Law

(a) Civil justice rests (i.e., is non-existent).

---

[2] "AOK 6, O Qu/Qu 2, "Einzelanweisungen betr. Verwaltung des Gebiets zwischen Dnjestr und Bug," March 20, 1944, CRS, AOK 6, 59352/8.

(b) Punitive authority against the civilian population is exercised by administrative procedure by the rayon chiefs (up to four weeks of forced labor and monetary fine up to RM 1000) and the district commandants (for all cases meriting higher punishment). Death sentences and sentences to over one year of forced labor require confirmation by the (German) field commandant...

(3) *Civil health and veterinary service:* to be continued by the Romanians under direction of army doctors and veterinarians.

(4) Direction of *propaganda and cultural institutes* is taken over by the (army) propaganda agencies, to be financed by rayons or cities.

Bibliography

Note on Primary Sources

(1) The printed collections of documents, such as *Trial of the Major War Criminals* and other materials emanating from the Nuremberg trials, contain only a minimum of pertinent information. Among the useful items are affidavits and depositions made to the Soviet authorities by Gheorghe Alexianu, wartime governor of Transnistria, and by other Romanian officials; these are available at the National Archives, Washington, D.C. The records introduced in evidence at other, and more directly relevant, war crimes trials, particularly in Romania and Odessa itself, are not available and are known only from brief accounts in the Soviet press. The pertinent unpublished documents introduced at the subsequent Nuremberg trials are of relatively low caliber.

(2) The German records at the Captured Records Section, Departmental Records Branch, The Adjutant General's Office, U.S. Army, Alexandria, Virginia, are rather voluminous but, proportionately, of small value. They include the incomplete files of the *Deutsche Heeresmission in Rumänien* (the German military liaison staff in Bucharest during the war) and of some of its subordinate units in occupied Soviet territory[1]; some materials directly from German army units and an occasional folder of the economic liaison staff stationed in Odessa. All in all, these records are of interest for the formal and administrative arrangements governing the Romanian occupation and Romanian-German dealings, primarily for 1941 and 1944. They are particularly poor in information on attitudes and in political reporting; they skip almost entirely the crucial period from late 1941 to early 1943.

(3) German diplomatic records seem to have been of high quality. However, by far the best single collection — the reports and records of the German Consulate General in Odessa, 1942-1944, under Dr. Werner Stephany — have not been located. Whether they were lost or were captured by the Soviet authorities cannot be ascertained. Excerpts or copies found in other files indicate, despite notable blind spots, a considerable measure of perspicacity. Some other German diplomatic records, available on microfilm in the Historical Branch, U.S. Department of State, have likewise been of interest and value.[1]

(4) Other contemporary documents have yielded little. Romanian records are virtually unavailable; U.S. diplomatic and other wartime reports are of practically no value — a few documents from the former O.S.S. files include translations and paraphrases from newspapers and dispatches not otherwise available; Italian diplomatic files[2] could not be utilized. Romanian documents which found their way into German files have also been used.

(5) Published contemporary materials, other than Soviet sources, include several books and pamphlets produced in wartime Romania, such as historical-ethinic accounts of Transnistrian history, tailor-made to fit Romanian imperialist ambitions; several German and other Axis descriptions of Transnistria; descriptions of military events; and some rather pedestrian pieces on the reception accorded the Romanians and on their accomplishments. Of considerably greater value are the periodicals and newspapers. A search of the accessible libraries and a check by mail with various overseas depositories have revealed no copies of any of the newspapers published in the Odessa area under Romanian occupation, except for a complete set of the German-language paper, *Der Deutsche in Transnistrien*, which, however, was not only empty and inferior, but also tended to

---

[1] The files of the Volksdeutsche Mittelstelle (brief, VoMi) are located in Berlin. To judge from a few excerpts introduced at the Nuremberg trials, they contain a good deal of material on Transnistria, largely, however, on the ethnic Germans there. Because they were SS-oriented and concerned primarily with topics not germane to this study, and because of difficulties of access, no attempt was made to exploit them for the present paper.

[2] So far as the Italian consulate general in Odessa is concerned, the former consul (now Italian ambassador to Switzerland) writes that "all the archives of the Odessa office as well as my personal records had to be destroyed when I had to leave Odessa after the Italian armistice, in order to avoid that such material should fall in the hands of German police... I am also given to understand that the existing archives of the Foreign Ministry in Rome are rather incomplete for the period, as a consequence of what happened during the months of German occupation in Rome." (Maurilio Coppini, letter to author, January 14, 1956.)

ignore events that did not involve ethnic Germans. Files of Bucharest papers, however, contain a number of pertinent items, as do such unlikely newspapers as the Belgrade *Donauzeitung,* the Zagreb *Neue Ordnung,* the Madrid *Arriba,* and various German papers whose reporters periodically visited Odessa. Also, the Russian-language and Ukrainian press in Axis Europe, particularly the Berlin *Novoe Slovo,* contained useful dispatches from or about Odessa.

Note on Secondary Sources

(1) Scholarly studies on the subject are non-existent. Special aspects, however, have received attention. The fate of the Jews has been discussed in a number of serious pieces of research (see Chapter V above); agricultural production has been examined somewhat (Karl Brandt, ed., *Management of Agriculture and Food in... Fortress Europe,* Stanford, 1953); and church history has been surveyed) Friedrich Heyer, *Die orthodoxe Kirche in der Ukraine,* Cologne, 1953). Finally, the general problem of German-Romanian relations during the war has been thoroughly covered by Andreas Hillgruber in his *Hitler, König Carol und Marschall Antonescu* (Wiesbaden, 1954).

(2) Soviet sources include a few contemporary accounts, interesting largely as an index to the propaganda reaction which the occupation provoked. More valuable are postwar publications. Though obviously one-sided, the report of the Extraordinary Commission on Axis atrocities is noteworthy. The most substantial body of data is contained in the volumes of documents published in Odessa after the war *(Odessa v velikoi otechestvennoi voine Sovetskogo Soinza; sbornik dokumentov i materialov,* 3 vol., Odessa 1947-1953). Only the first two volumes have been available, the third having apparently been withdrawn (cf., however, its mention in *Voprosy istorii*, No. 12, 1953, p. 180). Some useful data, particularly on the underground, are to be found in Kiev and Odessa newspaper articles; pertinent published memoirs are strikingly rare. Finally, there are a few brochures that deal with military developments, and Kataev's much-discussed novel, *For Soviet Power,* contributes to an understanding of the Soviet view of Transnistria.

(3) Memoir material is also rather poor on the German and Romanian sides The announced second volume of Barbul's political apologia of the Antonescu regime, which was to discuss the Transnistrian issue, never appeared. Some increasing information is to be found in such refugee

memoirs as Vladimir Petrov's *Retreat from Russia* (New Haven, 1950). However, the second part of the Fevr memoirs, which was to contain his account of a prolonged sojourn in Odessa, was never published.

Interviews and Written Materials

In view of the inadequacy of the materials discussed above, a special effort was made to supplement them with data from interviews or written communications. For this purpose, various institutes, libraries, and refugee organizations were contacted. Four manuscripts by refugees resident in Odessa during the war were found. At the author's suggestion, a brief one was produced by Eugene Tverskoi in Munich in 1951 for the Harvard Refugee Interview Project. Another, much longer and more substantial, was produced in 1952 for the Research Program on the U.S.S.R. by Michael Manuilov, a defector who, until his death, lived in Canada. The Institute for the Study of the U.S.S.R. in Munich commissioned two useful, though not fully reliable, manuscripts. A refugee from Odessa, I. Peterle, published an excellent article on the war years in the New York Russian-language newspaper *Novue Russkoe Slovo* (June 1, 1952); and an unpublished novel by Peter Ershov, *Strannyi konets*, is based on first-hand experience in Transnistria. In addition, several persons had notes or clippings from the period. Finally, personal interviews with a few refugees from the Odessa area and former Romanian officials proved quite helpful.

I. Bibliographies

Library of Congress, Division of Bibliography, *The Balkans: IV. Rumania: A Selected List of References,* Washington, 1943.

Yiddish Scientific Institute (YIVO), New York, *The Jews in Transnistria* (special YIVO file in bibliography project).

II. Books

Akademiia nauk SSSR, Institut istorii, *Ocherki istorii Velikoi Otechestvennoi voiny 1941-1945,* Akademiia nauk, Moscow, 1955.

(AOK 11, Ic), *Bessarabien-Ukraine-Krim,* Erich Zande, Berlin, 1943.

Armstrong, John A., *Ukrainian Nationalism, 1939-1945,* Columbia University Press, New York, 1955.

(Barbul, Gheorghe) *Mémorial Antonesco — le IIIe homme de l'Axe,* Vol. 1, Ed. de la Couronne, Paris, 1950.

Boldur, Alexandru, *Românii și strămoșii lor în istoria Transnistriei,* revised and enlarged ed., Liga culturală, Iași, 1943 (1942 ed. in Russian not located).

Borisov, A.D., *Odessa — gorod-geroi,* Voenizdat, Moscow, 1954.

Bova Scoppa, Renato, *Colloqui con due dittatori,* Ruffolo Editore, Rome, 1949.

Brandt, Karl, et al., Management of Agriculture and Food in the German-Occupied and Other Areas of Fortress Europe, Stanford University Press, Stanford, 1953.

Carp Mathias, *Cartea neagră: suferințele evreilor din România 1940-1944,* Socec & Co., Bucharest, 1946-1948, Vol. 3, 1947, *Transnistria* (also translated in Yiddish as *Transnistrie,* Buenos Aires, 1950).

Chekaniuk, A., *Narodne opolchennia v heroichnyi oboroni Kyeva i Odesy,* Ukrvidav, Moscow, 1943.

Chubai, Mstislav A., *Reid orhanizatoriv OUN vid Popradu po Chorne more,* Cicero, Munich, 1952.

Cornățeanu, Nicolae D., *L'organisation de l'agriculture roumaine en temps de guerre,* "La Roumanie et la guerre," Bucharest, 1943.

Dallin, Alexander, *German Rule in Russia, 1941-1945,* MacMillan, London, 1957. Second edition, 1981.

Dol'nik, A., *Bessarabiia pod vlastiiu rumynskikh boiar,* Gospoitizdat, Moscow, 1945.

Ehrenburg, Il'ia, *Voina,* Vol. 3, OGIZ, Moscow, 1944.

Fadeev, Anatolii Vsevolodvich, *Geroicheskaia oborona Odessy v 1941 g.,* Gospolitizdat, Moscow, 1955.

Fevr, Nikolai, *Solutse voskhodit na zapade,* Novoe slovo, Buenos Aires, 1950.

Geroicheskaia Odessa al'manakh, Odessa, 1945.

Gheroghe, Ion, *Rumäniens Weg zum Satellitenstaat,* Verlag Weisermühl, Wels (Ausrria), 1952.

Goroda geroi, OGIZ, Leningrad, 1943.

Great Britain, Ministry of Economic Warfare, (Basic Handbooks) Rumania, *London,* 1943.

Heyer, Friedrich, *Die orthodoxe Kirche in der Ukraine von 1917 bis 1945,* Rudolf Müller, Cologne, 1953.

Hillgruber, Andreas, *Hitler, König Carol und Marschall Antonescu,* Steiner, Wiesbaden, 1954.

Hoffmann, Walter, *Rumänien von heute,* 2d rev. ed., Felix Meiner, Leipzig, 1942.

Kataev, Valentin Petrovich, *Za vlast' sovetov,* Detizdat, Moscow, 1949. Red. ed., Sov. pisatel', Moscow, 1953.

Kononenko, V.M., *Chernomortsy v boiakh za osvobozhdenie Kryma i Odessy,* Voenizdat, Moscow, 1954.

Laeuen, Harald, *Marschall Antonescu,* Essener Verlagsanstalt, Essen, 1943.

Landra, Guido, *Il problema della razza in Romania,* Istituto italo-romeno di studi demografici e razziali, Bucharest, 1942.

Lauterbach, Richard R., *These Are the Russians,* Harper & Bros., New York, 1945.

Lebed', Mykola, *UPA,* Vol. 1, *Nimets'ka Okapatsiia Ukraïny,* UHVR, 1946.

Lee, Arthur G., *Crown against Sickle,* Hutchinson, London, 1950.

Lemkin, Rafal, *Axis Rule in Occupied Europe,* Carnegie Endowment, Washington, D.C., 1944.

Leverkuehn, Paul, *German Military Intelligence,* Weidenfeld & Nicolson, London, 1954.

Malaparte, Curzio, *Kaputt,* Dutton, New York, 1946.

Manstein, Erich von, *Verlorene Siege,* Athenäum-Verlag, Bonn, 1955.

Nistor, Iancu, *Asepecte geopolitice și culturale din Transnistria,* Bucharest, 1942.

Odessa, Obl. Komissiia po istorii Otechestvennoi Voiny, *Odessa v velikoi otechestvennoi voine,* 3 Volumes (Vol. 3), Odesskoe obl. izdat., Odessa, 1947-1953/

(Odessa, Serviciul de presă și propagandă a Municipiului Odesa), *Ein Jahr rumänische Verwaltng in Odessa,* (Municipality), Odessa, 1943.

Ogni Chernomoria, Odessa, 1949.

Penezhko, G.I., *Zapiski sovetskovo ofitsera, Son. pisatel',* Leningrad, 1949.

Penzin, K.V., Cheniomorskii flot v geroicheskoi oborone Odessy, Voenizdat Moscow, 1955.

Petrov, Vladimir, *My Retreat from Russia,* Yale University Press New Haven, 1950.

Pihido, Fedor, *Velykn vitchyzniana vuna,* Vydannia "novoho Shliakhu," Winnipeg, 1954.

Popp, Nicolae M., *Transnistria. Incercare de monografie regională,* Dacia Traiana, Bucharest, 1943.

Prost, Henri, *Destin de la Roumanie, 1918-1954,* Berger-Levrault, Paris, 1954.

Reitlinger, Gerald, *The Final Solution,* Beechhurst Press, New York, 1953.

Roberts, Henry L., *Rumania,* Yale University Press, New Haven, 1951.

Rumania. Trei ani de guvernare, Imprimeria Națională, Bucharest, 1943.

Rumäniens heiliger krieg im Spiegel der deutschen Presse, Bucharest, 1942.

Rumänisches Blut für das neue Europa: Rumäniens heiliger Krieg im Spiegel der italienischen Presse, Bucharest, 1943.

Senkevich, V.M., *Sovetskaia Moldaviia v bor'be protiv fashistskikh zahvatchikov,* Gosppolitizdat, Moscow, 1944.

Smochină, Nicolae P., *Die Rumänen in Sowjetrussland,* Iași, 1939.

Sobolev, Leonid, *Dorogami poobed v Bukhareste,* Voenizdat, Moscow, 1944.

Stepanov, M.A., ed., *Deistviia voenno-morskogo flota,* Voenizdat, Moscow, 1956.

Toynbee, Arnold and Veronica, eds., *Hitler's Europe 1939-1946* (Survey of International Affairs), Oxford University Press, London, 1954.

Transnistria, 1941-1943, Odessa, 1943.

United States, Office of Strategic Services, Research and Analysis Branch, "Population Movements of Black-Sea Germans," No. 2611, November 13, 1944.

Vielvölkerheere und Koalitionskriege, Leske, Darmstadt, 1952.

Virski, Fred, *My Life in the Red Army,* Macmillan, New York, 1949.

Vorob'ëv, F.D. and V.M. Kravtsov, *Pobeda sovetskikh vooruzbennykh sil v Velikoi Otechestvennoi Voine, 1941-1945,* Voenizdat, Moscow, 1953.

Werner, Paul, *Ein schweizer Journalist sieht Russland,* O. Walter, Olten, 1942.

Wolff, Robert Lee, *The Balkans in Our Time,* Harvard University Press, Cambridge, 1956.

Zagorov, Slavcho, *et al., The Agricultural Economy of the Danubian Countries, 1935-1945,* Stanford University Press, Stanford, 1955.

III. Series and Articles

Alliba (Madrid):
De la Aldea, Juan Manuel, "Odessa — la ciudad ha sido incorporada a nuestra civilización," December 5, 1943.

Berliner Börsen-Zeitung (Berlin):
Riedl, Franz, "Aufbau am Dnjestr," December 9, 1942.

Biulleten' odesskogo zemliachestva (New York):
Peterle, Iak., "Odesskaia tragediia," No. 6, 1953.

Bol'shevistskoe znamia (Odessa), February-May, 1945.

Bukarester Tageblatt (Bucharest), 1941-1944 incomplete.

Bukarester Woche (Bucharest), 1944 incomplete.

Chornomors' ka Komuna (Odessa), 1944-1945 incomplete.

Curentul (Bucharest), 1943 incomplete.

Deutsche Allegemeine Zeitung (Berlin):
    Schumacher, Hans, "Im Gouvernement Transnistrien," October 14, 1943.

Deutsche Arbeit (Berlin):
    Puls, Willi, "Wieder deutsche Schulen in Transnistrien," Vol. 42, No. 8, August, 1942, pp. 235-237.
    Wolfrum, Gerhard, "Deutsche Aufbauarbeit in Transnistrien," Vol. 42, No. 12, December, 1942, pp. 370-376.

Deutsche Bug-Zeitung (Nikolaev), 1942-1943.

Der Deutsche in Transnistrien (Odessa), Weekly, Vol. 1, No. 1, July 19, 1942, to Vol. 2, No. 49, December 12, 1943.

Deutsche Post aus dem Osten (Berlin):
    Lang, Gustav, "Transnistrien," Vol. 14, 1942, July, pp. 32-33.

Deutsche Ukraine-Zeitung (Rovno):
    Muller, Karl J., "Das Land zwischen Dnjestr und Bug," July 26, 1942.
    Poppenberger, Fritz, "Das Land am Ostufer des Dnjestrs," September 12, 1942 (also in *Hamburger Fremdenblatt*, September 10, 1942).
    "Friedliches Odessa," January 10, 1943.

Deutsche Zeitung im Ostland (Riga):
    Kausch, Hans-Joachim, "Rumäniens Anteil: Der Aufbau in Transnistrien," August 17, 1943.

Donauzeitung (Belgrade):
    "Anbauplan für Transnistrien," April 9, 1942.
    Editorial, December 24, 1942.
    Herrmann, Gerhart, "Dornröschen Odessa," August 8, 1943.

Economia română (Bucharest):
    "Agricultura sovietică in Transnistria, Vol. 24, No. 1, 1942, p. 40.
    "Aspectul economic al Transnistriei," *ibid.,* No. 2, p. 33.

Egység (Cluj):
    Sztern, Ignác, "Transznisztria" (Diary), May 30, 1946, and ff.

Europäische Revue (Berlin):
    Gheorghe Dabija, "Rumänien an der Ostfront," Vol. 19, February, pp. 57-84.

Excelsior (Bucharest):
    Codrescu, Florian, "Transnistria," October 25, 1942.

Frankfurter Zeitung (Frankfurt):
    hn., "Die Aulbauarbeit in Transnistrien," November 10, 1942.

Harmburger Fremdenblatt (Hamburg):
    Sedlatzek, Karl, "Siegreicher Einzug in Odessa," October 18, 1941.

Internationale Kirchliche Zeitschrift (Bern):
    Spuler, Bertold, "Die orthodoxen Kirchen," a semi-annual survey, Volumes 32-34, 1942-1944.

Izvestiia (Moscow):
    Gordienko, V, "Odesshchina nakanune uborki urozhaia," July 6, 1944.
    (Odessa Military District, Tribunal, Reports), January 11 and 18, 1946.

Krakauer Zeitung (Cracow):
    "Zwei Jahre Transnistrien," August 21,1943.
    "Transnistrien liefert bereits für Rumänien," September 12, 1943.

Krakivs'ki Visti (Cracow), 1942-1943.

Krasnaia Zvezda (Moscow):
    Petrov, General-maior I., "Pravda o bor'be za Odessu," October 22, 1941.
    Kurbatov, V., "V Odesse," November 16, 1945.

Mitteilungeti der Geographischen Gesellschaft (Vienna):
    "Transnistrien," Vol. 86, Nos. 4-6, 1943, pp. 198-200.

Molva (Odessa), 1942-1944. Only individual clippings available.

Monatshefte für auswärtige Politik (Berlin):
    G.E.U., "Transnistrien," Vol. 8, No. 12, December, 1941, pp. 1025-1026.

Münchner Neueste Nachrichten (Munich):
    W.A.B., "Transnsitrien als Teil Rumäniens," September 4-5, 1943.

Der Nahe Osten (Istanbul), 1943.

Nation und Staat (Vienna), 1941-1944.

Neue Ordnung (Zagreb):
    Bauer, Ernest, "Odessa," March 22 1942.
    Bauer, Ernest, "Das rumänische Transnistrien," August 16, 1942.
    Berge, Ferdinand, "Besuch in Odessa," October 18, 1942.
    Bauer, Ernest "Odessa — die Stadt hinter der Front," November 28, 1943.

The New York Times (New York), 1943-1944.

News Digest (London, HMSO), (E.H. series), 1941-1944.

Novoe Russkoe Slovo (New York):
    Nikolaevski, B., "Vnutrennaia liniia i Kap KA 1950. Foss," April 16, 1950.
    Peterle, Ia., (pseud.), "Odessa — stoliatsa Transnistrii," June 1, 1952.
    Solonevich, Ivan, letter to the editor, May 24, 1950.

Novoe Slovo (Berlin), 1941-1944.

Odessa (Odessa), 1941-1944.

Odesskaia gazeta (Odessa), 1941-1944 (Clippings only available)

Oktiabr' (Moscow):
    Bubennov, M., "O novom romane Valentina Kataeva 'Za vlast' sovetov," No. 2, February, 1950, pp. 3-19.

Osteuropa-Institut, *Jahrbuch* (Breslau):
    Sztuka, Alfred, "Wirtschaftskundliche Grundlagen des nordöstlichen Karpatenvorlandes einschliesslich Transmstriens, 216.

Osteuropa-Institut, *Ostraum-Berichte* (Berlin):
    Breckner, Friedrich A., "Rumänien," N.F., 1942, pp. 192-212.
    Die Ostkartei (Berlin)
    Heft 6: "Transnistrien," (1944).

Ostland (Berlin)
    "Transnistrien und die Rumänen," Vol. 20, No. 24, December 15, 1941, pp. 428-432.

("Government of Transnistria"), Vol. 22, No. 3, February 5, 1943, pp. 54-55.

Parizhskii Vestnik (Paris), 1942-1944.

Pravda Ukrainy (Kiev):
Prisiazhniuk, A., M. Genkin, and Gr. Limonov, "Partizanskaia Iskra," May 7 and 8, 1955.

Pribngskie izvestiia (Golta), 1942-1943.

Das Reich (Berlin):
gh. "Transnistrien: Das Werk des Guverneurs Alexianu," August 1, 1943.

Revaler Zeitung (Reval):
Koepp, Friedrich, "An der Bugbrücke," November 13, 1942.

Rivista di studi politici internationali (Florence):
Alvus (pseud.), "Il maresciallo Antonescu e la guerra contro l'URSS," Vol. 15, 1948, pp. 335-376.

Romania. *Monitorul Oficial* (Bucharest), 1941-1944.

Rumänischer Wirtschaftsspiegel (Bucharest):
"Die Wirtschaft Transnistriens," March 1, 1942.
"Güterverkehr in und mit Transnistrien," November 20, 1942.
"Schafe aus Transnistrien," November 20, 1942.

Soviet War News (London), 1941-1944:
Vilenski, E., "What I Saw in Odessa," No. 51, September 8, 1941. Petrov, Major-General, "The Defense of Odessa," No. 69, September 29, 1941.
Krylov, Colonel N., "Enemy Tactics in the Battle for Odessa," No. 80, October 11, 1941.
Krieger, Evgeny, "Odessa's Night and Morning," No. 841, April 24, 1944.

Südost-Echo (Budapest-Vienna):
Dr. B., "Wiederaufbau in Transnitrien," Vol. 12, No. 43, October 23, 1942.
—th., "Die Rumänen in Transnistrien," Vol. 12, No. 45, November 6, 1942.

VRR Klüber, "Leiwährung in Transnistrien," Vol. 12, No. 51, December 18, 1942.

Transnistrien, (Bucharest), 1941-?.

Transnistria Cristiană (Odessa) 1942-1944.

Universul (Bucharest), 1941-1944. Scattered issues.

Volk and Reich (Berlin):
Christoph, Gerhard, "Bessarabien und Transnistrien," Vol. 18, 1942, pp. 99-103.

Völkischer Beobachter (Berlin):
Theil, Karl Hermann, "Rumänen jenseits des Dnjestr," July 23, 1941.
Zierke, Fritz, "Jenseits des Dnjestr," July 19 and 20, 1943.

Volkstum im Südosten (Vienna).
"Rumänen im ehemaligen Russland," Vol. 18, 1942, pp. 194-195.

Voprosyy istorii (Moscow)
Shternstein, Ia. M., "Rabochie odesskogo porta v oborone goroda v 1941 godu," No. 6, 1956, pp. 99-109.

Wirtschaftsdienst (Hamburg)
W.M., "Wiederraufbau in Transnistrien," Vol. 27, No. 8, February 20, 1942, pp. 114-115.
"Aufbau in Transnistrien," Vol. 27, No. 42, October 16, 1942, p. 783.

YIVO *Annual of Jewish Social Science* (New York)
Schechtman, Joseph B., "The Transnistria Reservation," Vol. 8, 1953, pp. 178-196.

IV. Unpublished Documents

Individual documents are cited in full in footnote to the text. The following indicates the broad categories of documents surveyed.

German Foreign Office, records in custody U. S. Department of State Historical Division:

Microfilm reels 244, 1273, 2066, 5078-5088.

Harvard University Refugee Interview Project:

Interview protocol series B6: Nos. 96, 314, 542.

Nuremberg Military Tribunals:
- USSR series (particularly official Soviet reports)
- PS series (particularly on high-level and intra-Axis relations)
- NO series (particularly on ethnic Germans)
- NG series (particularly on forced labor and treatment of Jews)
- EC series (particularly on Army Group "A").

YIVO Archives, New York:
- Series Occ E 4 (Romania and the Balkans).

Captured Records Section, DRB, The Adjutant General's Office, Alexandria, Va.
- Deutsche Heeresmission in Romäneien (DHMR)
- Ministry for the Occupied Eastern Territories (EAP 99)
- Economic agencies (Wi/ID)
- Himmler files (EAP 161)

SS/SD reports from the occupie Eastern territories Military records, particularly Heeresgruppe A and Heeresgruppe Süd, AOK 11, AOK 6 and subordinate units (LIV Ak, LXXII AK, XXX AK, 50 ID, 132 ID, and others)
- Kdt. Dt. Truppen vor Odessa and VSt Wehrmacht fur Transnistrien (Russia Collection)
- Miscellaneous German Abwehr and Fremde Heere Ost reports

Italy, Ministry of Foreign Affairs, miscellaneous records, National Archives, Washington, D.C.

Major collections *not* consulted include:
- Bavarian Military Archives, Munich (records of Heeresgebiet Süd)
- Hauffe, Gen. der Inf. Artur, "Nachlass," Koblenz Bundesarchiv.
- Institut für Weltwirtschaft, Kiel, Bibliothek (file of documents and clippings on Transnistria)

V. Manuscripts

Anonymous, "Odessa: Poslevoennyi period," Research Program on the U.S.S.R., New York, 1952.

Bräutigam, Otto, Überblick über die besetzten Ostgebiete während des 2. Weltkrieges," Institut für Besatzungsfragen, Tübingen, 1954.

Bussmann, Walther, "Deutsch-rumänische Verhandlungen über das Gebier zwischen Dnjepr und Dnjestr," Germany, 1941 (Cited in Hillgruber, p. 359).

Desenko, L.I., "Narodnoe opolchenie v geroicheskoi oborony Odessy (Iun'— oktiabr' 1941 g.)," Candidate's disseration, Institute of History, Academy of Sciences of the Ukrainian S.S.R., 1953.

Ershov, P(etr), "Strannyi konets (povest')" (Germany, 1948 ?).

I.G. Farben A.G., Wirtschaftliche Abteilung, "Transnistrien (Gebiet, Bevölkerung, Wirtschaft)," Microfilm PB 73518, frames 185-196, Library of Congress, July, 1942.

Karov, D.P. (pseud.), "Sovetskoe podpol'noe i partizanskoe dvizhenie v Odesse i odesskoi oblasti v voinu 1941-1945 gg.," Institute for the Study of the History and Culture of the U.S.S.R., Munich, 1955.

Mamukov, E.I., "Rumvnskaia okkupatsii Odessy i 'Transnistrii' v 1941-1944 gg.," Institute for the Study of the History and Culture of the U.S.S.R., Munich, 1955.

Manuilov, Mikhail, "Odessa during World War II," Research Program on the U.S.S.R., New York, 1952 (Typescript in Russian).

Miiller-Hillebrand, General-major Burkhart, "Germany and Her Allies in World War II," MS P-108, Part II, Chapter 5: "Rumania," Office, Chief of Military History, U.S. Army, 1954, pp. 152-180.

Tverskoi, Evgenii, "Rumynskaia okupatsiia oblasti mezhdu Bugom i Dnestrom v 1941-44 gg.," Russian Research Center, Harvard University, 1951.

U.S. Army, Office, Chief of Military History, "Supply in Far-Reaching Operations," Vol. 19, Annex C, "Supply Difficulties of Army Group A, 1943-1944," Ms T-8, 1951, pp. 113-154.

World Jewish Congress, Romanian Section, "Bréviaire des souffrances des juifs en Transnistrie 1941-44," Bucharest, n.d. (1946?).

VI. Informants

To preserve anonymity, informants have been referred to in the text by alphabetical letter only, A through K. Notes taken at oral interviews and letters from informants are retained by the author.

Index

A

Abramov, General 187, 189
Aizenberg 223
Alexianu, Gheorghe 76, 77, 80, 85, 96, 99, 102, 126, 135, 138, 142, 148, 149, 153, 159, 161, 162, 164, 165, 200, 201, 205, 207, 209, 212, 214, 240, 243, 245, 252, 277
Ancharov 158
Andreev, Vasily 234
Antim, Archimandrite 164
Antonescu, Ion 14, 18, 22-24, 26, 41, 55-61, 67-69, 75, 77-79, 85, 90, 96, 99, 102, 106, 113, 120, 130, 131, 142, 143, 152, 156, 162, 170, 180, 182, 187, 199, 200, 205, 212, 238-243, 252
Antonescu, Mihai 61, 76, 212, 213
Auleb, Lt. General 239
Avdeev, V.D. 235

B

Babel', Isaak 11
Badaev (see Molodtsov)
Badoglio 197, 238
Bandera, Stepan 246
Belavski 273
Belkovski, M.N. 153, 154
Belousov 223
Berger, Gottlob 202, 238

Bian, Nicolae 163
Boiko-Fedorovieh 230
Bondarchuk 158, 195
Borisov 48, 49
Budennyi, Marshal 38

C

Cantacuzino, Alexandrina 80
Carol II, King 23
Cassulo, Mgr 162
Cercavski, Emil 76,
Chasovnikov, Pavel 147, 250
Chavra 273
Cherniatinski, Nikolai 156, 159
Chernomorski (see Avdeev, V.D.)
Chiorescu, Vladimir 83
Chubai, Mstislav 195
Ciobanu, Ștefan 88
Consolarino, Cleopatra 84, 85, 161
Coppini, Maurilio 197
Corănfeanu, Minister 200
Courbiére, L'Homme de 38, 40, 67
Crainic, Nichifor 80
Cundert, Vladmir 83

D

Dallin, Alexander 13, 15, 16, 20-22, 25, 26
Danidov 273

Despotuli (Kirsanov) 148
Diakonov 86, 249
Diehl, Albert Georg 218
Dorpmüller, Msinisrer 67
Drozdov, S.I. 231, 235
Dumitraşcu 153
Dumitrescu, General 98

E

Eichmann 208
Elena, Queen Mother 55, 85, 212, 242
Eristov, Count 192
Ershov, P. 186
Eugenia 225

F

Fans, Ivan 147
Fedorov, Fedor Kuz'mich 223
Fevr, Nikolai 188
Filatov, V.P. 33
Foss, Klavdii Aleksandrovich 189

G

Garnoshenko 273
Gheorghiu, General 180
Gimpu, Victor 148
Glasser, Markus 162
Glogoianu, Gl. 220
Glogoşeanu, General 81
Goering, Marshal 60
Goldhagen, Daniel Jonah 15
Golopenţia, Anton 89
Goralov-Gottlieb 123
Gunther, Franklin Mott 19

H

Halder, Franz 41
Häuffe, Major General 59
Herşeni, Troian 80, 152
Heydrich 207
Himmler 23, 202, 203, 238
Hitler, Adolf 19, 23, 38, 56-59, 64, 85, 238, 239
Hoffmeyer, Colonel 200, 201, 209, 239

I

Iablonovski, N. 148
Iacobici, Iosif 23-25
Ion, A.M. 232, 233
Ishtovenko 273
Izverezhnik 274

J

Jacobici, Minister 40

K

Kataev, Valentin 32, 50, 53, 85, 116, 117, 121, 123, 168, 220, 222, 223, 226, 227, 231, 232, 253, 254
Keitel, Marshal 64, 66
Khrushchev, Nikita 227, 235, 249
Killinger, Ambassador von 67, 96, 200, 212
Kirillovich, Vladimir 191
Kiritsa, Varlaam 163
Kleist, Field Marshal von 239
Kolb, Charles 213
Komanov, I.I. 273
Körner 238

Korotchenko, Demian 235
Kostiuk, Nikolai 229
Kovpak 234
Kozishkurt 273
Kretsenko 218
Kukharenko, I.A. 229
Kulakov, N.M. 38
Kutsov, Grigori 218
Kuznetsov (see Lazarev)

L

Lauterbach, Richard E. 252
Lawrence, W.H. 252
Lazarev, S.F. 223, 224, 226
Lazurski, Vladimir Feodorovich 147
Lebed', Mykola 196
Leibbrabdt, Georg 57
Leshchenko, Pëtr 168, 186
Likhtengaus, Isaak 218
Lipkovskaia, Lydia 159, 186
Lorenz, General 67, 202
Lozurski, Professor 249
Lutz, General 67

M

Makkaveiskii 157, 250
Maksiuk 273, 274
Malinovski, Marshal 249
Maniu, Iuliu 57
Manuil, Sabin 89
Manzhos 273, 274
Maslennikov, Anatolii 154
Mertsalova 157, 250
Metz, Colonel 41
Miaskovski 223

Michael the Brave 90
Mihai, King 55, 60, 85, 153
Moisev, Professor 147
Molodtsov, Vladimir Alexandrovich 220, 230, 231
Molotov, Viacheslav 31
Molov 249
Morhunenko, Vladimir 230
Mussolini 139

N

Nagel, Major General 214
Naumov 234
Neame, Lieutenant Colonel 19
Nesterenko, V.E, 229
Nikodemus, Patriarch 162

O

Oktiabr'ski, F.S. 37
Onipko, Evgenii 158
Ovcharenko 231

P

Pântea, Gherman 80, 82, 146, 153, 160, 233, 244
Panfil, S. 148
Pershin, Petr 157
Petrov, I.E. 38, 48
Petrov, Vladimir 87, 190
Petushkov, Ivan 244
Pflaumer, Minister 67
Pihido, Fedor 52
Pius (pseudonym) 218
Polomarchuk, Ivan 155
Popescu-Buzău 169

Posidelski 273
Potapenko 147
Potopeanu, Lt. General 243, 244
Pustovoitov, Nikolai Lukich 191, 192

R

Ranevskaia, R.M. 158
Reitlinger, Gerald 26
Romanov 274
Rosenberg 57, 64, 208, 238, 241
Rothkirch, Lieutenant General von 67
Rundstedt, Marshal von 41

S

Safronov, G.P. 37, 38
Savchenko 187
Schobert, General 68, 69
Scriban, Iuliu 163, 164
Seliavin, V.A. 156, 210
Shevchenko 273
Sinicliu, Elefterie 83
Smochin, Nicolae 88
Solonevich 155
Stalin 11, 21, 31, 70
Stepanov 273
Stephany, Werner 67
Strelets 273
Strokach, Timofei 235
Suvorin 154

T

Țabrea, Ilie 78
Tătăranu, General 59
Tarapanov 52

Tetradu, Professor 148
Thomas, General 61
Timiriazev 154
Timoshenko 225
Trestorianu, General 252
Trotsky, Leon 30
Tsibulka 273

V

Varneke, Boris Vasil'evich 147, 173, 250
Vasili, Dean 252
Verbitski 188
Vesnenko, N. 273
Vidrașcu, K. 171, 83-85
Vissarion, Metropolitan 80, 163, 164, 166, 191
Vlasov, Andrei A. 192
Vorakov, Vasilii 223
Vronskii, Vasilii 156-158, 186, 210

W

Wittgenstein, Prince 203

Z

Zaevloshin, M. 83
Zalevsky, Sr. Lt. 189
Zelinski, Mikhail Ivanovich 65
Zhdanovich 154
Zhilin, Professor 147
Zhukov, G. 37, 38
Zubov 157

HISTRIA BOOKS

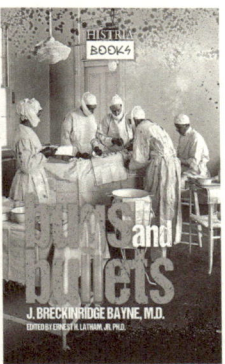

HistriaBooks.com